The Werewolf in the Ancient World

The Werewolf in the Ancient World

DANIEL OGDEN

OXFORD
UNIVERSITY PRESS

OXFORD

UNIVERSITY PRESS

Great Clarendon Street, Oxford, OX2 6DP,
United Kingdom

Oxford University Press is a department of the University of Oxford.
It furthers the University's objective of excellence in research, scholarship,
and education by publishing worldwide. Oxford is a registered trade mark of
Oxford University Press in the UK and in certain other countries

First Edition published in 2021

Impression: 1

Published in the United States of America by Oxford University Press
198 Madison Avenue, New York, NY 10016, United States of America

British Library Cataloguing in Publication Data

Data available

Library of Congress Control Number: 2020935095

ISBN 978–0–19–885431–9

Printed and bound by
CPI Group (UK) Ltd, Croydon, CR0 4YY

わが最愛の妻
江里子に

Preface

The origin of this book lies in the course I have been teaching to my undergraduate students from *c.*2000, first at Swansea and latterly at Exeter, 'Magic, Witchcraft and Ghosts in the Greek and Roman Worlds'. The sourcebook I developed in connection with the course, first published in 2002, carries the same name. I tentatively included some passages on werewolves in the book's first edition, not initially being confident that they fell properly within its purview. In 2009, when I had the opportunity to publish a second edition, I added a few more werewolf passages, having come by that point to feel more confident about their title to belong, and in any case encouraged by the students' evident enthusiasm for the topic. It is this same enthusiasm that now, at last, impels me to produce the current monograph. A trace of this development history can still be seen in its structure, with the first two chapters after the Introduction asking, respectively, what ancient werewolves have to do with witches, and what they have to do with ghosts.

Acknowledgements

I thank the Leverhulme Trust for supporting the writing of this book with a one-year Research Fellowship, 2018–19. I am most grateful for active support for the project to James Davidson (Warwick), Debbie Felton (University of Massachusetts at Amherst) and Susan Deacy (Roehampton). For useful references and discussions I thank Jan Bremmer (Groningen) above all, and also Elizabeth Baynham (Newcastle, NSW), Aude Doody (UCD), Richard Flower (Exeter), Johannes Heinrichs (Cologne), Sabine Müller (Marburg), Arthur Pomeroy (Wellington), and Richard Stoneman (Exeter). I would also like to record a more general debt of gratitude to Graham Anderson (Kent), for his inspiration over many years. A *Vorstudie* for this book, anticipating part of Chapter 4, has been published as Ogden 2019a: I am most grateful to Mr Roelf Barkhuis for permission to reproduce a revised and expanded version of that material here. At the Press I would like to thank Charlotte Loveridge, Georgina Leighton, and Karen Raith, as well as its anonymous but most helpful readers. Finally, thanks also, for reasons given, to my students in Swansea and Exeter.

Iidabashi, 2019

LEVERHULME
TRUST _____

Canis lupus, a European grey wolf

Contents

List of Abbreviations   xiii

Note on Orthography and Translations   xv

Note on Conventions in Relation to the Alexander Romance   xvii

Introduction: Petronius, Werewolves, and Folklore   1

1. The Curse of the Werewolf: Witches and Sorcerers   18

2. Werewolves, Ghosts, and the Dead   60

3. The Werewolf, Inside and Out   82

4. Werewolves and Projected Souls   109

5. The Demon in a Wolfskin: a Werewolf at Temesa?   137

6. The Werewolves of Arcadia   166

Conclusion: The World of Ancient Werewolves and their Stories   206

Appendix A: Homer's Circe as a Witch   211

Appendix B: Cynocephali   216

Appendix C: False Werewolves: Dolon and the Luperci   220

References   225

General Index   255

List of Abbreviations

AJA	*American Journal of Archaeology*
ANRW	*Aufstieg und Niedergang der römischen Welt.* Berlin 1972–
ATU	Uther 2004 (i.e. 'Aarne-Thompson-Uther')
BICS	*Bulletin of the Institute of Classical Studies*
BNJ	*Brill's New Jacoby.* 2006– (online resource)
CIL	*Corpus inscriptionum Latinarum.* Berlin 1863–
CMG	*Corpus medicorum Graecorum.* 1907–
CP	*Classical Philology*
CPG	Leutsch and Schneidewin 1839–51
CQ	*Classical Quarterly*
CR	*Classical Review*
CSCA	*California Studies in Classical Antiquity*
CW	*Classical World*
DNP	*Der Neue Pauly.* Stuttgart, 1996–2003
FGrH	Jacoby et al. 1923–
GRBS	*Greek, Roman and Byzantine Studies*
JdI	*Jahrbuch des Deutschen Archäologischen Instituts*
JHS	*Journal of Hellenic Studies*
JRS	*Journal of Roman Studies*
KA	Kassel and Austin 1983–
LIMC	Kahil et al. 1981–9
LSJ	Liddell et al. 1968
MI	Thompson 1955–8
ML	Roscher 1884–1937
OLD	Glare 1982
PF	Hallock 1969
PG	Migne 1857–1904
PL	Migne 1884–1904
PMG	Page 1962
PP	*La Parola del Passato*
QUCC	*Quaderni Urbinati di Cultura Classica*
RA	*Revue archéologique*
RE	Pauly et al. 1894–1978
REG	*Revue des études grecques*
RhM	*Rheinisches Museum für Philologie*
TAM	*Tituli Asiae Minoris.* Vienna 1901–

TAPA   *Transactions of the American Philological Association*
TrGF   Snell et al. 1971–2004
VC   *Vigiliae Christianae*
WS   *Wiener Studien*
ZPE   *Zeitschrift für Papyrologie und Epigraphik*

Note on Orthography and Translations

To spare the tedious bromides about the impossibility of full consistency in the transcription of Greek, my standing preference in this work, as in all my publications, has been for maximal Latinization or, as I would prefer to think of it, anglicization. I consider this not only to be the more aesthetic approach (those *k*s are so ugly), but also to give out the important message that classical antiquity is at home within our own culture and that, for all its delightful oddities, it is fundamentally the same, not different. (I make this claim not on the basis of any supposed nebulous continuity but because the culture of classical antiquity and the post-classical culture of early Christianity have been repeatedly folded into our own.). On this occasion, alas, I have felt compelled to compromise the (relative) purity of this approach in order to expose clearly for Greekless readers the connections or similarities between a series of Greek names and words (hence *Lykaon*, not *Lycaon*, to match *lykos*, etc.). Amongst the further anomalies to which this policy gives rise, the son of Periander, a character in our drama, must appear as 'Lykophron', whereas his namesake Hellenistic poet, a mere quarry of material, may continue to relax as 'Lycophron'.

All translations from Greek and Latin texts (in all phases of these languages) are my own, but not separately indicated to be such. Where relevant, these generally correspond with translations previously supplied in my sourcebooks Ogden 2009 and Ogden 2013b, though usually with some minor adaptation. The authorship, including my own on occasion, of translations from other languages is indicated with the quotations.

Note on Conventions in Relation to the *Alexander Romance*

AR   The *Alexander Romance*, MS A (α recension). Cited in accordance with the Kroll text, 1926, which also forms the basis, with slight modifications, of the Stoneman 2007– text; for an English translation, see Haight 1955.

AR   The Armenian *Alexander Romance* (α recension). Cited in accordance
Arm.   with the Wolohojian English translation, 1969; for the text, see Simonyan 1989.

AR β   The *Alexander Romance*, β recension. Cited in accordance with the Bergson text, 1965.

Introduction

Petronius, Werewolves, and Folklore

The Ancient Werewolf Introduced: Petronius

If a jobbing classicist were asked to compile a list of good werewolf stories from the ancient world, the initial result would doubtless resemble a list of the sort for which the British satirical magazine *Private Eye* is well known:

1. Petronius *Satyricon* §61
2. er...
3. that's it.

There is in fact quite a lot of ancient evidence for the subject of werewolves, be it of central or penumbral relevance, but, it must be conceded, at first glance the ancient world has bequeathed us only one really good, corking story about them, and Petronius supplies it in the 'Cena Trimalchionis' section of his comic Latin novel of *c.* AD 66, the *Satyricon*.[1] By the end of this study we will hope to have raised the profile of at least three more decent werewolf tales from antiquity but, for now, let Petronius' tale be our starting point.[2] The tale in question is one of a pair of what might be termed 'campfire horror stories' exchanged at a tastelessly extravagant dinner party thrown by Trimalchio for his fellow nouveau-riche Campanian freedmen, and it is told by Niceros. The responding story, a glorious one about witches, is to be told by Trimalchio himself, and will be considered in its own right in Chapter 1. Niceros proceeds as follows:[3]

---

[1] Cf. the observations of Summers 1933:153, Eckels 1937:32. For a statement of the standard view of the date and authorship of the *Satyricon*, see Rose 1971.

[2] See Conclusion. The three further tales in question are that of the werewolf deprived of his clothes (Chapter 4), that of the Hero of Temesa (Chapter 5), and that of Damarchus (Chapter 6).

[3] Technical commentaries on the tale: Friedlaender 1906:313–18, Maiuri 1945:196–9, Perrochat 1952:107–10, Marmorale 1961:119–27, Smith 1975:169–75, Schmeling 2011:252–60. There have been numerous discussions of the tale's folkloric aspects (whether these are perceived to be genuine or artificial). Amongst the more significant are: Pischel 1888, Schuster 1930:149–65, Scobie 1982:66–70, McDougall 1984:68–146 (NB 83–5, where the motifs of Petronius' tale, together with those of the Lykaon tales of Ovid, Apollodorus and Pausanias—for which see Chapter 6—are analysed against the grid of Thompson's *Motif-Index*, 1955–8), Bettini 1989–91:72–7, Bronzini 1990:22–8, Salanitro 1998, d'Autilia 2003. More minor contributions on this theme include: Rini 1929, Johnston 1932, Crum 1933, Spaeth 1933, 1935, Kroll 1937, Borghini 1991. Discussions of the related question of the linguistic style in which the story is told: Blänsdorf 1990, Gaide 1995, Boyce 1991:85–7.

When I was still a slave, we lived in a narrow street. The house is now Gravilla's. There, by the will of the gods, I fell in love with the wife of Terentius the inn-keeper. You knew Melissa of Tarentum, that gorgeous creature. But, by Hercules, I didn't love her just for her body or for sexual reasons, but because she had such a nice personality. If I asked her for anything, I was never refused. If she made tuppence, she gave me a penny. She kept my money for me, and never cheated me. Her husband met his end one day out on the estate.[4] I did everything I could to get to her. It's in times of need that you realise who your friends are. By chance the master had set off on his way to Capua to deal with some odds and ends.[5] I seized the opportunity and persuaded our guest to come with me to the fifth milestone. He was a soldier, as brave as Orcus. We shifted our butts just before cock-crow.[6] The moon was shining like the midday sun. We arrived among the tombs.[7] My man went for a pee against a gravestone.[8] I held back, singing and counting the stones. Then, when I looked back at my companion, he had taken all his clothes off and laid them beside the road. I almost died of fright, and I stood there like a dead man. He peed a circle around his clothes and suddenly

Discussions of further aspects of the tale in the Petronian literature: Miller 1942, Pinna 1978 [*non vidi*], Valentini Pagnini 1981:16–20, Baldwin 1986, Pàroli 1986, Fedeli 1995, Panayotakis 1995:92–93, Lefèvre 2003. Bouquet 1990 argues, on the basis of Petronius' werewolf, Pliny the Younger's haunted house (7.27) and Apuleius' witches Meroe and Panthia (*Metamorphoses* 1), for the existence of a litera-ture of the 'fantastique' (cf. 'Gothic') in the Roman world, by which he means a literature in which the supernatural is shown to intervene, in shocking fashion, in the familiar, realistic world of the quotid-ian and the banal. It is to be regretted that the tale goes unmentioned more often than not in the modern monographs devoted to Petronius, despite it being his finest episode.

Discussions of the tale in studies devoted to the ancient werewolf: Buxton 1987:97, Metzger 2011:233–6, Gordon 2015:46; a comment on these contributions below. Discussions of the tale in broader werewolf studies: (e.g.) Smith 1894:5–10, Summers 1933:153–6, Douglas 1992:41–4, Sconduto 2008:10–12.

[4] I consider the attempt of Smith 1975:171 and Schmeling 2011:255 to differentiate Terentius, to whom Melissa is *uxor* ('wife'), from her *contubernalis* (the word translated here as 'husband') to be sophistic; contrast Friedlaender 1906:315 and Marmorale 1961:121–2.

[5] This implies that the setting of the tale is somewhere in Magna Graecia. Smith 1975:173 (on §62) contends that such a setting is designed to suggest that it is an example of *Graeca credulitas* ('Greek gullibility').

[6] For Borghini 1991:29–32 and Gordon 2015:47, 51 n.34, 59 n.136 this (*galicinia*) is a knowing ref-erence to the Greek term for 'twilight', *lykophōs*, literally 'wolf-light', so-called because wolves were held to have sharp sight even at night (Aelian *Nature of Animals* 10.26).

[7] Petronius imagines a highway lined with tombs, on the model of the well-known Via Appia Antica; cf. Smith 1894:6, Smith 1975:172, Schmeling 2011:256.

[8] Cf. Petronius *Satyricon* 71, where Trimalchio proposes to establish one of his freedmen as a guardian of his tomb, so that people may not run up and defecate against it. Note also a genre of inscription or graffiti protecting buildings: *CIL* iv.7714 and 7715 (Pompeii), *Cacator cave malum* ('Shitter, look out for trouble'); *CIL* iv.7716 (Pompeii), *Cacator cave malum aut, si contempseris, habeas Iovem iratum* ('Shitter, look out for trouble; or, if you scorn this warning, may the anger of Jupiter fall upon you'); *CIL* vi.13740 (Rome), *qui hic mixerit aut cacarit, habeat deos superos et inferos iratos* ('If anyone pees or poos here, may the anger of the gods above and below alike fall upon him'); *CIL* vi.29848b (Rome), *duodeci(m) deos et Deana(m) et Iovem Optumu(m) Maximu(m) habeat iratos quisquis hic mixerit aut cacarit* ('If anyone pees or poos here, let the anger of the twelve gods, Diana and Jupiter Best and Greatest fall upon him'). See Clarke 2007:60–2, Schmeling 2011:256.

became a wolf. Don't think I'm joking. No one's inheritance is worth so much to me as to make me lie. But, as I'd begun to say, after he had become a wolf, he began to howl and ran into the woods.[9] At first I didn't know where I was, but then I went to his clothes to pick them up. They had turned to stone.[10] Whoever died with fright, if I didn't then? But I drew my sword and † hacked at the shades,[11] until I arrived at my girlfriend's house. I was like a ghost when I got in, and almost bubbling out my final breath. My groin was awash with sweat, my eyes were dead, and I have barely recovered from the experience even now. Melissa expressed amazement that I'd walked there so late and said, 'If you'd come earlier, at least you could have helped us. For a wolf got into the estate and among the flocks. He was draining the blood out of them like a butcher. But even if he got away, the last laugh was ours, for our slave managed to get a spear through his neck.' When I heard this, I could not even think of sleep, but when it was fully light I ran off home like the robbed innkeeper.[12] When I came to the place where the clothes had turned to stone, I found nothing but blood. But when I arrived home, my soldier was lying on his bed like an ox, and a doctor was attending to his neck. I realized that he was a skin-changer/werewolf [*versipellis*], and I could not thereafter bring myself to taste bread with him, not even if you had forced me on pain of death. Others can make up their own mind about this, but if I'm lying, may your guardian spirits exercise their wrath upon me.[13]   Petronius *Satyricon* 61–2

It has not proven possible to trace any direct antecedents to this tale in the extant literary record. Costas Panayotakis certainly goes too far in claiming that the tale was already to be found in Novius' *c.*30 BC Atellan farce *Fullones feriati* or *Fullers on Holiday*, this on the meagre basis of a fragment reading, 'He turns himself into all beasts and eats anything he can as much as touch.'[14] We shall revisit Petronius' story throughout the volume.

---

[9] Smith 1894:9 contends that in some medieval cases of werewolfism the howl completes the act of transformation, but decisive examples are wanting.

[10] This interesting magical feat is explained in Chapter 3.

[11] The sole MS gives *gladium tamen strinxi et* †*matavita tau*† *umbras cecidi, donec ad villam amicae meae pervenirem.* I can find neither contextual nor palaeographical merit in Miller's attempt (1942) to emend this phrase to *gladium tamen strinxi et maturavi et evitavi umbras*, which he then translates as 'I drew my sword, hurried along and avoided dark spots', removing mention of the ghosts. Bücheler's conjecture of *in tota via* for †*matavita tau*†, 'the whole way along', has proven popular. Was the original phrase here Greek? See Tremoli 1975. For the ability of iron to resist ghosts, see Homer *Odyssey* 11.48, Virgil *Aeneid* 6.260, Apuleius *Metamorphoses* 2.32.6, Lucian *Philopseudes* 15; cf. Schmeling 2011:258.

[12] This curious expression is discussed in Chapter 4.

[13] The notion of transformation is jokingly taken up by Petronius' narrator Encolpius at §64, when he observes that Niceros' and Trimalchio's stories were making the number of lamps multiply and the dining room change shape for him (*triclinium esse mutatum*)—i.e. their silliness was making his head swim or spin.

[14] Novius *Fullones feriati* F i (Frassinetti 1955:54): *vortit se in omnis bestias, comest quidquid tetigit tantum.* Panayotakis 1995:92.

Terms and Definitions

It could be said that the ancient world did not have a proper term for 'werewolf', or at any rate an exclusive one. Most of the Greek texts discussed in this book employ no special term for the phenomenon but merely speak of people—always men, in fact[15]—turning into a wolf (*lykos*). Only in the second century AD did the medical poet Marcellus Sidetes develop the term *lykanthrōpos*, 'lycanthrope', together with its corresponding abstract, *lykanthrōpia*, 'lycanthropy', to describe what we would today consider to be a variety of mental illness. Thereafter these terms remained almost wholly confined to the narrow medical tradition that recycled Marcellus' original work (for which see Chapter 2).[16] Only two uses of the term *lykanthrōpos* before the fall of Constantinople invite further comment at this stage. First, the (fourth-century AD?) amulet handbook, *Cyranides*, tells that *lykanthrōpoi* can be cured if they fast for three days and then eat the heart of a (pure) wolf.[17] Let us note that, despite the visceral imagery, the context remains one of healing, albeit of a magical variety. Secondly, the early-ninth-century AD chronicler Theophanes the Confessor tells how in AD 803 or 804 the Byzantine Emperor Nikephoros I sent some like-minded partisans, 'Lykaonians or *lykanthrōpoi*', to blind the failed usurper Bardanes Turcus in the monastery to which he had retired. Here the use of the term is prompted primarily by Lykaonia's evocation of the name of Lykaon, who famously transformed into a wolf, and its function is to serve as a colourful image for cruelty and violence. George the Monk (a.k.a. George the Sinner) redeployed Theophanes' wordplay for his own chronicle later in the century, although he protested that the Lykaonians were acting without the authority of their emperor.[18] Both of these contexts, the *Cyranides*

---

[15] But there are female werewolves in the Latin tradition: the witches discussed in Chapter 1.

[16] See *Suda* s.v. Μάρκελλος Σιδήτης (for Marcellus' work); Aëtius of Amida *Libri medicinales* 6.11 (4th c. AD); Oribasius *Synopsis* 8.9 (late 4th c. AD; cf. Photius *Bibliotheca* cod. 218); Paul of Aegina 3.16 (7th c. AD); Paul Nicaeus 24 (9th–11th c. AD); Psellus *Ponema iatrikon* 837–41 (11th c. AD); Joannes Actuarius *On Diagnosis* 1.35 (c. AD 1300); Anon. Περὶ λυκανθρωπίας (probably post-Paul Nicaeus at least; at Ideler 1842:ii, 282).

[17] *Cyranides* 2.23, p.152 Kaimakis; see further Chapter 3.

[18] Theophanes the Confessor *Chronicle* p.480 de Boor; George the Monk p.772 de Boor, recycled (again) at Constantine VII Porphyrogenitus' (excerpta) *De insidiis* 44. Lykaonia is in southern Asia Minor. For the historical context, see Treadgold 1988:131–5.

I cannot forbear to mention here the story of the werewolves of Constantinople recorded by the Lutheran natural philosopher Hiob Fincel (Jobus Fincelius), which is much cited in the werewolf literature, albeit everywhere tralatitiously, either by means of the wholly misleading references provided by Baring-Gould 1865:64–5 (who assigns it, unintelligibly, to Fincel's '*de Mirabilibus*, lib. xi') and Summers 1933:146, 174 n.67 (who appears to imagine that it derives from Fincel's 1556 book, published in Jena, *Wunderzeichen: Warhafftige* etc.), or by means of the indirect allusions made to Fincel's work in other early modern authors, such as Jean Bodin (1580:195). Let us put it back on track. The story is actually to be found in Fincel's 1559 book, published in Leipzig, *Der ander Teil Wunderzeichen* (at pp.150–1 in the online facsimile provided by the Martin-Luther-Universität, Halle-Wittenberg, Universitäts- und Landesbibliothek, Sachsen-Anhalt). According to this, Constantinople fell victim to a great plague of werewolves (or just wolves tout court after all?) in 1542. They did much harm and caused the inhabitants to barricade themselves in their own homes. Mustafa Pasha fortified and cure and the Bardanes Turcus tradition, entail that the term *lykanthrōpos* is deployed (at last) to signify or at any rate evoke a werewolf proper.

Turning to Latin now, while the term *versipellis*, literally 'skin-changer', may carry the specific connotation of 'werewolf' in our Petronian passage, other attestations indicate that it could also have a wider application.[19] In one further passage at least it does seem to carry the specific connotation of 'werewolf' again. Pliny, writing before AD 79, introduces his words on the rites and myths of the Lykaia, to which werewolfism is central, in the following terms:

> We should be confident in the belief that it is untrue that men are turned into wolves and restored again to their own form. Otherwise, we should believe everything that we have learned to be fabulous over all these centuries. All the same, we will indicate the origin of the popular superstition that skin-shifters/ werewolves [*versipelles*] are among those subject to a curse [*maledictis*].
>
> Pliny *Natural History* 8.80[20]

In three texts the term is applied to those that can change an outer form either into a different humanoid shape or into a variety of animal shapes. In his *Amphitruo* (c.190 BC) Plautus describes Zeus as *versipellis/vorsipellis* as he changes his form into that of Amphitryon, in order to sleep with the latter's wife, Alcmene, and sire Heracles.[21] In his *Metamorphoses* (later-second-century AD) Apuleius applies the term to the witches of Thessaly that change themselves into the forms of different animals, specifically birds, dogs, mice, flies, or, as the unfolding narrative reveals, weasels.[22] In his *Against the Pagans* (c. AD 300) Arnobius applies *versipellis* as an epithet to Circe. While it could be intended here merely in the degraded sense of 'deceitful' (which we shall discuss next), it is strongly tempting to read the term as making allusion to her transformations of men into animals (for which see Chapter 1). It could be that the term is therefore used to signify 'a changer of the skins of others', but it is also possible that Arnobius infers that Circe must have had the ability to change her own form too.[23] As we shall see (in Chapter 1 again), both the witches of Thessaly and Circe may be more closely associated with wolf transformation than is immediately apparent.

---

manned the city walls, and then swept through the city so as to corral the wolves in a corner of the fortifications, where he surrounded them. Facing death, the wolves leapt over the wall, never to be seen again in the city or the region.

[19] For discussion of the significance of term *versipellis*, see Summers 1933:18–19, Valentini-Pagnini 1981:6–8 (with care), McDougall 1984:131–5, Pàroli 1986:288–91, Metzger 2011:237–42.

[20] A fuller quotation of this passage is supplied in Chapter 6, where it is given detailed discussion. Cf. the corresponding phrase in the contents list in Book 1: *de lupis. unde fabula versipellium.*

[21] Plautus *Amphitruo* 123.

[22] Apuleius *Metamorphoses* 2.22; cf. 2.25. See van Mal-Maeder 2001 *ad loc.*, esp. 318.

[23] Arnobius *Against the Pagans* 4.14.

But in extant Latin texts the term is more often deployed, rather, to describe someone capable of adapting their own personality and therefore of being deceitful. Plautus provides the earliest example of this usage too: in his *Bacchides* he applies the term to a slave who is able to change his personality in order to deal with different types of individual.[24] The bulk of the remaining examples of this personality-changing usage are late, mainly from the fourth and fifth centuries AD.[25] Despite its relative popularity, the usage looks secondary. It looks like a metaphorical adaptation of the outer-form-changing uses, and indeed a rather poorly conceived one: one who changes his personality surely changes not his carapace but his core.

One small point of light in the yawning silence on werewolves in the Latin west between the end of late antiquity and their twelfth-century renaissance (of which more anon) comes in one of the brief dramas of Hrotswitha, the learned nun of Gandersheim (*c.* AD 935–75). In her *Sapientia*, Hope addresses Antiochus: 'You speak, Antiochus, with the deceit of a fox, and flatter with the cunning of a *versipellis.*'[26] Here the general significance of deceitfulness is evidently uppermost

---

[24] Plautus *Bacchides* 658.

[25] Thus:

- Lucilius *Carmina* Book 26 F34 Charpin = ll. 669–70 Marx = ll. 652–3 Warmington = ll. 647–8 Krenkel (2nd c. BC). In this rather obscure fragment of the Roman satirist the speaker seems to be claiming to be able to adapt his personality in the same way as the slave of the *Bacchides*: 'But a freedman-agent, a "Tricorian", a very Syrian, a whipping boy – with whom I'll become a *versipellis* and with whom I'll transform everything' (*at libertinus, Tricorius, Syrus ipse, at mastigias, quicum versipellis fio et quicum commuto omnia*). The Tricorii were a people of Gallia Narbonensis, but the term is deployed here to suggest a miscreant so vile that his punishment will wear out three whips (cf. Plautus *Poenulus* 139: *tris...corios*). Presumably the speaker means that he will change himself into the 'freedman-agent (etc.)'. The fragment is preserved by the (4th–5th c. AD) grammarian Nonius Marcellus (38.5), who introduces it with the explanation, 'People that change themselves in any way they wish are called *versipelles*' (*versipelles dicti sunt quolibet genere se conmutantes*). See Marx 1904–5:ii, 244–5, Christes 1971:40–2, Charpin 1978–91:ii, 281–2, Metzger 2011:239.
- Prudentius *Cathemerinon* 9.92 (later 4th c. AD). Prudentius refers in passing to the Serpent of Eden's exhortation of Eve as *versipellis*, inevitably 'deceitful'.
- *De physiognomonia liber* 78 (text at Foerster 1893:3–145; 4th c. AD?). This anonymous tract *On Physiognomony* observes that those that produce a 'sharp and dry voice' are '*versipelles* and tricky' (*qui acutam vocem cum siccitate promunt, versipelles ac subdoli sunt*), implying a meaning along the lines of 'deceitful'.
- Servius on Virgil *Aeneid* 6.724 (*c.* AD 400). Servius' commentary on Virgil's *Aeneid* treats us to a version of the old theory that the dispositions of the peoples of the world are shaped by the climates in which they live. Hence, the Greeks are inconstant, the Gauls lazy, while the Africans are *versipelles*—presumably again something along the lines of 'deceitful'.
- Jerome *Vulgate*, Proverbs 14:25 (*c.* AD 405). In his 'Vulgate' Latin translation of the Bible, Jerome offers the following proverb: 'A faithful witness liberates souls and a *versipellis* one brings forth lies.' This corresponds to the Greek Septuagint's 'A faithful witness will deliver a soul from evils, but a tricky one [δόλιος] kindles lies', and to the Hebrew Bible's 'A truthful witness saves lives, but one who utters lies is a betrayer' (here quoted in the Revised Standard Version).
- Martianus Capella *De nuptiis Philologiae et Mercurii* 4.330 (early 5th c. AD). In his *Marriage of Philology and Mercury* the Platonist Capella supplies an allegorical biography of Dialectic. Before she had acquired the greatness of Socrates and Plato, she had dwelled with Parmenides, where she had been subject to the calumny that she was a 'skin-shifting pursuit' (*versipellis studii*), i.e., presumably, a deceitful one.

[26] Hrotswitha *Sapientia* scene v: *vulpina fraude loqueris, et versipelli astutia, Antioche, adularis.* Shortly afterwards werewolves receive another mention—without the use of *versipellis*—in the

again, but the parallelism of the second phrase with the first, where *versipellis* stands opposite 'fox', impels us to find a werewolf lurking here too.

For the purposes of definition for this project, the term 'werewolf' will be taken to define a creature that changes form, or appears to do so, or can be inferred to do so, in whole or in part, between the humanoid and the lupine. I do not make any assumptions about which of these two forms is the base form; about the relationship between the two forms within a single body; about the permanence, impermanence, or duration of the switch; about the cause of the condition; about the modus oper-andi of those affected; or about whether they are living or dead.[27] I sympathize a little with Jost's protestation that Lykaon, who—arguably—is simply changed, in a one-off transformation, from a pure man into a pure wolf, is not thereby a werewolf. But when one then asks what the critical distinctions would be between the case of Lykaon and the cases of those one would describe as werewolves instinctively and without hesitation, it is difficult to settle upon anything compelling or satisfactory.[28]

The derivation of the English word *werewolf* (likewise German *Werwolf*), which is first attested, in the form *werewulf*, in the writings of Bishop Wulfstan (*c.* AD 1000)[29] and then in an Anglo-Saxon ordinance of King Canute (r. AD 1017–35),[30] is not itself of great moment for this study, but a few words may be said. The former element remains mystifying and controversial. The old explan-ation—which goes all the way back to Gervase of Tilbury (AD 1210–14)—derives it ultimately from Latin *vir*, 'man', or from an English form cognate with it, so that *werewulf* would literally mean 'man-wolf', and here we might compare the stand-ard Italian term *lupo mannaro*, where the second word in the expression is bor-rowed from the German 'Mann'.[31] The more recent and now generally accepted

---

(*c.* AD 1012–20) *Corrector sive Medicus* that forms the nineteenth book of Burchard of Worms' *Decretorum libri xx*: here there is (post-Augustinian) censure for the belief that 'whenever a man should wish it, he may be transformed into a wolf, or into a "Werewulf" as it is called in German, or into some other form' (ch. 5, at *PL* cxl, 971); cf. Kratz 1976:63.

[27] For problematization of the definition of the werewolf see de Blécourt 2015b esp. 1–4. Taxonomies of werewolfism were once popular in the scholarship: (i) voluntary vs involuntary; (ii) fixed-term vs cyclical; (iii) congenital/'constitutional' vs acquired. See Smith 1894:5, 8, 19, 20, 22–4, 40, Eckels 1937:40–4. Only occasionally is it possible to situate ancient werewolves in parts of this grid—and Petronius' werewolf not at all.

[28] Jost 2005:14; see Chapter 6. Of course, the picture becomes murkier when we consider that, as we have just seen, Greek effectively did not possess a term for 'werewolf' distinct from that for 'wolf'. Whether or not Lykaon is a satisfactory werewolf himself, he was unquestionably both an aetiology and a paradigm for a series of most satisfactory Arcadian ones, and so well earns his place in this volume.

[29] Wulfstan *Homilies* xli p.191 Napier. However, its usage here seems broad: Wulsftan speaks of the importance of the clergy protecting the flock of the faithful from the *wodfræca werewulf*, the 'raging Devil'. See Jacoby 1974:77.

[30] Text at Thorpe 1840:160–1, reproduced at Otten 1986:5; cf. Pluskowski 2006:175. The context is an odd one, with the term not obviously signifying anything more than 'wolf' tout court.

[31] Gervase of Tilbury *Otia Imperialia* xv: *vidimus enim frequenter in Anglia per lunationes homines in lupos mutari, quod hominum genus* gerulfos *Galli nominant, Anglici vero* werewlf [*sic*] *dicunt: were enim Anglice virum sonat,* wlf *lupum*. Cf. Summers 1933:6, Jacoby 1977:78–9.

explanation has it that the *were* element derives rather from Anglo-Saxon *w(e)arg*, 'strangler', therefore 'outsider', in which case *werewulf* is to have signified 'outsider-wolf' in origin.[32] However, *wearg* was established in the sense of 'wolf's head' already by the eleventh century,[33] while the Old Norse equivalent, *vargr*, which designated the familiar concept of the 'outlaw', was used to denote 'wolf' too[34] (and indeed *varg* has now become the standard word for 'wolf' in modern Swedish). Saxo Grammaticus tells that in thirteenth-century Denmark Frothi required thieves to be hanged with a wolf also hanged at their side, to give out the message of their true nature.[35] One wonders, then, whether there was an element of the meaning 'wolf' in *wearg* and its cognates across the Germanosphere from a point prior to the eleventh century,[36] and whether *werewulf* might accordingly rather have signified in effect 'wolf-wolf' at its point of coinage—which would also make sense, albeit in accordance with a different logic: 'that man is really a wolf I tell you, a very wolf!'[37]

Folklore First: the Project of the Book

The position adopted in this book is as follows. The ancients already cherished a rich folklore of werewolfism that broadly resembled the one copiously attested for the central medieval period in Europe.[38] Our best access to the sort of narrative that underpinned such folklore comes precisely in Petronius' tale, which shares some striking motifs with the equally famous AD 1160–78 Anglo-Norman tale of Bisclavret by Marie de France—even if Petronius' narrative is tricksier than its

---

[32] See Gerstein 1974 (with a wealth of evidence), Jacoby 1974 esp. 77–93, Lindow 1977 (reviewing Jacoby), Otten 1985:5–8, Douglas 1992:96, de Blécourt 2015b:2, 19, Pluskowski 2015:93–4. *W(e)arg* is further thought to be cognate with French *garou*, so that the English term aligns perfectly with the standard French term for 'werewolf', *loup-garou*.

[33] Hough 1994–5.

[34] E.g. Snorri Sturluson *Prose Edda* Skáldskaparmál p.168 Jónsson; cf. Jacoby 1977:117.

[35] Saxo Grammaticus *Gesta Danorum* 5.137; note also 8.232; cf. Davidson and Fisher 1980:ii, 89 n.137, 137 n.109.

[36] But not necessarily anciently. The earliest extant Germanic text, Wulfila's fourth-century AD translation of the Bible into Gothic, deploys a series of words built on the root *warg* in senses associable with outlawry but not self-evidently with wolfhood: e.g. Mark 10:33, *gawargjand*, 'condemnation'; see Gerstein 1974:132–4.

[37] Gerstein 1974 esp. 134–5 takes a stronger position than this, contending (with some difficulty, to my mind) that the meanings of both 'wolf' and 'strangler' had been present already in the antecedent Proto-Indo-European form *Hwergh-*, this on the basis of comparative evidence (linguistic and cultural) from Hittite.

[38] For folklore in general see Thompson 1955–8 and Uther 2004, the twin pillars of reference on which the folklore movement stands, and the discussions of its concepts and problems in Ranke 1934, Propp 1958, 1984, Dundes 1965, 1980, Thompson 1977, Oring 1986 (a collective pedagogical volume; see especially Oring's own contributions), Davidson and Chaudri 2003 and Bronner 2017 (esp. 62–7). For folklore in a specifically ancient context, see Hansen 1988, 2002 (esp. 1–19), Anderson 2000, 2007, 2019.

folky veneer initially indicates.[39] It was, accordingly, folklore that determined the ancients' conception of what a werewolf actually was. Almost all the evidence for werewolfism in antiquity should be regarded either as folkloric in nature or as secondary to and refractive of a folkloric core. The ancients redeployed, finessed, and parlayed this focal conception in distinct ways in diverse cultural contexts. Notions, themes, and images were borrowed from this folkloric home and transferred, in as it were a metaphorical fashion (as with the term *versipellis* just considered), to other realms of human experience and endeavour, be this aetiological myth, in the case of the material bearing upon Lykaon; rites of passage or of maturation, in the case of the material bearing upon the Lykaia rite; or medicine, in the case of the medical writers' identification of the disease of 'lycanthropy.' It is this that accounts for what initially appears to be the incoherent, chaotic, and centrifugal nature of the evidence field for werewolves that the ancients have bequeathed to us.[40]

A failure to appreciate the nature and structure of the evidence in this way, together with the ancient historian's default affinity for the 'drunkard's search' (the drunk loses his wallet in a dark alley, but goes to look for it under the street lamp where the light is better) has led to classical scholarship's enthronement of the Lykaon myth and the Lykaia rite as the focal and determinative phenomena of ancient werewolfism.[41] This is strikingly apparent in what may be regarded as the four standard modern studies of the werewolf in the ancient world. Arcadia is the prime subject of Richard Buxton's (lucid and valuable) 1987 article, within which only a single sentence is devoted to Petronius. Alain Moreau's two-part article of 1997 and 1998 devotes eight pages to Arcadia and just two to Petronius. In her 2011 book Nadine Metzger can devote a nineteen-page chapter to Arcadia, but only four pages to Petronius. Richard Gordon's dense 2015 essay can devote eleven pages to Arcadia, but just a fraction of a single one to Petronius.[42]

---

[39] Cf. McDougall 1984:83–5.

[40] Indeed the field of *ancient* evidence for the werewolf presents us in microcosm with some of the problems faced by those attempting to analyse the werewolf in larger scope, which drives de Blécourt 2015b to contend that we are wrong to look for a unitary werewolf in Western (let alone world) culture, and to insist rather that the evidence for werewolves should be considered in separate 'clusters'.

[41] For discussions of werewolves in the ancient world, with particular reference to the Lykaian material throughout, see in particular Böttiger 1837:135–8 (already a profound and scholarly contribution to the subject), Smith 1894, Cook 1914–40:i, 63–99, Frazer 1929:ii, 317–20, Schuster 1930, Eckels 1937:32–69, Miller 1942, Piccaluga 1968, Kratz 1976, Tupet 1976:73–8, 1986:2647–52, Gernet 1981:125–39, Burkert 1983a:84–93, Mainoldi 1984:11–35, Jost 1985:258–67, Pàroli 1986, Buxton 1987, Moreau 1997, 1998 (cf. 1989, 1990a, 1990b—a linked suite of articles published in *Connaissance héllénique*), Forbes-Irving 1990:51–7, 90–5, 216–18, Hughes 1991, Johnston 1991, Kunstler 1991, Gantz 1993:725–9, Marcinkowski 2001, Veenstra 2002, Zolotnikova 2005, Bremmer 2007b, Metzger 2011, 2012, Gordon 2015.

[42] Buxton 1987 (Lykaian material: 67–75; Petronius: 69; in fairness to Buxton, it should be made clear that the subject of his article is explicitly the Greek world as opposed to the Roman one). Moreau 1997 and 1998 (Lykaian material: 1997:72–9; Petronius: 1998:6–7). Metzger 2011 (Lykaian material: 198–216; Petronius: 233–6). Gordon 2015 (Lykaian material: 34–44; Petronius: 46).

My own drift is antithetical in particular to that of the (nonetheless important) work of Mauriz Schuster and to that of Moreau. In 1930 Schuster contended that Petronius' tale was inspired by accounts of the Lykaia rite of the sort subsequently supplied by Pliny (and he has been followed in this view more recently by Barry Baldwin).[43] Moreau begins his 1997-8 article pair on the ancient werewolf with the bold programmatic subtitle 'Les origines: les rituels', before going on to describe the folkloric werewolf, as found in Petronius, as a mere 'degradation' of the ritual one.[44] The Lykaia and other rituals do constitute a large and valuable part of the evidence for ancient werewolfism (and we will spend much time with the Lykaia itself in Chapter 6 in particular), but it is important to accept their derivative and secondary nature for the concept.

Accordingly, I will extend the field from which I draw data for *prime* consideration across the Dark Age gap to embrace also the very rich folkloricly determined werewolf material produced in the Latin West and the Norse realm in the eleventh, twelfth, and thirteenth centuries AD.[45] This later evidence does, I believe, help us to expose trends already present in the ancient material, and it helps us to trace a coherence of sorts within the ancient material that it is otherwise hard to detect. The medieval material will be adduced on the basis that it is an independent witness to the sorts of folkloric beliefs and narratives that already thrived in antiquity and that indeed were already old at that stage: it is a maxim of folklore studies that tale types should be considered ancient already by the point of their earliest attestation. This is not the first time I have had cause to quote a useful paragraph penned by William Hansen, one of the modern doyens of the study of the folktale in ancient context:

Being a small sample of the whole, each record [*sc.* of any given folktale performance] must stand for hundreds of thousands of unrecorded tellings in the career of an oral tale. In any assemblage of narrations of the same tale type, whether recent or old or both, it is therefore safest to assume that the texts are independent realisations of the tradition, unless particular relationships can actually be demonstrated to be otherwise.[46]

---

[43] Schuster 1930:158-62 and Baldwin 1986:9; Pliny *Natural History* 8.80-2.

[44] Moreau 1998:6-7, for 'degradation'.

[45] *In primis*: Bishop Patrick of Dublin *De mirabilibus Hiberniae* (AD 1084); Marie de France *Bisclavret* (AD 1160-78); *Lai de Melion* (AD 1190-1204); *Guillaume de Palerne* (AD 1194-7); Gerald of Wales *Topographia Hibernica* (c. AD 1188); Gervase of Tilbury *Otia imperiala* (AD 1209-14); Guillaume d'Auvergne *De universo* (earlier 13th c. AD); *Völsunga saga* (late 13th c. AD); *Arthur and Gorlagon* (13th-14th c. AD).

[46] Hansen 2002:8; cf. Ogden 2013a:22. For the notion of the werewolf as a folkloric concept deeply embedded before records begin, see Smith 1894:40-1, Summers 1933:1; cf. Pischel 1888:69. Thompson's standard motif index for folklore cites werewolf tales in the following categories (1955-8 D113.1.1, Werwolf): Irish, Icelandic, Norwegian, Finnish, German, Dutch, English, Swiss, Breton, Gascon, Estonian, Livonian, Lithuanian, Slavic, Jewish, Indian, North American Indian, South American Indian, African.

It is indeed most unlikely that our medieval authors were themselves aware of and directly reworking Petronius' story: there is no indication that manuscripts of the *Cena* portion of the *Satyricon* circulated widely in the central medieval period. The *Cena* survives to us only in a single manuscript, H, the so called Traguriensis that was discovered in 1650 at Trau in Dalmatia (Paris. lat. 7989), with its *editio princeps* (a poor one by Mentel) following in 1664.[47] The manuscript in question was written in 1423 and is assumed to be closely connected with a manuscript known to have been in the hands of Poggio Bracciolini in that year. Prior to that, in the eleventh century John of Salisbury had cited Petronius for the *Cena*-located tale of the unbreakable glass, which is not found in any of the Petronian fragment collections and so may have derived from a manuscript similar to H, whether or not its direct antecedent.[48] (John of Salisbury's free version of the tale actually plays an important role in reconstituting what Petronius himself originally wrote.)[49] At any rate, it is only after 1664 that Petronius' werewolf tale can be considered to have entered truly wide circulation. It is intriguing to note, nonetheless, Nicolas Rémy's 1592 report of the case of a sheep-worrying werewolf heard in Lorraine in 1581: the werewolf in question had rejoiced in the name of Petronius.[50]

In this regard my drift is antithetical also to that of Gordon's 2015 essay. In the few words he devotes to the Petronius tale, he takes the elaborate literary artifice in which the tale is undeniably clothed all the way to its very core. Evidently, there is no folktale here for Gordon. Concomitantly he must understand the relationship of this story with the earliest medieval material to be one of simple literary allusion, and he must accordingly assume—against the evidence—that there was widespread access to the *Cena* in the central medieval period.[51] A further consideration against Gordon's position is the presence in Petronius' tale of trace versions of motifs that are of central importance in the medieval material: it is easier to infer that these traces represent refractions of motifs already well established in the folkloric tradition that the medieval authors will inherit than that they constitute specific and direct literary inspiration points for the medieval authors (see Chapters 3 and 4).

---

[47] For the details see Schmeling and Stuckey 1977:18, Schmeling 2011:xx.

[48] Petronius *Satyricon* 51; cf. Rose 1971:25.

[49] A glass-blower presents an emperor with an example of the unbreakable glass he has invented, in anticipation of rich rewards. Instead, the emperor beheads him, in order to preserve the value of gold. The tale is also told at Pliny *Natural History* 36.195 and Cassius Dio 57.21.7, both of whom identify the emperor in question as Tiberius. Cf. Miller 1942:319, Smith 1975:xi, xxii–xxiii, 136–7, Schmeling 2011:xx. John of Salisbury *Policraticus* 4.5 (i. p.248 Webb), reproduced at Smith 1975:xxvi–xxvii.

[50] Rémy 1592 (Latin ed.) and 1595 (French ed.) ii.5 (p.210 of Boës' 1998 ed. of the French text; p.108 of the Ashwin-Summers 1930 trans.); so too Guazzo 1608 i.13; cf. Summers 1933:252, de Blécourt 2015b:7 (correcting some earlier misapprehensions).

[51] Gordon 2015:46–7 and 54 n.66, citing de Blécourt 2013b in support (p.977, presumably), though the latter neither asserts nor argues for the dependence of *Bisclavret* on the *Cena*.

The principal arguments made here are mounted on the basis, as indicated, of Western material produced up until the thirteenth century A D. This is relatively easy to encompass. I shall make more limited and circumspect references to werewolfism in the early modern period and since, and, to the extent that I do make such references, they will be more decorative than probative in intent. This is for two reasons. First, from this point the notices of werewolfism mushroom in a remarkable way. A daunting statistic to contemplate is that, as of 2015, the Flemish Folk Tale Bank alone boasted a collection of no fewer than 1,845 were-wolf legends (977 of them were from the single province of Limburg).[52] Secondly, it is recognized that the phenomenon of werewolfism takes on a rather different flavour from this time onwards (one might point to the rise of werewolf trials in particular here).[53] It will be noted that, despite this, Chapter 4 includes an extended foray into the soul-projecting werewolves of the early modern period and after. I have permitted myself this indulgence in the light of the peculiar rich-ness of the comparative evidence available here for one of the book's main con-tentions. Even so, the argument advanced at this point remains well capable of standing on the medieval comparanda alone. I make no mention of werewolves in the cinema. However, I will make occasional reference to Guy Endore's 1933 novel *The Werewolf of Paris*, which has exercised a particular influence on the movie-house werewolf (in this regard at any rate it perhaps stands beside Mary Shelley's *Frankenstein* and Bram Stoker's *Dracula* as the catalyst of one of the main subgenres of traditional cinematic horror), and which commands the name—amongst werewolf aficionados at any rate—of being the only werewolf novel of any literary merit.[54]

I have said something of the study of the ancient werewolf from the perspec-tive of classical scholarship, partly to its discredit. There is also, of course, a pre-dictably enormous literature devoted to the study of the werewolf in wider purview, much of which makes at least glancing reference to antiquity. The qual-ity of this literature is every bit as variable as one might predict. Between compe-tent studies on the one hand and worthless ones on the other lies a frustratingly broad band of work in which insight jostles with silliness.[55]

---

[52] De Blécourt 2015b:13.   [53] Cf. Donecker 2012:293.

[54] Cf. Copper 1977:138–59 and Frost 2003:145–51. But the early cinematic werewolf was evidently heavily influenced also by late-nineteenth-century and early-twentieth-century pulp-fiction stories of the sort published in *Weird Tales* and exemplified in Frost's 1973 collection.

[55] For werewolves in broader scope see, *inter multa alia*, Böttiger 1837, Hertz 1862, Baring-Gould 1865, Roberts 1999, Summers 1933, Eisler 1951, Villeneuve 1960, Russell and Russell 1978, Otten 1986, Douglas 1992, Milin 1993, Epstein 1995, Frost 2003, Bourgault du Coudray 2006, Sconduto 2008, de Blécourt 2013b, 2015a. I offer observations on some of these. A good many of the *loci* rehearsed still in the scholarship of ancient werewolfism were brought together in German by Hertz 1862 and then in English three years later by Baring-Gould 1865. The latter book is now often dismissed as outmoded, or even moved back over the line from being an incunabular contribution to modern scholarship to being a quaint object of study in itself for the history of werewolf thought (Copper 1977:232 even contrives to classify the work as 'fiction'!). This is unfair: subsequent

The present book proceeds in the following fashion. The first two chapters look at two persistent (and related) folkloric contexts for werewolfism in the ancient world. Chapter 1 looks at its association with witchcraft, magic and cursing, with particular attention to Homer's Circe, Herodotus' Neuri, Virgil's Moeris, the tradition of the intriguing *strix*-witch in Latin poetry and Latin fiction, and finally the notion of the werewolf's curse. Chapter 2 looks at its equally persistent association with ghosts, with particular attention to the general association between wolves and death in Italy, and then the writings of Herodotus, Virgil, Tibullus, Petronius, Marcellus of Side, and Philostratus. The associations documented in these two chapters tell us something of the story world in which the ancient werewolf dwelled. Chapter 3 then considers a range of themes in the evidence for ancient werewolfism, all of which share the conceit of a polarity between an inside and an outside, and all of which are shared with the medieval tradition (and beyond): the inner core versus outer carapace, sometimes linked by an identifying wound; the werewolf's movement between the inside of the home or the city and the outside of the woods or the wilderness; and the werewolf's taking of transformative material inside himself by means of ingestion. Chapter 4 builds on Chapters 2 and 3 to contend that the ideas of soul projection strongly associated with werewolfism in the medieval and early modern periods were already associated with it in the ancient world: a telling parallelism obtained between the ancient werewolf's shedding of his outer human carapace, identified with his

---

Anglo-Saxon scholarship has remained heavily dependent upon Baring-Gould's work (often, as we have already noted, tralatitiously). Summers 1933 is a work of immense and profound learning but of utterly chaotic and rebarbative presentation. Nonetheless, it remains the single most valuable repertorium of sources for the subject, that too despite the author's undisguised commitment to the belief that werewolfism is characteristically, *re vera*, a form of demonic possession. (A reasonably sympathetic approach to both of these English texts may be found at de Blécourt 2009:192–6.) Copper 1977 and Woodward 1979 are alike under-referenced and often derivative of Summers; the former is distinguished by its belletristic appreciations of werewolf novels, the latter by its good illustrations. Otten 1986 offers an oddly structured but nonetheless useful and indeed widely cited reader of original texts in translation and of scholarship upon them. Douglas 1992, written in an accessible style, is less scrupulous in its documentation than it might be and often derivative, but for all that offers some valuable insights, not least in relation to the significance of shamanistic thinking for post-classical werewolfism. Milin 1993 surveys werewolfism in the West over the last millennium, with particular attention to the medieval romances and to early modern demonology. Frost 2003 reliably surveys the scholarship and subscholarship of werewolves (30–49) and devotes a few words to the ancient and medieval traditions (50–5), but the author's principal interest lies in the werewolves of pulp fiction, his knowledge of which is impressive (note also his highly readable 1973 anthology of such material). His succinct and engaging summaries of werewolf stories published, mainly in English, in the century between 1820 and 1920 are of considerable interest (55–106). The object of Bourgault du Coudray 2006, a work of the postmodernist school, eludes me; its value for the study of the ancient werewolf may be gauged from its opening references to the works of 'Pausanius and Appollodorus' (12). Sconduto 2008 wears its learning lightly to offer an admirably engaging reading of the principal medieval French texts on werewolfism. De Blécourt 2015a presents a collection of serious and scholarly articles on the European werewolf with focuses from antiquity (Gordon 2015) to the modern period. Its claims (de Blécourt 2015b:2) that 'no academic history of werewolves' has preceded it and that 'werewolves on their own have not yet become a genuine subject of academic historical study' are unworthy, though no doubt good for marketing (cf. also de Blécourt's own suite of essays on comparative werewolf studies of one sort or another, including 2007a, 2007b, 2009, 2013a, 2013b).

clothing, in order for his inner wolf to run free, and the ancient Greek 'shaman' figure's shedding of his outer human carapace in the form of his physical body, in order for his soul to fly free. Consideration of these themes prompts the further suggestion that Petronius' tale retains the traces of and therefore testifies to the existence of a traditional werewolf tale type in the ancient word that ran along the lines of Marie de France's *Bisclavret*. Chapter 5 also builds on Chapters 2 and 3 to reconstruct the traditions pertaining to the athlete Euthymus and the Hero of Temesa, the 'demon in a wolfskin', and to contextualize them both against a further range of Greek traditional narratives and against the Italian iconography of death. Chapter 6 finally returns to the hoary subject of the confused and conflicting werewolf traditions of Arcadia and Mount Lykaion. It attempts to make sense of them by disentangling and disaggregating them, and most importantly so in the light of the folkloric and traditional themes considered hitherto, including those bearing upon athletes, building on Chapter 5 in this regard. It is possible to salvage the elements of a further folkloric werewolf tale here too from the midst of this compromised data, one focusing upon the figure of Damarchus.

A secondary purpose of this book is to provide a comprehensive sourcebook for werewolfism in Graeco-Roman antiquity, a purpose consonant with my long-established predilection for letting the ancient sources speak for themselves wherever possible.[56] To this end, I have sought to integrate full translations of all passages of importance under this head in display-quote format at the most appropriate point of the book. I apologize here for the fact that this technique may become a little cumbersome in those parts of the study for which there is a plenitude of data, most notably the copious traditions of the human sacrifice made by Lykaon (Chapter 6): the technique remains preferable, in terms of lucidity, convenience, and economy, to the obvious alternative, that of confining all the translations to a source catalogue or appendix at the rear.[57] It should be made clear that not all the passages of text in display quotes relate (directly) to the ancient world: some are reproduced for comparative purposes.

Why Werewolves?

Why, one may well wonder, did the Greeks and Romans develop the notion of the were*wolf* specifically? Why develop a tradition of men transforming into wolves in particular, as opposed to other animals? Of course the question is bigger than the classical world, just as the phenomenon of werewolfism is. Nor is the wolf the only animal of choice in such transformations in other cultures: in the Norse

---

[56] Cf. Ogden 2009, 2013b.
[57] Similarly, I attempted to reproduce full translations of all ancient passages bearing upon the legend of Seleucus at the appropriate points in Ogden 2017.

world, for example, were-bears are as frequent as werewolves (see Chapter 4). But let us, nonetheless, suggest a few words of justification for the particular significance of the wolf in this role in a specifically classical context.

There has been a tendency in discussions of ancient werewolfism to latch onto the wolf as the ultimate icon of wildness, as, that is to say, the nicely antithetical pole to the civilized human, taking inspiration from such texts as (the second-century AD) Artemidorus' *Oneirocritica*, in which a dream of a wolf signifies a person who is hostile, violent, and villainous.[58] So it is that, amongst more recent scholars, for example, Metzger declares, 'The wolf had a very strong cultural image and was seen as the direct opposite of man: his behaviour transgressed all the laws of human civilization.'[59] So too Gordon: '...the Greeks regularly distinguished between: (1) the city proper...; (2) the cultivated land surrounding the city, settled with villages; and (3) the largely uninhabited and prescriptively "unproductive" area beyond this, mainly hilly or mountainous.... Wolves belonged to this sphere of the wild....'[60] One can sympathize here to some extent. As we shall see in Chapter 3, the motif of the man transforming into a wolf and at that point running off into the wild, the woods, or the wilderness (or otherwise running off into these places in order to transform into a wolf there) was a persistent one in ancient and medieval werewolf literature.

But it is surely significant that, for the ancients, the wolf could also be, oppositely, a paradigm of human-style intelligence, civilization, and cooperation within the animal world.[61] What other large animals, relatable in size to a human scale, could be seen to fashion such a structured, orderly, and collaborative society for themselves?[62] And had not the wolves given mankind the dog, not merely the only creature capable of full and syntagmatic integration into human society, but actually in so many ways an exponent of the best of human virtues?

Already the *Iliad* sees a wolf pack hunting down and devouring a stag together as a suitable simile for Achilles' successful if not necessarily well-disciplined Myrmidons.[63] Xenophon speaks of a wolf pack sharing out duties when they wish

[58] Artemidorus *Oneirocritica* 2.12 (103). For Greek and Roman wolves and wolf-lore in general see de Block 1877, Eckels 1937, Richter 1978, Buxton 1987:60–7, Mainoldi 1984:11–35, 97–104, 127–41, 187–209, Maisonneuve 1985 [*non vidi*], Detienne and Svenbro 1989:148–55, 157–8, Marcinkowski 2001, Metzger 2011:171–9, Metzger 2012:142–5, Gordon 2015:26–31.

[59] Metzger 2012:135 (abstract).

[60] Gordon 2015:26. Previously, Detienne and Svenbro 1989 had lain great emphasis on the ancient conceptualization of the wolf as an asocial animal.

[61] For the quasi-human, intelligent, and civilized wolf in ancient thought see Buxton 1987:62–3, Gordon 2015:29–30. For modern thinking on the sociability, civilizedness, and structuredness of wolf (predominantly grey-wolf) society, see Lopez 1978:31–52, 59–60, 67–9 (wolves can even form relationships with ravens!), Mech and Boitani 2003b, Packard 2003, Harrington and Asa 2003, Spotte 2012:141–2, 193–238.

[62] Bees were also famous in the ancient world for their well-ordered society, as, classically, in Virgil *Georgics* 4; cf. Davies and Kathirithamby 1986:47–82. But bees are hardly on the human scale, and are rather less easy to relate to.

[63] Homer *Iliad* 16.156–65.

to seize some protected animal: some of them drive off the guard while others seize the prey.[64] Apollodorus' account of the myth of Athamas features a wolf pack sharing portions of slain sheep between themselves.[65] Babrius (c. AD 200) retells a remarkable fable of Aesop: the leader of an army of dogs of diverse breeds expresses his despair at the prospect of going into battle against a wolf army in which all the soldiers are identical, the implication being, of course, that the wolf army will act with the discipline of a well-drilled phalanx.[66] Timothy of Gaza (c. AD 500) notes that, 'If two wolves snatch a sheep together and slaughter it by shaking it in their teeth, the distribution is on equal terms.'[67]

Aelian (early third century AD) provides us with a wealth of material in this regard. He tells how wolf packs can get themselves safely across broad and fast-flowing rivers by swimming in a chain, each wolf clamping the tail of the one in front in its jaws.[68] The pack can use a similar technique again to extract (before devouring) an ox stranded in a pool: the first of the chain clamps onto the ox's tail, and then they all drag it out backwards.[69] In an example that nicely unites the wolves' cooperativeness with their cannibalistic savagery, Aelian notes that, when the hunt has been unsuccessful for Egyptian wolves and they must eat one of their own, they find the weakest member of the pack by running in a circle until one of them collapses from dizziness.[70]

Sometimes wolves are attributed with social interaction even with humans. Aelian again knows of a wolf that saved the life of Gelon of Syracuse when he was a schoolboy: it seized the writing tablet from his hands as he sat in his school and ran off. Gelon left the school to chase after it, whereupon the roof fell in.[71] He also tells that at Conopium on the Maetis (the Sea of Azov) wolves serve as the faithful companions of fishermen, being explicitly compared to house-guarding dogs in this respect.[72] And sometimes too the civilizedness of wolves can even extend to piety. Aelian knows of a particular pious wolf that located the gold that had been stolen from Apollo's temple at Delphi: it dragged a priest along by his robe to the spot at which it had been concealed and started to dig with its paws; a bronze statue was duly erected in its honour.[73] He also knows that wolves in general

---

[64] Xenophon *Hipparch* 4.19–20.
[65] Apollodorus *Bibliotheca* 1.9.2. Detienne and Svenbro 1989: 152 go so far as to compare this to an 'isonomic' distribution between hoplites; cf. Buxton 1987:76.
[66] Aesop 343 Perry = Babrius 85.
[67] Timothy of Gaza *On Animals*, excerpt printed at Haupt 1869:8; cf. Buxton 1987:62.
[68] Aelian *Nature of Animals* 3.6. This was a favourite paradigm of lupine cooperation: a poem of the *Greek Anthology* tells that wolves could successfully hunt down men that jump into the Nile to escape them by means of a similar technique (9.252); cf. also Artemidorus *Oneirocritica* 2.12 (103).
[69] Aelian *Nature of Animals* 8.14; cf. 5.19 for a clever technique an individual wolf can employ to fell a bull on land.
[70] Aelian *Nature of Animals* 7.20.
[71] Aelian *Nature of Animals* 13.1; cf. Marcinkowski 2001:23–6.
[72] Aelian *Nature of Animals* 6.65.
[73] Aelian *Nature of Animals* 10.26 and 12.40; a broadly similar story at Pausanias 10.14.7, which includes the wolf killing the thief.

respect the sanctuary offered to their prey by the shrine of Pan at (Arcadian) Aule, and decline to enter it in pursuit of the animals that have fled there.[74]

Perhaps this, after all, is why werewolves are wolves, why, in other words, the ancients chose the wolf to be the animal of transformation: the wolf does not merely represent the crude alternative pole to humanity, as its notable savagery might invite us to suspect, but rather it already embodies in itself a straddling of the divide between savagery and civilization. Werewolves are wolves because there is a sense in which wolves are in and of themselves werewolves already— insofar, that is, as they combine the qualities of the wildest and most lawless of animals with those of civilization and humanity.[75]

---

[74] Aelian Nature of Animals 11.6.

[75] One could contend, I suppose, that the primary affinity of werewolves is not with the quasi-human, cooperative wolves of the pack but with the supposedly more savage lone wolf. Most of the ancient werewolves we encounter, it must be admitted, are seemingly solitary as they run off into the wilderness alone (for which see Chapter 3; cf. Alcaeus 130b.16–25 LP, which seems to associate the wilderness life with the lone wolf in particular, in speaking as it does of an exile life amongst the 'wolf thickets', lykaimiais). Much would depend here on taking Aristotle very seriously when he claims that 'It is lone-hunter wolves rather than hunting packs that eat people' (ἀνθρωποφαγοῦσι δ' οἱ μονοπεῖραι τῶν λύκων μᾶλλον ἢ τὰ κυνηγέσια, History of Animals 594a30); cf. Eckels 1937:9–11, Buxton 1987:62–3, 75, 79 n.59, Detienne and Svenbro 1989:156. We do hear occasionally of lone wolves devouring people in ancient literature beyond this (e.g. the great red wolf that devours Publius at Phlegon Mirabilia 3.11–12, for which see Chapter 2; and the wolf that eats the Delphic temple robber at Pausanias 10.14.7, to which we have just referred—though both of these examples are rather odd ones). However, Tibullus 1.5.47–60 seems to imagine his transformed bawd-witch in the company of other wolves, and Pliny Natural History 8.80–2 tells that the werewolves of the Arcadian Anthid rite run with other wolves once transformed. And we do hear equally of wolf packs devouring people too: Milo of Croton was devoured by a pack of wolves once he had foolishly trapped his hands in a tree trunk (Pausanias 6.14.8; cf. Chapter 6), and the Greek Anthology (9.252) tells, as we have just seen, of wolves (most cooperatively) forming a lupine chain in order to get at the man who had jumped into the Nile to escape them.

1

The Curse of the Werewolf:
Witches and Sorcerers

'By their friends shall ye know them,' as Matthew didn't quite say. The purpose of this chapter and the next is to establish the two principal (and related) contexts of werewolves in ancient thought: that of magic and witchcraft on the one hand, and that of ghosts on the other, both of them eminently folkloric subjects in themselves. Here we review the evidence for the association with witches and sorcerers, in broadly chronological order.[1]

Homer's Circe

The first text of potential interest for ancient werewolfism is a complex one. It derives from the seventh-century BC *Odyssey*. In their attempts to make their way home to Ithaca, Odysseus and his men have arrived at Circe's island.[2] Plans are made to explore:

> But I counted off all my well-greaved companions into two groups, and I gave both groups a leader. I led one, and godlike Eurylochus the other. We quickly shook lots in a helmet fitted with bronze. Out jumped the lot of great-hearted Eurylochus. He set out, and with him twenty-two companions, weeping. They left us behind, and we were wailing too. In the glens they found the house of Circe, built with polished stones, in a sheltered place. Around it there were wolves of the mountain and lions, which Circe herself had enchanted, for she had given them evil drugs. But they did not attack the men; rather, they stood on their hind legs and fawned around them [*perissainontes*] wagging their long tails.[3]

---

[1] For the syndrome of werewolves and magic in ancient literature see the brief words of Metzger 2011:225–6; for the syndrome in broader contexts, see Summers 1933 *passim*, Ginzburg 1990:153–82, de Blécourt 2009.

[2] For Circe in debates about ancient werewolfism, see Douglas 1992:54–6, Metzger 2011:227–8. For general commentaries on the scene see Kaiser 1964:200–13, Heubeck and Hoekstra 1989:55–6, Parry 1992:173–95.

[3] The key lines, 211–14:

> ἀμφὶ δέ μιν λύκοι ἦσαν ὀρέστεροι ἠδὲ λέοντες·
> τοὺς αὐτὴ κατέθελξεν ἐπεὶ κακὰ φάρμακ' ἔδωκεν·
> οὐδ' οἵ γ' ὡρμήθησαν ἐπ' ἀνδράσιν ἀλλ' ἄρα τοί γε
> οὐρῇσιν μακρῇσι περισσαίνοντες ἀνέσταν·

As when dogs fawn on their master as he comes from dinner, for he always brings them tid-bits to cheer their heart, in this way the strong-clawed wolves and lions fawned on them [sainon]. But the men took fear, when they saw the dreadful wild animals.[4]   Homer *Odyssey* 10.203–19

The only key Homer provides to this—quite mysterious—passage is the words he subsequently puts into Eurylochus' mouth, as he expresses dismay at the prospect of returning to Circe's house after witnessing his comrades turned into pigs:

Ah, wretches, where are we going? Why do you yearn after the disaster that will ensue from going down to the hall of Circe, who will make us all pigs or wolves or lions, to have us, by force, as guards for her great house?

Homer *Odyssey* 10.431–4

No alternative perspective is supplied and so, in the first instance, we must understand that the nature of the enchantment to which the wolves and the lions outside Circe's house have been subject is that of transformation by Circe into their current animal forms from humans, just as, in the striking central vignette of this famous episode, Odysseus' companions themselves are transformed into pigs by her with a magic potion.[5] The analogy works well: when Circe proceeds to transform the companions into pigs, we are told that 'They had the heads, voices, bristles, and bodies of pigs, but their minds remained unchanged and just as they were before.'[6] It seems that a lekythos-painter working in around the last decade of the sixth century BC also read the nature of the wolves in this way: amongst the transforming creatures with which he surrounds Circe, potion in hand, is a figure with a human body and a wolf's head.[7] And this was evidently the way Dio Chrysostom understood the action here, observing as he does that 'The ancient myth tells that Circe effected transformations by means of drugs, with the result that pigs and wolves were created from humans.'[8] It was also the way that the Homeric scholiasts and in due course Eustathius read the scene, both making appeal to Eurylochus.[9] The paradoxical gentleness and friendliness

---

[4] The key lines, 218–19:

ὡς τοὺς ἀμφὶ λύκοι κρατερώνυχες ἠδὲ λέοντες
σαῖνον·

[5] Homer *Odyssey* 10.229–43.   [6] Homer *Odyssey* 10.39–40.

[7] Taranto, Museo Nazionale 20,324 (9887) = *LIMC* Kirke no.5 = Touchefeu-Meynier 1968:88 no. 174 with plate xiii.3–5; cf. Mainoldi 1984:103. A lion-headed man is present too, which further points to the fact that the artist has the *Odyssey*'s wolves-and-lions scene in mind.

[8] Dio Chrysostom *Orations* 33.58: ὁ παλαιὸς μῦθός φησι τὴν Κίρκην μεταβάλλειν τοῖς φαρμάκοις, ὥστε σῦς καὶ λύκους ἐξ ἀνθρώπων γίγνεσθαι· Cf. Kaiser 1964:203–5.

[9] Schol. vet. Homer *Odyssey* 10.213 (τοὺς αὐτὴ κατέθελξεν] ἐξ ἀνθρώπων εἰς φύσιν λεόντων καὶ λύκων μετέβαλεν. Q. οὐκ ἐξ ἀγρίων τιθασεύουσα, ἀλλ' ἐξ ἀνθρώπων θῆρας ποιήσασα. λέγει οὖν ὁ Εὐρύλοχος ἑξῆς (443) 'ἢ σῦς ἠὲ λύκους ποιήσεται ἠὲ λέοντας.' H.T.); Eustathius on Homer *Odyssey* 10.213 (p.377 Stalbaum).

of the wolves and the lions may be readily explained by the fact that, like the pigs, they retain human minds within.

And further, pleasing implications follow from the assumption that the wolves and the lions represent the crews of previous ships that had had the misfortune to visit Circe's island. In this case the fawning is surely to be read, in retrospect at any rate, no longer as the unquestioning, exuberant affection of a pet dog but as a desperate plea—either a warning to Odysseus' men lest they suffer the same fate of animal transformation, or a request for help from these victims in recovering their own human forms. And if these animals have been transformed from humans by Circe, what of the other animals on the island? Had they all once been humans? Again, a pleasingly sinister implication follows for the first animal Odysseus himself has encountered on the island, the great stag that runs across his path as he returns from his initial reconnaissance, which he kills and eats with his men: might we understand, in retrospect, that this stag too was a man transformed and was trying to communicate with Odysseus, and might we understand that Odysseus has accordingly been tricked into cannibalism?[10]

We encounter the stag first, but it is only when we meet the wolves, named before the lions, that we are introduced to the notion of transformation from the human. Perhaps it is significant that it is the wolf that is used to introduce the broader idea, human-to-wolf-transformation—werewolfism—already being a well-established notion in its own right.

The distinguished Roman scholar Varro wrote in the first century BC, and is cited for us by Augustine in his *City of God*, written in 413–23 AD. They both bracket the animal transformations of Circe, now presented by Augustine as a 'woman-mage', closely together with the phenomenon of Arcadian werewolfism (for which see Chapter 6):

> ...Varro mentions other things, these no easier to believe, in connection with that most famous woman-mage [*maga*] Circe, the one who also transformed Odysseus' companions into beasts, and in connection with the Arcadians. These, chosen by lot, would swim across a certain pool, and they were changed into wolves there....[11]
>
> ...Wherefore, as to the claim that has been entrusted to writing, that men are habitually transformed into wolves by the gods, or more properly the demons, of Arcadia, and as to the claim that Circe transformed the companions of Odysseus – it seems to me that these things could have been effected by the means I have stated, if indeed they have happened at all.[12]
>
> Augustine *City of God* 18.17 and 19

---

[10] Homer *Odyssey* 10.156–84.
[11] A fuller version of this first passage is supplied in Chapter 6.
[12] This 'means' will be discussed in Chapter 4.

And so too Isidore of Seville, writing in the early seventh century A D, in a section of his work headed *De magis*, 'On mages':

> A certain very famous woman-mage [*maga*] Circe is also spoken of, who trans-formed Odysseus' companions into beasts. Spoken of too is the sacrifice the Arcadians used to perform to their god Lycaeus. Any people that ate from it were transformed into the shapes of beasts.   Isidore of Seville *Etymologies* 8.9.5

None of these last three authors come close to attributing wolf transformations directly to Circe, but it is evident that for them she inhabits the same *imaginaire* as the werewolf.

But the *Odyssey* is an open text and other readings remain possible. Eurylochus' words at ll. 431–4 could be discounted as a misinterpretation on the part of the character, while ll. 203–19 could rather be construed to mean that Circe's enchant-ment has been of a much more limited kind, merely taming the minds of original wild animals.[13] This reading does not invigorate the surrounding text in the same way as the werewolf line of interpretation, but that is no final argument against it, and it raises interesting possibilities of another kind, namely that Circe refracts a goddess-type familiar in the Near East and early Greece alike, the so-called 'Mistress of Animals' (*potnia thērōn*).[14] This goddess-type exercises mastery over animals and in her iconography is traditionally represented as a standing figure with a pair of wild animals fawning upon her from either side. Artemis is often so portrayed in early Greek art, from the seventh century B C on.[15] Of course, the parallel with Circe's case is not exact here, since Circe's animals are only seen to fawn upon Odysseus' men, not upon Circe herself. Mistresses of Animals are fur-ther known for taking human lovers (though this would hardly suit the chaste Artemis), whom they then maim, and here we recall that Hermes advises Odysseus to exact from Circe an oath to the effect that she will not leave him 'cowardly and unmanned' if he sleeps with her.[16]

The classic example of a Mistress of Animals in Greek literature is that of Aphrodite in the *Homeric Hymn to Aphrodite* (7th–6th c. B C):

> Aphrodite came to Ida of the many springs, Ida the mother of beasts, and she made straight for the house across the mountain. And there followed after her,

---

[13] The interpretation favoured by Mainoldi 1984:102 and Heubeck and Hoekstra 1989:55–6, the latter on the spurious basis that the verb *thelgein* exclusively denotes a transformation effected on the mind rather than upon an outer form; but Homer uses the same verb less than a hundred lines later to describe Circe's attempt to transform Odysseus himself into a pig (291, 327).

[14] For Circe's relationship with Mistress of Animals figures in the Near East and the Greek world, see Mainoldi 1984:102–3, Crane 1988:61–85, Yarnall 1994:26–52, Marinatos 2000 esp. 32–45 and Ogden 2008:7–27.

[15] *LIMC* Artemis nos. 2–70; cf. Kahil 1984:624–9.

[16] Homer *Odyssey* 10.301 and 341: κακὸν καὶ ἀνήνορα.

fawning upon her, grey wolves and fierce-eyed lions, bears and swift leopards, hungry for deer. She delighted in her heart to see them, and cast desire into their breasts, and they all lay together, two-by-two in the shady haunts.

Homeric Hymn (5) *to Aphrodite* 69–74

We note that wolves are mentioned first in this list too. We are further told here that Aphrodite takes a human lover, Anchises, the father of Aeneas, only to render him 'feeble'.[17] Subsequent sources specify that she rendered him paraplegic, the condition in which he is famously found in Virgil's *Aeneid*.[18] Such, indeed, was her unmanning of him.

But perhaps the distinction between the two paradigms adumbrated here, transformer of men into wolves and Mistress of Animals, need not be all that great. The classic example of the Mistress-of-Animals type in Near Eastern literature is represented by the figure of Ishtar in the standard Akkadian version of the *Gilgamesh* epic (second millennium BC). In the sixth tablet Gilgamesh rejects Ishtar's attempts to seduce him with the promise of bestowing fecundity upon his animals, reminding her of the doom that her former lovers have met: she had turned the gardener Ishullanu into a frog; she had broken the wing of the *allallu*-bird while condemning the lion to the hunter's pit and the horse to the whip. These three persecuted animals seem also to have been former lovers, and to have been subjected at once to both animal transformation and maiming. Most interestingly of all for us:

> You loved the shepherd, the grazier, the herdsman, / who regularly piled up for you (bread baked in) embers,/ slaughtering kids for you day after day. / You struck him and turned him into a wolf, so his own shepherd boys drive him away, and his dogs take bites at his thighs.
>
> *Gilgamesh* (Standard Version) vi.58–63 (George trans.)[19]

Another Greek manifestation of the Mistress-of-Animals goddess-type, and one of particular relevance for us, relates to Leto:

> This is told by the Xanthian Menecrates in his *Lysiaca* [*FGrH/BNJ* 769 F2; 4th c. BC] and by Nicander [*FGrH/BNJ* 271/2 F23; 2nd c. BC].[20] When Leto had given birth to Apollo and Artemis on the island of Asteria, she came to Lykia bringing

---

[17] *Homeric Hymn to Aphrodite* 161–7, 180–90, esp. 188, ἀμενηνόν.

[18] Virgil *Aeneid* 2.707 etc.

[19] For translations see Dalley 1989:77 and George 2003:i, 623 (cited; a slightly different version at George 1999:48–50). NB Dalley has Ishullanu turned (uncertainly) into a frog, whereas George has him turned (uncertainly) into a dwarf; discussion at George 2003:ii, 836. For a comparandum from Chinese mythology in which a one-night assignation with a witch-like goddess leads to emasculation ('Madame White Snake') see Lai 1992.

[20] Cf. Jenkins, *BNJ ad loc.*

her children to the baths of the river Xanthus. As soon as she arrived in Lykia, the first thing she encountered was the spring of Melite, and she was keen to wash the children there before going to the Xanthus. But oxherd men drove her off, so that their oxen could drink from the spring. Leto abandoned Melite and went off, but wolves [*lykoi*] met her, fawned upon her [*sēnantes*], showed her the way and took her to the river Xanthus. She drank its water, washed her children, and declared the Xanthus sacred to Apollo. The land, which had been called Tremilis, she renamed Lykia from the wolves that had escorted her. She returned to the spring and exacted justice from the oxherds that had driven her away. They were washing their oxen beside the spring. Leto transformed them and turned them all into frogs. She struck their backs and shoulders with a rough stone and cast them all into the spring. She gave them a life in the water, and still now they call out in the rivers and the lakes.

Antoninus Liberalis *Metamorphoses* 35 (2nd c. AD)[21]

Here, then, we seem to have a Greek example of a Mistress of Animals fawned on specifically and significantly by wolves, who transforms human men into animals. The herdsmen are no lovers of hers, in contrast to the case of Ishtar, but it may be indicated that they are also maimed as well as transformed: what, otherwise, is the significance of Leto striking them with a rough stone?

Needless to say, the etymology of 'Lykia' offered here is a false one (the name is rather derived from a term similar to the indigenous Luwian 'Lukka').[22] But Leto enjoyed her escort of wolves beyond the confines of the claim that she bore her children in Lykia, and wolves were held to have escorted her also to Delos, the more canonical birthplace of Apollo and Artemis. Aristotle cites a myth designed to explain why wolves only whelp within a twelve-day period each year: the number of days salutes the time it took Leto's lupine escort to bring her, in her pregnant state, from the land of the Hyperboreans to the island of Delos, during which time she herself also took on the form of a she-wolf in order to conceal herself from Hera's wrath.[23] Aelian tells us that it was for this reason that Homer applies the epithet *Lykēgenēs*, which he interprets as 'Wolf-born' (as opposed to 'Lykian-born'), to Apollo, and that it was for this reason also that Leto was honoured with

---

[21] For discussion of this text, see Summers 1933:143–4, 173–4, Eckels 1937:66–9, Papathomopoulos 1968:148–9, Bryce 1983, Keen 1998:194–7, Jenkins on *BNJ* 769 Menekrates F2 and *BNJ* 271/2 Nikander F23. Ovid *Metamorphoses* 6.313–81 has a more expansive but wolfless version. The 2nd-c. BC Polycharmus *FGrH/BNJ* 770 F5 (= *TAM* ii.1, no. 174) specifies that Leto gave birth at Araxa on the Xanthus; cf. also Diodorus 5.56; but according to Strabo C639–40 the Lykian river in question was, rather, the Cenchrius.

[22] See Melchert 2003:107–14, Jenkins on Menecrates *BNJ* 769 F2. Aeschylus *Seven Against Thebes* 145–6 already makes explicit play with the term *Lykeios* as signifying at once both 'Lykian' and 'wolf-like'. It has been suggested that the name 'Lykaon' is actually derived from the Hittite word for 'Lykian', *Lukkawanni*: see Lebrun 2001:252; Bremmer 2019:369.

[23] Aristotle *History of Animals* 580a (6.35); cf. Plutarch *Natural Questions* 38 (= *Moralia* p.517), Aelian *Nature of Animals* 4.4, Antigonus *Mirabilia* 56 Giannini. See Eckels 1937:66–9.

a bronze statue of a wolf at Delos.[24] The Greeks developed other wolf-themed aetiological tales too to explain why Apollo should have been *Lykios* or *Lykeios*. Delphic Apollo had once spared the Sicyonians from the depredations of the local wolves on their sheep by giving them a bit of dry wood from his shrine; they were able to poison and deter the wolves by mixing this wood with sheep flesh.[25] And Apollo was said to have adopted the form of a wolf to kill the malevolent Telchines.[26]

At any rate, in view of the cases of Circe, Aphrodite, and Leto, it seems that wolves—and that too anthropomorphic ones—figured prominently in the entourage of the Greek reflex of the Mistress-of-Animals figure.

These considerations bear upon the hoary old issue of whether the Homeric Circe should actually be seen as a 'witch', at any rate for those who insist on formulating the issue in the exclusive and reductive terms of 'either witch or goddess'. This is, however, a false dichotomy based upon a category mistake, since goddesses are perfectly capable of deploying witchcraft.[27] It must also be borne in mind once again that the *Odyssey* is an open text, the characters and episodes of which were pulled in different directions towards a range of competing paradigms, sometimes compatible with each other, sometimes less so, in the long period of its oral gestation. In including discussion of Homer's Circe here, I have not doubted that it is indeed right and proper to see her as—whatever else she might also be—a 'witch', as she so clearly was for Varro, Augustine, and Isidore of Seville, and as she will self-evidently be for most readers. But given the contentiousness of this view in the context of modern debates about ancient magic, I justify it (once again) in Appendix A.

Herodotus' Neuri

The historical race of the Neuri were a mobile population in antiquity, but they are now primarily identified with the Milograd culture that existed 'in the wooded regions between Ukraine and Bielorussia, along the Pripjat and the upper Dnieper'.[28] Herodotus, writing before 425 B C, has this to say of them:

---

[24] Aelian *Nature of Animals* 10.26; Homer *Iliad* 4.101, 119.
[25] Pausanias 2.9.7.
[26] Servius on Virgil *Aeneid* 4.377. For Apollo Lykeios and the ancient interpretation of terms such as *Lykēgenēs*, see Eckels 1937:60–6, Mainoldi 1984:22–8, Graf 1985:218–27, Gershenson 1991 esp. 1–23 (a book of deep but undisciplined learning; the challenging contention is made that Apollo Lykeios is the god of the 'wind-wolf'), Keen 1998:197–201, de Roguin 1999, and Gordon 2015:28–9.
[27] E.g. Aphrodite's erotic-amulet girdle, the *kestos himas* also borrowed by Hera at Homer *Iliad* 14.197–222; cf. Bonner 1949 and Faraone 1999: 97–110.
[28] See Corcella at Asheri et al. 2007:552–8 (with several maps guessing at their location), 589 (the quote), 656, 662. For general discussion of the Neuri in relation to werewolfism, see Summers 1933:133–4, Metzger 2011:217–24, Donecker 2012:298–9, Gordon 2015:40–1, 44.

105. The Neuri have Scythian customs...These people [the Neuri] may well be sorcerers [goētes]. It is said by the Scythians and the Greeks living in Scythia that every year each of the Neuri at one point becomes a wolf for a few days, before returning to his previous form. They don't persuade me of it, but they certainly say it, and they swear to what they say. 106. The Androphagoi ['Man-eaters'] possess the wildest customs of all men. They neither practise justice nor make use of law. They are nomads, and the clothing they wear resembles the Scythian, but they have a separate language of their own. These are the only one of all these peoples to eat men. 107. The Melanchlainoi ['Black-cloaked'] all wear black clothes, and it is on the basis of these that they have their name. They practice Scythian customs.   Herodotus 4.105–7

Herodotus associates the Neuri tightly with the Androphagoi and the Melanchlainoi once again in a subsequent chapter.[29] The Neuri were to be spoken of in similar terms in the Latin tradition:

For individual Neuri there is a fixed time for them, should they wish, to turn into wolves and then back into the people they were.

Pomponius Mela 2.1.14 (AD 43)

The river Borysthenes rises amongst the Neuri. It contains fish of excellent flavour, but they have no bones, just very soft cartilage. But the Neuri, as we understand, are transformed into wolves at fixed times. Then, when the time given to this fate has passed, they return to their original form. These peoples have Mars for their god. They worship swords instead of images. They use people as sacrificial victims. The fires of their altars grow great with bones [ossibus adolent ignes focorum].   Solinus 15 (mid 3rd c. AD)

It is not clear that Mela has any ultimate source other than Herodotus, but Solinus has evidently found some at least of his material elsewhere.

Herodotus declares the Neuri to be 'sorcerers', goētes. We will speak at some length of this word's etymology and semantic field in Chapter 2. It is particularly significant here that Herodotus regards transformation into a wolf not as something merely practised by this single group of 'sorcerers' but rather as something characteristic of sorcerers in general.

The neighbouring peoples Herodotus (twice) identifies for the Neuri, the Androphagoi and the Melanchlainoi, might both be thought to make very suitable neighbours for werewolves. The relevance of the 'Man-eating' Androphagoi in this regard is readily apparent.[30] When Solinus then attributes human sacrifice

---

[29] Herodotus 4.125.3, where he also mentions their (former) homeland, Neuris; cf. also 4.17.2.
[30] So Buxton 1987:68, Moreau 1997:78.

to the Neuri, it seems that he is bringing the conceit of man-eating fully home to them too (even if he does not explicitly state that they actually proceed to eat their sacrificial victims). There may well be some contamination here from the traditions associated with the Arcadian Mount Lykaion, where werewolfism and human sacrifice were famously brought together; the seeming reference to an ash altar, such as was used on Mount Lykaion, does suggest this (see Chapter 6). But the 'Black-cloaked' Melanchlainoi too are suggestive in relation to werewolves, when we consider that Pausanias describes his Hero of Temesa as a demon wearing a wolfskin and as 'terribly black' in his skin (Chapter 5).[31]

Virgil's Moeris

Virgil's (c.39–37 BC) adaptation of Theocritus' second *Idyll*, in which an amateur witch weaves spells to bring home her errant lover, cites the precedent of what is evidently a master sorcerer:[32]

> *Bring Daphnis home, my spells, bring him from the city.* These herbs and these drugs [*venena*], picked in Pontus, were given to me by Moeris himself (they grow in profusion in Pontus). By their power I often saw Moeris change into a wolf and hide himself in the woods, and I often saw him use them to rouse ghosts from the bottom of their tombs, and spirit sown crops away into another field. *Bring Daphnis home, my spells, bring him from the city.*
>
> Virgil *Eclogues* 8.94–100

What can we say of Moeris? In the first instance his name has an appropriately pastoral resonance, being borne by one of the speakers in the following *Eclogue*.[33] But a (Hellenized) Italian shepherd does not make for a very good master magician. More suitably to this context, the name also had strongly Egyptian affinities. Herodotus was already speaking of Egypt's Fayyum Canal, the *Mer-Wer*, as Lake Moeris, and giving the same name also to the pharaoh that dug the lake out, Amenemhet III (r. c.1860–1814 BC).[34] Egypt had been regarded as an ancient home of magic since the time of the *Odyssey*, in which Polydamna, wife of Egypt's

---

[31] Pausanias 6.6.11: 'His skin was awfully black and he was utterly terrifying to see; he had a wolf-skin for his clothing' (χρόαν τε δεινῶς μέλας καὶ τὸ εἶδος ἅπαν ἐς τὰ μάλιστα φοβερός, λύκου δὲ ἀμπίσχετο δέρμα ἐσθῆτα).

[32] For Moeris and his werewolfism see Douglas 1992:56–8, Sconduto 2008:8–9, Metzger 2011:228–30, Gordon 2015:45–6.

[33] Cf. also [Virgil] *Catalepton* 9.18.

[34] Herodotus 2.13 (with miscalculated dating), 69, 101, 148–9, 3.91. Coleman 1977 on *Eclogues* 8.96 prefers to explain the name with reference to the Greek word *moira*, 'fate', unpersuasively, to my mind; Clausen 1994 has nothing to say.

king Thon, had given Helen a selection of drugs both beneficial and deleterious,[35] and it came particularly to be so regarded in the literature of the imperial age.[36] But somehow this well-travelled master magician of Virgil's had contrived to get himself to another of the great homes of magic, the Black Sea, the location of Medea's own Colchis, no less; and Medea too was famously a collector of drugs (*venena,* that is *pharmaka*) of the sort that we are told grow in profusion in the region.[37] One thinks of an intriguing deracinated fragment from one of Sophocles' tragedies that evidently attempts to build up the qualifications of another master magician by associating him with a diverse series of magical homelands: 'a man Colchian, Chaldaean and Syrian by race'.[38] Moeris further declares himself to be a master magician with his expertise in the commonplace activities of the ancient magical repertoire, crop-charming and necromancy, the latter of which will be discussed further in Chapter 2.[39] He recalls Herodotus' Neuri inasmuch as he is a sorcerer who seemingly concentrates on turning himself as opposed to others into a wolf. The Moeris of *Eclogues* 9, as indicated, cannot be supposed to be the same character, but Virgil perhaps seeks to make an artful allusion back to his *Eclogues* 8 namesake by putting the word 'wolf' into his mouth: he explains his loss of voice with reference to the already old proverb in accordance with which it was the lot of those that were seen by a wolf before they saw it themselves to lose their voice.[40]

[35] Homer *Odyssey* 4.219–39.

[36] For some superb portraits of Egyptian sorcerers in Greek and Latin literature of the imperial period see, e.g., Lucian *Philopseudes* 33–6 (Pancrates, he of *The Sorcerer's Apprentice*); Apuleius *Metamorphoses* 2.28–30 (Zatchlas, of whom more below); Antonius Diogenes *Wonders Beyond Thule* at Photius *Bibliotheca* cod. 166 (the wicked Paapis); [Thessalus of Tralles] *De virtutibus herbarum* 1–28 Friedrich (a ghost-raising chief priest); *Alexander Romance* (A) 1.1–12 (Nectanebo, pharaoh and mage); Heliodorus *Aethiopica* 3.16 (a general characterization).

[37] Medea was at the heart of Sophocles' lost tragedy *Rhizotomoi.* 'Root-cutters' (on which see further below); later on, Ovid *Metamorphoses* 7.179–237 gives us an expansive scene in which Medea goes about collecting the drugs she will need to rejuvenate Aeson, roaming the earth in her serpent-drawn flying chariot to do so.

[38] Sophocles *Tympanistai* F638 TrGF.

[39] Crop-charming belonged particularly to the Roman magical world. It was prescribed against already in the Twelve Tables, supposedly compiled in 451 BC (viii.8a–b = Crawford 1996 no.8.4). Pliny *Natural History* 18.41–3 (incorporating L. Calpurnius Piso Frugi F33 Peter = F35 Cornell) preserves the apocryphal story set in the earlier second century BC of an honest man, Cresimus, accused of the practice. See Tupet 1976:181–7, 1986:2610–17, Graf 1997:62–5, Ogden 2009:277–8.

[40] Virgil *Eclogues* 9.53–4 (with Servius *ad loc.*); cf. Plato *Republic* 336d, Theocritus *Idylls* 14.22–3, Aristophanes of Byzantium (et al.) *Aristophanis historiae animalium epitome subjunctis Aeliani Timothei aliorumque eclogis* 2.229 (3rd–2nd c. BC and later), Pliny *Natural History* 8.80, Solinus 2.35 (3rd c. AD), Ambrose (late 4th c. AD) *Hexaemeron* 6.4.26–7 (*PL* 14.252), *Expositio evangelii secundum Lucam* 7.48 (*PL* 15.1711), *Expositio de psalmo* cxviii 10.24 (*PL* 15.1339), Symphosius *Aenigmata* 33.3 (4th–5th c. AD?), Timothy of Gaza 8.10 (5th–6th c. AD), Isidore of Seville *Etymologies* 12.24 (early 7th c. AD), *Geoponica* 15.1.8 (10th c. AD); see Smith 1894:3, Johnston 1931, Crum 1933, Summers 1933:72, Eckels 1937:25–9, Valentini Pagnini 1981:13, Gordon 2015:29–31. Gordon makes the dubious contention that the wolf is to be thought of as casting the 'evil eye' in such circumstances; for the evil eye in antiquity see Dickie 1990, 1991, 1995.

The *Strix*-witch (i): Witches, Screech Owls and Werewolves in Early Imperial Latin Literature

In this section we address the associations, direct and indirect, of the *strix* or *striga* with the werewolf. The term literally denoted a 'screech owl', but it was used in the texts of interest to denote a wicked witch that flew by night in the form of said screech owl, or at any rate in a monstrous form in some way evocative of it, or just possibly sometimes a bat, in order to kill or snatch children or to harvest their body parts.[41] She can be seen to anticipate the modern Western stereotype of the witch, hideous and flying (on a broom) by night, and also that of the vampire. The *striges* were not the first witches to be identified with birds of prey in the classical tradition: the name of our own Circe (*Kirkē*) is thought to derive from *kirkos* ('hawk'), not that Homer seems to make anything of this.[42] One key question is this: was there a notion that a *strix*-witch might have, beyond her focal propensity to transform herself into a screech owl (or something akin to it), a secondary propensity to transform herself also into a wolf? Before we look at the key texts for the question, it will be helpful to establish the paradigm of the *strix* more fully and also to adumbrate another Roman witch paradigm too, that of the bawd-witch that stalks the pages of Latin love elegy.

The Paradigm of the *Strix*-witch

First, a pair of ancient definitions. Festus (later second century AD) cites the first-century BC Latin author Verrius for a popular Greek charm. The texts both of Verrius' words and of the charm he quotes have unfortunately become corrupt, but Festus seems to have said something along the following lines:

> As Verrius says, the Greeks call a *strix* [Lat.] a *strinx* [Gk.] ... the name is applied to evil-doing women, whom they also call 'flying women' [*volaticae*]. And so the Greeks have the custom of, as it were, averting them with these words: '[Gk.] Send away the *strinx*, the long-eared-owl *strinx*, from people, the bird that

---

[41] In Greek we find the terms *strinx* (*stringes*), *strix* (*striges*), *stlix* (*stliges*), *stryx* (*stryges*), *styx* (*styges*), *strigla* (*striglai*), and *striglos* (*strigloi*); in Latin *strix* (*striges/striges*), *striga* (*strigae*), *styx* (*styges*), and *stria* (*striae*). For general discussion of *striges* see in particular the recent overlapping series of publications by Cherubini: 2009a, 2009b, 2010a (a full-length monograph on the subject), and 2010b (an account of her views in English); see further Lawson 1910:179–84, Oliphant 1913, 1914 (the standard collation of the evidence, with arguments for seeing the *strix* as, at least in part, a bat), Boehm 1932, Scobie 1978, 1983:21–30, Curletto 1987: esp. 150–6, West 1995:309–11, McDonough 1997 (arguing that the term denotes some sort of fantastical, hybrid creature), Gordon 1999:204–10, Spaeth 2010, Pater 2015: esp. 224–8, Björklund 2017, Hutton 2017:67–72, Paule 2017:65–79.

[42] See the discussions at Deroy 1985:185–6, Yarnall 1994:28–35, West 1997 408, Marinatos 2000:32–45. Nor were the *striges* the last witches to be so conceptualized: for witch-as-raptor as a folktale motif, see Thompson 1955–8 G211.

should not be named, onto swift-faring ships [*sc.* to carry her away to a desolate place where she can do no harm].'   Festus p.414 Lindsay = *PMG* 858

In another portion of potentially corrupt text, Hesychius' dictionary (*c.* AD 500) offers the following gloss for *striglos*, although it is possible that it was originally attached to a different, adjacent headword, such as *strinx*: '…the "night-wanderer"; it is also called the "little owl" [*nyktoboa*, lit. 'night-shouter']; according to others, the "long-eared owl" [*nyktikorax*, lit. 'night-crow'].'[43]

For the *strix*-witch three texts are of particular value, two early-imperial Latin ones, and a mid-Byzantine Greek one. Ovid puts some flesh on the bones of the phenomenon with an aetiological tale focusing on the boy Proca (a future Alban king) in his *Fasti* of AD 8. He tells us that it is uncertain whether *striges* are natural birds or are witches that have so transformed themselves by their magical arts. Either way, they fly by night and attack children unguarded by nurses; they snatch them from their cradles, rend their flesh with hooked claws, take their innards, and drink their blood:

There are some rapacious birds. These are not the ones that cheated Phineus' mouth of his table [i.e. the Harpies], but they derive their descent from them. They have a large head, their eyes stand proud, their beaks are suited to snatching. There is greyness in their wings and there are hooks on their talons. They fly by night and seek out children without a nurse. They snatch their bodies from their cradles and mar them. They are said to tear apart the innards of suckling babies with their beaks, and their throats are engorged with the blood they have drunk. They are called screech-owls [*striges*]; the reason for the name is that they are accustomed to screech [*stridere*] in dreadful fashion during the night. Whether, then, these creatures are born in avian form, or they are created by means of a spell, and Marsian[44] dirge transmutes old women into birds, they came into Proca's bedchamber. The boy had been born just five days before, and now he was a fresh prey for them. They sucked out his infant breast with eager tongues. The unfortunate child wailed and called for help. Alarmed at the cry of her charge, his nurse ran to him. She found that his cheeks had been gored by hard talons. What could she do? The colour of his face was that one sometimes finds in late leaves that have been damaged by the new frost. She went to Carna [a.k.a. Cranae] and told her all. She said, 'There is no need to be frightened: your charge will be safe.' She came to the cradle. His mother and his father were weeping. 'Hold back your tears: I myself will heal him,' she said. At once she

---

[43] Hesychius s.v. στρίγλος; cf. Hansen's 2005 edition *ad loc.*
[44] The Marsi were an Italian people based at Marruvium, on the shore of Lake Fucinus; for the Romans they were ever associated with magic. See Letta 1972 esp. 139–45, Tupet 1976:187–98, Dench 1995: 159–66.

touched the doorposts, thrice over, with an arbutus branch, and three times she marked the threshold with her arbutus branch. She sprinkled the doorway with water (the waters contained an infusion) and she held the uncooked entrails of a two-month old sow. This is what she said: 'Birds of the night, spare the child's innards; for a small boy a small victim is sacrificed. I pray, take this heart for his heart, these liver-lobes for his liver-lobes. We give you this life to preserve a better one.' When she had made her offering, she laid out the parts she had cut in the open air and forbade those attending the rite to look back at them. A rod of Janus, taken from a whitethorn bush, was put where the small window allowed light into the bedchamber. It is said that after that the birds no longer invaded the cradle, and the boy's former colour returned to him.

Ovid *Fasti* 6.131–68[45]

Petronius reports Trimalchio's tale of *strigae*, whom he also describes as *plussciae* ('women that know something more') and *nocturnae* ('night-women'),[46] this being told in response to, and forming a narrative diptych with, Niceros' werewolf tale:

I myself will tell you a tale to make you shudder: an ass upon the roof-tiles. When I still had my hair long (for from being a boy I led a life of 'Chian' luxury), our master's favourite boy died. He was a pearl, and delightful in every respect. While his pitiful mother was mourning over him, and many of us were feeling miserable about it, the witches [*strigae*] suddenly started to screech [*stridere*].[47] You would have thought it was a dog chasing a hare. We had at that time a Cappadocian slave, tall, quite daring, and strong. He boldly drew his sword and ran out of the door, carefully binding up his left hand to use as a shield. He ran one of the women through the middle, round about here—gods preserve the part of my body I indicate. We heard a groan, but—honestly, I won't lie—we did not actually see them. Our great hulk of a man returned within and threw himself down on the bed. His whole body was black and blue, as if he'd been beaten with whips (this was obviously because an evil hand [*mala manus*] had touched him).[48] We shut the door and returned to what we were doing, but, when the mother embraced the body of her son, as she touched it she realized that it was just a tiny thing made of straw. It had no heart or guts, nothing. You see, the

---

[45] For general discussion see Frazer 1929:iv, 141–4, Bömer 1958–63:ii, 344–5, Scobie 1978:76, Littlewood 2006:45–51, Cherubini 2010a:25–34, 2010b:66–7.

[46] Cf. Damigeron-Evax 28.1 (at Halleux and Schamp 1985:266–7; the text is a 5th–6th c. AD Latin adaptation of a Hellenistic Greek original), which prescribes an amulet against *nyktalōpes*, 'creatures that see by night', and explains the term with the words, 'which is to say, against nocturnal birds [*nocturnas aves*], i.e. *striges* or tawny owls [*cavanae*]'. However, Halleux and Schamp regard the words of explanation as an interpolation. Cf. Cherubini 2009b:80 n.8.

[47] This word is a (plausible) editorial conjecture.

[48] The bracketed portion of the text may be an interpolation.

witches had stolen the boy and left a straw doll in his place. I beg you to believe it. Women that know something more do exist, night-women do exist, and what is up, they can make down. But that hulking man never properly recovered after this adventure, and indeed he went mad and died a few days later.

Petronius *Satyricon* 63[49]

Trimalchio's words leave us uncertain precisely what the witches have done to the baby: either they have replaced the body in its entirety with a straw dummy, or they have extracted its heart and guts and stuffed the shell of the body with straw. Petronius briefly mentions *striges* again (indeed actually deploying the form *striges* as opposed to *strigae* this time). The text is damaged, and the context slightly obscure, but the old woman Proselenos seems to mock Encolpius for his impotence with a rhetorical question, 'What *striges* have devoured your nerves/ cock [*nervos*]?' Here Petronius seems to evoke a more Ovidian model in accordance with which the witches attack a living baby and devour its internal (or external) parts.[50]

Finally, a valuable Greek fragment attributed, perhaps spuriously, to the eighth-century AD John Damascene:[51]

I don't want you to be ignorant about this. Some less well-educated people say that there are women called *stryngai* and also *geloudes* [= *gellos*]. They say that they appear through the air by night. Arriving at a house, they find no hindrance in doors and bolts, but get in even when doors have been securely locked, and smother the children. Others say that they devour their liver and all their mois- ture[52] and impose a time-limit on their lives. Some insist that they have seen them, others that they have heard them. Somehow they enter houses, even though the doors have been locked, together with their body, or just by means of their bare soul. And I will declare that only Christ, Jesus Christ our God, was able to do this. After he rose again from the dead he entered through locked doors to meet his holy apostles. But if a woman mage [*magos*][53] did this, and does it, then the Lord no longer did anything amazing with the locked doors. If they were to say that a witch enters the house just as a bare soul, with her body resting on a bed, then hear what I have to say, which is what our Lord Jesus

---

[49] For general discussion see Cherubini 2010a:34–41, Schmeling 2011:260–4.

[50] Petronius *Satyricon* 134; cf. Friedlaender 1906:318–22, Cherubini 2010b:66, Schmeling 2011:581.

[51] John of Damascus was an Arab Christian, born *c.* AD 650 and dying seemingly a full century later, *c.* AD 750. For Geerard, *CPG* nos. 8040–70 are genuine, *CPG* nos. 8075–100 dubious, and *CPG* 8110–27 spurious. John's works are edited in Kotter and Volk 1969–2013. The current fragment is not yet included in this continuing edition.

[52] The slightly unexpected meaning of οἰκονομία in this context, as explained by *PG ad loc.*

[53] It is rare for the Greek term *magos*, 'mage', to be applied to a woman, as opposed to female-spe- cific terms like *pharmakis*, 'witch', etc. There is another example of the usage, however, at (the effect- ively undateable) Aesop *Fable* 56 Perry, where a 'woman mage' is confuted in court.

Christ said: 'I have the power to lay down my soul, and I have the power in myself to take it up again.'[54] And he did this once on the occasion of his holy passion. But if a disgusting woman mage can do this whenever she wishes, then the Lord did nothing more than what she does. And if she has devoured the child's liver, how is he able to live? All this is nonsense talked by some heretics opposed to the one and holy Church, with a view to diverting some people of the simpler sort from orthodoxy.

John Damascene *On Dragons and Witches* (*De draconibus et strygibus*),
PG 94, 1599–1604 = CPG 8087[55]

In their modus operandi *striges* strongly resemble two sets of female child-killing demons that stalked Graeco-Roman antiquity, the Gellos (or *gellos*—the term serves both as proper name and common noun)[56] mentioned by John Damascene and the closely similar but better known Lamias (or *lamias*),[57] who could feed not only on babies[58] but also on desirable young men.[59] Both of these demon-types had strong roots in Mesopotamia, being derivatives, respectively, of Gallû (who was actually male)[60] and Lamashtu.[61]

In the light of these three principal texts we can be fairly confident that the already-flourishing notion of the *strix* as a child-gutting witch lurks behind the

---

[54] John 10:18.

[55] It is not clear whether the fragment on dragons actually belongs, in any sense, with the fragment on witches translated here. Litavrin 2003:636–43 contends that the dragon portion of this material was actually written by (the 11th-c. AD) Kekaumenos, author of the *Stratēgikon*. For a complete translation of both portions and a commentary on them, see Ogden 2018.

[56] For Gellos as snatchers, devourers, and suffocators of newborns, and as killers of women in childbed, see Zenobius *Proverbs* 1.58 (inc. Sappho F178); *Cyranides* 2.40.35–8; Hesychius *s.vv.* Γελ(λ)ώ, Γελλώς; Michael Psellus (11th c. AD) *Opuscula psychologica, theologica, daemonologica* 164 (*De Gillo*); *Suda* s.v. Γελλοῦς παιδοφιλωτέρα.

[57] For general discussion of Lamias and related phenomena see Lawson 1910:173–9, Schwenn 1924, Rohde 1925:590–3, Fontenrose 1959:44–5, 100–4, 119–20, 1968:81–3, Boardman 1992, Burkert 1992:82–7, Spier 1993, Leinweber 1994, Johnston 1995, 1999a:161–99, Ting 1966, Hansen 2002:128–30, Resnick and Kitchell 2007, Viltanioti 2012, Felton 2013, Ingemark and Ingemark 2013, Ogden 2013a:86–92, 2013b:97–108 (nos. 68–74), Patera 2015, Björklund 2017, Eidinow 2018. For the explicit identification of Lamias (and also a third category of demons, Mormos) with *striglai*, see schol. Aelius Aristides *Panathenaicus* 102.5 (iii p.42 Dindorf).

[58] For Lamias as child-killing demons (often with a serpentine element) see: Aristophanes *Peace* 758, with schol.; Duris of Samos *FGrH / BNJ* 76 F17; Statius *Thebaid* 1.562–669 (for the application of term *lamia* to this wonderful monster see First Vatican Mythographer 2.66); Diodorus 20.41.3–6; Horace *Ars poetica* 340; Isidore of Seville *Etymologies* 8.11.102; schol. Theocritus 15.40; schol. Aelius Aristides (as cited); *Suda* s.v. Μορμώ.

[59] For Lamias rather as the killers of young men, see Dio Chrysostom *Orations* 5; Antoninus Liberalis *Metamorphoses* 8 Lamia (paraphrasing Nicander); Philostratus *Life of Apollonius* 4.25; Heraclitus *De incredibilibus* 34 Lamia.

[60] In Akkadian texts we read that 'The evil Gallû-demon roams in the city, he kills people without mercy...'; see West 1995:313.

[61] As child-killing demons and as devourers of young men alike, Lamias were derived from the Mesopotamian serpent-wielding demoness Lamashtu, described in Akkadian sources as a tearer of foetuses from pregnant women, a snatcher of children, a (deathly) suckler of them, a tormentor of little ones and a drinker or absorber of the blood of men: see the texts collected at West 1995:250–9, 276–7; cf. also West 1991, Farber 1983, and Wiggermann 2000.

tirade of the Cook in Plautus' 191 BC *Pseudolus*. He complains that his cheaper and inferior rival cooks season their food not with seasonings but with *striges*, which devour the diner's intestines while he is still alive.[62] Also in the second century BC, the comic playwright Titinius knew that boys (*puelli*) could be attacked by 'a black *strix*' that could drop milk from her/its fetid dugs between their tender lips, and noted that garlic should be worn as a defence.[63]

A theme that emerges strongly from all three of the principal texts is that the battle-line between the *striges* and their victims is the shell of the house. The challenge for the *striges* is to penetrate this boundary; the challenge for the house-holders is to keep it secure, with doors and windows constituting particular points of vulnerability. The significance of the boundary is conveyed by John Damascene's claim, evidently intended tendentiously, that locked doors present no hindrance to the *striges*. As he himself indicates, they may on occasion have to penetrate the house in question by means of projecting their soul alone—as a wisp that can no doubt flit through the tiniest of apertures or cracks (we shall have more to say on this in Chapter 4). Locked doors evidently did present an initial obstacle at least to Petronius' *striges*: we are to understand that they enabled themselves to enter the house in question by enticing the stolid Cappadocian slave to open the door so as to be able to come out and challenge them as they screeched, and then by slipping in invisibly while it remained open. From Ovid it is clear that one could protect doorways against the *striges* by brushing them with the arbutus branch and by sprinkling them with water, while windows could be protected against them with a rod made from a whitethorn bush.[64] The Mesopotamian Lamashtu demon had similarly been able to overcome such challenges as she sought to enter houses to kill babies etc.: 'she enters by the window, she glides like a serpent; she enters the house, she leaves the house'; 'She enters through the door of the house, she slips in past the door-pivot,[65] she has slipped

---

[62] Plautus *Pseudolus* 820–1: *non condimentis condiunt, sed strigibus, vivis convivis intestina quae exedint*; Scobie1978:98 is surely right to read the text in this way; cf. also Oliphant 1913:135–6, Cherubini 2009b:66.

[63] Titinius F ex incertis fabulis xxii Ribbeck (1873:159), as cited at (the 2nd c. AD) Quintus Serenus Sammonicus *Liber Medicinalis* 58 (1035–7); cf. Oliphant 1913:136, McDonough 1997:319, Cherubini 2010a:21–5, 2010b:71. Subsequently Pliny *Natural History* 11.232 notes, 'I consider it fantastical that *striges* should drop milk from their dugs into the lips of infants.' And then Isidore of Seville *Etymologies* 12.7.42: 'This bird [*sc. strix*] is commonly called *amma* [i.e. wet-nurse] from the fact that it loves [*amando*] little children, whence it is even said to offer them milk when they are born'; see the discussion at Curletto 1987:150.

[64] When Ovid introduces Carna/Cranae at *Fasti* 6.101, he himself offers an appropriate folk etymology of her name: she is 'the goddess of the door-hinge' (*cardo*). Insofar as this figure, as presented by the poet at any rate, protects both innards and hinges alike, she is the perfect opponent to the *strix* that penetrates through doorways with a view to stealing organs. In elucidation of Ovid, Macrobius *Saturnalia* 1.12.32 confirms that the goddess Carna presides over the safety of the internal organs such as livers and hearts, but he may not have any further evidence for this than the passage of Ovid before him, as McDonough supposes. See Pettazzoni 1940 esp. 164, McDonough 1997:328–30, Cherubini 2010b:67.

[65] I.e. through the crack at the back of the door between its hinged edge and the wall.

in past the door-pivot, she kills the little ones; she has given it (the child) a seizure in its abdomen seven times'; 'She enters the open house, she sneaks in by the door of the closed house.'[66]

The *strix* would prove a durable fixture in the *imaginaire* of the Latin west. In King Clovis' *Salic Law* of *c.* AD 507–11 a large fine—one might have expected more—is prescribed for the *stria* (an evolved version of the word) that eats people.[67] Later laws were more concerned with protecting individuals from the consequences of ignorant belief in such things. The AD 643 Lombardian Edict of Rothari prescribes that 'No one should take it upon himself to kill another person's serving-woman or maid on the basis that she is a *striga*, also called a *masca*, because such a thing should in no way be believed by Christian minds, nor does a woman have the ability to devour a person alive from the inside.'[68] Similarly, in making laws for the Saxons in AD 789, Charlemagne was concerned to punish those that, in their pagan ignorance, falsely imagined a woman (or a man) to be eating people qua *striga*, and rashly acted upon the belief.[69] Albeit without the explicit use of the term *strix* (*vel sim.*), the themes of our three principal texts are strikingly resumed in Burchard of Worms' *c.* AD 1012–20 *Corrector* sive *Medicus*, as the nineteenth book of his decrees is known:

> Have you come to believe what many women that have turned to Satan believe and declare to be true? Do you believe that, in the silence of a disturbed night, when you have put yourself to bed and your husband lies in your embrace, you are able to depart through closed doors, for all that you have a bodily form? That you have the power to travel considerable distances over the world, together with other women in the grip of a similar delusion? That, without any visible weapons, you have the power to kill people that have been baptized and redeemed by the blood of Christ? That you have the power to cook their flesh and devour them and to substitute their heart with straw or wood, or something else of this sort? That you have the power to restore them to life after you have eaten them, and allow them to live for a limited reprieve? If that is what you have come to believe, you should do penance for forty days, that is a diet of bread and water only, for forty days, for a series of seven years.
>
> Burchard of Worms *Decretorum libri xx* 19.5, *PL* cxl, col. 973[70]

---

[66] Akkadian texts collected at West 1995:250–9, 276–7.

[67] *Pactus legis Salicae* 64.3 apud *MGH* Leges nat. Germ. iv.1 p.231. For an English translation of the Salic Law, see Drew 1991.

[68] Edict of Rothari no. 376, *MGH* Leges iv, p.87; cf. Cherubini 2010b:68.

[69] *Capitularia regum Francorum, capitulatio de partibus Saxonicae* 6 apud *MGH* Leges ii.1, pp.68–9; cf. Cherubini 2010a:42, 2010b:68, 75 (who seems to me to mistranslate this text) and Hutton 2017:70–1.

[70] Cf. Cherubini 2010a:68–9, 75.

Gervase of Tilbury was still speaking (explicitly) of *striae* in his *Otia imperialia* of AD 1209–14, where he similarly attributes to them the characteristics we have observed in our three principal texts. For Gervase *stria* is a French term for the *lamia* he reports the belief that, *inter alia*, such creatures fly by night at great speed, enter houses, attack people in their sleep, inflict nightmares in such a way as to make people cry out, eat from the house, light lamps, take people's bones apart, sometimes putting them back together again in a confused order, drink human blood, snatch babies from their cradles, and move them from one place to another.[71]

But it is rather the *strix*'s cousin Gello, with her ancient Akkadian roots, that has been distinguished for true longevity, this in the Greek east. She is the demon to be deterred still from child-killing and child-snatching in the Melitene historiola ('story-let'), an expansive charm recurring in Greek manuscripts between the fifteenth and early twentieth centuries AD: here, just like the *striges*, Gello infiltrates Melitene's house by surreptitious means in order to kill her child, in this case by disguising herself as a clod of earth stuck to a horse's shoe.[72]

The Paradigm of the Bawd-witch

The second paradigm, that of the bawd-witch, can be introduced more succinctly.[73] She features in the poems of the three principal Augustan elegists, as we shall see, and represents a synthesis of two broader stock types of Latin poetry.[74] The first is the (drunken) bawd, the malign and self-serving old woman that keeps the poet's girl, the courtesan she controls, from his arms, prevails upon her to demand a heavy price for her favours, or presses her to redirect her attentions to a richer lover.[75] The second is the hag-witch, the crone devoted to magical rites of a cruel and disgusting kind, as best exemplified by Horace's Canidia, the subject of an interesting cycle of satirical poems,[76] and Lucan's Erictho, the grotesque figure that reanimates a corpse to provide a prophecy for Sextus Pompey.[77]

---

[71] Gervase of Tilbury *Otia imperiala* 3.85–6 (pp.39–40 Liebrecht); cf. Banks and Binns 2002:717–24 (notes) and Cherubini 2009b:92, 2010a:43, 2010b:69–70.

[72] For the Melitene text see Gaster 1900 esp. 143–9, Argenti and Rose 1949:42–5, Greenfield 1988, Viltanioti 2012 and Björklund 2017.

[73] See Ogden 2009 esp. 127–9.

[74] See also Ovid *Fasti* 2.571–83 (elegiac but not love elegy), where a drunken old woman is seen teaching young girls a spell to bind the tongues of their enemies employing a sown-up fish-head. It is easy to imagine that she is a madam passing on the ancillary tools of her trade. See Frazer 1929:ii, 446–52, Bömer1958–63:ii, 126–7 (both *ad loc.*)

[75] E.g. Tibullus 2.6; cf. Herodas *Mimambi* 1. See Myers 1996.

[76] Horace *Satires* 1.8, *Epodes* 3, 5, 17; cf. also *Satires* 2.1.48 and 2.8.95. For Canidia see, in particular, Watson's commentary on the relevant *Epodes* (2003), and now Paule's new monograph study, 2017.

[77] Lucan *Pharsalia* 6.413–830. See, in particular, Gordon 1987 and Korenjak 1996.

Tibullus' Bawd-witch

We may now at last return to werewolves. Tibullus, writing *c.*27 BC, finds a bawd-witch keeping his Delia from him, and he utters a curse upon her:

> A rich lover is now on the scene: a cunning bawd works toward my destruction. May she eat bloody feasts and with gory mouth drink joyless cups full of gall. May ghosts ever flit about her complaining of their fates and may the screech-owl [*strix*] call from her roof. May starvation goad her to madness and send her searching for herbs on graves and bones abandoned by fierce wolves. May she run bare-groined and howling through the cities, and may she be chased from the crossroads by a rough pack of dogs. It will happen. So indicates the god. The lover has his gods, and Venus can be cruel when she is unjustly neglected. But, Delia, cast the instructions of that greedy witch aside at once, for all love is overcome by gifts.   Tibullus 1.5.47–60[78]

No less than three competing narrative logics have been dashed together and concatenated here:

i. The Professional Witch Goes About her Business

The professional witch culls the drugs she needs for her operations, as had long been the practice for witches in the Greek tradition. Indeed these lines salute those found in a fragment of Sophocles' *Rhizotomoi* (*Root-cutters*), where a witch, presumably Medea herself, is described in the process of drug collection:

> Turning her gaze away from her hand as she did so, she caught up the milky juice from the cut in bronze jars....And the secret chests conceal the cut roots which she, shouting, howling and naked was reaping with bronze sickles.[79]
>
> Sophocles *Rhizotomoi* F534 *TrGF*

This witch collects drugs naked and howling. Furthermore, the terms used to convey the howling are reminiscent of each other in sound and structure: *alalazomenē, ululet.*

---

[78] For more general exegesis of this passage, see Smith 1913:301–5, Murgatroyd 1980:176–81, Maltby 2002:253–6; cf. Gordon 2015:59 n.130. The key portion reads as follows (1.5.53–6):

Ipsa fame stimulante furens herbasque sepulcris
Quaerat et a saevis ossa relicta lupis,
Currat et inguinibus nudis ululetque per urbes
Post agat e triviis aspera turba canum.

[79] The final part reads:

...αἱ δὲ καλυπταὶ
κίσται ῥιζῶν κρύπτουσι τομάς,
ἃς ἥδε βοῶσ' ἀλαλαζομένη
γυμνὴ χαλκέοις ἦμα δεπάνοις.

To the topos of drug collection the more gruesome and gothic witch of Latin literature added the topos of bone- and body-part collection too.[80] And noteworthy here, in light of Tibullus' words, is Lucan's grotesque witch Erictho, who is said to lie in wait beside abandoned bodies for the wolves to come, so that she can then snatch the scavenged body parts actually from the creatures' mouths.[81] This is evidently because the wolf confers a further degree of efficacy on the body part, in preparation for its role as a magical instrument or ingredient. The key thing was to acquire body parts connected to a vigorous restless ghost: restless ghosts were produced when their bodies were deprived of burial, and ever since the *Iliad* the most dramatic and symbolic means of depriving a body of burial had been to cast it out for the dogs and the birds to eat.[82] And no doubt the drugs that grow on graves similarly enhance their efficacy through contact with the dead, even if not, in this case, the unburied dead.

In this register, the dogs that are to chase the witch from the crossroads are ostensibly those of Hecate herself, who was worshipped at crossroads, and whose complex body incorporated the forms of dogs, the sound of whose barking precedes her arrival.[83] But that this should happen is a mark of the witch's failure in her craft, for Tibullus elsewhere speaks admiringly of the abilities of the witch that he himself has employed to aid his love affair with Delia, and in so doing specifies that 'She alone is said to possess Medea's evil herbs, she alone to tame the wild dogs of Hecate.'[84] We shall return to this second Tibullan witch below, when we speak of Propertius.

ii. The Starving Woman Scrabbles for Food

The destitution that Tibullus wishes upon the venal bawd leaves her so desperate that she must scrabble even for the rough plants that grow on graves, and she is even driven to a most miserable variety of cannibalism, gnawing old bones scorned even by wild animals. So poor is she that she must go naked. So poor is she too that she is driven to steal—sacrilegiously—the offerings left for Hecate at the crossroads, the so-called 'dinners of Hecate', the traditional resort of those reduced

---

[80] E.g. Horace *Epodes* 5, Lucan 6.529–68, Petronius *Satyricon* 63, Apuleius *Metamorphoses* 2.22, 2.30, 3.17. On the Greek side, note Hesychius *s.v.* τυμβὰς γυνή: 'They used to call witches "tomb-women" [*tumbades*] from the fact that they would hang around tombs [*tumboi*] and chop off corpses' extremities'; cf. also Michael Psellus (11th c. AD) *Poems* 21 ll. 177–84: *nuktitumbas*, 'night-tomb-witch'.

[81] Lucan 6.550–3.

[82] Homer *Iliad* 1.1–5, Sophocles *Antigone* 205–6, Thucydides 2.50, etc.; for the productive theme of dogs devouring cast-out bodies in Greek literature, see Burriss 1935:37–8, Mainoldi 1984:104–9, 176–80.

[83] An Attic Black Figure lekythos of *c*.470 BC, National Museum 19, 765 = *LIMC* Hekate 95 = Erinys 7, the earliest identifiable image of Hecate, depicts the goddess in anguipede form, with a pair of dogs projecting from her midriff; they tear an unfortunate human soul apart between themselves. This is precisely the form in which the goddess is subsequently described also by Lucian *Philopseudes* 22; here we learn that the dogs are the size of Indian elephants, and that the goddess's arrival is preceded by the sound of their barking. See Ogden 2013a:257–9.

[84] Tibullus 1.2.53–4.

to abject beggary.[85] And so in this register too it is entirely appropriate that she should be chased away from the crossroads by the goddess herself and her integrated dogs.

iii. The Witch Becomes a Wolf

According to a third logic, the witch transforms herself into a wolf, to keep company with the true wolves of the cemetery.[86] She transforms herself by means of the consumption of human flesh and prepares for the transformation or indeed effects it by divesting herself of her human clothing, so as to be naked (cf. Chapter 3 for both of these motifs). She howls as a wolf must. She runs through the town, but is chased out of its streets by the town's feral dogs, with whom she competes. And here it may be significant that one of the characteristics of those afflicted with the disease of lycanthropy is to have their shins covered in lacerations because 'they are continually falling down and being bitten by dogs'.[87]

The notion that the witch might transform herself into an animal is prepared for in the preceding reference to the *strix*, at once witch and screech owl, which Tibullus prays should cry from her roof.[88] The reference is somewhat impressionistic. On the face of it, Tibullus seems to be praying that the witch should herself become the victim of the *strix* (perhaps it might prey on the children of her household, though one would not normally imagine such characters to have children). But, given the context, it is difficult to avoid the vignette of the witch herself as the *strix*, newly transformed to owl shape and poised on her own roof, ready to fly off to do her mischief—just as Apuleius' Pamphile transforms herself into an owl in her upper room and then flies off from her balcony to meet her lover (we shall say more about this later in the chapter).[89]

Propertius' Bawd-witch Acanthis

Propertius' contribution to the canon of drunken bawd-witches in Latin love elegy is the figure of Acanthis ('Thistle'; *c.*16 BC). She is evidently based in Rome (she collects Colline herbs), though her Greek name, any irrecoverable tributes to Hellenistic models aside, may suggest that she belongs to the freedman stock one might have expected to populate the city's demi-monde. The many abilities

---

[85] Aristophanes *Wealth* 594–7, Lucian *Downward Journey* 7, *Dialogues of the Dead* 1.1; both of the Lucianic passages speak of these dinners being taken by beggarly Cynic philosophers. See Rohde 1925:322 n.88, Johnston 1991, 1999a:60–1.

[86] Schmeling 2011:256–7 at any rate perceives that the witch becomes a wolf herself at this point.

[87] Aëtius of Amida *Libri medicinales* 6.11.

[88] Tibullus 1.5.52: *semper et e tectis strix violenta canat.*

[89] Apuleius *Metamorphoses* 3.21–5; see Chapter 2.

Propertius attributes to her are mainly concerned with love magic. Amongst these he makes the following claim:

> Bawd, may the ground cover over your tomb with brambles, and may your shade go thirsty—the last thing you want! May your ashes' ghost find no peace, and may avenging Cerberus terrify your foul bones, howling with hunger. She knew how to break down even Hippolytus' resistance to Venus and, ever the worst bird of omen for a harmonious lover's bed, could compel even Penelope to disregard rumours of her husband and marry lusty Antinous.[90] If she wished, loadstone could fail to attract iron, and the bird could be a stepmother to the chicks in her nest. And if she brought Colline herbs to the trench, things standing solid would be dissolved into running water. She was bold enough to bewitch the moon and impose her orders on it, and to change her form into that of the nocturnal wolf [*nocturno lupo*], so that she could, by her craft, blind keenly watchful husbands. With her nail she tore out the eyes of crows—they did not deserve this—and asked the witches/screech-owls [*striges*] about my blood. She gathered *hippomanes*, the seed of the pregnant mare, to use against me.[91]
>
> Propertius 4.5.1-18[92]

Here again we have a magical professional transforming herself into a wolf and associating, at least, with *striges*; it is not excluded that she is also a *strix* herself.

Why does she turn herself into a wolf? Husband-blinding spells, whereby a husband is not literally blinded but somehow kept from noticing his wife's infidelity, were an established part of the magical repertoire, and not least in its manifestation in Latin elegy. In another poem of Tibullus the poet tells Delia that they will be able to carry out an illicit affair successfully because he knows a witch, a 'wise woman' (*saga*):

> She composed a spell for me by which you could deceive him. Sing it three times, and spit after each of the three singings. Then he will not be able to believe anyone who tells him about us. He won't even believe himself, if he sees us in our soft bed with his own eyes. But you must keep away from other men, for he will see everything else. About me alone will he perceive nothing.
>
> Tibullus 1.2.55-60

---

[90] Hippolytus and Penelope both serving as icons of chastity, in their different ways.

[91] *Hippomanes* is a stock item of erotic magic, variously conceived of as a herb, a growth on the head of a newborn foal, a discharge secreted by mares (as here), and a stallion's semen. See Aristotle *History of Animals* 572a, 577a, 605a; Virgil *Georgics* 3.274–83, with Servius *ad loc.*: Pliny *Natural History* 28.261. For discussion, see Tupet 1976:79–81, 1986:2653–7, Ogden 2009:242–3.

[92] For general discussion of this passage see Hutchinson 2006:136–42, Heyworth 2007:453–4.

But how could one effect such a spell by turning into a wolf? Perhaps they key term here is 'nocturnal'. Does the witch merely adopt the guise of the wolf so as to be able to travel stealthily and unseen by night to the husband and thus be in a position, having transformed herself back into humanoid form, to effect the blinding spell upon him?

At any rate, there is dense allusion here to Tibullus' bawd poem: we should note, *inter alia*, the recurrence and reworking of the following themes: bawd-witches; the worrying of bones (now by Cerberus, rather than the wolves or the bawd-witch herself); and, last but not least, the *striges*. This makes it possible to contemplate that Propertius' perhaps undermotivated transformation of his bawd-witch into a wolf may be determined by his reading of the wolf transformation in Tibullus' poem.

Ovid's Bawd-witch Dipsas (?) and Medea

Ovid too makes his contribution to the tight canon of Latin love elegy's drunken bawd-witches. In his *Amores* (also *c.*16 BC) we encounter yet another old witch specializing in love magic, as well as in the manipulation of ghosts. Like Propertius' Acanthis, she too has a Greek name, Dipsas, which signifies, appropriately enough, 'Drunken'. Ovid proceeds as follows:

> There is this (listen up, if you want to learn about a bawd!), there is this old woman called Dipsas. Her name is a significant one: she has never seen roseate-horsed Dawn, the mother of black Memnon, in a state of sobriety. She knows the craft of magic and Aeaean incantations. By her craft she turns flowing waters back to their source. She knows all too well the powers of the herb, the threads twisted by the spinning *rhombus*-wheel, and the secretion of the mare in love. At her wish, clouds crowd over the entire heaven; at her wish, the daylight shines in a clear sky. If you believe it, I have seen the stars dripping with blood. The face of the moon was deep red with blood. I suspect that she shape-shifts [*versam*] and flits about among the shades of the night and that her old body is covered with feathers.[93] This is what I suspect, and this is what they say. Also, double pupils flash from her eyes, and the beams shine from twin circles. She calls forth great-grandfathers and the great-grandfathers of great-grandfathers from their ancient tombs and cleaves open the solid ground with a protracted incantation. This woman set herself the task of violating the chastity of my girl's bedroom [*thalamos temerare pudicos*]. It must be said, her tongue does have a destructive eloquence.   Ovid *Amores* 1.8.1–20[94]

[93] The key lines, 12–14, read: *purpureus Lunae sanguine vultus erat./hanc ego nocturnas versam volitare per umbras/suspicor et pluma corpus anile tegi.*

[94] For general discussion see McKeown 1989:198–212.

Dipsas is another self-transforming *strix*-witch ('she shape-shifts and flits about among the shades of the night and that her old body is covered with feathers'). The suggestion that she metaphorically violates the bedroom in her role as a bawd gains colour from the notion that she is also a *strix*, the creature that violates bedrooms by night in a more direct and ruinous fashion. Now there is a faint intimation of werewolfism on Dipsas' part. We are eventually told in line 111 that her hair is white (*albam comam*): this retrospectively prompts us to read a self-referential significance into the proverb she utters at line 56: 'It is in the flock that the hoary wolves (*canis...lupis*) find bountiful prey.' There may also be an intimation of werewolfism in the fact that the reference to Dipsas' shape-shifting in the passage quoted is immediately preceded by a (potentially scene-setting) reference to the moon. In light of the connections subsequently to become apparent in Petronius' tale, the moon that brings on a change of shape is a moon evocative of werewolfism. The simple term *versam* may, furthermore, evoke the compound term *versipellis*, which seems to have been associated with werewolves in particular (see Introduction).

We are on firmer ground with some of Ovid's lines on Medea in his *Metamorphoses* (AD 8). He supplies a protracted list of the bizarre ingredients that Medea throws into her cauldron to make a magical rejuvenation liquid with which to restore Aeson's youth. Amongst these:

> She added frosts collected under the all-night moon, the notorious wings of the screech owl [*strix*], together with its flesh, and the entrails of the shape-shifting wolf, which changes its wild-animal form into a man.
>
> Ovid *Metamorphoses* 7.268–71[95]

Here we have yet another emphatic association between a witch, a werewolf, and indeed a screech owl, but it is of a different kind to what has gone before. The witch is not turning herself or anyone else into a werewolf or a screech owl, but is seemingly using pre-existing body parts to make her magical liquid. Presumably the prime function of the werewolf parts here is to serve as an impossible or near-impossible ingredient, as are some of the others also listed, for example the beak of a crow that had lived for nine generations.[96] One might be tempted to imagine that Medea had herself manufactured the werewolf before deploying its parts in magic (we are reminded of the fashion in which Simon Magus manufactured a boy out of thin air, only to sacrifice him to the ghosts with whom he wished to

---

[95] *addit et exceptas luna pernocte pruinas/et strigis infamis ipsis cum carnibus alas/inque virum soliti vultus mutare ferinos/ambigui prosecta lupi.* For discussion of this passage in the context of ancient werewolfism, see Tupet 1976:401–8, Metzger 2011:230–1.

[96] Ovid *Metamorphoses* 7.274. Erictho also uses a series of impossible magical ingredients in preparing the liquid with which to reanimate a corpse at Lucan 6.667–718 (including ship-stopping fish, Arabian flying snakes, and phoenix ashes). One of the Greek Magical Papyri, *PGM* XII.401–44 (4th c. AD), offers a convenient list of more obtainable substitutes for such impossible ingredients.

confer).[97] And are we then to think that the screech owl she has caught is a fellow witch in transformation? However, that is all to go beyond what we are told, and the implication of the brief words upon which we depend seems to be rather that the werewolf has a separate existence prior to its exploitation.[98]

Another potentially interesting implication of Ovid's phraseology is that the default form of his werewolf is the wolf rather than the man, which has certainly been the case with all the other examples considered so far. But it is the nature of the werewolf, whatever their base form, to switch back and forth between the shapes of man and wolf, and Ovid may be focusing here on the transition from wolf to man merely for the sake of variation. (We shall approach the question of 'base forms' from a rather different perspective in Chapter 3.)

We may briefly note that Lucan was subsequently to bring screech owls and wolves (*tout court*) together again in association with another witch's spell. His Erictho initiates the imprecation of her great reanimation spell with a series of inarticulate sounds: 'Then her voice, mightier than all the herbs in the bewitching of the gods of Lethe, poured out, first, mutterings that were discordant and not all of which sounded like the products of a human tongue. The voice contained the barking of dogs and the howling of wolves, the complaining cries of a scared *bubo*-owl and the night's screech owl, the screeching and bellowing of wild animals, and the hissing of the snake.'[99]

Petronius' Niceros and Trimalchio

With Petronius we find a rather different kind of relationship again constructed between werewolf and witch. Witches—specifically *strigae*, *strix*-witches—and werewolves are the respective stars of the pair of fantastical, campfire-horror-style

---

[97] [Clement of Rome] *Recognitions* 2.13 (4th c. AD, based on an early 3rd-c. AD *Grundschrift*).

[98] Ovid's conceits are seemingly kaleidoscoped in Seneca's description of the ingredients used by Medea in the fiery poison with which she will imbue Creusa-Glauce's wedding dress: 'She crops death-bringing herbs, expresses venom from serpents and mixes evil birds in with them, the heart of the mournful eagle-owl [*bubo*] and the innards cut from a raucous screech owl [*strix*] whilst it yet lives' (*Medea* 731–4). In a witty twist here, the *strix* is subject to the process—the extraction of internal organs while it yet lives—to which it itself typically subjects others.

[99] Lucan *Pharsalia* 6.685–90: the key lines run *latratus habet illa canum gemitusque luporum,/quod trepidus bubo, quod strix nocturna queruntur*. Cf. also 6.627–8, where Erictho descends upon a battlefield to pick out a corpse suitable for magical exploitation: 'The wolves fled at once and the birds fled too, withdrawing their talons, and still hungry' (*continuo fugere lupi, fugere revolsis/unguibus inpastae volucres*). Presumably vultures are intended here, in the first instance. Ovid's words and Lucan's alike put us in mind of the list of magical ingredients Horace's hag-witch Canidia had called for in his *Epodes*, as she worked with her coven of three companions to manufacture a gruesome love potion (5.15–24): 'Canidia, small vipers entwined in the unkempt hair on her head, ordered wild fig trees, torn up from graves, funereal cypresses, eggs pasted with the blood of the foul frog, a feather of the nocturnal screech owl [*plumamque nocturnae strigis*], herbs which Iolcus and Iberia, fertile in poisons, export, and bones snatched from the mouth of a ravening dog [*ossa ab ore rapta ieiunae canis*] to be burned in Colchian flames.'

stories exchanged over dinner by Trimalchio and his guest Niceros, both of which we have quoted above (in this chapter and in the Introduction respectively). These two stories, told by different men, are completely separate, and no syntagmatic relationship is constructed within them between the werewolf and the witches. Even so, given that these entities are the focal stars of this diptych of rival, similarly atmospheric horror stories, Petronius gives out a clear message that *strix*-witches and werewolves belong together in the same story world.

The *Strix*-witch (ii): Apuleius' Thessalian She-wolves

Lupulae

There is reason to think that a characteristic animal form of the various Thessalian witches of Apuleius' (later-second-century AD) *Metamorphoses* was that of the she-wolf. Photis explains to Lucius that she cannot protect him from the witches in the following terms:

> I can hardly preserve you, in your unarmed state, from those little Thessalian she-wolves [*lupulae*].[100]   Apuleius *Metamorphoses* 3.22

Apuleius' witches live in a demi-monde, and one could well make the argument that this unique use of *lupula*, the diminutive of *lupa*, 'she-wolf', carries the connotation here of prostitution that *lupa* itself would normally do when applied to women.[101] However, the immediate context is one of animal transformation: Pamphile has transformed herself into a *bubo*-owl in the preceding chapter and Lucius will transform himself into an ass in the following one. In such a context, one cannot avoid the implication that these witches are indeed, *inter alia*, she-wolves.

Pamphile's Transformation into an Owl

The model of the *strix* also lurks behind a number of the activities of the Thessalian witches in the *Metamorphoses*, even though the term does not appear in the text. First and foremost, Lucius' famous, focal transformation into an ass is preceded by the Thessalian witch Pamphile's transformation of herself into an owl—indeed it is precisely this feat that Lucius is attempting to replicate. However, her purpose

---

[100] *Sic inermem vix a lupulis conservo Thessalis.*
[101] See LS and *OLD* s.v. *lupa* and its derivatives; cf. Summers 1933:66–9, Mazzoni 2010:112–16.

is not to tear children. Rather, it is to fly to meet a lover.[102] In the parallel scene in the Lucianic *Onos*, which may well reflect the terminology deployed in the original Greek version of Apuleius' novel,[103] the corresponding witch, the wife of Hipparchus, transforms herself into a *korax nykterinos*, a 'night crow'. The ancients did not have a settled idea as to what creature this last term denoted, but the *strix* does indeed seem to have been amongst the alternatives here.[104] The term deployed by Apuleius is not *strix* either, but *bubo*, 'eagle owl'. The use of this term may be due, as Scobie suggested, to Apuleius' desire to 'inflate' his inherited materials and also to his taste for irony.[105] But, in any case, the kindred nature of *strix* and the *bubo* is often adverted to in Latin poetry. For example, Ovid describes an evil tree in the following terms: 'It provides foul shade to screeching *bubo*-owls (*raucis bubonibus*); in its branches it holds the eggs of the vulture and the *strix*.'[106] Pliny indeed describes the *bubo* in terms that would be particularly fitting to the *strix*: it is funereal, it inhabits frightful places and it is regarded as portentous of evil when it settles on a private house.[107] And it is surely significant that Apuleius describes owl-Pamphile as emitting a 'screech' (*stridore*) as she departs.[108]

Meroe and Panthia as *Lamias*

Two more of Apuleius' Thessalian witches, the striking Meroe and Panthia, are explicitly described as *lamias*.[109] One of the highlights of the novel is the early tale of them recounted by Aristomenes. He explains how Meroe had enslaved his

[102] Apuleius *Metamorphoses* 3.21–5.

[103] Photius *Bibliotheca* cod. 129 (at ii pp.103–4 Henry) ascribes to one Lucius of Patras a novel entitled *Metamorphōseōn logoi diaphoroi* (*MLD*) and claims that Lucian of Samosata copied the first two books (only, oddly) of it for a much-reduced version, his *Onos* (*Ass*). This *Onos* is transmitted with the oeuvre of Lucian, and declares itself at its close to be, precisely, the work of Lucius of Patras (55). The *Onos* as a whole is more easily seen as an abridgement of the *MLD* as a whole. Apuleius' *Metamorphoses* is seemingly an adaptation of the *MLD*, with, to judge from the *Onos*, the insertion of, *inter alia*, many additional witch tales (all those, in fact, not bearing upon the key character of the wife of Hipparchus/Pamphile). Some significant scholars, including Perry 1967:211–82, Bowie 1994:444, and Anderson 1976:34–67, hold that Lucian was actually the author of the *MLD*, which is quite possible: 'Lucius of Patras' could have been the adapted version of his own name that Lucian bestowed upon his semi-alter-ego first-person narrator figure (*Loukianos*, *Loukios*), much as he bestows the similarly adapted name Lycinus (*Lukinos*) upon a semi-alter-ego figure in a wide range of his works (*Dance, Dipsads, Hesiod, Eunuch, Hermotimus, In Defence of Portraits, Lapiths, Lexiphanes, Portraits,* and *Ship*; cf. also *Cynic*, which is probably spurious, and *Loves*, certainly so). For a convenient parallel printing of the texts of Apuleius' *Metamorphoses* and the *Onos*, see van Thiel 1971–2; for a more recent summary analysis of the differences between these two texts, see Frangoulidis 2008:13–45.

[104] [Lucian] *Onos* 12; cf. Scobie 1978:77–80.   [105] Scobie 1978:77–80, again.

[106] Ovid *Amores* 1.12.19–20. See also Lucan *Pharsalia* 6.685–90, quoted above, and Statius *Thebaid* 3.508–12 (*strix* and *bubo* brought together again). Cf. Oliphant 1913:138–9, 146–7.

[107] Pliny *Natural History* 10.34–5; cf. Tibullus 1.5.47–60 (quoted above): 'may the screech-owl [*strix*] call from her roof.'

[108] Apuleius *Metamorphoses* 3.21; cf. Curletto 1987, Cherubini 2010a:9–16 for the relationship between *strix* and *stridere*.

[109] Apuleius *Metamorphoses* 1.17.

friend Socrates to herself, reducing him to beggary; he had resolved to help him escape from Thessaly and her clutches. Here Meroe and Panthia catch up with the fugitives as they rest overnight in an inn:

But I shut the door, made the bolts fast, and pushed my pallet-bed tight up behind the hinge, and laid myself upon it. To start with I was awake for quite a while because of my fear. Then, at around the third watch [i.e. midnight] I managed to shut my eyes for a bit. I had only just got off the sleep when the doors suddenly flew open with greater force that you would have thought robbers could muster. Indeed they were actually broken open, torn right out of their hinge-sockets and flung onto the floor. My pallet-bed, which was an insubstantial thing anyway, rotten and with one leg too short, was also flung forward by the strength of the force used. I was thrown out of it, but it landed back on top of me upside down, and covered me and hid me.... Down there in the dirt, I looked out sideways to see what was going on, shrewdly shielded by my bed. I saw two rather old women. One was carrying a bright lamp, the other a sponge and an unsheathed sword. With this paraphernalia they stood over Socrates, who was still fast asleep.... Meroe pushed Socrates' head to one side and plunged the whole sword into the left side of his neck, right up to the hilt. She carefully applied a leather bottle to his neck and carefully caught up the blood that welled out, so that there was not a drop to be seen anywhere. I saw this with my own eyes. Because, I believe, the good lady Meroe did not wish to depart in any way from sacrificial observance, she stuck her right hand into the wound and, delving down to his innards, probed about and pulled my poor companion's heart out. With that Socrates brought forth a noise, or rather an indistinct screech, through the wound in his throat that the sword had hacked open, and gurgled out his last breath. Panthia used the sponge to stop up the wound at its widest point and said, 'Now, sponge, born in the sea, cross not over a river!' ... They had just stepped through the doorway when the doors leaped back into position, undamaged. The hinge-axles slotted back into their sockets, the bars returned to the posts, and the bolts ran back to do their locking.... [Aristomenes, after much consternation, discovers that Socrates remains alive after all, despite his. As the two men proceed with their escape in the morning, they take a snack beneath a plane tree.] But when Socrates had chomped through enough food, he was seized by an unbearable thirst. He had, after all, greedily gulped down a healthy helping of excellent cheese. Not far from the roots of the plane tree there dawdled a small stream, as calm as a pool, and looking like silver or glass. 'See,' I said, 'refresh yourself with the milky water from this spring.' He rose to his feet and found a place where the bank had an even edge. Then he got down on his knees and brought himself close to the water in his eagerness to get a drink. He had hardly touched the water's surface with the tips of his lips, when his throat-wound yawned open and deep, and the sponge suddenly bounced out of it, followed by just a bit of blood. Then his lifeless corpse almost fell headlong into the river, but I managed to hold onto one of his feet and, with an effort, drag him back up the bank. Once there, I wept over the poor little man, as much as I could under the circumstances, and covered him with the sandy earth. He will lie forever beside that river.   Apuleius *Metamorphoses* 1.11–19[110]

Once again here the doorway represents a boundary of particular interest and attention. Having got in, Meroe proceeds (a) to jugulate Socrates and catch up every last drop of his blood in a leather bottle; (b) then to reach down through the wound and extract his heart (we are not told what she does with it); (c) finally, to insert a magic sponge into the neck wound and sing an incantation over it, as a result of which Socrates, initially alive still, subsequently does indeed die, at the point of which he cranes his neck over a river to drink from it.[111] These gestures all form a striking parallel to John Damascene's observations that *striges* (a) devour all the moisture of the children they attack; (b) devour their livers too, perhaps in such a way that they continue, at least temporarily, to live ('How is he able to live?', John protests); and (c) impose a time limit upon their lives.

This story seems to refract the motifs of a well-known folktale in the Grimm collection, that of 'The Wolf and the Seven Young Kids' (see Table 1.1).[112] While the mother goat is away, the wolf attempts to trick her seven kids into letting him through the door of their house (the challenge-of-the-boundary motif). He eventually manages to get in at the third attempt by disguising himself as a human. As the kids realize their mistake, they dive for cover in various places, with one going into the bed and another going under the table, but the wolf overturns all the furniture and devours them all save for the one that successfully hides in the clock case (cf. Socrates' companion Aristomenes' attempt to hide from the witches under the bed they have overturned upon blasting open the door, where they do indeed discover him). The mother goat returns, is told all by the surviving kid, tracks down the wolf, now sleeping in his satiety, and opens his stomach with a pair of scissors to release the six kids still alive, before filling the now empty stomach with stones and sewing it up again.[113] When the wolf wakes he is rendered thirsty by the stones and so leans over a well to drink, but the weight of the stones pulls him down into it and he drowns. The correspondences between the motif sets here are surely too profound to be accidental, for all that Apuleius' tale kaleidoscopes them in relation to the folktale, in that the role of the original wolf passes from the witches (in overcoming the challenge of entry to their victims

---

[110] For a general discussion of this episode, see Frangoulidis 2008:46–68.
[111] Apuleius *Metamorphoses* 1.13, 17, 19.   [112] Grimm (1986) no.5 = ATU no. 123.
[113] Cf. Grimm no. 26 = ATU no. 333 ('Rotkäppchen', i.e. 'Little Red Riding Hood') for this particular motif: after the wolf has been split open by the woodman to release the grandmother, Little Red Riding Hood fills its belly with stones she has collected. When the wolf regains its senses and tries to run off, it falls down dead.

within) to Socrates (who is split open, has something removed from within and substituted, is then sewn back together and made to perish as he cranes his head over water). Nonetheless, we are left to ponder whether this glorious wolf story, or something akin to it, lurks significantly behind Apuleius' tale: did the wolf lead him to the witch? The plausibility of this comparison will increase when we realize that the next of Apuleius' witch tales we are to consider also bears a strong but similarly kaleidoscopic relationship in its motifs with another Grimm tale.

The Thelyphrons

Thirdly, Apuleius gives us yet more Thessalian witches contriving to penetrate a locked room to steal body parts, as in the *strix*-witch's speciality. His Thelyphron tells how, as an eager and gauche young man, he had agreed a sum with a new widow for guarding the corpse of her husband overnight before its burial, lest the local witches should attempt to steal its extremities for use in their spells. As it was explained to him,

> They [sc. the witches of Thessaly] are dreadful skin-changers [*versipelles*] and they creep in secretly after changing their appearance into that of any animal they wish. They could deceive the very eyes of the Sun or Justice. For they put on the shapes of birds, or alternatively dogs or mice, or even flies.
>
> Apuleius *Metamorphoses* 2.22[114]

We may take it that, so far as Apuleius is concerned, the Thessalian witches can transform themselves not only into the animals named here, but also into owls, asses, and (as we shall see) weasels. We may probably infer that they can also change themselves into beavers, frogs, and rams given that the Thessalian Meroe

---

[114] For discussion of this passage in the context of ancient werewolfism, see Metzger 2011:231–3; cf. also van Mal-Maeder 2001:318. The Thessalian witches' general ability to transform themselves into multiple different kinds of animal was anticipated in Roman geographical traditions about Sena, the tiny Île de Sein or Enez Sun, off Finistère. Pomponius Mela (writing *c.* AD 43) offers the following note on it, 3.48: 'The island of Sena is situated in the British sea opposite the Ossismician shores. It is distinguished for its oracle of a Gaulish god, the priestesses of which are said to be nine in number and hallowed by perpetual virginity. They call them Gallizenae, and they believe that they are endowed with the exceptional abilities to stir up the seas and the winds with their incantations and to turn themselves into whichever animals they wish [*seque in quae velint animalia vertere*], to cure illnesses which are incurable for others, and to know and predict the future. But they deliver their prophecies only to those who set out to sail to their island with the sole purpose of consulting them.' The reading of the name given to the priestesses is a matter of great controversy, though it hardly matters for our purposes: MSS offer, *Gallizenas* aside, *Galligenas* ('Gaulish-born women'), *Gallicenas, Galicenas, Gallicinas* ('Singers of the cockerel-song'?). Suggested editorial emendations include: *Galli Senas, Barrigenas* (cf. Baragoin), *Galli cenas, Galli Benas, Galli Zenas*. Discussion at Tzschucke 1806–7:iii, 159–63.

Table 1.1 'The Wolf and the Seven Kids' and Apuleius' Meroe and Panthia episode

Motif	'The Wolf and the Seven Kids' (Grimm no. 5/ATU no. 123)	Meroe and Panthia (Apuleius *Metamorphoses* 1.11–19)
1. The villain must overcome the challenge of a locked door to gain entry to the victims.	The wolf must make three attempts before he persuades the kids to open the door to him.	The witches use magic to blast the hotel room door off its hinges.
2. Furniture is overturned.	The wolf overturns the furniture in looking for the kids.	The magical blast overturns Aristomenes' bed.
3. A (potential) victim hides underneath something.	One kid hides in the bed, another under the table.	Aristomenes hides under the overturned bed.
4. A body is split open.	The mother goat scissors open the wolf's stomach.	The witches jugulate Socrates.
5. Something is removed from within the body.	The mother goat retrieves her kids from the wolf's stomach.	The witches pull out Socrates' heart.
6. The items removed from the body are substituted.	The mother goat replaces the kids with stones.	The witches replace Socrates' heart with a magic sponge.
7. Death follows when the split person cranes over water to drink.	The stones in his stomach pull the wolf down into the well from which he attempts to drink, and he drowns.	In accordance with the witches' spell, the magic sponge leaps out when Socrates attempts to drink from a river; he dies and begins to fall in.

is said to have transformed other people into these things.[115] But it does of course remain possible that the term *versipellis* here as elsewhere carries a particular (though evidently not exclusive) connotation of wolf transformation.

To return to Thelyphron's story, having made his agreement, he is locked into a chamber (*incluso custode cubiculo*) with the corpse in the widow's house. As he watches, the room is penetrated by a tiny weasel, which stares at him and casts sleep upon him. From outside the chamber the witches attempt to reanimate the corpse by calling its name and then walking it to the wall of the chamber from where they can slice off its nose and ears through a chink, covering their tracks by replacing the parts with wax prostheses. However, the corpse's name is also Thelyphron and, as they call it, the more lithe, merely sleeping Thelyphron responds to the call first, and it is his parts that they (unwittingly) slice off and replace. When the living Thelyphron wakes in the morning, he is relieved of his initial panic upon checking that the corpse remains intact. Only later does he

---

[115] Apuleius *Metamorphoses* 1.9.

realize what has happened to him when the corpse is successfully reanimated by the Egyptian magician Zatchlas, who revives it by laying a herb on its mouth and another on its chest: the dead Thelyphron explains what had happened during the night, and also that he himself had been poisoned by his wife and her lover.[116]

It is strongly tempting to imagine that Apuleius' weasel is none other than the heartless widow herself: there is not much distance between the witch and the lady-poisoner in the ancient world.[117] At any rate, the weasel is a particularly apt animal for a witch to transform herself into: in a fable recounted by Aelian, the weasel was once a human sorcerer (*goēs*) or a witch (*pharmakis*) who was transformed into animal shape by Hecate.[118]

The problem of the locked chamber's penetrability to the witches lies at the heart of this fascinating tale. The witches seemingly do not have the power to *enter the room in human form*, which is why they have to harvest the body parts through the chink in the wall. This conceit is fundamental to the tale, of course: it is needed to explain how they could mistake the living Thelyphron (whose body parts will be useless to them) for the dead one. Even so, one wonders why this weasel-witch could not simply transform herself back into human form once inside the room, in order to proceed with the harvesting in untrammelled fashion. (Let us note also that this tale gives us the theme, once again, of substitute body parts, as in the case of the straw-baby of Petronius' *striges* and Apuleius' own magic sponge.)

Like Apuleius' tale of Meroe and Panthia at the inn, this tale too refracts and reconfigures the themes of another folktale, one with almost universal coverage, and typified by 'The Three Snake Leaves' tale in the Grimm collection (Table 1.2).[119] According to this, a doting husband is sealed into the tomb with his dead wife. As he waits to die himself, a snake penetrates the tomb and he kills it, for fear it may mar the corpse. But then a second snake penetrates the tomb, finds the first one dead, departs briefly, and returns with three leaves, which it lays on the dead one's body, thereby reanimating it and allowing it to scuttle off alive. The husband lays the abandoned leaves on his dead wife, similarly bringing her back to life. They shout to be released from the tomb, but the revivified wife has changed personality and in due course murders her husband in league with a new lover.

---

[116] Apuleius *Metamorphoses* 2.21–30; for a detailed commentary on this episode see van Mal-Maeder 2001:307–95; for a general discussion see Frangoulidis 2008:85–107; for a minute study of the reanimation sequence in particular, see Stramaglia 1989.

[117] The basic terms for 'witch' in both Greek and Latin, *pharakis* and *venefica*, respectively also signifying 'poisoner': witches and poisoners alike manipulate dangerous drugs. See the entries for the terms in LSJ and *OLD*, and also Bernand 1991:47–8, Graf 1997:46–9, Stratton 2007:26–30, Collins 2008:58–63.

[118] Aelian *Nature of Animals* 15.11. According to Antoninus Liberalis *Metamorphoses* 29 (after Nicander), the Fates turned the girl Galinthias into a weasel for aiding Alcmene in the birth of Heracles; Hecate took pity on her and adopted her as her own special servant. Cf. van Mal-Maeder 2001:342.

[119] ATU no. 612; Grimm (1986) no. 16.

Table 1.2 Apuleius' Thelyphrons episode and 'The Three Snake Leaves' (etc.)

ATU no. 612: Motifs	Three Snake Leaves (Brothers Grimm no.16)	Polyidus (Apollodorus Bibliotheca 3.3.1-2, Hyginus Fabulae 136, etc.)	The Thelyphrons (Apuleius Metamorphoses 2.21-30)	Alexander the Great and Ptolemy—a vestigial refraction (Diodorus 17.103.4-8, Curtius 9.8.22-8)	Eliduc's wives (Marie de France Eliduc)	Sigmund and Sinfjötli (Völsunga saga ch.8)
1. Person is shut in with a corpse.	Husband is shut in with corpse of his princess wife.	Seer Polyidus is shut in by Minos with corpse of his son Glaucus.	Thelyphron 1 is shut in with the corpse of Thelyphron 2.	[Ptolemy is dying from poison arrow.]	Eliduc's second wife attends the corpse of his first.	[Wolf-Sigmund retires to a forest house with dying wolf-Sinfjötli after biting out his throat.]
2. Animal penetrates the chamber, threatens the corpse (and is killed).	Snake penetrates tomb and is killed by the husband, to prevent it harming the corpse.	Snake penetrates tomb and is killed by Polyidus.	Weasel (witch in disguise) penetrates the room, with ultimate purpose of marring the corpse (but is not killed).		Weasel penetrates chapel and is killed by the second wife's squire for running over the corpse.	Two weasels penetrate the hut and fight; one rips out other's throat.
3. Second animal reanimates the first by bringing a herb in its mouth and laying it on it.	Second snake lays three snake leaves on the first.	Second snake lays a herb on first.	Weasel (witch in disguise) proceeds with other witches in an attempted reanimation.	Alexander sees a dream vision of a snake bringing him the antidote-herb in its mouth.	Second weasel lays a crimson flower on first.	The first weasel fetches a leaf to heal the second one.

4. Reanimation of the human corpse by the watcher.	Man lays three snakes leaves on his wife's eyes and mouth.	Polyidus lays the herb on Glaucus.	Zatchlas lays herbs on the mouth and breast of Thelyphron 2.	Alexander has men search for the herb locally; it is brought and Ptolemy is healed.	The second wife lays the crimson flower on first wife.	The same kind of leaf is then brought to Sigmund by a raven in its mouth; he draws it across Sinfjötli's throat to heal him.
5. The wife and her lover kill the husband.	The reanimated wife has changed personality, she kills her husband with her lover (but he is in turn reanimated by the leaves).	—	The wife of Thelyphron 2, it transpires, has poisoned him with her lover.	—	—	—

The greater part of this tale was well known in classical antiquity. Minos' little son Glaucus died and was lost when he fell into a pot of honey. The seer Polyidus located the body for Minos, but the king, in a fit of pique when Polyidus could not also restore him to life, had him sealed into the tomb with the dead boy. Again he kills a snake that penetrates the tomb, and again it is restored when a fellow snake lays a magic herb upon its body. Polyidus uses the herb to revivify Glaucus, and both are released from the tomb.[120] The same core tale finds its way into Marie de France's (AD 1160–78) *Eliduc* too, but here we have a weasel, as in Apuleius. Eliduc's second wife is attending the corpse of his first in a chapel when a weasel runs over it, and she has her squire kill it. A second weasel brings a crimson flower to revivify the first. She takes the flower and uses it to bring the first wife back to life. The central core of the tale is also deployed in the (mid thirteenth-century) *Völsunga saga*'s story of Sigmund and Sinfjötli and again here the animal concerned is a weasel (this will be discussed in Chapter 3). Apuleius' tale of the Thelyphrons takes a kaleidoscopic approach to many of these constituent motifs: a living man is shut in with a dead man; a weasel penetrates the chamber with a view to marring the corpse; an attempt is made to bring the corpse back to life in the chamber; and then a second, more successful attempt is made, outside the chamber, to bring the corpse back to life, specifically by laying a pair of herbs on it; and a wife murders her husband in conjunction with her new lover.[121] There are no werewolves in the tale of the Thelyphrons, but they are indeed to be found in the Sigmund and Sinfjötli version of this tale, as we shall see.

The werewolf—or the practice of transformation into a wolf—seems to lurk in different ways around the evidence for *strix*-witches in earlier imperial Latin literature, but firm conclusions remain out of reach. It could well be, to formulate the strongest available conclusion, that behind these texts lies a notion of what might be termed a triangular phenomenon, that of a human witch whose two primary animal transformations of choice were screech owl and wolf. Or, to formulate the weakest one, it could be that, for the creative writers of the Roman world, the imagery of one distinctive animal-transformation theme (the *strix*-witch) tended to invite associative reference to that of another one (the werewolf).

---

[120] Polyidus and Glaucus: Apollodorus *Bibliotheca* 3.3.1–2, Hyginus *Fabulae* 136; cf. Euripides *Polyidus* FF634–45a *TrGF*. The same tale of Glaucus appears to have been told with a heroic Asclepius himself in the role of Polyidus: Amelesagoras *FGrH* 330 F3 *apud* Apollodorus *Bibliotheca* 3.10.3, Hyginus *Astronomica* 2.14 and schol. Euripides *Alcestis* 1. The myth's central vignette is beautifully illustrated on a *c.*460–450 BC white-ground kylix attributed to the Sotades Painter in the British Museum (BM 1892, 0718.2): inside a conical tomb Polyidus sits opposite the boy Glaucus, revivified but still wrapped in his tight shroud, while the two snakes depart. Elements of the tale found their way also into the Alexander tradition: Diodorus 17.103.4–8 and Curtius 9.8.22–8 (i.e. Clitarchus?) tell how, at Harmatelia, when Ptolemy is dying of a wound from a poison arrow, the grieving Alexander is visited in his sleep by a serpent carrying a special herb in its mouth. Upon waking he sends his men in search of the herb; it is located and an antidote is made for Ptolemy.

[121] Cf. Ogden 2013a:345–6.

The *Strix*-witch (iii): the 'Were-women' of Mount Lebanon

Let us now look briefly across to the other side of the classical world, indeed just beyond it, and to a remarkable episode in the Syriac *Life of Simeon Stylites* composed shortly after the saint's death in AD 459. The *Life* tells how the villages on Mount Lebanon are being attacked by evil creatures, which kill two or three people a day. Sometimes these creatures manifest themselves as women shorn of their hair, wandering about and howling in lamentation, and sometimes they manifest themselves as beasts. They enter houses, snatch babies from mothers' breasts, tear them apart, and devour them before them, or drag the corpses off. Simeon advises the people to surround the borders of their villages with stones inscribed with the cross three times over. The creatures wander about the stones wailing and howling for ten days, whereupon the menace comes to an end. Some of them burst open around the stones, others disappear off, never to be seen again. In their final wailing they blame Simeon for their tortures. The grateful villagers bring three of the pelts to Simeon: they are multicoloured, and resemble neither those of bears nor those of leopards.[122]

In making a fleeting reference to this episode, Peter Brown describes the entities in question as 'were-women'.[123] One can understand why: the transitions between humanoid and beast forms, and the howling. But *we* must be more scrupulous. The motif of the howling seems, deliberately, to point in two directions at once: it is the cry of a beast, yes, perhaps indeed a broadly lupine one, but it is also the lamenting of a mourning woman—of which the shorn hair is also a basic marker in the ancient world. The beasts into which the entities transform themselves are (we infer) large and man-eating, but their multicoloured pelts do not sound like those of wolves (and the text seems to want to tell us that they resemble those of no known creatures whatsoever, not just those of bears and leopards).

As lamenting female humanoids, with some sort of animalian aspect, penetrating the shells of houses to snatch, rend, and devour babies, these entities in the first instance resemble, rather, the *striges* and the *lamiai* we have been discussing in the last two sections, not least given that the archetypal Lamia was held to have been rendered monstrous through grief after Hera destroyed her own children, and for this reason to have snatched up and destroyed the children of other women.[124] Even if we cannot, in good conscience, affirm that the specific beasts into which creatures of Mount Lebanon transform themselves are wolves, they would seem to be partly wolflike. At the very least, this episode should be taken to

[122] *Syriac Life of Simeon Stylites* 97, pp.589–92 Bedjan; for text see Bedjan 1890–7:iv, 507–644; for translations see Hilgenfeld 1908 (German) and Lent 1915 (English).
[123] Brown 1971:90; I thank my colleague Richard Flower for this reference.
[124] Schol. Aelius Aristides *Panathenaicus* 102.5 (iii p.42 Dindorf); cf. n. 57 above.

document a broad intercultural phenomenon in which *strix*- or *lamia*-like entities are associated with transformation into furry man-eating beasts *of some sort.*

The Curse of the Werewolf

Akin to the notion that a werewolf transformation could be effected by magic is the notion that it could be effected by a divine curse. As we have already noted, Pliny introduces his discussion of the rites and myths of Zeus Lykaios with the assertion, 'We will indicate the origin of the popular superstition that skin-changers/ werewolves [*versipelles*] are among those subject to a curse [*maledictis*].'[125] In context this can only refer to a divine curse proceeding from Zeus, a curse imposed in response to the attempt of Lykaon or his sons to feed him the flesh of a human sacrifice. The earliest mention of this tale is probably the Hesiodic *Catalogue of Women*'s glancing reference to Lykaon's 'trangression' (*paraibasia*).[126] But the world of magic and witchcraft does not seem far away, for a *maledictum* is normally a curse made within the human realm, not the divine one.[127]

Of interest here too is an Aesopic fable found in a sixteenth-century manu-script (Codex Laurentianus 57.30) of the collection made by the later-thirteenth-century AD Maximus Planudes, and not otherwise securely dateable: it may be ancient, or it may be Byzantine.[128] We shall quote the tale in full in Chapter 3, but let us focus here on the explanation that its protagonist thief offers for his (pretended) werewolfism:

> Now, my good man, I do not know for what reason the urge to yawn comes upon me, be it for my errors [*dia tas hamartias*] or for some other reason unknown to me. But whenever I yawn three times, I become a man-eating wolf.
>
> Aesop *Fable* 419 Perry = 196 Halm = 301 Hausrath and Hunger

Since he is lying, the thief is understandably vague about the origin of his pre-tended affliction, but the term *hamartiai* suggests some offence against the gods and that the werewolfism accordingly results from a divine curse.[129]

---

[125] Pliny *Natural History* 8.80.   [126] Hesiod *Catalogue of Women* F164 MW = 114 Most.
[127] See LS and *OLD* s.v.
[128] Cf. Smith 1894:10–11, Summers 1933:145; Gordon 2015:58 n.126 contemplates that the Aesopic story may be pre-Petronian.
[129] A striking example of the manufacturing of 'the curse of the werewolf' in the modern age is found in Guy Endore's 1933 novel *The Werewolf of Paris*. Here (ch. 1) the werewolf curse is inflicted across the generations of the Pitamonts by their rivals the Pitavals, when the latter imprison one of the Pitamont men for life in a darkened well, alternately starving him and feeding him on raw meat, until he begins to howl like a dog. The mechanism by which the curse takes effect is intriguingly obscure, not least given that the imprisoned Pitamont is (inevitably) without issue. The curse manifests itself most directly in the novel's final chapter (ch. 18) when the werewolf Bertrand finds himself confined in an all-but windowless cell in a lunatic asylum, where he is similarly alternately starved and fed on raw meat.

Magic and Werewolfism in Medieval Texts

The association between werewolfism, witchcraft, and magic persisted into the medieval period. Three of the texts of interest here, the *Topographia Hibernica*, the *Lai de Melion*, and *Guillaume de Palerne*, were all produced within a short space of time at the turn of the thirteenth century, and derive from the earliest band of extant medieval werewolf tales (along with Marie de France's *Bisclavret*).

Gerald of Wales's Latin *Topographia Hibernica* (*c.* AD 1188) tells that the people of Ossory, who were ever bound to supply a pair of themselves to serve as werewolves, had been placed under a curse by Natalis, the abbot and saint (the tale is summarized more fully in Chapter 3). This is quite mysterious. Are we to presume that the curse (a saint's) is endorsed and enacted by God, for all that, without any further context, it would appear to be a malicious one, and one aligning more with the magical realm?[130] Half a century later, a version of this tale found its way into the Old Norse *Konungs skuggsjá* (*Speculum regale*, King's Mirror; *c.* AD 1250). In this version the curse originates not with Natalis but with St Patrick himself, no less, and his reason for imposing it had been the disrespectful behaviour of the people of Ossory towards him as was trying to convert them. His audience had howled at him like wolves, and so the punishment was a thematically appropriate one:

> There is another quite extraordinary phenomenon in that land, which must seem wholly unbelievable to many. Even so, the inhabitants of the land assert that it is absolutely true, and that its cause is the anger of a holy man. It is said that when St Patrick was preaching Christianity in the land, one particular clan resisted him more strongly than other the folk in it. These people sought to heap insult upon him in all sorts of ways, the holy man himself and God too. When he was urging the Christian faith upon them as he did other men, and came to their meetings and to the assemblies they held, they devised the scheme of howling at him like wolves. When he saw that he could achieve little of his mission with these people, he became very angry and asked God to exact revenge upon them by means of some scourge, so that their descendants might have a reminder ever after of their refusal to obey him. Their descendants subsequently suffered a mighty and an appropriate form of vengeance, albeit an extraordinary one, inasmuch as it is said that all the people that come from that race become wolves at some point, run in the forest and feed upon the same things that wolves do. But actually they are worse, insofar as they have a human understanding underpinning all their cunning, but a hunger and a greed for human beings as much as for other living creatures. It is said that some of them

[130] Gerald of Wales *Topographia Hibernica* ch. 19; cf. Summers 1933:207–10, Otten 1986:57–61, Douglas 1992:110–12.

experience this affliction every seventh year, being men in the intervening period, whilst others experience the affliction for a continuous period of seven years, but never again thereafter. *Konungs skuggsjá* 11 (Ogden trans.)[131]

In the Picard French *Lai de Melion* (*c.* AD 1190–1204) the transformation of King Arthur's knight Melion into a wolf and back again is dependent upon a magical object.[132] One day, when he and his wife, the daughter of the King of Ireland, are hunting together, she sees an enormous stag and declares she will never eat again unless she has some of it. Melion shows her his ring, with a red and a white stone. He tells her that, if she touches him on the head with the white stone when he is naked, he will turn into an enormous wolf, and thus be able to catch the stag and bring her some of its flesh. The red stone will transform him back. He begs his wife to guard his clothing. The wife duly transforms him, in a process which is a physical ordeal for him. As soon as he begins to chase after the stag his wife, though hitherto seemingly completely loyal and loving, turns tail, rides off with Melion's squire, and takes him back to her father's court in Ireland. Melion returns from the hunt with the meat to find his wife gone, and himself accordingly trapped in wolf form. After some adventures he is adopted, as a tame wolf, by his own Arthur, and he comes to share his food and drink. When Arthur takes him along with his retinue to visit the Irish court, he attacks the squire, now living there. Since this is out of character for the wolf, Arthur forces the squire to explain the beast's actions, and he reveals all. The Irish king makes his daughter surrender the magic ring, which he passes to Arthur. Gawain persuades Arthur to accomplish the transformation in a private room, for the sake of Melion's shame. Arthur puts the ring to his head, and he is transformed back to a man, face first, before being covered with a cloak. The Irish king delivers his daughter over to Melion to do with her as he will. Melion initially wishes to touch her with the ring and so turn her into a wolf for life, but Arthur's knights dissuade him from doing so. So here we have what is evidently a magical tool. The final episode, in which Melion has to be dissuaded from applying it to his former wife, tells us that its effect is a general one and not in any way confined to him alone. There are no sorcerers or witches as such here, though one must imagine that the ring had initially been the product of one, while in her malicious, callous, and deceitful use of it, and with her inscrutable and undermotivated change in personality, Melion's wife does come to resemble a witch.[133]

---

[131] For the text see Jónsson 1920; for a full translation Larson 1917 (Meyer 1894 has the Irish marvels only). Discussion at Summers 1933:20–6, Sconduto 2008:32–3, Douglas 1992:111, Pluskowski 2015:96.

[132] I summarize this tale and also that of Arthur and Gorlagon a little more fully than is strictly needed here in order to pave the way also for arguments made in Chapter 4.

[133] For text and translation see Hopkins 2005:51–82, Burgess, Brook, and Hopkins 2007:413–66; further discussion at Milin 1993:81–5, 102–12, Sconduto 2008:57–75, Boyd 2009 (the latter arguing for significant Irish-cultural influence).

We find many similar themes also in the Picard French *Guillaume de Palerne* (*William of Palermo*; AD 1194–7). Here Alphonse, eldest son of the King of Spain, is transformed into a wolf by his wicked stepmother, Brande, using a lotion, so that she can promote her own son to be crown prince in his place. After many adventures, in which he has served as protector to Guillaume, wolf-Alphonse is reunited with his father when the latter visits the Palermo court. The king recognizes his son upon remembering the rumour that Brande had turned him into a wolf. Brande is now summoned, made to confess all and to turn him back. She does so by hanging a golden ring with a magic stone around his neck on a scarlet silk thread, and then reading out a spell from a book. As a manipulator of magic lotions, magic rings, and verbal spells, as well as a wicked stepmother, it is fair to say that Brande too is cast as a witch.[134]

Moving on a century or so, we come to the Latin romance of *Arthur and Gorlagon* (thirteenth–fourteenth century AD), in which again we find many themes familiar from the two Picard romances. Arthur goes on a quest to discover the nature of women. King Gorlagon tells him the story of a king (who eventually turns out to be Gorlagon himself), at whose birth there appears a sapling in his garden. Fate decrees that if someone cuts this down and strikes another person on the head with it, saying 'Be a wolf and have the understanding of a wolf', he will indeed turn into one. Gorlagon accordingly encloses the garden in a high wall, and allows only one trusted servant to enter. He refuses to eat each day until he has checked that the sapling is safe. His beautiful wife, who loves another, a pagan, asks him why he goes to the garden so much. He declines to tell her, whereupon she refuses to eat until he does. She then cuts the branch and strikes him with it, but in her haste mispronounces the spell: 'Be a wolf and have the understanding of a *man*.' So transformed, Gorlagon flees into the forest with his own hounds in pursuit. The treacherous wife immediately marries her pagan lover and makes him tyrant in Gorlagon's place. After many adventures Gorlagon is adopted as a tame wolf by his brother Gargol, also a king, and dines at his table. Gargol's wife too is faithless, carrying on an affair with her steward, and wolf-Gorlagon finds a way to reveal this to Gargol after she has tried to frame him for the supposed murder of her son. These events lead Gargol to conclude that Gorlagon is a human in lupine form. He follows him to his former kingdom, where the people tell how the queen had turned the former king into a wolf. He returns with his troops and captures both the queen and her tyrant lover.

---

[134] *Guillaume de Palerne*, esp. ll. 274–307 and 7728–842 for Brande's magic (cf. also l.58, where the ladies-in-waiting at Palermo plot to kill Guillaume with a herbal potion). For the text see Michelant 1876 and Micha 1990; for an English translation see Sconduto 2004; for a modern French translation with a substantial introduction, see Ferlampin-Acher 2012. At l.9660 (cf. ll.276, 293) the anonymous author claims his poem is translated from a Latin source, but this may simply be a pseudepigraphic conceit, of a sort familiar enough from ancient literature. General discussion at Summers 1933:220–22, Dunn 1960, Kratz 1976:69–70, Douglas 1992:119–21, Sconduto 2004:1–10, 2008:90–126, McCracken 2012, Hogson 2016.

She is pressed to produce the sapling, which she at first refuses to do, claiming that it has been broken up and burned, but after much torture and deprivation of food and drink she does so. The king strikes Gorlagon on the head with it, with the words, 'Be a man and have the understanding of a man.' Gorlagon returns to being human, more beautiful than before. Recovering his throne, he now has the tyrant put to death, and divorces his wife. He decapitates the tyrant's body, embalms the head, and ordains that his former wife should ever sit beside him with the head in a dish. Whenever he kisses his replacement wife, his former wife is to kiss the head. (It is not made explicit whether Arthur concludes from this tale, as well he might, that his own wife, Guinevere, is betraying him with Lancelot, but this is something that the reader certainly knows.) Once again, we have a magical tool, though one produced under mysterious and unexplained circumstances, and not by any human hand. Its manipulator is not really charac-terized as a witch, though once again she is a deceitful woman with a lover.[135]

In the late-thirteenth-century Old Norse *Völsunga saga*, Siggeir captures Sigmund and his nine brothers in battle; their sister Signy, Siggeir's wife, prevails upon him not to execute them at once. With some misgivings, he lays them out in stocks in the forest instead. Thereupon a great wolf presents itself each night and devours one of the nine, until only Sigmund remains. At this point Signy then sends her servant to him with a pot of honey, which he smears over Sigmund's mouth and face. When the wolf appears, it makes to lick the honey from his face before devouring him. This gives Sigmund the opportunity to grab its tongue in his teeth; as the wolf resists him, he is able to wrench it out, killing the beast. The author concludes his story by observing that some believed that the wolf was Siggeir's own mother, who had changed herself into this shape by means of 'trolldom and sorcery [*fjölkýngi*, literally "much-knowing"]'.[136]

In a *c.* AD 1400 Norse saga, *Ala flekks saga*, 'The Saga of Spotted Ali', we find the condition of werewolfism inflicted by a sorcerer. The sorcerer Glodarauga curses Ali, the lost son of King Richard, on his wedding night, compelling him to take to the woods and become a wolf, whereupon he marauds England in terrible fashion. The curse also entails that he can only escape death (and, seem-ingly, his lupine form) if someone begs for pardon for him when he is captured. When he is eventually taken by the king, his foster mother Hildr duly does so, having recognized his eyes. She takes the wolf back to her home. When she wakes in the morning, she finds Ali lying in the bed, and the wolfskin on the floor

---

[135]   For the text see Kittredge 1903; for an English translation see Milne 1904 (= Otten 1986:234–55). Discussion at Kittredge 1903:162–75 (including the theory that the text has Welsh origins), Douglas 1992:117–19, Harf-Lancner 1985, Milin 1991, 1993:85–95, 113–15 (*inter alia*, comparing ATU no. 449), Sconduto 2008:76–89.

[136]   *Völsunga saga* 5; cf. Douglas 1992:67–8.

by his side. Ali's foster father Gunni burns it. All is revealed to the king, the sorcerer is hanged, and Ali eventually inherits his father's throne.[137]

Conclusion

It has been the task of this chapter to trace the persistent association between werewolves on the one hand and witches and sorcerers on the other in the ancient world (and finally to do the same, in a brief way, for the earliest medieval were-wolf tales). The Homeric Circe's wolves should be understood as men transformed by the witch. Despite some modern claims, this was the position of the *Odyssey* itself, as well as the subsequent ancient tradition. The text may have introduced us to the notion of Circe's transformation of men into animals more generally by means of the wolf example actually because there was already an established notion that witches were inclined to transform men into that animal in particular. Herodotus' treatment of the Neuri not only asserts that they are sorcerers that turn themselves into wolves, but also implies that transformation into a wolf is a thing more generally characteristic of sorcerers. Like the Neuri, Virgil's (Egyptian?) Moeris is projected as a sorcerer that specializes in turning himself into a wolf. Imperial Latin literature provides us with examples of individual witch-figures transforming into wolves, notably Tibullus' bawd-witch and Propertius' Acanthis, but, beyond this, there seems to have been a set of thematic associations between werewolfism and the terrible *strix*-witches. It may have been thought, in particular, that they had a propensity to transform themselves not only into child-stealing and child-maiming screech owls or screech owl-like crea-tures, but also into wolves. Apuleius characterizes his *strix*-like Thessalian witches in general as *versipelles* and 'she-wolves', and wolf imagery seems to lurk in the folkloric background to one if not two of the marvellous tales he tells about them, those of Meroe and Panthia and that of the Thelyphrons. The notion that were-wolfism could sometimes be effected by a divine curse, as in the Arcadian tradi-tions and as in Aesop's fable, was perhaps a variation or extension of the more typical and established idea that it could proceed from the cursing of a witch or a sorcerer. We shall have more to say about the significance of this thematic associ-ation in the general Conclusion.

---

[137] *Ala flekks saga* 6–7; for the text see Lagerholm 1927:84–120; for an English translation see Bachman and Erlingsson 1993:41–61; for a summary see Kittredge 1903:255–6 and for scholarship see Glauser 1993.

2

Werewolves, Ghosts, and the Dead

In the last chapter we saw that the ancient world associated werewolves on the one hand with witches and with sorcerers on the other, in both a direct fashion (that is, by constructing tales in which the two categories interacted with each other) and in a broader thematic fashion (that is, by more loosely featuring the two categories in the same texts). Similarly, the ancient world also associated werewolves with ghosts in both direct and thematic ways.[1] Once again, we will review the evidence in broadly chronological fashion, after first considering the case for the general associations between wolves and death in the ancient world.

Wolves and Death in Greece and Italy

There is significant evidence for an association between wolves and death in the ancient world, this relating principally to the non-Latin parts of Italy.

Wolves and Death in the Greek world?

Both Carla Mainoldi (in 1984) and Daniel Gershenson (in 1991) have maintained that the wolf had a particular association with death for the Greeks, as is more obviously true for the dog (their devouring of corpses cast out, Cerberus, the *Aidos kyneē*, etc.).[2] But the case for the wolf is not a strong one. None of the examples Gershenson adduces in support of his thesis seem to me to be cogent (most of his discussion devoted to the Lykaia). More promisingly, the principal example in Mainoldi's portfolio is the Hero of Temesa, mentioned later in this chapter and then discussed more fully in the dedicated Chapter 5. However, we must exclude him from our considerations at this point if we are to avoid *petitio principii*. Beyond this, the only significant wolves Mainoldi can point to in association with death have the look of being minor and exotic variations of dogs in similar roles. Thus, in Aeschylus' *Seven Against Thebes,* Antigone protests that she will not leave her brother's body exposed to be devoured by wolves, this instead of

---

[1] We shall articulate this point in a slightly more formal way in the Conclusion.
[2] Mainoldi 1984:28–30 (for the wolf) and 37–51 (for the dog); Gershenson 1991:98–117.

the more usual dogs.[3] In the fourth-century AD Great Magical Papyrus in Paris, Hecate, the underworld goddess of the all-pervasive canine imagery, is given (amongst a great many others) the epithets *Lykō* and *Lykaina*, which may both be construed as 'She-wolf'.[4] In the later fifth century BC Sophron had already described Mormolyke ('Bogey-wolf'), a member of Hecate's entourage, as 'the nurse of Acheron' (Acheron being one of the fabled underworld rivers).[5]

Etruscan Aita-Calu

Etruscan art reveals a profound association between wolves, death, and the dead in that culture. The Etruscan reflex of the Greek Hades was Aita/Eita, and he was identified with the indigenous Calu.[6] Examples abound from the fourth century BC onwards of his depiction in head or bust only wearing a wolf-head cap. It is possible that the latter is the Etruscan version of the dogskin cap of invisibility attributed to Hades in Greek mythological sources.[7] Of particular interest are a pair of fourth-century BC tomb paintings, one from the Golini I tomb at Orvieto and one from the *c.* 340–320 BC Orcus II tomb at Corneto (Tarquinia). In both images Aita is accompanied by his wife Persephone ('Phersipnai'), both figures being named. In the Golini tomb the pair reclines at a banquet with the dead man and his family, and Aita wears a wolf-head cap, while holding a sceptre around which there winds a snake.[8] In the Corneto tomb Aita and Persephone are housed in a cave within the underworld, and he sits on a rock throne. He again wears a wolf-head cap.[9] The notion that Aita-Hades might dress in a wolf-head cap might suggest an ironic reading of the assertion of Petronius' Niceros that his soldier companion was 'as brave as Orcus [i.e. Hades again]', just prior to his wolf transformation.[10]

Also of great interest here is the striking series of eight scenes on second-century BC Etruscan cinerary urns in alabaster or terracotta. On these a wolf, sometimes a quite terrifying one, a wolf-headed humanoid, or a humanoid wearing a wolfskin, with the head as cap, precisely à la Aita, attempts to emerge from a puteal

---

[3] Aeschylus *Seven Against Thebes* 1041–2; for dogs as the traditional and iconic devourers of the cast-out or the battlefield dead, see Homer *Iliad* 1.1–5; further references in Chapter 1.

[4] Lyko: *PGM* IV.2276 (4th c. AD). Lykaina: *PGM* IV.2546. Cf. Mainoldi 1984:29.

[5] Sophron F4B KA/Hordern (cf. Apollodorus of Athens *FGrH* 244 F102a, *apud* Stobaeus *Anthology* 1.49–50, pp.418–20 W). For Mormolyke see Hordern 2004:137–8, Johnston 1999a:161–99, Patera 2005 esp. 377–81, 2015:106–44. Note also the *mormolykeion*, referred to at Aristophanes *Thesmophoriazusae* 413–17, Plato *Phaedo* 77e, Heliodorus *Aethiopica* 6.2.1, Proclus *Commentary on Plato's Republic* 180.19, Hesychius s.v. μορμολυκεῖα, schol. Aelius Aristides *Panathenaicus* 102.5 (iii p.42 Dindorf), etc.; cf. Mainoldi 1984:29.

[6] For Aita and his place in the Etruscan underworld, see Cook 1914–40:i, 98–9, Krauskopf 1987, 1988, Jannot 2005, 54–71, Rissanen 2012:129–34.

[7] E.g. Homer *Iliad* 5.845, Hesiod *Shield* 227, Aristophanes *Acharnians* 390, Plato *Republic* 612b.

[8] *LIMC* Aita/Calu 5.

[9] *LIMC* Aita/Calu 6. Weber-Lehmann 1995:72–100, with pl. 21–4, offers a detailed analysis of this tomb's images.

[10] Petronius *Satyricon* 61–2.

(a well head), perhaps symbolic of an exit from the underworld, but is prevented from doing so by a group of men around it, who strenuously hold the creature back with a chain round its neck or by threatening it with weapons. A calmer man holds a *patera* over it and Vanth, the Etruscan female underworld demon and psychopomp, winged and torch-bearing, often attends the scene. The scene evidently represents some sort of dangerous ritual, and it is usually thought to represent an offering to the ghost of a dead man. Chierici, a little ambitiously, regards these scenes as representing, more specifically, Etruscan versions of scenes from Greek myth in which groups of warriors make offerings to dead heroes: Odysseus and his men with the ghost of Elpenor, or the Argonauts with the ghost of Sthenelus.[11]

The Etruscan Tityos Painter's Wolfman

Surely relevant here too—somehow or other—is a much older Etruscan image, the superb 'wolfman' painted by the Tityos Painter (c. 540–510 BC) on the tondo of a Pontic Plate found in Vulci and now in Rome's Museo Etrusco di Villa Giulia. This perky running figure has a wolf's head and a humanoid body covered in wolfskin (see Figure 5.1).[12] We shall speak of him again in Chapter 5.

The Faliscan Hirpi Sorani of Soracte

Ancient authors were intrigued by the cult performance of the Hirpi Sorani on Mount Soracte, in the Faliscan region 45 kilometres north of Rome, who would walk barefoot over wood embers in honour of Apollo of Soracte.[13] The first extant

---

[11] (1 and 2) Volterra, Museo Guarnacci, inv. 350–1 = *LIMC* Olta nos. 3 and 5 (from Volterra); (3) Florence, Museo archeologico, inv. 5781 = *LIMC* Olta no. 2 (from Chiusi); (4) Pisa, Camposanto, inv. 1906/117 = *LIMC* Olta no. 4 (from Volterra); (5, 6, and 7) Perugia, Museo archeologico, inv. 107 (or 341, from San Sisto), 367 = *LIMC* Olta no. 8 (from Palazzone?) and a lost item without inventory number; (8) Gubbio, Palazzo dei Consoli, inv. 5801 (unknown provenance). Images of all these items except (7) are reproduced at Chierici 1994:355–61; cf. also Szilágyi 1994, Elliot 1995 and Rissanen 2012:130–4. For Elpenor, see Homer *Odyssey* 11.1–83 and the Elpenor vase, Boston, Museum of Fine Arts 34–79 = *LIMC* Odysseus 149; discussion at Ogden 2001 esp. 43–60, with further references. For Sthenelus see Apollonius *Argonautica* 2.911–29, Valerius Flaccus *Argonautica* 5.87–95; perhaps he is the perky warrior emerging from his barrow on an *askos* lid in Boston, Museum of Fine Arts 13.169, as Schefold and Jung 1989:30 suggest (there is no entry for this Sthenelus in *LIMC*).

[12] The plate was found in Vulci's Osteria Necropolis, Tomb 177. See Elliot 1995:24–7, Rissanen 2012:133–4. We might also point to two humanoid figures with wolf-heads attending scenes of Achilles' ambush of Troilus on Etruscan Black Figure vases, illustrated at Simon 1973:39 figs. 8–9; cf. Mainoldi 1984:29.

[13] Virgil *Aeneid* 11.784–8, Strabo C226, Pliny *Natural History* 7.19, Silius Italicus 5.175–183, Solinus 2.26. For general discussion, see Wissowa 1894–90, Otto 1913, Franklin 1921:29–31, Piccaluga 1976, Negri 1982, Rissanen 2012 (where these texts are conveniently reproduced), di Fazio 2013, Vé 2018:172–8. Strabo identifies the deity in receipt of this sacrifice rather as a goddess, Feronia, this seemingly a mistake arising from the name of the local town, Lucus Feroniae; cf. Rissanen 2012:119 n.30.

author to mention them is Virgil in his *Aeneid*. His Arruns prays on the battlefield to 'Apollo, guardian of sacred Soracte', of whom he declares himself to be a primary devotee and for whom he professes to walk through the embers. He then asks the god to help him kill Camilla, and his prayer is granted. But when her companions rally to her as she dies, 'Arruns fled...and in a state of confusion removed himself from sight, in just the same way as the wolf immediately makes for the pathless places and hides himself in the high mountains after killing a shepherd or a great steer, before he can be pursued with hostile weapons. With a feeling of guilt for his act of audacity, he slackens his tail and tucks it under his belly as it trembles, and seeks out the woods.'[14]

Virgil's commentator Servius offers the following explanatory note on the prayer and the rite:

'Apollo, guardian of sacred Soracte.' Mount Soracte is located on the Via Flaminia amongst the Hirpini. Once on this mountain, when a sacrifice was being made to Father Dis [Dis Pater] – for it was sacred to the ancestral dead – wolves suddenly arrived and snatched the entrails from the fire. After the shepherds had followed them for a long time, they were brought to a certain cave, which emitted a pestilential gas, so lethal that it killed anyone that stood near it. A pestilence arose from there, because they had followed the wolves. When they consulted an oracle they were told that the pestilence could be brought under control if they imitated wolves, that is, if they lived by rapine. After they turned to this, those peoples were called 'the Hirpi Sorani'. For in the Sabine tongue wolves are called *hirpi*. They are called 'Sorani' because of Dis, for the father of Dis is called Soranus. They are effectively being called 'the wolves of Father Dis [*or:* the wolves of the father of Dis].' Virgil is mindful of this when a little later on he compares Arruns to a wolf, inasmuch as he is a 'Hirpinus Soranus.'

Servius on Virgil *Aeneid* 11.785

Hirpus is indeed the Faliscan dialect equivalent of Latin *lupus*.[15] But Servius also makes some confusions here: first, he confuses the Hirpi with the Hirpini, who lived some 200 kilometres distant, around Ampsanctus; secondly, after correctly explaining the name phrase Hirpi Sorani, in which Sorani is a genitive singular, 'the Hirpi of Soranus', he immediately proceeds in the final words here as if Sorani is, rather, a masculine plural adjective agreeing with Hirpi.[16]

Servius' notion that the Hirpi Sorani lived by plundering is probably a fallacious explanation added by the commentator himself (or a prior source) into the

---

[14] Virgil *Aeneid* 11.784–815 (785, 806, 809–14 quoted).
[15] See Strabo C226, Festus p.106M; cf. Rissanen 2012:117, with further references.
[16] Rissanen 2012:117, 123–4.

traditional aetiology. Rather, the Hirpi resembled wolves because, in memory of the wolves' original raid upon the fiery altars, they imitated them by walking through fire (there is no particular reason to suppose that, beyond this, they actually dressed up as wolves for the purpose, or that they had anything to do with werewolfism as such).[17] An Etruscan vase in a private collection in Basel, made half a millennium before Virgil, c.500 BC, seems relevant here: on one side a man tends an altar; on the other side brands burn on another altar, which is surrounded by images of creatures that could be either dogs or wolves standing on or running over sticks or plants lying at different angles. Do these represent the original wolf-thieves walking over the wood embers to steal the meat, or the Hirpi Sorani-as-wolves doing the same? Or do they represent a similar myth or rite practised by another Italian people?[18]

For Servius, the sacrifice is no longer to Apollo but to Dis Pater, god of the underworld, and the wolves are accordingly his servants. The god Soranus was identified with Apollo from at least the fifth century BC, but Servius' words suggest rather an identification—perhaps rather an original identity—with the Etruscan god Śuri, who was indeed oracular like Apollo, but also, like Dis Pater, a god of the underworld.[19] A series of bronze figurines perhaps representing Dis Pater bear a superficial resemblance to the image of Aita: he too is shown as a bearded figure wearing a wolfskin, the wolf's head serving as the cap in familiar fashion, and holding a bowl.[20]

Herodotus' Neuri (again)

We return now to Herodotus' Neuri (see Chapter 1), whom the historian describes as goētes.[21] What did he mean by this? His own work affords us no further clues, unfortunately. He only applies the term elsewhere to a remote race of pygmies living south of the Libyan desert, without further elaboration.[22]

---

[17] So Marbach 1929:1131 and Rissanen 2012:121. Rissanen further makes the tendentious claim (124–6) of a certain parallelism between the myth of the Hirpi Sorani and the rite of the Roman Lupercalia, in which, as he sees it, 'wolves', the *luperci*, emerge from and return to the Lupercal cave, supposedly also an underworld entrance. For the Lupercalia see Appendix C: I consider that the association of this rite with wolves and certainly with anything resembling werewolves has been overstated.

[18] Etruscan late black-figure neck amphora, c.500 BC. Private collection, Basel; the vase is reproduced at Rissanen 2012:120–1, figs. 1–2.

[19] Colonna 1985:76–7, 2007:113–14, Rissanen 2012:122–3, 129.

[20] Cook 1914–40:i, 96–8; but scepticism from Belloni 1986.

[21] Herodotus 4.105–7: κινδυνεύουσι δὲ οἱ ἄνθρωποι οὗτοι γόητες εἶναι. Metzger 2011:220–4 discusses Herodotus' use of the term here in some detail, without, it seems to me, hitting the key points.

[22] Herodotus 2.32–3. It is conceivable that the race's small stature was a factor in Herodotus' decision to deploy the word here, given the term's application, already in the *Phoronis*, to the tiny Idaean Dactyls: see below.

The term *goēs* (this is the singular form) is conventionally translated as 'sorcerer'. The (10th-c. AD) *Suda* contends, however, that '*Goēteia* is applied to the bringing up of a dead man by calling upon him; the term is derived from the wailings [*gooi*] and the lamentations of people at the tomb.'[23] Modern historians of religion and—more reassuringly—comparative philologists agree that the term is indeed derivative of the noun *gooi* (singular *goos*) and the verb *goaō*, which refer to the wailing of grief, and they hold, accordingly, that it originally designated a practitioner that specialized in manipulating the souls of the dead.[24] Let us briefly consider the usages of the terms built on the *goēt-* root from their earliest attestation in the *c.*500 BC *Phoronis*, down to the works of Plato, who exploits them voraciously. Beside the noun *goēs* itself, attention must be given to the derived verb *goēteuō* (with its compounds *ekgoēteuō* and *katagoēteuō*), and to the abstract nouns *goēteia* and *goēteuma*.[25]

Diogenes Laertius cites Satyrus for the information that Gorgias had claimed to be present when Empedocles was being a *goēs* (*goēteuonti*). He then reproduces a fragment of Empedocles that Satyrus had adduced to lend credence to Gorgias' claim. In this fragment Empedocles proclaims that he will teach his followers spells (*pharmaka*) against ills and old age, the ability to control rain and the winds, and finally the ability to 'bring from Hades the strength of a dead man.'[26] If we can trust this chain of Chinese whispers, it would seem that Gorgias considered the manipulation of the souls of the dead to be part of the work of a *goēs*. It is noteworthy that Empedocles is elsewhere associated with other early Greek soul-manipulating 'shaman' figures and other shamanistic tendencies.[27] And here let us note that the Tiberian Strabo was subsequently to invoke the greatest of the early Greek shaman figures, Aristeas of Proconnesus, as the *goēs* par excellence (see Chapter 4 for more on Aristeas).[28] Phrynichus Arabicus (2nd c. AD) may indicate that the necromantic 'Evocators' or, more literally, 'Soul-drawers' of Aeschylus' play *Psychagōgoi* employed *goēteiai* in order to summon up souls from the underworld.[29] In the *Laws* Plato does indeed associate the verb *goēteuō* with

[23] *Suda* s.v. γοητεία: γοητεία δὲ ἐπὶ τῷ ἀνάγειν νεκρὸν δι᾽ ἐπικλήσεως, ὅθεν εἴρηται ἀπὸ τῶν γόων καὶ τῶν θρήνων τῶν περὶ τοὺς τάφους γινομένων.

[24] Reiner 1938 *passim*, Vermeule 1979:17–19, Burkert 1962 esp. 44–5, Johnston 1999a:103, 1999b:96, Ogden 2001:110–12, Chantraine 2009 s.v. γοάω, Beekes 2010 s.v. γοάω. Some scepticism from Bremmer 2016:64–5.

[25] It is a pity that the fragments of Aristomenes' lost comedy *Goētes* are so uninformative for their subject.

[26] Diogenes Laertius 8.58, incorporating Satyrus F6 Kumaniecki, Gorgias A3 DK and Empedocles B111 DK/F101 Wright.

[27] Porphyry *Life of Pythagoras* 28–9 (Pythagoras, Abaris, Epimenides); cf. Burkert 1962, Ogden 2009:9–16, Ustinova 2009:186–7, 194–6, 209–17. I explain my use of the term 'shaman' in Chapter 4.

[28] Strabo C589: ἀνὴρ γόης, εἴ τις ἄλλος.

[29] Phrynichus Arabicus *Praeparatio sophistica* p.127 de Borries, reproduced (without being classified either as a fragment or a testimonium) at *TrGF* iii p.370: οἱ δ᾽ ἀρχαῖοι τοὺς τὰς 'ψυχὰς' τῶν τεθνηκότων γοητείαις τισὶν 'ἄγοντας'. τῆς αὐτῆς ἐννοίας καὶ τοῦ Αἰσχύλου τὸ δρᾶμα 'Ψυχαγωγός' [*sic*]; cf. Aeschylus *Psychagogoi* FF273-5 *TrGF*.

the verb *psychagōgeō* and apply it to sorcerers that claim (*inter alia*) to be able to draw up the souls of the dead. Here the term *psychagōgeō* is also used in a vivid metaphorical fashion to describe the 'soul-drawing' deception practised by such sorcerers on the souls of the living, inasmuch as they bamboozle them with their bogus arts.[30] Elsewhere, Gorgias (twice) and Plato himself (twice) use words of the *goēt-* root in similarly vivid metaphors to describe the effect of deceitfully persuasive, manipulative speech upon the souls on the living. In particular, in Plato's *Meno* Meno asserts that his soul and his mouth have been paralysed by Socrates the *goēs*.[31] In the *Phaedo* Plato further uses the term to speak of the bewitching effect of pleasures upon the souls of the living.[32]

Beyond this, from Euripides onwards, words of the *goēt-* root are frequently applied, in a partially derived usage, to deceitfully persuasive, manipulative speech directed towards the living, albeit without the explicit specification that their effect is upon the soul itself. This application is particularly common in Plato, where the words are often associated with the term 'sophist'.[33] Plato similarly applies the root twice also to the bewitching effect of pleasures on the living, again without specification of the soul.[34] In further derived usages, Xenophon applies *katagoēteuō* to the deceitful effects of Cyrus' Median dress, and Plato applies it to the deceitful effects of lifelike painting.[35]

It is of particular interest for the present study that a strong secondary association of the *goēt-* root is the transmutation of forms. Fragments of the *c.*500 BC *Phoronis*, the *c.*456 BC Pherecydes, and of Hellanicus, who wrote shortly after Herodotus, all preserved by a scholiast to Apollonius' *Argonautica*, apply the term *goētes* to the tiny 'finger-sized' Idaean Dactyls specifically in respect of their ability to transform base ore into brilliant metal objects.[36] Even more germanely, Plato applies the term in the *Euthydemus* to the shape-shifter par excellence of Greek myth, Proteus, and in the *Republic* three times to the gods themselves, this in the context of the (rejected) notion that they might manifest themselves before men in a range of different forms.[37] Why would such a significance sit comfortably with that of soul manipulation? Presumably because there is an underlying notion that when a form is transmuted an inner core is made to pass, as it were, between outer carapaces, like a soul in metempsychosis or reincarnation.

---

[30] Plato *Laws* 909b.   [31] Gorgias *Helen* 10, 14; Plato *Menexenus* 235a, *Meno* 80a–b.
[32] Plato *Phaedo* 81b.
[33] Euripides *Hippolytus* 1038, *Bacchae* 234; Xenophon *Anabasis* 5.7.9; Plato *Euthydemus* 288b (sophist), *Gorgias* 483e–484a, *Laws* 922a, *Hippias Minor* 371a, *Republic* 412e–413d (repeatedly), 598d, *Sophist* 234c–235a (sophist), 241b (sophist), *Statesman* 291c (sophist), 303c (sophist), *Symposium* 203d (sophist).
[34] Plato *Philebus* 44c, *Republic* 584a.   [35] Xenophon *Cyropaedia* 8.1.40; Plato *Republic* 602d.
[36] Scholiast Apollonius *Argonautica* 1.1128, incorporating, *inter alia*, *Phoronis* F2 West, Pherecydes *FGrH* 3 F47/Fowler and Hellanicus *FGrH* 4 F89/Fowler. With some weariness I must point out that, *pace* Johnston 1999b:96 and (tralatitiously, I presume) Stratton 2007:28, the *Phoronis* was a poem, not a poet.
[37] Plato *Euthydemus* 288b; *Republic* 380d, 381e, 383a.

Let us note also, for completeness' sake, the frequent association of the *goēt-* root with other magic-related terms. In particular, it is frequently associated with words of the 'drug'/'spell' root, *pharmakon, pharmakeus* (the male equivalent of *phamakis*) and *pharmassō*, from Pherecydes onwards,[38] and also with words derived from the 'incantation' root *epaoid-*, from Gorgias onwards.[39] It is associated once with *kēleō*, 'charm',[40] once with both *manganeiai*, 'trickeries', and *katadeseis*, '(magical) bindings',[41] and only once too, a little surprisingly, with *mageia* ('magic') itself, this last by Gorgias.[42]

So Herodotus' description of the werewolf Neuri as *goētes* is potentially very rich: it may well imply an understanding that they *transmute their own forms* primarily by means of *the manipulation of their own souls*.

Virgil's Moeris and Tibullus' Bawd-witch

Let us return briefly to two of the passages of Latin poetry considered in the last chapter. As we saw there, Virgil (39 BC) closely associates Moeris' turning of himself into a werewolf with his raising of ghosts: 'By their [*sc.* Pontic herbs'] power I often saw Moeris change into a wolf and hide himself in the woods, and I often saw him use them to rouse ghosts from the bottom of their tombs.'[43] Tibullus prays that his bawd-witch should scrabble for her herbs (the tools of her witchcraft and a wretched meal alike) on graves, and scrabble also for bones abandoned by her fellow wolves, perhaps in the same place, before transforming into a wolf: 'May starvation goad her to madness and send her searching for herbs on graves and bones abandoned by fierce wolves. May she run baregroined and howling through the city....' There surely is an association here between the graves and the werewolfism, though Julia Doroszewska may read these lines a little too reductively in asserting that the witch actually transforms into a wolf in the graveyard itself.[44]

---

[38] Pherecydes *FGrH* 3 F47 Fowler; Gorgias *Helen* 14 (cf. A3 DK); Plato *Laws* 649a, 933a, *Meno* 80a-b, *Symposium* 203d.

[39] Gorgias *Helen* 10; Euripides *Hippolytus* 1038, *Bacchae* 234; Plato *Gorgias* 483e-484a, *Laws* 909b, 933a, *Meno* 80a-b, = *Symposium* 202e-203a.

[40] Plato *Republic* 413b.   [41] Plato *Laws* 933a.

[42] Gorgias *Helen* 10. However, Xenophon's reference to Cyrus' adoption of Median dress as an act of *katagoēteuein* (cited above) brings us close to the realm of the mages (*magoi*) of the Persian empire, whom Herodotus held to originate in Media (1.101, 107–8, 120, 128), seemingly correctly, even if his explicit reason for making the connection is his supposition that they took their origin from the witch *Med*ea (7.62; cf. Hesiod *Theogony* 956–62, this passage evidently being a post-mid-sixth-century BC interpolation). Scholars now hold that the *magos* (Persian *makuš*) had initially been a priest of a local Median religion centred around the god Zurvan. For the historical mages of the Persian empire see Benveniste 1938, Bickerman and Tadmor 1978, Burkert 1983b, Handley-Schachler 1992: 39–69b, 367, Briant 2002:94–6, 130–4, 244–6, 266–8, Bremmer 2008:235–48, Panaino 2011, and Trampedach 2017.

[43] Virgil *Eclogues* 8.94–100.

[44] Tibullus 1.5.53–4; the fuller context and the Latin are supplied in Chapter 1; Doroszewska 2017:15; Schmeling 2011:256–7 ('Werewolves are believed to haunt graveyards').

Petronius' Niceros

In the superb werewolf tale Petronius gives to Niceros, with which we began, ghosts and the underworld assert themselves repeatedly and prominently.[45] Before the featured soldier is shown to turn himself into a werewolf, Niceros describes him as 'as brave as Orcus', the king of the underworld, as we have already noted.[46] In travelling with the soldier, he tells that they moved amongst the tombs (which would have been lining the road) in the moonlight, where the soldier made his transformation. Niceros says of himself, as he saw the transformation, 'I almost died of fright [*literally*: my soul was in my nose],[47] and I stood there like a dead man.' Thereafter, he tells us, 'I drew my sword and † hacked at the shades...I was like a ghost (*in larvam*) when I got in, and almost bubbling out my final breath...my eyes were dead.' Niceros concludes his narrative by asserting its truth in a forceful way: 'But if I'm lying, may your guardian spirits exercise their wrath upon me (*genios vestros iratos habeam*).'[48] The ghostly context could not be stronger: not only does Niceros, in experiencing the werewolf, imagine that he is confronted by ghosts from all directions, and that his own soul is on the point of departing his body to become one, but he also invokes them in his para-narrative.

Phlegon of Tralles' Red Wolf and the Talking Head of Publius (potential case)

The paradoxographer Phlegon was a freedman of the emperor Hadrian. The third of his delightful *Marvels* brings together two stories of prophecies of doom issued to the Romans under Glabrio after their defeat of Antiochus III at Thermopylae and the Aetolians at Heraclea in 191 BC. Phlegon claims to have taken them from one Antisthenes, possibly the second-century BC historian Antisthenes of Rhodes. Their ultimate origin must have been in Aetolian resistance propaganda.[49] In the second of these stories the Roman general Publius (his name perhaps intended to evoke the historical Publius Cornelius Scipio) goes mad and starts uttering prophecies for his fellow Romans, first of a further victory for them against Antiochus, but secondly of an eventual vengeful doom to return upon

---

[45] Petronius *Satyricon* 61–2; cf. Bettini 1989–91:73.

[46] Donecker 2012:293 strangely takes 'Orcus' to be the soldier's personal name.

[47] As Smith 1975 *ad loc.* observes, the departing soul is supposed to leave through the nose (appropriately enough, given its assimilation to breath). We may note also that when the Jewish exorcist Eleazar exorcized a demoniac before Vespasian, he drew the demon out through the patient's nose with the help of a magic ring (*Jewish Antiquities* 8.42–9).

[48] For the significance of the *genius*, the spirit of an ancestor often (curiously) embodied in the form of a serpent, see Hild 1877–1919, Otto 1910, Rose 1923, Latte 1967: 103–7.

[49] See Jacoby (*FGrH*) *ad loc.*, Gauger 1980, Hansen 1996:101–12 and McInerney (*BNJ*) *ad loc.*

them from Asia. He then climbs a tree, from which he proclaims that the truth of his prophecies will be guaranteed by the fact that a huge red wolf (*lykos pyrrhos*) will now come and devour him. The wolf duly appears and Publius presents himself to it for consumption. The wolf leaves behind his head, which then proceeds to spout yet more prophecies of doom for the Romans. They build a shrine to Apollo Lykios, the epithet here evidently to be read as signifying 'Of the Wolf',[50] in the place the wolf has deposited the head, and return to their own country. The key passage reads as follows:

'Men of Rome and other soldiers, it is for me to be killed and devoured by a massive red wolf on this very day. You must recognise that what I have told you will all come to pass for you. Take the imminent manifestation of the beast and my own death as proof of the fact that I have told you the truth, which has come to me from a divine revelation.' After saying this, he ordered them to stand at a distance. He told them that none of them should interfere with the beast's arrival and that it would not turn out well for them if they drove it off. The crowd did as he asked, and it was not long before the wolf arrived. When he saw it, Publius came down from the oak and lay down supine. The wolf tore him open and feasted upon him whilst all looked on. It consumed the entirety of his body, save for his head, and then turned to the mountain.

Phlegon of Tralles *Mirabilia, FGrH/BNJ* 257 F3.11–12

This story aligns closely with another that Phlegon tells in the second of his *Marvels*, this one derived from an unidentifiable Hieron of Ephesus or Alexandria, and in this case the story evidently originated rather in anti-Aetolian propaganda. Here Polycritus the Aetolarch (a fictionalized version of Polycritus of Callion) has died, leaving his wife pregnant. As the local townspeople hold a debate in the agora about what to do with the ensuing baby, which they find to constitute an ill omen as being hermaphrodite, the ghost or revenant of the Aetolarch manifests itself, seizes the baby, devours its body, and leaves its head behind on the ground. This head then proceeds to utter prophecies of doom for the Aetolians.[51] In this way, we can see that the big red wolf of the Publius tale is structurally equivalent to the ghost in the Polycritus tale. We may also note that some have contended that the colour red could in itself also be particularly associated with the dead in the ancient world.[52]

---

[50] Cf. the discussion of this term in Chapter 1.

[51] Phlegon of Tralles *FGrH/BNJ* 257 F2; cf. Proclus *Commentary on Plato's Republic* 2.115, who tells that Hieron wrote about these matters to Antigonus—presumably Antigonus II Gonatas. See Jacoby (*FGrH*) *ad loc.*, McInerney (*BNJ*) *ad loc.* and Hansen 1996:85–101; cf. also Brisson 1978.

[52] So Gauger 1980:237–8, with further references in n.36; Hansen 1996:111.

Both of these stories fit comfortably into a tradition of necromantic talking heads.[53] Aristotle tells of the decapitated head of a priest of Zeus Hoplosmios in Arcadia that sang the name of his killer, Cercidas.[54] Aelian tells that the supposedly mad King Cleomenes I of Sparta discussed all his plans with the decapitated head of his friend Archonides, which he preserved in a jar of honey.[55] Philostratus tells that, after he was beheaded by the Thracian women, Orpheus' head took up residence 'in a nook, in a cranny' in Lesbos, from where it issued prophecies.[56] A recipe in a fourth-century AD grimoire amongst the Greek Magical Papyri provides instructions for the practical manufacture of such a talking head: one performs the rites prescribed upon a skull and then is visited in one's sleep by the associated ghost.[57]

There is, let us be clear, no attempt on Phlegon's part to identify the wolf here more specifically as a werewolf. Are there any indications that it could have been one? There is perhaps a vague one from a folkloric perspective. A French werewolf tradition from admittedly long after the period of our primary focus is suggestive. Pierre de Lancre, writing in 1612, reports the notorious case of Jean Grenier, subject of the last werewolf trial to take place in western Europe, at Coutras in 1603. A girl of 13 testified that a large red wolf had grabbed her and torn her dress, but that she had beaten it off with a stick; Grenier, a boy of 13 or 14, had, she said, admitted to being the creature; she had heard that Grenier had also eaten a boy, a girl, and some dogs. A girl of 8 testified that he used a red wolfskin to transform himself into a wolf. After arrest Grenier confessed that in a forest he had met a man in black, on a black horse, who had kissed him with an extremely cold mouth. This was the Lord of the Forest, and he had promised him money if he would serve him; he gave him wine and marked him on the buttocks with a pin. Grenier further confessed to killing more children. He told that he transformed himself by rubbing on some grease that the Lord of the Forest had given him, and then by donning the wolfskin. He could not produce the skin or the lotion, as the Lord of the Forest kept them. His stepmother had left his father when she had seen him vomit up the paws of dogs and the hands of children. He was sentenced to death, but the Parlement de Bordeaux intervened, reinvestigated the case, and resolved instead to lock him up in a monastery for the rest of his life. Pierre de Lancre visited him there in 1610, where he continued to confess to his crimes, and declared that he was still possessed by the desire to eat little girls.[58] (Other werewolves too manifest themselves in the forms of wolves of distinctive

---

[53] See Deonna 1925, Nagy 1990, Ogden 2001:208–16, 2009:202–5.
[54] Aristotle *Parts of Animals* 673a.   [55] Aelian *Varia Historia* 12.8.
[56] Philostratus *Heroicus* 28 (p.172 Kayser); the scene is illustrated on a fine red-figure Hydria, Basel, Antikenmuseum, BD 48 = *LIMC* Orpheus 68, Mousa/Mousai 100; cf. Schmidt 1972.
[57] *PGM* IV.1928–2240. Cf. Apuleius *Apology* 34 (with Hunink 1997 *ad loc.*) and Hippolytus *Refutations* 4.41.
[58] De Lancre 1612 §4.2–4; cf. Baring-Gould 1865:67–76, Summers 1933:231–4, Otten 1986:62–8, Douglas 1992:147–50, Milin 1993:129–33, Sconduto 2008:169–78.

colour, as for example in the case of the French folktale 'The White Wolf' collected by Cosquin and published in 1887.)[59]

However, even if we exclude all suspicion of werewolves from Phlegon's story, it retains some value for us insofar as it does at least seem to provide us with a ghostly wolf, and this in itself will resonate with the arguments advanced in Chapter 4.

Marcellus of Side's Medical Lycanthropes

Marcellus of Side's earlier-second-century AD hexameter poem on medicine is lost, but his words on medical lycanthropy are refracted in a series of later authors, with Aëtius of Amida's mid-fourth-century AD summary constituting the most important witness to them:[60]

> Marcellus On Lycanthropy or On Cynanthropy ['Were-dog-ism']. Men afflicted with the disease of so-called cyanthropy or lycanthropy go out by night in the month of February[61] in imitation of wolves or dogs in all respects, and they tend to hang around tombs until daybreak. These are the symptoms that will allow you to recognize sufferers from this disease. They are pallid, their gaze is listless, their eyes are dry, and they cannot produce tears. You will observe that their eyes are sunken and their tongue is dry, and they are completely unable to put on weight. They feel thirsty, and their shins are covered in lacerations which cannot heal because they are continually falling down and being bitten by dogs.

[59] A father is about to set out on a journey. He asks his three daughters what gift they would like him to bring back. The elder daughters ask for dresses, but the youngest asks for a talking rose. He despairs of satisfying her request but at long last comes across a beautiful castle. Hearing voices from within, he enters and finds himself in a courtyard with a rose bush full of talking flowers. He picks one for his daughter, whereupon a white wolf falls upon him and threatens to kill him for taking one of his roses. Upon hearing of the man's daughter, however, the wolf relents and lets the man go, and take the rose, on condition that he brings back to him the first person he meets on his return. This is indeed his youngest daughter, whom he duly takes back to the wolf. The wolf says he has no intention of harming them: he tells them that he is a fairy condemned to be a wolf by day, but that everything will turn out well for them if they keep his secret. He gives them a splendid dinner and by night shows himself to them in the form of a handsome lord. He tells the girl he will marry her and she will be queen of his castle. The father returns home, whereupon his wife and other daughters press him for the where-abouts of the girl. He eventually tells them, with the result that one of the elder daughters goes to visit her and demands to know what is going on. Eventually she reveals her lord's secret, at which point she hears a terrible howl and the white wolf comes to her only to fall dead at her feet. See Cosquin 1887:ii, 215–17 (no. lxiii), with commentary at 217–30.

[60] For Marcellus of Side and his medical poem, see Metzger 2011:150–2.

[61] Burkert 1983a:89, Bremmer 2007b:72 and Metzger 2011:161–2 find the significance of February here in the fact that this was the month of the Roman Lupercalia, but the role of wolves in this festival has been significantly over-egged (see Appendix C). One might, rather, be tempted to find significance in the Feralia festival, which took place on 21 February: while the name Feralia signifies 'Festival of the beasts', it was in fact a festival of the dead: Ovid Fasti 2.533–70; cf. Frazer 1929 ad loc. (ii, 431–46), Wiseman 1995b:70–1.

Such are their symptoms. One must recognize that lycanthropy is a form of melancholia. You will treat it by opening a vein at the time of its manifestation and draining the blood until the point of fainting. Then feed the patient with food conducive to good humours. He is to be given sweet baths. After that, using the whey of the milk, cleanse him over three days with the gourd-medicine of Rufus or Archigenes or Justus. Repeat this a second and third time after intervals. After the purifications one should use the antidote to viper bites. Take the other measures too prescribed earlier for melancholia. As evening arrives and the disease manifests itself, apply to the head the lotions that usually induce sleep and anoint the nostrils with scents of this sort and opium. Occasionally supply sleep-inducing drinks too.[62]   Aëtius of Amida *Libri medicinales* 6.11

Let us note also the words of the eleventh-century AD Psellus:

Lycanthropy is a matter of black bile. It is absolute misanthropy. You will know a man that has fallen into it because you will see him running around tombs by night, pale, dejected, dried up, apathetic.

Psellus *Ponema iatrikon* 837–41[63]

In fact the second passage quoted here is ultimately derivative of the first.[64] We are told baldly that sufferers of lycanthropy go about in imitation of wolves in all respects, but beyond this there is little attempt to describe precisely how their symptoms relate to wolves or werewolves. Indeed, the most significant point of contact with werewolves would seem to be, precisely, the sufferers' propensity to hang around tombs. If this is indeed the principal justification for designating their disease lycanthropy, then it at least indicates that the association between werewolves, ghosts, and their haunts was a fundamental one. A lesser point of contact with wolves or werewolves might be the harrying dogs: as we saw in the previous chapter, Tibullus' witch is to be harried by dogs upon transformation into a wolf.[65]

This venerable tradition of, as it were, medical lycanthropy continued into the twentieth century, or at any rate was recreated then. In *Old Calabria* Norman

---

[62] For this text see Metzger 2011:152–64   [63] Cf. Metzger 2011:256–7.

[64] Marcellus' words are also refracted at Oribasius *Synopsis* 8.9 (late 4th c. AD; a less accurate representation of the original text than Aëtius'; cf. Photius *Bibliotheca* cod. 218); Paul of Aegina 3.16 (7th c. AD; dependent upon Oribasius); Paul Nicaeus 24 (7th–9th c. AD; in turn dependent upon Paul of Aegina). Psellus is similarly dependent upon Paul of Aegina. Note also Joannes Actuarius *On Diagnosis* 1.35 (c. AD 1300) and anon. Περὶ λυκανθρωπίας (probably post-Paul Nicaeus; at Ideler 1842:ii, 282). See above all Metzger 2011:150–70, 256–9 and 2012:137–42, 150–3; cf. also Roscher 1897, Summers 1933:38–51, Eckels 1937:45–8, Burkert 1983a:89, Gordon 2015:31. For a medieval Arabic reflex of Greek medical lycanthropy see Ullmann 1976.

[65] Tibullus 1.5.43–60; cf. *Gilgamesh* (Standard Version) vi.58–63, where the herdsman transformed into a wolf by Ishtar is harried by his own dogs (also discussed in Chapter 1).

Douglas reports an incident as he was driving by night in the summer of 1911 from Spezzano to Vaccariza:

> We passed a solitary man, walking swiftly, with bowed head. What was he doing there?
>
> 'Lupomanaro,' said the driver.
>
> A werewolf...
>
> I had always hoped to meet with a werewolf on his nocturnal rambles, and now my wish was gratified.   Douglas 1915:176[66]

Omnia in peiora ruunt. The modern psychiatric literature devoted to medical lycanthropy as a going concern appears by and large to lack scientific rigour—admittedly to one without medical training.[67] When contemporary patients present themselves to the authorities with the claim of being werewolves, their primary source of inspiration transpires to be the cinema.[68]

Pausanias' Hero of Temesa

Pausanias' intriguing (later second-century AD) tale of the Hero of Temesa, the wolfskin-sporting ghost of Polites, should feature next here in our chronological review: indeed, it is the star witness for the association between werewolves and ghosts in the ancient world. But, given both its complications and its points of interest, discussion of it is deferred to a dedicated chapter, Chapter 5.[69] We will, however, need to make comparative reference to it in the section immediately following.

Philostratus' Dog-demon of Ephesus

In his *Life of Apollonius*, written after AD 217, perhaps with some irony, Philostratus ascribes many miracles to the sage, the Neo-Pythagorean from Tyana. Amongst them is the following:

> When the plague fell upon the Ephesians, and no defence could be found against it, they sent to Apollonius, and made him their doctor for the disease. He

---

[66] Douglas 1915:176; cf. Johnston 1932. We will encounter a nineteenth-century medical lycanthropy patient in C. R. Maturin's 1824 novel *The Albigenses* in Chapter 3.

[67] E.g. Coll et al. 1985, Keck et al. 1988, Fahy 1989, Koehler et al. 1990, Blom 2014, Moselhy and Macmillan 2014; cf. Douglas 1992:1–19.

[68] De Blécourt 2015b:19.   [69] Pausanias 6.6.7–11.

thought that this was a trip he could not put off, but on saying 'Let us go' he was already in Ephesus.[70] I think he did the same thing as Pythagoras, who contrived to be at once in both Thurii and Metapontum. Apollonius assembled the Ephesians and said, 'Do not worry, for I will put an end to the disease this day.' Saying this, he led all the people into the theatre, where the statue of the Averter is now sited. There he found what appeared to be an old beggar contriving to squint. He carried a wallet and morsel of bread in it.[71] He was dressed in rags and had a squalid face. Apollonius grouped the Ephesians around the beggar and said, 'Collect as many stones as you can and throw them at this enemy of the gods.' The Ephesians were taken aback by this instruction, and thought it terrible to kill a stranger in such an unfortunate condition. The beggar himself was beseeching Apollonius and begging for pity, but Apollonius was insistent and urged the Ephesians to get on with the job and not to let the man go. When some of the people began to pelt him with stones, the man who had been pretending to be squinting suddenly looked up at them and showed that his eyes were full of fire.[72] The Ephesians then recognized that he was a demon [daimōn] and so they stoned him to death so thoroughly that they built up a heap of stones over him. Apollonius waited a little and then asked them to remove the stones and see what creature they had killed. When they got down to what they thought was the man they had stoned, he had disappeared, but they saw a dog resembling the Molossian breed in form, but the greatest lion in size. It had been crushed by the stones and was spitting foam from the side of its mouth, like those that are rabid [lyttōntes]. The statue of the Averter, that is, Heracles, is set up in the place in which the apparition/ghost [phasma] was pelted to death.

Philostratus Life of Apollonius 4.10

We may wonder whether it is appropriate to consider a dog entity, such as we seem in the first instance to have here, in the context of werewolfism.[73] But, for what is it worth, Marcellus Sidetes, and after him Aëtius of Amida, in their treatments of the medical reflex of werewolfism, unselfconsciously identify lycanthropy with cynanthropy, the latter being the canine equivalent of the former, as we have just seen.[74] More generally, the Greeks do seem to have recognized the sometime close affinity between wolves and dogs. Plato notes that wolves are very similar to dogs, the wildest of animals resembling the tamest of them. Aristotle is aware that wolves and dogs can interbreed. Diodorus explains that the Egyptians

[70] See Chapter 4 for this mysterious detail.
[71] πήραν ἔφερε καὶ ἄρτου ἐν αὐτῇ τρύφος.
[72] Cf. the case of the mid-nineteenth-century Portuguese werewolf-woman Joana, who was similarly said to have sported fiery eyes. See Latouche 1875:25–34. Further discussion of this tale in Chapter 3.
[73] For dogs in the ancient world generally see Orth 1910, Mentz 1933, Burriss 1935, Scholz 1937, Hull 1964, Merlen 1971 (unreferenced), Lilja 1976, Bodson 1980, Zaganiaris 1980, Mainoldi 1984, Phillips and Willcock 1999.
[74] Aëtius of Amida Libri medicinales 6.11.

honour wolves because their nature is so similar to that of dogs (for him, seemingly in all respects), and again he refers to their ability to interbreed.[75] The problem of the extent to which wolves and dogs are the same or different is well articulated across the range of Aesop's *Fables*.[76] In some of these the cunning wolf is contrasted with the more stolid dog: wolves attempt to make peace with the sheep, on condition that they surrender their sheepdog guards;[77] the wolf refuses to accept the dog's easy meals at the price of wearing his enslaving collar;[78] dogs are set on a wolf to protect goats.[79] In another fable the fundamental affinity of the two creatures is assumed: a wolf reared with the sheepdogs ends up filching from the flock and sharing the meat with the dogs.[80] Other fables again turn on the very ambiguity of the relationship: the wolves persuade the sheepdogs to betray the flock and share it with them on the basis of their kinship, but then destroy the dogs before taking the flock for themselves;[81] a dog general compares and contrasts his dog army with that of the wolf army ranged against him;[82] a wolf helps an underfed sheepdog to secure better meals from his owner, but once the dog has succeeded in this he repays the wolf in a half-hearted way which culminates in the latter's capture and death.[83]

Returning to Philostratus' tale, of all the common dog breeds in the ancient world the large, fierce mastiff-like Molossians were probably the most lupine, even when not supernaturally inflated to the size of a lion. And wolves do in any case lurk just beneath the surface of the Greek text here. The verb utilized to signify 'to be rabid', *lyttaō/lyssaō*, is derived directly from the word for wolf, *lykos* (via **lykiaō*), and would certainly have been heard and read as such: literally, and manifestly, 'to go wolf'.[84]

The passage is included in this chapter on the basis that the beggar-dog is some sort of ghost or revenant, or is akin to such. This may at first seem odd given that

---

[75] Plato *Sophist* 231a; Aristotle *Generation of Animals* 2.7, 5.2, *History of Animals* 6.35, 8.28; Diodorus 1.88.6; cf. Eckels 1937:13, Mainoldi 1984:193, Buxton 1987:65, 76 n.16, Gordon 2015:27. Dogs and wolves can and do interbreed both in the wild and domestically (today hybrids are deliberately created to serve as pets). Indeed, all members of the *Canis* genus are interfertile, with the only obstacle to interbreeding being the disproportionate sizes of individual animals: Musiani et al. 2010b:3–4, Coppinger *et al.* 2010:45. The 'genetic distance tree' of European wolf and dog populations reproduced at Wayne 2010:27 (after Luchini et al. 2004) demonstrates that (a) dogs as a group are no further removed from wolves than different subsets of European wolves are from each other; and (b) Spanish wolves are particularly close to dogs as a group. Neither archaeologists nor biologists can decide when dogs were first bred out of wolves, possibly in two separate episodes: guesses range between c.15,000 BP ('before present') and c.40,000 BP; see Spotte 2012:19–32.

[76] General discussion of dogs and wolves in the *Fables* at Mainoldi 1984:201–9.

[77] Aesop 153 Perry.   [78] Aesop 346 Perry.   [79] Aesop 699 Perry.

[80] Aesop 267 Perry.   [81] Aesop 342 Perry.   [82] Aesop 343 Perry

[83] Aesop 701 Perry. The perceived similarity between wolves and dogs justifies the inclusion of the brief Appendix B on the ancient world's Cynocephali, 'Dog-heads'.

[84] The verb is built on the intermediate noun *lyssa*, 'wolf-madness', <*lykia*. See above all Chantraine 2009 and Beekes 2010 s.v. λύσσα (the latter even going so far as to suggest that *lyssa* originally signified 'she-wolf' in itself); cf. also Latouche 1875:30, Lincoln 1975, Mainoldi 1984:175–6, Marcinkowski 2001:20 n.97.

the entity is seemingly killed within the tale, but some contextual details in the beggar's description point strongly to this: the description 'He was dressed in rags and had a squalid (*auchmērōs*) face'[85] is suitable enough for a beggar, but it is particularly appropriate also to the traditional representation of ghosts. The house-haunting ghost faced down by Arignotus in Lucian's *Philopseudes* is described as 'squalid (*auchmēros*), dishevelled and blacker than the dark'.[86] And this is how Apuleius describes the ghost or revenant of a woman sent by a witch to murder the miller in his *Metamorphoses*:

> She was only semi-clothed, with a pitiful piece of patchwork. Her feet were bare and uncovered. She was yellow like boxwood and foully emaciated. Her unkempt hair was partially grey and caked in the ashes that had been scattered over it. It hung down and covered most of her face.
>
> Apuleius *Metamorphoses* 9.30

Before this, in Euripides' *Orestes*, when Orestes had declared himself metaphorically dead, Menelaus had told him, 'Your squalid (*auchmēros*) hair has gone wild, wretched one.'[87] Clothing of rags, foul face, and unkempt hair are clearly standard *topoi* for ghost descriptions.

The term *phasma*, applied to the creature, may also of course specifically designate a 'ghost'. And there are a great many instances in Greek literature where this is plainly and simply the case: it is used for, *inter alia*, the ghost of Orpheus' wife Eurydice in the underworld, the ghosts that occupy haunted houses, and the ghosts of the vengeful dead and the sex-starved.[88] But the word admittedly has a broad and complex semantic field. The long-standing need for a detailed study of it has at last been addressed by Flaminia Beneventano della Corte in a University of Siena thesis. The term is a *nomen rei actae* derived from the verb *phainō* and so can designate anything that has been shown. Generally speaking, it can designate

---

[85] ῥάκεσί τε ἠμφίεστο καὶ αὐχμηρῶς εἶχε τοῦ προσώπου.

[86] Lucian *Philopseudes* 31: αὐχμηρὸς καὶ κομήτης καὶ μελάντερος τοῦ ζόφου; cf. Ogden 2007:216, 223 n.40.

[87] Euripides *Orestes* 385–91 (387 cit.).

[88] Thus: Euripides *Alcestis* 1127 (the possibility that Alcestis, delivered from clutches of Death, is merely a ghost); Plato *Symposium* 179d (the ghost of Eurydice in the underworld); Philemon *Phasma* (the 'ghost' comedy adapted by Plautus for his haunted-house play *Mostellaria*); Menander *Phasma* (the 'ghost' comedy summarized by Donatus on Terence *Eunuch* 9, in which a living girl is mistaken for a ghost); Memnon *FGrH/BNJ* 434 F1 (the tyrant Clearchus is terrified by the ghosts of those he has killed); Plutarch *Cimon* 6 (the ghost of Cleonice harries her murderer, the regent Pausanias), *Theseus* 35 (the ghost of Theseus appears before the Athenians at Marathon), *Moralia* 1105e (visions of dead friends), Lucian *Philopseudes* 14 (the summoned-up ghost of Alexicles), 15 (ghosts deterred by the clanking of metal), 16 (exorcism of ghosts), 29 (*phasmata* associated with *daimones* and 'the souls of the dead' in a context that implies the three terms to be equivalent), 31 (the house-haunting ghost laid to rest by Arignotus), *Menippus* 7 (the ghosts that might harm Menippus as he enters the underworld); Phlegon of Tralles *Mirabilia* 1 (the ghost/revenant of Philinnion returns to sleep with her parents' lodger). Some of these examples are discussed at Beneventano della Corte 2017:79–104.

'apparition', 'spectral appearance', 'phantom', 'vision', 'omen', 'monster', 'prodigy'. More specifically, the term is likely to be used in the following contexts: supernatural entities delivering instructions to human addressees or siring extraordinary children; prophetic visions seen in dreams; and ghosts and revenants of all sorts. A more particular use of the term is to designate brightly shining meteorological or celestial phenomena and Beneventano della Corte proceeds from this to show the importance of brightness, shiningness, and clarity in almost all entities designated as *phasmata*, not merely the celestial ones: it is noteworthy that *phasmata* visions consisting of fiery weapons and fiery phalluses abound.[89] In this regard, the beggar's fiery eyes again catch our attention.

Philostratus' own usage of the term *phasma* unhelpfully spans a spectrum. In this same text it is used to designate a number of manifestations that are supernatural but not ghostly as such: Proteus;[90] a satyr;[91] an entity described as an *empousa* and a *lamia*;[92] and another entity described as an *empousa* tout court (which is, however, specifically compared to a 'ghost', *eidōlon*, in context).[93] But it is also used to designate the avenging ghost of the Indian Ganges.[94] In the same author's *Heroicus* the term is similarly applied both to a manifestation of the goddess Thetis[95] and to the ghost of Protesilaus.[96]

But perhaps the strongest case for finding intimations of werewolfism and ghostliness in this episode lies in a certain parallelism between Philostratus' narrative and Pausanias' account of the Hero of Temesa, the vengeful ghost that is the subject of our Chapter 5. In both cases:

- The troublesome entity is (a) presented as displaying lupine–canine characteristics; (b) explicitly described as a 'demon'; and (c) described as a ghost, if indeed we may take *phasma* that way in the Philostratus passage.
- The entity is clothed in a rough fashion: the Ephesian beggar in rags, the Hero of Temesa in a wolfskin.
- The presence of the entity in itself constitutes a curse to the community, in this case manifesting itself in plague, while the Hero of Temesa must be prevented from random attacks on his community with annual offerings.
- The deliverer is a man of shamanic powers (cf. Chapter 4). Apollonius was a great soul-manipulator, as is made clear in the opening section of this

---

[89] Beneventano della Corte 2017 *passim*. Fiery weapons and phalluses: e.g. Plutarch *Romulus* 2.4–7; Dionysius of Halicarnassus 4.2.1–2, 5.46.1–3. Beneventano della Corte also examines *phasmata* as facilitators of communication between this realm and other realms. Their role in this regard is helpfully crystallized in the distinction between *phasma* and *deigma* (the *nomen rei actae* derived from *deiknumi*, also 'show'): a *phasma* opens up a question or a possibility; a *deigma* determines or confirms the answer.

[90] Philostratus *Apollonius* 1.4.   [91] Philostratus *Apollonius* 6.27.
[92] Philostratus *Apollonius* 4.25.   [93] Philostratus *Apollonius* 2.4.
[94] Philostratus *Apollonius* 3.20.   [95] Philostratus *Heroicus* 45.2
[96] Philostratus *Heroicus* 2.4.

passage, in which he teleports himself and his companions to Ephesus; the shamanic associations of Euthymus, the deliverer of Temesa, will be discussed in Chapter 5.

- The theme of stoning is prominent: here the Ephesian beggar-dog is stoned 'to death'; the vengeful ghost of the Temesa story is created when the locals had stoned the miscreant Polites to death. Pelting with rocks is a striking token of the technique of *pharmakeia*, scapegoating.[97]

The central motif of Philostratus' tale is saluted (consciously or otherwise) in the appendix to Guy Endore's 1933 novel *The Werewolf of Paris*. Here Bertrand, the werewolf, is seemingly buried, after his suicide, in humanoid form. When his coffin is accidentally opened some years later, it is found to contain only the remains of a dog.

A Christian refraction of a tale of this sort is to be found in the (5th-c. AD?) *Passion of St Trypho*. Gordiana, cherished daughter of the emperor Gordian III, is possessed by a demon (*daimōni, pneuma*) that ever cries out the name of Trypho the gooseherd with dread. Troops eventually track this Trypho down to an obscure Phrygian village and bring him to Rome. Upon arrival he calls the demon out in the name of Christ and it emerges in the form of a black dog with (NB) fiery eyes. Trypho compels it to confess its identity—the son of Satan, it transpires—and sends it off to the place of fiery punishment.[98] While demons were often portrayed as black in early Christian thought, the pagans before them had characteristically conceived of ghosts as black too, as we have just seen in the case of Lucian's *Philopseudes*.[99]

Later Comparanda

Readers from the Balkans may find much of the preceding material in this chapter quaint, the association between werewolves and the dead being self-evident, given that for them the werewolf has effectively morphed into or merged into the vampire. The terms generally in use for the demonic dead—'vampires'—in the Balkans, including the Serbo-Croat *vukodlak* and the Greek *vrikolakas*, the latter well known from folklore, are thought to derive from the reconstructed Slavic term *vъlk*, 'wolf', and the South Slavic term *dlaka*, 'fleece'. The *vrikolakas* will still occasionally turn into a wolf, though on the whole his lupine qualities have dissipated, apart, of course, from his fundamental craving for human blood.[100]

---

[97] For scapegoating, see Chapter 6.

[98] *Passio S. Tryphonis* 1–2 (*BHG* no. 1856); for the text see Franchi de' Cavalieri 1908:45–74 (at pp.45–54) and for the tradition of Trypho's life see now Macchioro 2019.

[99] For the blackness of pagan ghosts see further Chapter 5 n.78. For the early Christian assimilation of demons with black-skinned peoples see, e.g., Boulhoul 1994:286–7 and Verkerk 2001.

[100] Lawson 1910:376–412, 385 (cf. 239), Summers 1933:14–18, 146–7, Pasarić 2015:239–42. For the *vrikolakas* more generally in modern Greek folklore, see Blum and Blum 1970 esp. 70–6.

This relationship between the werewolf and the vampire is saluted in Bram Stoker's *Dracula*, for which our own Sabine Baring-Gould's 1865 *The Book of Werewolves* was an important source.[101] Dracula escapes from the wreck of the schooner *Demeter* at Whitby in a form initially identified as that of great dog;[102] Van Helsing subsequently expresses the view that he had taken the form rather of a wolf.[103] More generally, Dracula's peculiar affinity for wolves and his power over them is well evidenced throughout the novel: while masquerading as his own coachman, he dismisses an encircling pack that gathers to devour Jonathan Harker;[104] the howling of wolves prompts him to observe, 'Listen to them – the children of the night. What music they make!';[105] he summons another pack of wolves to devour a peasant woman who has had the temerity to come to his castle to complain that he has taken her baby;[106] he summons them again as Jonathan Harker threatens to walk out of his castle;[107] he deploys a normally harmless and genial wolf ('Bersiker', that is 'Berserker') from London Zoo to break Lucy Westenra's garlic-protected window for him, so that he may enter it in the form of a bat;[108] finally, he summons wolves through the snow to his aid as Van Helsing's team converges on the gypsy party escorting his coffin; they slink away again once he is destroyed.[109] Dracula's most striking personal manifestation in wolf form was lost from an early draft of the novel, only to be published posthumously by Stoker's widow in the form of the atmospheric short story 'Dracula's Guest'.[110] In this Jonathan Harker, while en route to Dracula's castle (probably situated in Austrian Styria at this point), finds himself wandering in an abandoned cemetery outside Munich on Walpurgis night. He is saved from its vampire occupants, who rise from their graves en masse, and from a beautiful female vampire in particular, the Countess Dolingen of Gratz, by a great wolf that lies on his chest, a wolf that sports the fiery eyes we associate with the Count in the novel.[111] Soldiers arrive to chase it off, and they subsequently report that it was 'a wolf – and yet not

---

[101] The notes Stoker took from Baring-Gould are reproduced in facsimile at Eighteen-Bisang and Miller 2013:128–31; cf. 284.

[102] Ch. 8, Cutting from *The Dailygraph*, 8 August. In Stoker's notes for the novel, Dracula had been projected to appear at Whitby first as a man, then as a wolf, and then as a flying creature of some sort: Eighteen-Bisang and Miller 2013:142.

[103] Ch. 18, Mina Harker's Journal, 30 Sept.; ch. 26, MH's Memorandum, 30.

[104] Ch.1, Jonathan Harker's Journal, 5 May; ch. 3, JH's Journal, 8, 16 May.

[105] Ch. 2, JH's Journal, 5 May; the line is faithfully and famously reproduced by Bela Lugosi in the 1931 Universal *Dracula*.

[106] Ch, 4, JH's Journal, 24 June.   [107] Ch. 4, JH's Journal, 29 June.

[108] Ch. 11, *The Pall Mall Gazette*, 18 Sept., Memorandum left by Lucy Westenra, 17 Sept. Stoker evidently found the name 'Berserker' appropriate for a wolf after perusing Baring-Gould 1865:34–42; cf. Eighteen-Bisang and Miller 2013:128–9.

[109] Ch. 27, MH's Journal, 6 Nov.; cf., further, ch. 15, Note left by Van Helsing, 27 Sept.; ch. 18, MH's Journal, 30 Sept.; ch. 19, JH's Journal, 1 Oct.

[110] Stoker 1914. The status of this literary fragment is no longer in doubt: Eighteen-Bisang and Miller 2013:278–80.

[111] Ch. 2, JH's Journal, 8 May; ch. 3, JH's Journal, 16 May; ch. 4, JH's Journal, 28 May, 30 June.

a wolf', and that it has disappeared amongst the tombs; their bullets have no effect on the creature, since they are not 'sacred' ones. We are left to infer that the wolf was none other than Dracula himself in lupine form, protecting his important guest from his lesser rivals.[112]

Finally, I indulge myself with another modern British tale. In his 1912 book *Werwolves* [*sic*] Elliott O'Donnell gives us a tale of werewolfism set in Cumberland, supposedly reported to him the previous year. The telling of the story is clearly O'Donnell's own; one suspects the formulation of it to be equally so. According to this, the Andersons' newly built house in the country was long beset by nocturnal lupine howlings, causing the servants to depart. Eventually on Christmas night the family encountered in the children's bedroom a huge, terrifying, nude grey form with a wolf's head, which disappeared when the mother brought a candle into the room. Bones were subsequently discovered in a cave in the hills behind the house: a human skeleton without a head, together with a wolf's skull. These were burned, and the hauntings duly ceased.[113] Many will recognize the bones of the ancient world's favourite haunted-house story here.[114]

Conclusion

This chapter has traced the persistent association between werewolves, ghosts, and the dead in the ancient world. There is a weak basis for thinking that a general association obtained between wolves *tout court* and the dead in the Greek world, but a stronger one for thinking that such an association did indeed obtain in the Italian world, given that the Etruscan reflex of Hades, Aita/Calu, could sport a wolfskin, and that wolves come to serve as the emissaries of Dis in the aetiological myth of the Hirpi Sorani. As to werewolves proper, Herodotus' application of the word *goētes* to his werewolf Neuri, in addition to saluting their ability to transmute their form, probably also implies that they engaged in ghost or soul manipulation. Virgil's werewolf Moeris is a raiser of ghosts. Petronius' werewolf story is richly decked out with the imagery of ghosts and the underworld. Marcellus of Side's medical 'lycanthropes', sufferers from the disease of 'lycanthropy', roll around in graveyards, and indeed it would appear to be on the basis of this symptom in particular that the victims of the disease are considered to be werewolves: their projection as such is essentially metaphorical, and they should not be seen as the origin point or the key to ancient werewolfism. Pausanias' Hero of Temesa is a ghost or a revenant dressed in a wolfskin, while Philostratus'

---

[112] The episode in a sense duplicates those of the novel in which Dracula warns his three brides to stay away from Harker: ch. 3, JH's Journal, May 16; ch. 4, JH's Journal, 29 June.

[113] O'Donnell 1912:97–103; Summers 1933:189–91, Frost 1973:31; Rini 1929:83 notes the Italian superstition that those born on Christmas night become werewolves.

[114] Discussed, with references, in Chapter 4.

pestilential beggar of Ephesus, revealed to be a terrible dog in his true form, is also projected as some sort of ghost or revenant. As with the thematic association between werewolves and witches discussed in the previous chapter, I shall have more to say about the significance of the thematic association between werewolves and ghosts too in the general Conclusion. In the meantime, the establishment of the association between werewolves and ghosts importantly paves the way for Chapter 4's investigation into the association between werewolves and the world of the soul-projecting shaman figures.

3
The Werewolf, Inside and Out

This chapter offers three studies on the persistent articulation of ancient werewolf lore in accordance with an axis between an inside and an outside of various kinds. Together with the following chapter, it will adduce a little more post-medieval comparanda than has been done hitherto, given the richness of the material available.

Inside and Out (i): Carapace and Core

A werewolf must inevitably comprise at once both human and lupine elements. What was the arrangement between these elements, and by what means did one or other of them come to the fore?

Human Carapace around a Wolf Core

The principal notion in antiquity at any rate seems to have been that a werewolf comprised of an inner wolf core contained within an outer human carapace, this human carapace often being identified not, as one might initially expect, with his skin, but, by something of a sleight of hand, with his clothing. The werewolf doffs his clothing to become a wolf and must recover it if he is to be able to retrieve his human form.[1] Of course this conceptualization of the werewolf makes easy sense at a symbolic level, the clothing signifying a belonging to the human world of culture and civilization, in contrast to the wolf's world of the naked and the wild. The key examples are as follows:

- In Tibullus' tricky imprecation against the bawd-witch, the witch is to run howling through the city 'with naked groin'. According to the werewolf-reading of this complex text, she is naked precisely because she has transformed herself into a wolf, seemingly by divesting herself of her clothes in the midst of other wolves (cf. Chapter 1).[2]

---

[1] Buxton 1987:69 discusses stripping as a prelude to animal metamorphosis, and compares the actions of Lucius prior to becoming an ass (while expecting to become a bird) at Apuleius *Metamorphoses* 3.21 and 3.24.
[2] Tibullus 1.5.55–6.

- Petronius' soldier divests himself of his human clothing in the cemetery in order to become a wolf; he evidently recovers his clothes and with them his human form after having taken the precaution of keeping them safe by turning them to stone. The werewolf turns his clothes to stone here by the magical method of urinating in a circle around them.[3] The restraining use of urine magic to render the clothes immovable was explained by Alex Scobie:[4] earlier in the *Satyricon* a fellow freedman of Trimalchio abuses Giton with the remark, 'If I pee around him, he won't know how to escape';[5] and when Apuleius' horrid witches Meroe and Panthia empty their bladders over Aristomenes in the inn after murdering his companion Socrates, the intention is to keep him trapped in the building until daybreak, allowing them sufficient time to escape the scene, while causing suspicion to fall upon him.[6] The significance of the outer carapace in this transformation is further highlighted by Petronius' application of the word *versipellis* to the soldier, literally 'skin-changer' (cf. Introduction).
- According to Pliny's account of the Arcadian Lykaia rite, men of the Anthid clan divest themselves of their clothes, hang them on a tree, swim across a pool and become wolves; in due course, provided that they have not in the meantime tasted human flesh, they return from across the pool, recover their clothes from the tree and with them their human form (cf. Chapter 6).[7]
- In the undateable Aesopic tale referred to briefly in Chapter 1, the thief, pretending that he is about to be transformed into a werewolf, asks the innkeeper to keep his human clothes safe for him, evidently so that he too can recover his human form:

> A thief stayed in an inn. He passed a few days there with the hope of stealing something, but he could not manage to do so. Then one day he saw the innkeeper wearing a smart new cloak (there was a festival on) and sitting in front of the inn gate. There was no one else about. The thief approached, sat down beside the innkeeper and started a conversation with him. After talking for some time the thief yawned and at the same time howled like a wolf.

---

[3] Petronius *Satyricon* 62. The motif is saluted in Guy Endore's 1933 novel *The Werewolf of Paris* (chs. 9 and 18), where the werewolf Bertrand is compelled to remove his clothes and urinate beside them for a feeling of liberation as he begins to transform into a wolf; in the latter chapter the Petronian precedent is explicitly acknowledged.

[4] Scobie 1982:68; subsequently McDougall 1984:120–7 and Watson 2004 (who seems to have been unaware of Scobie's work). On this passage cf. also Smith 1894:8, Schuster 1930:162, Summers 1933:155, Smith 1975:173, Schmeling 2011:257–8.

[5] Petronius *Satyricon* 57.3: *si circumminxero illum, nesciet qua fugiat.*

[6] Apuleius *Metamorphoses* 1.11–17 (esp. 13). Russell and Russell 1978:155 and Gordon 2015:59–60 n.137 contend rather that the urination reflects a dog's marking of its territory (the man being on the point of turning into a wolf, at any rate), while the motif more generally reflects a Roman anxiety about having one's clothes stolen, an anxiety usually focused, for obvious reasons, on bathhouses in particular (Catullus 33, Seneca *Letters* 56.2; cf. Tomlin 1988 *passim*, esp. pp.79–81).

[7] Pliny *Natural History* 8.81.

The innkeeper asked him why he was doing this. The thief replied, 'I'll tell you, but I must ask you to look after my clothes, for I shall leave them here. Now, my good man, I do not know for what reason the urge to yawn comes upon me, be it for my errors or for some other reason unknown to me. But whenever I yawn three times, I become a man-eating wolf.' With this he yawned a second time and howled again, just like the first time. The innkeeper, hearing this and believing the thief, took fright, and got up with the intention of running off. But the thief seized hold of him by the cloak and besought him with the words, 'Stay, my good man, and take my clothes, so that I don't lose them.' As he besought him he opened his mouth and began to yawn a third time. The innkeeper was terrified that he would eat him, abandoned his cloak, bolted into the inn and secured himself within. The thief went off with the cloak. This is what happens to those that believe lies.

Aesop Fable 419 Perry = 196 Halm = 301 Hausrath and Hunger

The motif of divesting one's human form with one's clothes to become a werewolf continues strongly in medieval texts. We shall defer discussion of the important examples of the twelfth-century romances *Bisclavret* and *Melion* until the next chapter, where indeed we will have more to say too of the ancient material already mentioned. But here let us at least note the description of the werewolf Chaucevaire (Calcevayra, Claceveyra) of Luc in Gervase of Tilbury's *Otia imperialia* of AD 1209–14:

There was an inhabitant of the town of Luc, on the border of the see of Viviers and Mende, called Chaucevaire, who had a similar lot. A victim of fate, he claimed that, on the occasion of the new moon, when the time came, he would abandon all his associates and set his clothes aside under a bush or a remote rock. Then he would roll around naked in the sand for a long time and put on the form and the ravening hunger of the wolf. He would gape after prey, distending his mouth and spreading his jaws wide.

Gervase of Tilbury Otia imperialia 3.120 (p.51 Liebrecht)[8]

To dip briefly into the modern period, the reliable Brothers Grimm published a folktale in their 1812–15 collection associated with Bibesheim and Wernigerode. In one of the tellings they heard, a soldier recounted a supposed experience of his grandfather. One day, when pretending to doze after cutting wood in the forest, he had seen one of his companions take off his belt, become a wolf, and devour a foal, before putting the belt on again and resuming human form. Once they had returned to the town, the grandfather had let the man know what he had seen.

---

[8] For text and translation see Banks and Binns 2002. Cf. Smith 1894:20–1, Kratz 1976:60–1, Milin 1993:67–9, Sconduto 2008:37, Pluskowski 2015:97–8.

The man replied that if he had told him this in the forest, he would not have been in a position to be telling it him now.[9]

Augustine's conceptualization of the werewolf and related phenomena would seem to salute the notion of an outer human carapace and an inner wolf core too, but in a slightly different way. He seems to speak of an outer human shell from which its inner soul is projected outwards in the (illusory) form of a wolf.[10] The same is true of Guillaume d'Auvergne's werewolf story in his thirteenth-century AD *De universo*.[11] We shall consider both these texts in some detail in the following chapter too.

Hairy Hearts

It is just possible that this inner wolf was sometimes conceptualized in more directly physical terms as it lay within its human covering. Much depends upon what we think of the tradition of the hairy heart possessed by Aristomenes of Messene, legendary hero of the Messenian resistance against the Spartans, to whose marvellous adventures Pausanias devotes much of his fourth book:[12]

> The Spartans wondered at him, since he had beaten them so many times. When they finally defeated him in the Messenian wars, they cut him open to see if they could find anything to use against the remaining Messenians, and they found his innards to be extraordinary and his heart to be shaggy, as Herodotus, Plutarch and Rhianus say.
>
> Stephanus of Byzantium s.v. Ἀνδανία (6th c. AD)
= Rhianus FGrH/BNJ 265 F46/F53 Powell (2nd c. BC)

> More remarkable...was the heart of Aristomenes of Messene. The Athenians [*sic*] cut it out because of his extreme cunning and found it stuffed with hair. This was when they caught him after he had escaped from several previous captures through his slyness.   Valerius Maximus 1.8 ext. 15 (Tiberian)

> It is known that some men are born with a hairy heart, and that none are of braver application. An example is Aristomenes of Messene, who killed three hundred Spartans...When they had captured him for the third time the

---

[9] Grimm 1986 no. 214; cf. Hertz 1862:80, de Blécourt 2007a:23–4.

[10] Augustine *City of God* 18.16–18.

[11] Guillaume d'Auvergne *De universo* 2.3.13 at *Opera omnia* (1674) i,1043b; cf. Summers 1933:222–3; Sconduto 2008:22–3, Pluskowski 2015:96.

[12] For all things Aristomenes see principally Ogden 2004 and Casevitz and Auberger 2005. Some subsequent bibliography is accessible through Langerwerf 2009. Amongst earlier material see *in primis* Shero 1938, Pearson 1962, Musti and Torelli 1991, Auberger 1992, 2000. For Aristomenes' hairy heart and lupine qualities in particular see Ogden 2004:113–22.

Spartans cut open his chest whilst he was still alive and his heart was discovered to be hirsute.   Pliny *Natural History* 11.185 (AD 79)

But I fear lest long hair is of no help to fools, not even if they become shaggy in their very hearts, as they say Aristomenes of Messene was found to be when at last was killed. He had caused the Spartans a great deal of trouble, and though repeatedly captured had escaped from them.

Dio Chrysostom *Orations* 35.3 (*c.* AD 100)

Nothing here or indeed elsewhere in the rich traditions bearing upon Aristomenes states that he was a werewolf, though he evidently possessed a number of qualities that might be described as broadly lupine (his bravery, his cunning), as the brief texts collected here indicate.

And wolf imagery does lurk elsewhere in the Aristomenes tradition. As a guardian of the Andanian mysteries, Aristomenes is aligned with a pair of wolf-named figures. Pausanias tells that these mysteries were supposedly first imported to Andania from Eleusis by the hierophant Caucon, son of Celaenus: Caucon initiated the eponymous Messene, who established the rites in her country. Messene was wife to Polykaon, whose name evidently derives from *poly-* and *kaōn* (cf. *kaiō*), and signifies 'Much-burning', 'Much-scorching', but it is nonetheless evocative of that of the famous Arcadian Lykaon, 'Wolfy'.[13] This point would be nugatory, were it not for the fact that, according to Apollodorus, Caucon was not the son of Celaenus but actually one of the sons of this same Arcadian Lykaon. Such a filiation may well imply, further, a tradition that Caucon imported the mysteries not from Attica but from Arcadia, with its gods, myths, and rites so deeply infused with the imagery of the wolf and the werewolf (see Chapter 6 *passim*). Pausanias goes on to tell that the Andanian mysteries were subsequently promoted to a position of greater standing by another Athenian, Lykos (simply 'Wolf') the son of Pandion, supposedly a member of the *Lyko*mid clan (*genos*) that controlled a mystery cult at Attic Phlya: the Andanians of Pausanias' own day still called the wood in which he purified the mystery-initiates the 'Wood (*dry-mos*) of Lykos'. The periegete also cites the mention made of this wood in Rhianus of Bene's Hellenistic epic *Messeniaca*.[14] (The importance of woods to wolves and werewolves is discussed later in this chapter.) This Lykos left the Messenians with an oracle to the effect that the preservation of the mystery rites would ensure the eventual recovery of their country when it was conquered by the Spartans. It was on the basis of this that, as the city of Messene was about to fall, Aristomenes concealed the all-important record of the rites, written on a tin lamella and enclosed in a bronze water jar, on Mount Ithome. When it was finally time for

---

[13] Cf. Pape and Benseler 1911 s.v. Πολυκάων.
[14] Pausanias 4.1.2–4.2.2 (incorporating Rhianus *FGrH/BNJ* 265 F45/F55 Powell) and 4.2.6; Apollodorus *Bibliotheca* 3.8.1. For the Lykomids, see Parker 1996:305.

Messene to rise again, the ghost of Caucon appeared in a dream to its Theban deliverer, Epaminondas, and to its Argive refounder, Epiteles, and showed them where to find Aristomenes' deposit.[15]

It must be conceded, however, that Aristomenes' signal adventure brings him together not with a wolf but with another canid, a fox. On one occasion when the Spartans had captured him, they threw him, shield and all, down the Caeadas crevasse, supposedly to his death. But he arrived at the bottom without harm because an eagle materialized from somewhere and bore him gently down. Almost certainly this bird should be understood to have been his own eagle shield blazon mysteriously come to life. As he lay amid the mouldering bodies of the others that had been cast down, he noticed a fox nuzzling amongst them, and realized that the animal had a way in to the pit, and therefore a way out of it. Grabbing its tail, and allowing himself to be bitten the while, he had the fox guide him out as it fled.[16]

Some other humans are also said to have been possessed of hairy hearts too:[17] Stichius of Aetolia, a beloved of Heracles;[18] Leonidas, the Spartan victor of Thermopylae;[19] Lysander, the Spartan victor of the Peloponnesian War;[20] and the second–third-century A D sophist Hermogenes of Tarsus.[21] Alas, in none of these cases do our sources give us enough context to enable us to understand the significance of the hearts.

A text that might initially appear to frustrate the line of reasoning that makes of a hairy heart an inner animal is the second-century A D Ptolemy Chennus' *New History* (or perhaps better *Strange History*). Photius' substantial summary of this lost work tells that, according to Chennus, Ptolemy I Soter had a Molossian dog, Briareus, that proved to have a hairy heart (*kardian…tetrichōmenēn*) upon being cut open.[22] Eustathius' claim that Alexander the Great himself had had a dog with a hairy heart (*tetrichōtai to kēr*) may well also derive ultimately from Chennus.[23] What is the point of a dog having a hairy heart? Is it to be taken as a dog within a dog? In all probability we are not supposed to be able to resolve the conundrum of Soter's dog, just to enjoy it. It is difficult to characterize the nature and tone of Ptolemy Chennus' work in short compass (and it does not help that the book

[15] Pausanias 4.20.4, 4.26.6–8, 4.33.4–6. For exegesis of the traditions associating Aristomenes with the mysteries, see Ogden 2004:89–103. For Lykos see also Gershenson 1991:67–9.
[16] Pausanias 4.18.4–4.19.1 (cf. 4.16.7 for the blazon) and Polyaenus *Strategemata* 2.31.2. The story type is delightfully revived in the *Fourth Voyage of Sindbad* from the *Arabian Nights*. Discussion at Ogden 2004:70–4, 119–20, 211–15.
[17] Cf. Heath 1998:52–4, Ogden 2004:114–17.
[18] Ptolemy Chennus at Photius *Bibliotheca* cod. 190, 152b36–8.
[19] [Plutarch] *Parallela minora* 306d; Stobaeus *Florilegium* 3.7.65; John Lydus *De mensibus* F5; Aristides of Miletus *FGrH* 286 F20a, b and c.
[20] Eustathius on Homer *Iliad* 1.189.
[21] *Suda* s.v. Ἑρμογένης.
[22] Ptolemy Chennus *New History*, as summarized at Photius *Bibliotheca* cod. 190,148a23–6.
[23] Eustathius on Homer *Iliad* 1.189.

itself is lost). But it may be said that he was a playful controversialist, one who delighted in setting his readers intriguing but irresolvable conundrums by giving a slight tweak to established traditions and by making claims that, while fantastical in themselves, retained some sort of link with what people knew, or thought they did. Take, for example, his claim that the Athenian politician Ephialtes was found to have been reading Eupolis' comedy *Hybristodicae* on his deathbed, this comedy being devoted to those that refused to bring lawsuits: sure enough, Ephialtes had a famous death in 461 BC (though given that it was an assassination, it is not certain that he had a deathbed); and, sure enough, the law courts were of particular interest to him, given his famous reforms of them.[24] But, disorientingly, Eupolis did not debut as a dramatist before 430–424 BC! However, what Ptolemy Chennus' little hairy-heart puzzle may succeed in revealing to us— especially when taken together with Aristomenes' association with his fox—is that hairy hearts were generally imagined to be *canid*: this may be the peg of established tradition upon which Chennus hangs this particular novelty.[25]

There are no direct medieval comparanda for the particular notion of inner fur of this sort. But some early modern comparanda deserve brief mention. The Lutheran natural philosopher Hiob Fincel (Jobus Fincelius) recorded in his 1559 *Der ander Teil Wunderzeichen* the trial of a werewolf that had taken place in Padua in 1541. After a career of killing, the werewolf was caught in human form. He insisted to his captors that he was in effect a real wolf, save for the fact that his fur grew inwards from his skin instead of outwards. His limbs were chopped off in an attempt to test the claim, and he died in the process.[26] In John Webster's 1623 *The Duchess of Malfi* we are told that those with *licanthropia* are overcome with melancholy and imagine themselves to be transformed into wolves. They steal forth into churchyards by night and dig up bodies. Duke Ferdinand had on a recent night been encountered in this condition behind a church, a human leg over his shoulder. He had howled and said he was a wolf: 'onely the difference / Was, a Woolffes skinne was hairy on the out-side; / His on the in-side.'[27] More

---

[24] [Aristotle] *Constitution of Athens* 25.2.

[25] For Ptolemy Chennus and the nature of his work, see Tomberg 1968, Hartley 2014, ní Mheallaigh 2014: 116–26, Ogden 2017:253–9, the last with a number of examples of Ptolemy Chennus' tweaking of established traditions.

[26] Fincel 1559 (*Der ander Teil Wunderzeichen…*) at pp.135–6 in the online facsimile provided by the Martin-Luther-Universität, Halle-Wittenberg, Universitäts- und Landesbibliothek, Sachsen-Anhalt. The garbled version of this reference at Baring-Gould 1865:64–5 (cf. Introduction, p.4), which, *inter alia*, contrives to turn Fincel's Padua (Patavium) into Pavia, expands tralatitiously through the modern popular scholarship on the werewolf. The references made to this episode by Summers 1933:160–1, 176–7 and Duni 2015:129 are misleading in other ways, the first suppressing the citation and the second failing to realize its origin in the work of Fincel as opposed to Johann Wier's *De praestigiis daemonum* of 1563.

[27] John Webster *The Duchess of Malfi* Act 5 Scene 2; cf. Summers 1933:161–2, Douglas 1992:230–1, Moreau 1998:12. Summers and Douglas adduce similar material from other Jacobean dramatists.

recently, in the Irish novelist C. R. Maturin's 1824 novel *The Albigenses* a victim of the disease of lycanthropy is encountered in a castle dungeon:

> 'Examine me,' said the unhappy wretch; 'I tell thee I am a wolf. Trust not my human skin – the hairs grow inward, and I am a wolf within – a man outward only. Slay me, and thou wilt be satisfied of the truth. The hairs grow inward – the wolfish coat is within – the wolfish heart is within – the wolfish fangs are within.'
>
> Maturin *The Albigenses* ii, 263[28]

Baring-Gould seems to have been inspired by material of this sort in formulating his contention that the Latin term *versipellis* (for which see Introduction) should actually be construed to mean 'skin-*reverser*'.[29]

We shall return to the 'wolf-within' model in the following chapter, where it will form an important underpinning to the notion that werewolves were soul-projectors.

Wolf Carapace around a Human Core

The ancient world was a little less interested in and explicit about the alternative model, in accordance with which a werewolf consists of a human core and a wolf carapace, but we can point to two instances of this notion, both of which will be of primary concern to us in following chapters, where the evidence (in the first case copious) is laid out:

- Ovid's description of Lykaon's transformation into a wolf has his human clothes being transformed into an enveloping wolfskin: 'His clothes turned into tufts of hair, his arms into legs' (see Chapter 6).[30]
- Pausanias' Hero of Temesa is described as a *daimōn*, essentially a (we presume humanoid) ghost, in a wolfskin (see Chapter 5).[31]

This model came to be celebrated in medieval texts. In Gerald of Wales's wonderful AD 1187 tale of the werewolves of Ossory in Ireland (mentioned briefly in Chapter 1) we meet a priest travelling through the woods from Ulster to Meath with a boy companion. The setting, *c.* AD 1174, is just a few years prior to the time of writing. By night he encounters a wolf, which tells him not to be afraid. The wolf explains that the abbot Natalis has put the people of Ossory under a curse, and that every seven years two of them, a man and a woman, must put off human

---

[28] Cf. Summers 1933:263; cf. Bourgault du Coudray 2006:14–15.
[29] Baring-Gould 1865:65; cf. Smith 1894:10.
[30] Ovid *Metamorphoses* 1.226–39.   [31] Pausanias 6.6.11.

form, becoming wolves, and leave the dwellings of men. If they survive as wolves for seven years, they are restored to human form and then two other people of Ossory must take their place as wolves. The wolf goes on to explain that his wife and partner, transformed with him, is dying, and he asks the priest to give her the last rites. He follows the wolf in fear and duly does this. To convince the priest that he will not be committing blasphemy by bestowing the last rites upon an animal, the wolf rolls back his wife's wolfskin, from head to navel, to reveal that she is a human old woman beneath. The following morning the male wolf leads the priest and the boy out of the woods and gives him prophecies for the future of Ireland and the prospects for the English there. The priest is subsequently sent to the pope to account for his actions. If the male werewolf can roll back his wife's wolfskin, to reveal the human body beneath, one wonders why they cannot doff their skins completely. Perhaps, despite being able to open them up to a certain degree, they are nonetheless magically trapped within them (as in the next case); or perhaps they are merely forbidden to remove them completely by the terms of the curse.[32]

A yet more striking case is provided by the mid-thirteenth-century AD Norse *Völsunga saga*:

> Now it happened that on one occasion they [Sigmund and Sinfjötli] went again into the forest to acquire wealth for themselves, and they found a house. Two men were sleeping in it and they wore large gold rings. They were under a curse, for wolfskins [*úlfahamir*] hung over them in the house. Only once in every ten days could they get out of the skins.[33] They were princes. Sigmund and Sinfjötli donned the skins and could not get out of them: the skins' power was just as it had been before. When they tried to speak, they produced wolf-howls, but they both understood the howls. Now they went off into the woods, each taking his own path.... [After mixed adventures, the pair are anxious to shed their wolf-skins again.] After that they went into the subterranean house and remained there until they could get out of the wolfskins. Then they took them and burned them in the fire and bade them be of harm to no one any more. Under that curse they had performed many great deeds in the realm of king Siggeir.
>
> *Völsunga saga* 8 (Ogden trans.)[34]

---

[32] Gerald of Wales *Topographia Hibernica* 19; cf. Boivin 1985, Otten 1986:57–61 (for a convenient translation), Sconduto 2008:26–32. Knight 2001:68–73 discusses the illustration of the werewolf scene in the thirteenth-century manuscripts.

[33] For the motif cf. Grimm 1986 no.49. 'The Six Swans', in which we find six brothers trapped in shirts that transform them into swans. They are permitted to take them off for just a quarter of an hour each evening.

[34] For a full translation see Finch 1965 and Byock 1990. Cf. Smith 1894:22–9, Summers 1933:243–4, Davidson 1986 [1978]:151–2, Douglas 1992:64–8, Moreau 1997:78, Lionarons 1998:59–64, Sundquist and Hultgård 2004:8–9, Guðmundsdóttir 2007:283–90, Tuczay 2015:74–5, Pluskowski 2015:95, 98. Sinfjötli's werewolfism is alluded to also in the *Poetic Edda*'s First Lay of Helgi Hundingsbane, stanza 6 (where he is described as 'the friend of wolves').

We shall return to Sigmund and Sinfjötli shortly. Similarly, in the later medieval *Ala flekks saga*, 'The Saga of Spotted Ali' (discussed in Chapter 1), when Ali is finally able to rid himself of the werewolf curse inflicted upon him by a sorcerer, he is found lying in a human bed with the wolfskin sloughed on the floor beside him; his foster father Gunni burns it.[35]

We should probably conceptualize Alphonse's werewolfism in this way too in the Picard French lay *Guillaume de Palerne* (AD 1194–7), briefly summarized in Chapter 1. He is transformed into a wolf when the wicked Brande smears a lotion over his skin. The broader thematic context supports this interpretation: Guillaume and Melior, the lovers on the run that wolf-Alphonse makes it his mission to protect, are concealed first by being sewn into tightly fitting bearskins and then similarly into deerskins, the latter provided by Alphonse himself.[36]

This model is extraordinarily common in more recent narratives. *Exempli gratia*, we may note the following:

- The werewolf Peter Stubb (a.k.a. Stube, Stump, Stumpf) was executed in Bedburg near Cologne in 1589. He transformed himself into a werewolf by donning a special girdle given to him by the Devil, returning to human form upon putting it off again. Eventually he abandoned it, as he said, in a certain valley; but when the magistrate investigating his crimes sent men to retrieve it, they could find no trace of it, and it was inferred that the Devil had taken it back.[37]

- As we have seen (in Chapter 2), Jean Grenier was said to have transformed himself into a large red wolf by donning a red wolfskin at Coutras in 1603.[38]

- An Estonian folktale recorded by von Schlegel at the beginning of the nineteenth century tells how Estonia had been invaded by a plague of terrible wolves from Russia. Eventually a German hunter shot a massive one dead. The corpse was too big to shift. When the hunter invited the local peasants to skin it on the spot, they found within it a dead woman who had transformed herself through witchcraft.[39]

- In the collection of Swedish folktales Afzelius began to publish in 1839 he recorded a case from the Finnish War of 1808–9. A Swedish soldier from Kalmar had fallen homesick and made his way back to his native village in

---

[35] *Ala flekks saga* 6–7.
[36] *Guillaume de Palerne* ll. 274–307 (the magic lotion), 3012–4340 (the bearskins), 4341–5379 (the deerskins).
[37] See above all Kremer 2006 (incorporating the evidence); Summers 1933:253–9 and Otten 1986:69–76 reproduce an English pamphlet recounting the affair, translated from a German original and produced in 1590. See also Smith 1894:28, Douglas 1992:132–4, de Blécourt 2009, Voltmer 2015:169–72.
[38] De Lancre 1612 §4.2–4.
[39] Von Schlegel 1830:179–81; cf. Metsvahi 2015:211–12, with some further Estonian tales of interest also at 215–16.

the form of a wolf, but he was shot by a local hunter just as he arrived. When the wolf was flayed, his shirt was found between the outer wolfskin and the body. His widow recognized it as one she had made for him and sent him to war with.[40]

- At the end of the nineteenth century Pitrè recorded a Sicilian tradition associated with either Palermo or Salaparuta, in which a young man attacked by a werewolf slashed him with a blade on the forehead, in criss-cross fashion, whereupon the human head within protruded from the wound, and he recognized his friend.[41]
- In the wake of Jean Grenier, the tradition that werewolves were sorcerers that acquired their transformative wolfskins or other garments from the Devil, typically by performing a rite at a crossroads, continued to thrive into the twentieth century.[42] In 1907 the abbé Dambielle published a Gascon tradition in accordance with which it was believed that a sorcerer would spread a sheet at a crossroads at midnight and return to it at dawn to collect the wolfskin the Devil had left for him on it. He would then don the wolfskin, seemingly being trapped in it, and begin his reign of night-time terror. Should one of the people he attacked challenge him to take off his skin, he would be able to do so, and the two humans would then fight, with the loser being obliged to put the skin on and adopt or resume the same werewolf life.[43] An audio archive of Dutch folklore includes a recording of a tradition from Maastricht in accordance with which a man wanting to become a werewolf would sacrifice a black chicken at a crossroads, whereupon the Devil, dressed in black, would appear in a black coach drawn by black horses, to give him a belt or a shirt that would transform him.[44]

Unsurprisingly, wolfskins could be regarded as possessing magical properties in their own right in antiquity. In particular, a wolfskin drum could render sheepskin drums mute in their presence (and similarly a wolf-gut lyre string could mute sheep-gut lyre strings).[45] This notion evidently piggybacks on the one we have noted above (Chapter 1, in connection with Virgil's Moeris), that when a wolf looks at a man before he sees it, it deprives him of his voice.

The ancient texts, whatever their understanding of core and carapace, seem to imagine that the werewolf's default form is that of a man rather than a wolf.

---

[40] Afzelius 1842:ii, 361 (this is a German translation of the first two volumes of the Swedish original, 1839–70, which I have not been able to see); cf. Smith 1894:23 n.1.

[41] Pitrè 1889:463–70; cf. 164–5.

[42] For werewolves at the crossroads, cf. Tibullus 1.5.43–60, discussed in Chapter 1.

[43] Dambielle 1907:14–15; cf. Devlin 1987:73, Douglas 1992:166. Note also the role of the Devil in the nineteenth-century traditions from Périgord, discussed below, p.107.

[44] Audio recording, Archive Meertens Institute, Amsterdam, Collection Eggen 19.4, translated at de Blécourt 2015b:12–13.

[45] Oppian *Cynegetica* 3.282–7 (drums); Timothy of Gaza 8.17 (lyre strings); cf. Eckels 1937:24.

A rare ancient exception to this understanding seems to come in the ingredients Ovid gives to Medea for her rejuvenation potion for Aeson: 'the entrails of the shape-shifting wolf, which changes its wild-animal form into a man.' However, this phraseology may be determined by no more than the desire to produce a (characteristically Ovidian) witty inversion.[46] If we look again at Philostratus' dog-demon story, discussed in Chapter 2, we may imagine, on the basis of modern preconceptions, that it tells us that the dog is this creature's default form, somehow revealed in death. But modern preconceptions here may mislead. As we shall see, the piece of bread the beggar carries in his wallet may suggest that he deliberately effects a transformation from his default humanoid form into the dog form at the last minute, as he is killed.[47]

The Identifying Wound

Whatever their order of stacking, the two faces of the werewolf are commonly pinned together in their stories by what might be termed the 'identifying wound' (Adam Douglas deploys, rather, the term 'sympathetic wound').[48] This gratifying motif is already found in Niceros' tale:

> 'But even if he got away, the last laugh was ours, for our slave managed to get a spear through his neck.' ... But when I arrived home, my soldier was lying on his bed like an ox, and a doctor was attending to his neck. I realized that he was a werewolf/skin-changer [*versipellis*] ....   Petronius *Satyricon* 61

Leslie Sconduto notes the oddity that Niceros only recognizes that the soldier is a werewolf when he sees the wound, even though he has already actually watched him transform himself into a wolf at the tombstones.[49] An excellent point! This pleonasm allows us to observe the force of what must have been an already long-established, deeply familiar, and powerful motif, a motif which in other traditional werewolf tales would indeed have been the mechanism by which a mysterious werewolf was first identified. We begin to get a sense of the fashion in which a broader family of well-established werewolf tale types peeps through the cracks of Petronius' narrative; we will consider further examples of this important phenomenon in the following chapter.

It is just conceivable that a dim trace of this motif lurks already in the famous episode of the *Odyssey* in which the aged maid Eurycleia identifies her master

---

[46] Ovid *Metamorphoses* 7.268–701.   [47] Philostratus *Life of Apollonius* 4.10
[48] Douglas 1992:43. Note Thompson's *MI* (1955–8) here: motifs H56 (recognition by wound), and G275.12 (man in form of animal is injured or killed as a result of injury to animal); cf. Scobie 1982:69, McDougall 1984:127–31.
[49] Sconduto 2008:11.

Odysseus, despite his disguise as a beggar, by means of the scar on his thigh. The identification occasions a flashback to the context in which he sustained the wound in his youth: a boar hunt under the supervision of his maternal grand-father, Autolykos, whose name signifies 'Very-wolf' or 'Wolf-self', and who is said to have excelled in (wolfish?) thieving. If we follow Burkert's insistence that the grandfather's speaking name and modus operandi proclaim him to be a were-wolf—strong meat, perhaps—then we may also think that the Eurycleia episode has been shaped by the disaggregated elements of a traditional werewolf tale in which the werewolf is revealed by the recognition of his wound.[50]

The identifying-wound motif was to continue to flourish in the medieval trad-itions. Before AD 1084 Bishop Patrick of Dublin published his Latin hexameter poem *De mirabilibus Hiberniae* ('On the Wonders of Ireland'), in which he seem-ingly collects much Irish and Irish-language lore. He tells as follows of 'certain men of the Irish race' who 'wickedly change themselves into wolves':

> If anything harms them, or any wounds are inflicted upon them {by the people pursuing them}, they are in very truth always visible on their bodies. And so it is that raw meat {from the sheep that they devour} can be seen by their associates, remaining fast in the mouth of their body in its true form. I marvel at this, and so does everyone else.
>
> Bishop Patrick of Dublin *De mirabilibus Hiberniae* xvi, ll.76–9[51]

Here then we have not only the identifying wound tying wolf to human, but also an identifying gobbet of sheep's flesh. We shall focus more fully on this interesting text (and related medieval accounts of this Irish tradition) in the following chapter.

Gervase of Tilbury (writing in AD 1210–14) has the following delightful tale:

> One thing I know is that is that it is usual amongst our countrymen for certain men to turn into wolves at the full moon, if their fates so dictate. For I know that in the bishopric of Clermont in the Auvergne, Ponce de Castres outlawed a nobleman, Raimbaud de Poinet, the strongest of soldiers and well-practiced in arms. He was reduced to wandering over the earth as an exile. When he was roaming over the pathless places and through the woods, in the manner of a wild beast, one night he was disturbed by an excessive degree of fear, and he was turned into a wolf by the distraction of his mind. Such havoc did he wreak upon his country that he compelled many farmers to leave their steadings abandoned.

---

[50] Homer *Odyssey* 19.386–475; Burkert 1983a [1972]:120, 131, approved by Bremmer 1978:15–16; cf. also Moreau 1990a:32–4.

[51] The curly-bracketed portions of text represent Patrick's own glosses on his poem.

In his wolf form he devoured children, but he also tore apart those of advanced age with his wild bites. In the end he was vigorously attacked by a certain carpenter, and lost one of his feet to the blow of his axe, but in this way he recovered his former appearance and put on the identity of a man. Thereafter he openly declared that he was pleased by the loss of his foot for the very reason that, by means of its amputation, he had shed himself of his wretched condition, his curse and his damnation. Some assert that such men can be liberated from this sort of misfortune by the chopping off of limbs, and they have put it into practice too.   Gervase of Tilbury *Otia imperialia* 3.120 (pp.51–2 Liebrecht)[52]

The motif continues into more recent texts too:

- The Swedish priest Olaus Magnus recorded a Livonian tale in his 1555 Latin *History of the Northern Races* (*Historia de gentibus septentrionalibus*). According to this, a peasant demonstrated to a sceptical Livonian lady that he could become a wolf. In this form he was then attacked by her estate's dogs, which tore out one of his eyes. When he returned to human form, he remained without his eye.[53]
- In his *Discours exécrable des sorciers*, Henri Boguet, the persecutor of werewolves and witches, relates an event that had taken place in 1588 in a village near Apchon, also in the Auvergne. A gentleman asked a huntsman on his way to hunt on his land to give him part of his bag on his return. As the huntsman proceeded along a valley he was attacked by a large wolf. He was eventually able to hack a paw from it, and he put it in his bag. When he returned to the gentleman he found in his bag not the paw, but a human hand, and this bore the ring of the gentleman's wife. In the kitchen the gentleman found his wife nursing her arm, her hand cut off. She confessed that she was a werewolf, and was subsequently burned at Ryon.[54]
- In Richard Thomson's 1828 Gothic tale, 'The Wehr Wolf: A Legend of Limousin', the knight Saintefleur is attacked in a wood at night by a huge wolf, but is able to sever its foreleg and make his way back to an inn, where he shows it off. Shortly afterwards the foreleg mutates back into a human arm with an identifying brand on it, revealing it to belong to Gaspar, a fellow knight Saintefleur had falsely accused of treason. A hunting party sets out to kill him, but Gaspar is able to kill Saintefleur before dying himself.[55]

---

[52] At 2.93 p.45 Liebrecht Gervase similarly reports on women that prowl as cats by night and likewise exhibit their amputations when changed back; cf. Summers 1933: 185–7, 194.

[53] Magnus 1555: 643–4; cf. Summers 1933:246, Höfler 1934:21-30 (= Ginzburg and Lincoln 2020:33-40), Sconduto 2008:158, Donecker 2012:295–8, Pluskowski 2015:106, Metsvahi 2015:206–7.

[54] Boguet 1590 ch. 47, also including a similar identifying-wound story about the werewolf Michel Udon; translation at Ashwin and Summers 1929:140–1; cf. Summers 1933:228, 312–14, Milin 1993:128–9, Sconduto 2008:166, de Blécourt 2015b:7.

[55] Thompson 1828; cf. Frost 2003:56–8.

- In Oswald Crawfurd's (John Latouche's) mid-nineteenth-century tale of the Portuguese werewolf Joana, which we will shortly consider in more detail, we have as it were a double example of the identifying-wound motif: the nail wound, which she attempts to explain away, and the bruised arm, which she cannot.[56]
- In Eugene Field's short children's story 'The Werewolf', published posthumously in his 1896 *The Second Book of Tales*, a werewolf is dealt a mortal blow with a magic spear by his sweetheart unawares; she only realizes what she has done when his body, reverted to human form, is found with the corresponding wound.[57]
- J. C. Lawson recorded a tale collected from local workmen when the British Museum was conducting excavations in Cyprus in 1899. According to this, one village, subject to depredations from a night-time marauder, organized a watch committee, which duly espied a *vrykolakas* (which in this instance must retain its original significance of 'werewolf') and shot it. The monster disappeared off into the shadows, wounded. The next day a villager, one who had not been part of the watch committee, was found to be sporting a wound in exactly the same place as the wolf.[58]
- Finally, let us mention again Guy Endore's 1933 novel *The Werewolf of Paris*. Here we find an identifying wound once again, this time gratifyingly inflicted with a silver bullet.[59]

The power of this motif in medieval times can be observed from the expanded deployment of wounds in the werewolf stories of the period. At the culmination of Marie de France's *Bisclavret* (AD 1160–78), Bisclavret, in his final act as a wolf before being restored to his human form, bites off his unfaithful wife's nose. Thenceforth her female descendants were ever to be born without noses. It is noteworthy that even though the motif of the wound has been transferred here to a character other than the werewolf himself, it nonetheless retains its role of an identifying mark of sorts.[60]

It is time to return to the (mid-thirteenth-century AD) *Völsunga saga*'s Sigmund and Sinfjötli. While they are trapped in their wolfskins and living the lives of wolves, separately, roaming about the forest, they agree that they may each take on parties of up to seven men alone, but if they face more, they are to howl to the other for help, in the wolf language they both now understand. When

---

[56] Latouche 1875:25–34.   [57] Field 1896:243–56; cf. Frost 2003:87.
[58] Lawson 1910:379–80; cf. Summers 1933:17, 74. For the *vrykolakas* see Chapter 2.
[59] Endore 1933 chs. 6 and 7. In Stoker's short story 'Dracula's Guest' (published in 1914, but cut from an early draft of the 1897 novel; cf. Chapter 2), the soldiers regret that they have not been able to kill a werewolf for the want of a 'sacred bullet'. But the use of specifically silver bullets against a werewolf appears to have originated in a pulp-fiction short story by Jeremy Ellis, 'Silver Bullets', published in *Weird Tales* 15.4 (April 1930), and then in the denouement to Alfred H. Bill's 1931 novel *Wolf in the Garden*; Frost 1973:39, 43; Roberts 1999:578.
[60] Marie de France *Bisclavret* ll. 232–4, 309–14.

Sigmund encounters a party of seven, he howls, Sinfjötli runs to help, and between them they kill the men. But then, when the younger and more impetuous Sinfjötli encounters a party of eleven men, he takes them on single-handedly and without calling to Sigmund for help. While he is able to kill them all, he nonetheless emerges from the encounter wounded. Sigmund finds him resting under an oak in this condition, where he boasts that Sigmund needed help to deal with seven men, whereas he took on eleven on his own. Enraged at the insult, Sigmund bites Sinfjötli in the throat, but then carries him back to their forest house and tends him. Here he observes a pair of weasels: one of them bites out the other's throat, but then runs out into the woods to fetch a particular leaf, which it lays on the wound, whereupon the wounded weasel leaps up, restored to full health. As he leaves the house a raven flies to him with a similar leaf, which he then draws over Sinfjötli's throat, and Sinfjötli accordingly jumps up, similarly restored to full health. In due course, as we have seen, they are eventually able to throw off their wolfskins.[61]

In the case of this werewolf tale the distinctive motif of the wound has evidently become somewhat deracinated from its original function, for it is both inflicted and healed while Sinfjötli remains in wolf form and so serves no identifying purpose. Now, the story reminds us urgently, of course, of the ancient folktale of 'The Three Snake Leaves' investigated in Chapter 1.[62] It is by no means a full performance of the tale, but the central and distinctive motifs of it are present. Wolf-Sigmund retreats to an enclosed chamber, the forest house, with the dying (albeit not yet dead) Sinfjötli. The weasels (familiar from *Eliduc* and Grimm versions of the folktale, but also already from Apuleius' refraction of it in his Thelyphrons episode) duly make their demonstration with the magic, healing herb. (The harm is inflicted on the first weasel by the second as opposed to by the unwounded person (a) because Sinjötli is not dead, so there is no corpse for the weasel to mar; and (b) so that the situation of Sigmund and Sinfjötli might be more directly reflected, since it is wolf-Sigmund that has wounded his own fellow animal.) And then the healing herb Sigmund is actually to use is brought to him in the mouth of an animal, albeit a different one from the one that has made the healing demonstration, the raven taking over from the weasel in this regard (of course, since Sigmund remains a wolf at this point himself, he also represents a third example in the story of an animal bearing the healing herb in its mouth). So we can see that in this narrative one distinctive motif has ceded precedence to another: the motif of the identifying wound has ceded precedence to that of the healing animal.[63]

---

[61] *Völsunga saga* ch. 8.   [62] ATU no. 612; see in particular Table 1.2 pp.50–1.
[63] Clover 1986 contends that there is an (indirect) textual relationship between *Eliduc* and the *Völsunga saga* here, as opposed to a more intangible folkloric one, with the *Völsunga saga* reworking a lost Norse translation of the lai. It is a difficulty for this view, however, that *Eliduc* is the only one of Marie de France's twelve lais *not* to be included in *Strengleikar*, the translation of them commissioned by Haakon IV of Norway in the mid thirteenth century.

There is sometimes a further dimension to the motif of the identifying wound. According to some traditions, the infliction of the wound in itself breaks the werewolf's curse and permits him to transform back, once and for all, into human form.[64] We have already seen this in the case of the AD 1210–14 Gervase of Tilbury tale referred to above, in which the werewolf Raimbaud de Poinet is thereby liberated from his curse when he loses his foot to the carpenter's axe.[65] In a nineteenth-century tale from Arthex in France, a young man is pestered by a large dog and then a goat at a crossroads. Eventually he stabs the goat and it transforms back into his best friend, who thanks him for liberating him from the curse. But the young man swears (à la Niceros) that he will never drink with him again.[66] In 1867 Bonnafoux recorded some folk beliefs about werewolves in French La Creuse. According to these, werewolves were suffering unfortunates, doomed each night to don their accursed skin and run until they met some that would deliver them from their condition by dealing them a wound. They would thank the man brave enough to do it.[67]

Does this dimension to the motif have a wider currency than first appears? It is of course always true (except in the anomalous tale of Sigmund and Sinfjötli) that the werewolf turns back into human form as good as immediately after being dealt his wound. The prime function of this transformation, from a narrative perspective, is to permit the identification between the werewolf's two forms to be made. Nonetheless, given the inevitable persistence of the association between wound and transformation back to human, one has to wonder whether a more general notion may after all have obtained that a wound forces the werewolf back into human form, whether permanently or temporarily. And perhaps such a notion already lurks behind Petronius' story—in which, indeed, we do not know for sure whether the werewolf returns to human form on a temporary basis or a permanent one.

Inside and Out (ii): Ingestion

There is another sense in which the inside-outside axis comes into play in ancient werewolfism, and that is in the context of its sometime causation by means of ingestion.[68]

---

[64]   Cf. Hertz 1862:69, 78–83, Ginzburg 1990:247.

[65]   Gervase of Tilbury *Otia imperiala* 3.120 (pp.51–2 Liebrecht); cf. Summers 1933:113, 185–6, Banks and Binns 2002;814 n.5, Sconduto 2008:35, 138, Pluskowski 2015:82.

[66]   The tale is given at Laborde 1935–6:(1935) 115; cf. Devlin 1987:199–200, Douglas 1992: 186–7.

[67]   Bonnafoux 1867:27; cf. Smith 1894:34–5 (similar material relating to Germany); Summers 1933:113 (cf. 164–6, with two fine Sicilian stories).

[68]   For werewolfism as induced by cannibalism see Smith 1894:19.

From Man to Wolf

The clue that animal transformation might be effected by ingestion of a magical substance in the ancient world is given first by Homer, who shows Circe transforming men into pigs at any rate by feeding them a magic potion, a potage of cheese, barley-meal, honey, Pramnian wine, and baleful drugs,[69] and at the other end of antiquity by Augustine, who speaks of Italian landladies transforming their guests into beasts of burden by feeding them pieces of cheese.[70]

For werewolves and the like the substance in question may have been bread, magical or otherwise. When Philostratus tells us that the dog-demon of Ephesus had a morsel of bread in his beggar wallet (Chapter 2), the detail initially seems curiously superfluous. It becomes less so when we realize that the eating of some of this may be what has transformed him into the monstrous dog found beneath the rocks.[71] Corroboration for the notion comes when we turn again to Petronius. Niceros concludes his tale with the following affirmation: 'I realized that he was a werewolf/skin-changer [*versipellis*], and I could not thereafter bring myself to taste bread with him, not even if you had forced me on pain of death.'[72] This phrase signifies more, I think, than a metonymic rejection of the werewolf's society. It reflects a specific anxiety that the transformation may be effected by the eating of bread. It may also be that Niceros fears that he may also be transformed himself if he shares bread with the werewolf.[73]

There are early modern Livonian parallels for such notions. In his 1555 Latin *History of the Northern Races* (*Historia de gentibus septentrionalibus*) Olaus Magnus noted that werewolfism can be transmitted if a man shares a beer with an existing werewolf and he recites a certain spell at the same time.[74] This is precisely how the Livonian Thiess came to be a werewolf, according to his 1691 testimony.[75] In a trial of 1636 a woman of Kurna, Maret, claimed that she became a werewolf when another woman brought her into the forest and gave her a sweet root to eat, whereupon they both transformed together.[76] (But sometimes it can be safer to eat with a werewolf than not. The Estonian Folklore Archive contains thirty-five different versions of a tale first recorded in 1873. According to this, two girls travelling through the country bed down for the night. One secretly observes the other rise, turn herself into a wolf by making three somersaults, kill a foal, eat some of it, and then store some of the remaining meat in her food box. As they

---

[69] Homer *Odyssey* 10.234–6.   [70] Augustine *City of God* 18.18.
[71] Philostratus *Life of Apollonius* 4.10.
[72] Petronius *Satyricon* 62: *nec postea cum illo panem gustare potui, non si me occidisses.*
[73] In the nineteenth-century tale from Arthex in France just discussed, a man who has discovered his friend to be both a were-dog and a were-goat and has liberated him from the curse nonetheless refuses ever to drink with him again. See Devlin 1987, esp. 72–80, 198–202, Douglas 1992:186–7.
[74] Magnus 1555:643–4; cf. Metsvahi 2015:206, 210.
[75] The sources are laid out in Chapter 4.
[76] Winkler 1909:337, Madar 1990:270, Metsvahi 2015:210.

continue their journey the next day, the wolf-girl offers her companion some of her meat, but she refuses it, telling her she can eat the raw foal's meat herself, if she likes it, whereupon the wolf-girl tells her to see for herself whether it is raw, and casts it in her face: it is so hot that it burns her.)[77]

A further strand of ancient thought seems to have had it that the wolf transformation could be effected upon a human specifically if he ate human flesh. This makes good sense: it is wolves that are supposedly the man-eating creatures par excellence, and they can be imagined to be emblematic of the savagery associated with cannibalism. Aristotle asserts that wolves are man-eaters, noting that they will even go so far as to dig up graves in order to get at human flesh.[78] It is noteworthy in this context that Aesop's cloak thief, the pretended werewolf, declares that he will be transformed into a 'man-eating wolf'.[79]

The key evidence here relates to the Arcadian cult of Zeus Lykaios and its myths, which will be laid out more fully in Chapter 6. Here it suffices to note that Plato speaks of a 'myth' in accordance with which a man must by all means become a wolf if he tastes the entrails of a human sacrifice cut up amongst those of the animal sacrifices to Zeus Lykaios;[80] and that Varro, Pliny, and Augustine tell, after one 'Euagropas', that Demaenetus of Parrhasia was transformed into a wolf for ten years when he tasted the entrails of a boy at the sacrifice to Zeus Lykaios.[81] It is never stated explicitly, but it might be implied in the sources for the Lykaon's own myth (which are also laid out fully in Chapter 6) that he himself shares in the meat of the human sacrifice he makes to Zeus: if so, then that might offer a further or parallel explanation of his own transformation into a wolf.[82] Pausanias too *may* hint darkly at an association between the Anthid rite at the festival of Zeus Lykaios, in which a young man turns into a wolf, and the making of human sacrifices to this god: 'They sacrifice to Zeus Lykaios on this altar in secret fashion. I would prefer not to push my nose into the details of the sacrifice. Let it be as it is and as it was from the beginning.'[83]

---

[77] The summary reflects Estonian Folklore Archives H iii 25, 261/3 (9), translated and discussed at Metsvahi 2015:217–19. It was a common Livonian notion that werewolves could magically roast the meat of their kills.

[78] Aristotle *History of Animals* 594ab (he associates this tendency with lone wolves rather than with wolves hunting in packs); cf. Metzger 2011:174.

[79] Aesop *Fables* 419 Perry.

[80] Plato *Republic* 565d–566a: Ὡς ἄρα ὁ γευσάμενος τοῦ ἀνθρωπίνου σπλάγχνου, ἐν ἄλλοις ἄλλων ἱερείων ἑνὸς ἐγκατατετμημένου, ἀνάγκη δὴ τούτῳ λύκῳ γενέσθαι.

[81] Pliny *Natural History* 8.82 (incorporating 'Scopas' *FGrH* 413 F1); Augustine *City of God* 18.17 (citing Varro).

[82] See in particular [Hesiod] F163 MW = [Eratosthenes] *Catasterismi* 1.8, Ovid *Metamorphoses* 1.226–39, *Ibis* 431–2, Hyginus *Astronomica* 2.4, *Fabulae* 176, Clement of Alexandria *Protrepticus* 2.36.5, p.31 Potter, Arnobius *Adversus nationes* 4.24, Servius on Virgil *Eclogues* 6.41 and *Aeneid* 1.731, Anonymus Paradoxographus *De transformationibus* p.222, 3–5 Westermann, First Vatican Mythographer 1.17, schol. Germanicus *Aratea* pp.123–4 Breysig, schol. Lycophron *Alexandra* 481.

[83] Pausanias 6.8.2, 8.2.6, 8.38.7.

It is possible that it was (at least eventually) thought that the Scythian Neuri too effected their own lupine transformations by means of cannibalism, either directly or indirectly. As we have seen, Herodotus twice makes them the neighbours of race called the Androphagoi ['Man-eaters'], and Solinus (in the third century AD) then attributes human sacrifice to them. He does not make the point explicitly, but it is probable that he imagines that the Neuri devour the flesh of their human sac-rifices, as supposedly happened in Arcadia (see Chapters 1 and 6).[84]

Finally, Tibullus' imprecation against his bawd-witch (discussed in Chapter 1), when read in the werewolf register, has her scrabbling for human bones to eat, whether from a graveyard or from the leavings of actual wolves, or both, before being transformed into a wolf herself and running howling through the city.[85]

From Wolf to Man

Ingestion can be key to the reverse transformation too. In the Anthid rite of the Lykaia, as Pliny, Pausanias, and Augustine tell us (after Euanthes and Varro), it is precisely abstinence from human flesh on the part of the werewolf, once trans-formed into a wolf, that enables him to regain his human form; but if he does taste human flesh as a wolf, then he must remain trapped in animal form (the texts are, again, quoted in Chapter 6, with much further discussion).[86]

The (fourth-century AD?) amulet handbook *Cyranides*, however, inverts the logic of ingestion more perfectly:

> The roasted heart of the wolf cures fasting *lykanthropoi* [also known as *baboutzi-karioi*], if they have fasted for three days.   *Cyranides* 2.23, p.152 Kaimakis

The bracketed portion of the text is clearly an intrusion from a marginal note, the term *baboutzikarios* not being attested before the ninth century AD.[87] As to the simple, original claim of the *Cyranides*, we can see that the theme of abstinence recurs, but, more germanely, just as the devouring of human flesh turns a human into a wolf, so the devouring of wolf flesh turns the lupine werewolf back into a human (and note that the flesh involved is specifically the heart: cf. above on hairy hearts). The *Cyranides* also tells us here that dried wolf's liver is of help to the 'the moonstruck and the mad' (*selēniakoi kai mainomenoi*), which may also

---

[84] Herodotus 4.105–7, 4.125; Solinus 15.   [85] Tibullus 1.5.53–5; cf. Schmeling 2011:256–7.
[86] Pliny *Natural History* 8.81, Pausanias 8.2.6.
[87] Metzger 2011:243–9, Gordon 2015:31. See *Suda* s.v. Ἐφιάλτης and Psellus' minor demonological text τί ἐστι βαβουτζικάριος; The term is identified with Ephialtes, the name given to the night-terror incubus. Its form is reminiscent of those of other later Greek demon names such as καλλικάντζαρος, where the -*tz*- cluster represents a phoneme derived from Arabic.

be significant if we can associate the quality of being moonstruck with werewolfism (Chapter 6, again).

Moving forward in time, it is a common motif of Livonian werewolf legends that the wolf should be transformed back to human form by eating bread in the depth of the forest.[88] Thiess again spoke in 1691 of werewolves on occasion transforming back into human form *even without the use of bread*, thereby identifying such a use as the norm.[89] As the food characteristic of man and of civilisation, bread seems better suited to the wolf-to-man transformation than the man-to-wolf one of the ancient model.

Danish folk traditions recorded in the late nineteenth century, however, take what might be described as a 'doubling down' approach to the question of reversion by ingestion. In these the werewolf reverts to human form not by abstaining from human flesh but by eating human flesh in the most antinomian fashion possible: the werewolves attack pregnant women and tear open their stomachs so as to be able to secure release by eating the hearts of their unborn babies.[90]

A similar postulate underlies a Portuguese tale from the same century. In 1875 Oswald Crawfurd, writing as John Latouche, reported it from his earlier travels in Portugal. It had been told to him by a farmer who claimed to have been at the heart of the events in question, which had taken place near Ponte de Lima twenty years before, when he had been a farmhand. A sturdy peasant woman from Tarouca, Joana, strangely crop-haired and clad in a brown cloak, was taken in by his boss, the farmer, to help with the housework, since his wife had a new baby. But she turned out to be a werewolf. She tattooed (it is to be inferred) a devil's mark on the baby, a crescent moon between the shoulder blades. She evaded detection by a wise woman brought in to address the matter by refusing to let her see her eyes, which were fiery, narrow, and lupine. The peasant woman, however, told the parents that the child was destined to become a werewolf unless they performed an apotropaic rite, laying it out naked on a mountainside before the rise of the new moon, whereupon the moon would draw up the mark to itself as it draws up the tides. They proceeded to do this, but a huge, brown, fiery-eyed wolf grabbed the child before the moon had risen, jugulated it, and killed it. The farmer fired a nail at it from his gun, while the farmhand, our narrator, was able to bash its foreleg with a stick; nonetheless it managed to escape into the woods. The trail of the wolf's blood led them to the peasant woman, who had gone missing, and she was dying. She denied that she had been the wolf, but confected the lie that she had rather been secretly watching the rite from the edge of the woods, to protect the baby, and had accidentally caught the bullet the farmer had fired at the wolf; she declined, however, to account for the bruise on her right arm (an example, as we have noted, of the motif of the identifying wound). The priest was

---

[88] See Metsvahi 2015:218.
[89] Testimony at von Bruiningk 1924:205; see further Chapter 4.
[90] See the folktales recorded at Kristensen 1893:ii nos. 33–5; cf. Simonsen 2015:230–6.

sent for, but she died before he could arrive. A true devil's mark was found on her breast. The wise woman explained that people could free themselves of the werewolf curse by drinking the warm blood of a newborn child, and that this was what the peasant woman had been attempting to do. The priest chided the people for taking in a woman of Tarouca, for the place was well known to be a nest of witches. So here the ingestion of human flesh does not transform a human to a wolf, but rather transforms a lupiform werewolf back to a human, and indeed cures them of the condition.[91]

Inside and Out (iii): Civilization and the Wilderness Beyond

Into the Woods

A motif that strikingly endures from antiquity into the medieval period is that of the werewolf, as soon as he is transformed into a wolf, rushing off by reflex into the woods (or the wilderness), and indeed being inclined to do the same on other occasions too.[92] The inner, human home of civilization is abandoned for an outer world, a beyond suitable to wild animals. From the wolf's perspective, however, it may rather be that the woods should be seen as the inner place (*into*…), and the civilized world the outer one. Thus we have Virgil on Moeris again: 'By their [Pontic herbs'] power I often saw Moeris change into a wolf and hide himself in the woods.'[93] And, once more, Petronius on Niceros' werewolf: 'But, as I'd begun to say, after he had become a wolf, he began to howl and ran into the woods.'[94] But the most striking material here is the Arcadian (again to be discussed more fully in Chapter 6). Here is Ovid on the transformation of Lykaon, the founder, be it noted, of the world's first city, Lykosoura: 'Lykaon himself fled in terror. Making his way to the still of the countryside, he howled and tried in vain to make human utterance.'[95] And as to Arcadia's Anthid rite, according to Pliny, the young man becoming a wolf 'hangs his clothes on an oak tree, swims across the pool, goes off into the wilderness, is transformed into a wolf, and joins a pack with others of the same kind for nine years'; according to Augustine, such young men, 'chosen by lot, would swim across a certain pool, and they were changed into wolves there.

---

[91] Latouche 1875:25–34; the summary at Summers 1933:167–71 is inaccurate in some details.

[92] This is quite compatible with the Greek conceit that the lone wolf at any rate is a creature of the wilderness: Alcaeus F130b describes his 'rustic lot' as an exile as a life amongst the 'wolf thickets' (*lykaimiais*); cf. Burkert 1983a:91, Mainoldi 1984:28, Buxton 1987:63. For the wolf's folkloric associations with the wilderness more generally see Pluskowski 2005, 2006.

[93] Virgil *Eclogues* 8.97–8.   [94] Petronius *Satyricon* 61.

[95] Ovid *Metamorphoses* 1.232–3. For Lykaon's Lykosoura as the world's first city, see Pausanias 8.2.1, 8.38.1.

They would make their lives in the desolate parts of that region alongside similar wild animals.'[96]

As we move into medieval material, we find that in Marie de France's AD 1160–78 *Bisclavret*, when the hero confesses to his wife that he is a werewolf, he declares that he runs off directly into the woods upon transformation: 'My lady, I turn werewolf (*bisclavret*). I throw myself into that great forest and in the very depth of the wood I live from prey and rapine' (this text will be discussed at greater length in Chapter 4).[97] It is in the woods that the priest encounters the already long-transformed werewolves of Ossory, according to Gerald of Wales's story (*c.* AD 1187): these werewolves are compelled, upon transformation, to leave the dwellings of men; and the sick ones take up residence in a hollow tree.[98] In the related narrative of the *c.* AD 1250 Old Norse *Konungs skuggsjá* or *Speculum Regale* (*King's Mirror*), we are told that the men St Patrick cursed with werewolf-ism ran off into the woods as the curse took effect (cf. Chapter 1).[99] In the AD 1190–1204 *Lai de Melion*, the forlorn Melion is given a castle in the woods by the king. He is transformed by his wife with his magic ring while out hunting in these woods with her.[100] In the thirteenth-century *Völsunga saga*, 'Sigmund and Sinfjötli donned the skins and could not get out of them . . . Now they went off into the woods, each taking his own path.' The force of the motif is apparent here not least because the forest is already the setting of the transformation.[101] In the Picard French *Guillaume de Palerne* (AD 1194–7), when we first meet the werewolf Alphonse he is already long established in the lupine form in which he has been trapped. Even so, he is introduced with a run and an escape as he makes off with the child Guillaume, in his attempt to protect him from the dangers of the Palermo court, and it is in a great forest near Rome that his flight finally ends and he finds a suitable hiding place: the motif that more normally belongs with the initial act of transformation is saluted here.[102] In the

[96] Pliny *Natural History* 8.81–2; Augustine *City of God* 18.17. A further, indirect example may be given. In the previous chapter we encountered Virgil's Arruns, the Hirpus Sorani who would honour Apollo of Soracte by walking over wood embers in imitation of the god's wolves, which had once raided a burning sacrifice: after killing Camilla he flees 'in just the same way as the wolf immediately makes for the pathless places and hides himself in the high mountains after killing a shepherd or a great steer . . . he slackens his tail and tucks it under his belly as it trembles, and seeks out the woods' (*Aeneid* 11. 809–14).

[97] Marie de France *Bisclavret* ll.63–6 (Ogden trans.). So too in the derived (AD 1322) *Biclarel* 38–53 (cf. 282); more on this text too in Chapter 4.

[98] Gerald of Wales *Topographia Hibernica* 19.

[99] *Konungs skuggsjá* ch.11 (p.115 in the Larson 1917 trans.). Cf. Summers 1933:20–6, Douglas 1992:111, Sconduto 2008:32–3.

[100] *Lai de Melion* ll. 133–204.

[101] *Völsunga saga* ch. 8 (Byock trans.). Cf. also the later Norse saga, *Ala flekks saga*, 'The saga of Spotted Ali,' (discussed in Chapter 1), where a sorcerer compels Ali to take to the woods and become a wolf (6–7).

[102] *Guillaume de Palerne* ll.168–72. Later on, when Alphonse helps the adult Guillaume flee Rome with his lover Melior, he delivers them stolen food in their place of concealment before retreating once again into the forest (ll. 3296–8).

thirteenth–fourteenth-century French romance *Arthur and Gorlagon*, Gorlagon runs off into the forest as soon as he is transformed into a wolf by his treacherous wife with a magic sapling.[103]

Let us say a little about the later material. As we shall see in the next chapter, the supposed werewolf of the 1487 *Malleus maleficarum* also made for the woods, where he bedded himself down when in his imagined lupine phases.[104] And, as we have seen already in this chapter, Jean Grenier, the early-seventeenth-century werewolf of Coutras, was transformed after meeting a man in black in the forest, this being the Lord of the Forest himself. This Lord would compel him to don a (red) wolfskin to become a wolf, retaining the skin himself between Grenier's transformations, presumably in the forest again.[105] We have mentioned here too the Livonian Maret's 1636 claim that she became a werewolf when another woman brought her into the forest and gave her a sweet.[106] More recently, in Crawfurd's (Latouche's) mid-nineteenth-century Portuguese tale of the werewolf Joana, just mentioned, the lupiform Joana runs off into the woods as soon as she is shot.[107] More recently still Carlo Levi left us the following note on the werewolves of Gagliano (that is Aliano) in his *Christ Stopped at Eboli*, originally published in 1945: 'There is a need for great care when they return to their house. When the werewolves knock at their door for the first time, their wives must not open it. If a wife were to open it, she would see her husband a complete wolf still, and he would devour her and flee off into the woods forever' (Ogden trans.).[108]

Perhaps there is nothing very surprising about the content of this motif: after all, where else but in the forest or the wilderness should a wolf live? But the persistence with which the motif is explicitly performed in these narratives remains striking and seems to establish a strong thematic articulation between the wild world of the woods and the civilization of the world of the city, the village, or indeed just the farmstead.

Across the Water

As we have seen, a striking detail of the Arcadian Anthid rite as described by Pliny and Augustine is that the transformation into a wolf is effected at least in part by the young man crossing a pool en route to the wilderness, perhaps,

---

[103] For the details of this text, see Chapter 4.

[104] Kramer and Sprenger *Malleus maleficarum* part 1, question 10; the passage is quoted in Chapter 4. The motif of the woods is less apparent in the authors' source text for this tale, Guillaume d'Auvergne's *De universo* 2.3.13, also quoted in Chapter 4.

[105] De Lancre 1612 §4.2–4.   [106] Winkler 1909:337, Metsvahi 2015:210.

[107] Latouche 1875:25–34

[108] Levi 1945 ch. 12; for a complete translation see Frenaye 1947. A parallel Apulian superstition about the need for a wife to let her *lepomene*-werewolf husband knock three times before admitting him had already been recorded by la Sorsa 1915:54 (*non vidi*) and, after him, Rini 1929:83.

accordingly, to be seen as a boundary marker between the worlds of civilization and wilderness.[109] For this motif clear and independent ancient or medieval comparanda are wanting.[110] The good parallels for it begin to emerge, rather, in the early modern period. Turning once more to the Livonian werewolves discussed in the second, 1560, edition of Kaspar Peucer's work on divination, *Commentarius de praecipuis generibus divinationum*, we find some of the werewolves in question holding themselves to be so transformed after they are driven across a great river, parted for them by a tall man with an iron whip.[111]

But the most remarkable comparanda here are regrettably recent, deriving from nineteenth-century France. Carnoy recorded information about a peasant-werewolf in Picardy given to him in 1880 by one M. Jules Bonnel of Thièvres. Every Saturday, in the Fairy Wood (NB), he would take off his clothes, lay them under a bush, and roll around in its Fairy Pool. This quickly transformed him into the Werewolf of Bois d'Orville. The wolf would then take himself off to Thièvres or Orville and steal a sheep, which he would bring back to the Fairy Wood, where he would roast it and eat it together with the fairies, witches, and the Devil.[112] In 1897 Sébillot reported on the then contemporary folk-beliefs of Périgord as follows:

---

[109] For the notion that the pool functioned as the boundary between an inside and an outside see Buxton 1987:70.

[110] The word 'independent' is important here. We might otherwise look to two twelfth-century texts that, while speaking of transformations into other animals, are clearly derivative of Augustine's words on Arcadian werewolves (and in so being, of course, testify to the current and continuing meaningfulness of Augustine's words at some level). First, a tale from William of Malmesbury's *Gesta regum Anglorum* (2.171), completed before AD 1125, is clearly a descendant not only of Augustine's words on Arcadian werewolves but also of his words on Italian landlady-witches and additionally of Apuleius' *Metamorphoses*. According to this tale, in the reign of Pope Leo IX two such landlady-witches keep a pub on the road to Rome, and transform a travelling musician into an ass, in due course selling the performing creature on to a rich nobleman. The accompanying advice that the ass should never be allowed to set foot in water is in vain: he escapes his keeper and plunges into a lake, transforming himself back into human form. The women are arrested and confess.

Secondly, Gerald of Wales follows his tale of the werewolves of Ossory with a recycling of Augustine's words on the Arcadian werewolves and their water-induced transformation, to which he then adds the observation that even in his own time some people were able to use magic to transform any object at all into a fat pig, which they would then sell in the marketplace. The object would, however, only be able to retain its porcine appearance for a maximum of three days before reverting, and it would revert immediately upon being carried over water (*Topographia Hibernica* 19, AD 1187).

Douglas 1992:121–2 attempts to find direct medieval comparanda for the Arcadian rite's association between werewolfism and water crossings in the repeated sea crossings of the *Guillaume de Palerne*, *Melion*, and *Gorlagon* romances. Admittedly, *Guillaume de Palerne* does make something of the challenge for the werewolf Alphonse in crossing the straits of Messina, in both directions (ll.115–17, 4568–632), but even so one feels this is to over-egg the pudding: it can hardly be contended that the sea crossings directly effect the transformations either in this text or in the others.

[111] Peucer 1560 folio 141v: *Ad flumina ubi accesserunt, dux flagelli ictu aquas findit, ut dehiscere et discedere videantur, relicto sicco tramite, quo transeant. Exactis diebus duodecim dissipatur agmen rursus et ad se quisque deposita lupi et recepta hominis specie revertitur.* Cf. Smith 1894:19, Buxton 1987:70, Ginzburg 1990:156–7; Douglas 1992:153–4.

[112] Carnoy 1883:106–8; cf. Sébillot 1904–7:ii, 437, Crampon 1936:163, Armand 2013. It seems to be to this story that Douglas 1992:187 refers, albeit without citation.

Certain men, principally the sons of priests, are compelled to transform themselves into this variety of diabolical beast [the werewolf] upon each full moon. It is by night that the 'evil' seizes them. When they feel the attacks coming on, they spasm, leap from their bed, jump out of the window and throw themselves into a spring. After thrashing about in the water for a few moments, they get out of the spring on the opposite side to the one by which they entered it and find themselves wearing a goatskin [sic] given to them by the Devil. In this condition they are able to walk very easily on four paws and spend the rest of the night running through the fields, chasing the villagers and biting or eating all the dogs they meet. At the approach of day, they return to their spring, put off their white covering and go home.   Sébillot 1897:663 (Ogden trans.)[113]

Traditions of this sort were picked up by the eccentric Anglo-Russian author Count Eric Stanislaus Stenbock in his 1893 short story published in *The Spirit Lamp*, 'The Other Side: A Breton Legend'. In this tale one Gabriel is tempted by an enchanting blue flower, despite warnings, to cross a brook that separates his verdant village from a grim, wolf-inhabited wasteland beyond. So begins the process of his own eventual transformation into a wolf.[114] The correspondences in these cases are so striking that one has to wonder whether Pliny and Augustine do not lie directly at the root of the claims.

Conclusion

Ancient werewolf thinking was strongly articulated in accordance with an axis between an inside and an outside, in three ways. First, the werewolf was often understood as a combination of an outer carapace and an inner core: more often the human element formed the carapace, and the lupine element the core, but the opposite arrangement could also obtain. Usually the humanoid carapace was identified, awkwardly, with the werewolf's human clothing, and the wolf was revealed once this was shed; but sometimes, perhaps, the wolf could be more deeply buried within, as in the cases of those, like Aristomenes, that boasted a hairy heart. The inner and outer form could be pinned together, as it were, by an identifying wound; it is also possible that the belief that a wound could force a werewolf back into human form existed already in the ancient world. Secondly, a werewolf transformation, in either direction, could be effected by the taking of a foodstuff within the body: a man could be transformed into a werewolf by eating an (enchanted?) piece of bread, or the food most appropriate to a wolf, human

---

[113] Cf. Sébillot 1904–7:ii, 205, for similar practices in Montagne Noir. See Summers 1933:114 and 131 n.146 and Armand 2013, with further references.

[114] Stenbock 1893, reprinted at Otten 1986:269–80; cf. Frost 2003:87–90.

flesh; he could be transformed back into a man either by abstinence from human flesh or by the equal-and-opposite process of eating a wolf's heart. And, thirdly, it was the impulse of the werewolf, when transformed from man to wolf, to make a bolt from the inner places of humanity and civilization for the outer places of the wilderness and the forest. The themes discussed in this chapter, in particular that of the werewolf's conceptualization as an inner wolf contained within an outer human, and that of the passage from an inner place to an outer place in the course of wolf transformation, when combined with the theme discussed in the last chapter of the werewolf's associations with ghosts and detached souls, prepare the ground for the study of the shamanic aspects of the ancient werewolf that comprises the next chapter.

4
Werewolves and Projected Souls

From the earliest medieval werewolf material onwards there is a persistent association of werewolfism with soul-projection or soul-flying. It is the contention here that this association already obtained in antiquity.[1] This is suggested by similar patterns in the ancient evidence in the representations of the soul-projectors of the Pythagorean tradition and werewolves. It is important to bear in mind, however, that these patterns are latent and somewhat obscure: they could not in themselves have inspired and given rise to the medieval (and subsequent) connection between werewolfism and soul-projection. The latter cannot be seen as some sort of artificial literate revival. The only satisfactory explanation is that werewolfism and soul-projection were ever associated with each other in the West, and that this fact comes across faintly in the ancient evidence, before coming across loudly in the medieval and early modern evidence.

In this connection it is difficult to avoid the admittedly contested term 'shamanism'.[2] I use it here primarily as an anthropological shorthand to denote the practice (or notion) of, precisely, soul-projection. Its use is justified by two considerations in particular. First the (essentially mythical) soul-projectors of the Greek Pythagorean tradition, Aristeas of Proconnesus and others, who constitute an important part of our argument here, are regularly referred to in contemporary scholarship as 'the Greek shamans'. Secondly, 'shamanism' is also regularly deployed in modern discussions of the Norse and the Livonian phenomena to which we shall shortly turn our attention. In light of this, it seems that to avoid the term completely here would be likely to give rise to more confusion than it eliminated. However, I should make it clear that in applying the term to figures

---

[1] Bourgault du Coudray 2006:2 mistakenly imagines the explanation of werewolfism as mesmeric projection to be a late Victorian innovation.

[2] For the anthropological concept of shamanism in general see Eliade 1964 (1951), Burkert 1979:88–94, Hutton 2001, and Jackson 2016. Hutton offers a bracing starting point. Of the four broad definitions of 'shamanism' he identifies as in common use in scholarship (vii–viii), my own falls between his first three (his fourth relates specifically to the concept's supposed Siberian type societies, the Tungus, etc.): 'In one, shamanism is the practice of anybody who contacts a spirit world while in an altered state of consciousness. A second limits it to specialist practitioners who use such contacts at the behest of others. A third attempts to distinguish shamans from other such specialists, such as "mediums", "witch doctors", "spiritual healers" or "prophets", by some particular technique. This is the definition most commonly accepted amongst modern scholars, but there is no agreement on what that technique should be. To some the definitive characteristic is that shamans exert control over the spirits with whom they work while to others it is the ability to undertake a personal journey into an alternative reality and accomplish tasks there.'

from ancient Greek culture, I do not thereby seek to entail or imply the assumption that the relevant Greek practices and beliefs were derived either from predecessors of the Siberian Tungus, from whose language the word 'shaman' derives, or from any Scythian intermediaries.[3]

Werewolves and Projected Souls: Medieval, Early Modern, and Modern

Let us begin, back to front, with the post-ancient evidence for the association between werewolfism and soul projection, so as to be clear what it is we are looking for when, eventually, we turn back to the ancient evidence itself.

The Medieval Period (i): Latin and Irish Texts

A persistent notion in medieval and subsequent werewolf narratives and werewolf lore holds that the wolf form of the werewolf is a manifestation of the soul projected forth from his humanoid body as he sleeps or remains comatose. Let us return to the words 'on men who transform themselves into wolves' in Bishop Patrick of Dublin's 1084 AD Latin hexameter poem *De mirabilibus Hibernie* ('On the Wonders of Ireland'), which we mentioned briefly in Chapter 3. The following passage immediately precedes the one quoted there:

> There are some men amongst the Irish that possess a marvellous nature, which they derive from their first ancestors, in accordance with which they are able, when they wish, to change themselves instantaneously, in wicked fashion, into the shapes of {or into the characters of} wolves with rending teeth. In this way they are often seen killing complaining sheep. However, when the shouting or the approach of men with cudgels or weapons alarms them, they run off in flight {like actual wolves}. But when they do this, they leave their true {their own} bodies behind, whilst giving the command to their family {their wives} that no one should move them. For if that happens {the moving of their own bodies}, they will not have the ability to return into them again.
>
> Bishop Patrick of Dublin *De mirabilibus Hibernie* xvi, ll. 66–75[4]

---

[3] Cf. Bremmer 2016:67 ('In the end there is no early shamanistic detail left of Aristeas' legends that is credibly derived from the Scythians') and 2018. Bremmer himself more scrupulously deploys the arm's-length term 'shamanoid' for the Greek figures of interest: 2016: 61, 68–70, 85.

[4] Once again (cf. Chapter 3), the curly-bracketed portions represent Patrick's own glosses on his poem. For the text see Gwynn 1955:62–3; it is reproduced with a translation at Todd 1848:204–5. Cf. Summers 1933:206–7, Reinhard and Hull 1936, Lecouteux 2003 (1992):110–11, Carey 2002:48–64, esp. 53–6, Sconduto 2008:33–4, Boyd 2009:563–5, Pluskowski 2015:97. Carey and Sconduto make the important point that this exposition seems to be independent of Augustine (on whom see below), and so to report genuine folk beliefs.

This material was much recycled. It is found in the Middle Irish poem *De Ingantaib Érenn* ('On the Wonders of Ireland' again), which may indicate that it originated in an Irish medium.[5] It is also found in an anonymous thirteenth-century Latin poem, *On Men who Turn Themselves into Wolves* (*De hominibus qui se vertunt in lupos*), a version of which was added into the manuscripts of Nennius of Bangor's *History of the Britons* (*Historia Brittonum*).[6] The *De Ingantaib Érenn* account includes the additional information that these werewolves are the descendants of Laigne(ch) Faelad in Ossory, the werewolves of Ossory famously being the subject of an engaging exposition and narrative by Gerald of Wales, as we have also seen in Chapter 3.

Guillaume d'Auvergne, Bishop of Paris (AD 1228–49), has this tale to tell in his *De universo*:

> There was a man that was possessed. From time to time the evil spirit would possess him and derange him to such an extent that he believed he was a wolf. However, during the days in which he was possessed, the devil would cast him down in a concealed place and leave him there, just as if he were dead. But during the time of his concealment in this way the devil would enter a wolf, or show itself to people in the form of a wolf. It would make terrifying depredations upon men and animals alike, in such a way that people fled whenever it appeared, fearing that they would be devoured by it. And so the rumour arose that this man was becoming a wolf from time to time, and the man himself came to believe this, just as I said. He came to believe, furthermore, that he was the wolf that was making the depredations of that sort. A holy man heard about this and came to the region in which these things were taking place. He told the people that what they believed of that man was not true, namely, that he was becoming a wolf. He had himself brought to the place in which the man was lying as if dead, and showed him to the people that had come to look. He roused him from his sleep in front of them, liberating him from the ordeal of his possession. He also showed him, as well as those attending, the wolf that the man had been believing himself to be, with the result that he made confession before all that were present.
>
> Guillaume d'Auvergne *De universo* 2.3.13 at *Opera omnia* (1674) i, 1043b[7]

This looks like a theologically aware attempt to explain the same phenomenon of soul-projection: the action normally ascribed to the detached soul is transferred to a masquerading demon, just as in Christianized versions of traditional ghost

---

[5] Cf. Carey 2002:54.   [6] Nennius *Historia Brittonum* 76 (Mommsen).
[7] Cf. Summers 1933:222–3, Harf-Lancner 1985:214–15, Lecouteux 2003 (1992):117–18, Milin 1993:65–7, Sconduto 2008:22–3 (the English translation offered here, derived from a French intermediary, is not entirely accurate), Pluskowski 2015:96, Dillinger 2015:147.

stories the ghosts similarly tend to mutate, often at the expense of the tale's logic, into masquerading demons. Ghosts had always been problematic for Christianity: the New Testament repeatedly admonishes that the souls of the dead are confined, imprisoned, indeed, in the underworld (sometimes in their tombs, or in the sea) until the Day of Resurrection, whereupon they are to be roused by a clarion call.[8] Accordingly, Tertullian (c. AD 200) explains at some length that *apparent* ghosts, which he knows full well to be a genuine phenomenon, are not the souls of the dead themselves but actually demons, and specifically those demons that have been responsible for the deaths of the individuals concerned in the first place. They masquerade as their souls, as sometimes becomes explicit when a possessing demon is interrogated during exorcism and it claims to be the soul of its host's ancestor, or of a gladiator. They do this precisely so that they may interfere with good Christians' belief in the Day of Judgement and the Resurrection.[9] Pagan antiquity's favourite haunted-house story remains strikingly familiar to us today.[10] We have access to three versions (in the hands of Plautus, Pliny the Younger, and Lucian) of the tale in which a philosopher takes on the challenge of spending the night in a derelict house from which an occupying ghost has chased all previous comers or in which it has actually killed them. The philosopher braves the ghost's terrifying attack, and it then meekly leads him to a certain spot within the house before disappearing. Come morning, and the philosopher has the spot dug out. The mangled remains of a secret murder victim are exposed. They are given due burial, and the house is delivered of its terrors.[11] When the story type, far too good to abandon, came into Christian hands, revision was called for. In Gregory the Great's version (late sixth century AD), the hero has appropriately transmuted into a Christian bishop, Datius, and the ghost into a demon or a devil (a *diabolus*), though it retains characteristics from the ghosts of the classical tradition, such as being able to imitate animals (as in Lucian). But the cost of the latter transformation is that there is no longer a body to find, and Bishop Datius must content himself with an act of exorcism.[12]

---

[8] Luke 16:19–31 (the parable of Lazarus and the rich man); John 5:28–29, 11:24; 1 Corinthians 15:52; 1 Thessalonians 4:13–17; 1 Peter 3:19; Revelation 20:5, 11–13. Cf. Hippolytus' grim vision of the underworld prison-house: *Contra Platonem de causa universi*, PG 10, 796.

[9] Tertullian *On the Soul* 57; cf. Waszink 1947 *ad loc.* and Nock 1950.

[10] Cf. Oscar Wilde's *Canterville Ghost* (1887) and Bram Stoker's 'The Judge's House' (1891). Note also the modern Italian folktale reported at Rini 1929:85.

[11] Plautus *Mostellaria* 446–531 (*c*.200 BC, after Philemon's lost play *Phasma*, of the late fourth or early third century BC); Pliny the Younger *Letters* 7.27.5–11 (*c*. AD 107); Lucian *Philopseudes* 30–1 (*c*. AD 170–80). Cf., broadly, Grimm 1986 no. 4 = ATU no. 326 and, for the central motif, Thompson 1955–8 no. E235.2. For discussions of this story type see above all Nardi 1960:80–118, Felton 1999, Stramaglia 1999:120–69, and Ogden 2007:205–24.

[12] Gregory the Great *Dialogues* 3.4.1–3. Another early Christian version of the story type is found at Constantius' *Life of St Germanus* 2.10 (AD 480); his attempts to grapple with the tale's theological difficulties, while maintaining the story type's integrity, are more awkward. For a rather later Christian version of the story type, see Jacobus de Voragine's tale of St Ambrose's discovery of the bodies of the martyrs Gervasius and Protasius (*Golden Legend* no. 85, AD 1263–7; text at Graesse 1850; English trans. at Ryan 1993). Discussion of all these in Ogden 2019b.

We may compare here St Hildegard of Bingen's (*fl.* A D 1098-1197) explanation of the well-attested ancient superstition that a human was deprived of their voice when a wolf looked at them first (for which see Chapter 1):

> When a wolf looks at a man before the man sees him, it is the aerial spirits that accompany him that sap the man's strength, because at that point the man does not know that the wolf is looking at him. But when a man sees a wolf before it sees him, he holds God in his heart, and by virtue of that puts the aerial spirits to flight and the wolf with them.
>
> Hildegard of Bingen *Physica* 7.19 (*PL* 197, 1327)

The Medieval Period (ii): Werewolves, Were-bears, and Projected Souls in Norse Texts

Norse culture exhibits complexly intertwined traditions of werewolves and were-bears. We have already encountered some of its werewolves proper, in the cases of Siggeir's mother and of Sigmund and Sinfjötli.[13]

The berserkers, the famous wild warriors that whipped themselves up into an ecstatic trance to fight, may have derived their title from the bear (cf. *ber*), that is 'bear-shirts', though it is probable that it signified rather 'bare (of) shirts' (cf. *berr*). However, it is clear that they, or a class of them at any rate, were also held to exhibit important affinities with wolves, with them often being referred to actually as 'wolfskins':[14]

> The berserkers howled...the wolfskins [*úlfheðnar*] cried out, and brandished their weapons.
>
> Thorbjorn Hornklofi *Haraldskvæði/Hrafnsmál* 8 (*c.* A D 900; Ogden trans.)[15]

---

[13] For werewolves in Old Norse literature generally see Guðmundsdóttir 2007, Pluskowski 2006:179–90, 2015, Tuczay 2015. Old Norse appears to have had no word for werewolf as such until it coined *vargúlfr* ('outlaw wolf', or perhaps more simply 'wolf-wolf'—see Introduction) for the purposes of translating Marie de France's *Bisclavret* (as *Bisclaretz ljóð*) amongst the *Strengleikar*, the translation of twenty-one of Marie's lais made in the mid-thirteenth century for King Haakon IV of Norway.

[14] For berserkers see von See 1961, Boberg 1966:124–5 (a list of references to their appearances), Höfler 1976, Beard 1978, Blaney 1982, 1993 (with expansive bibliography), Davidson 1986:148–50, Douglas 1992:77–80, Milin 1993:18–22, Liberman 2003, 2005, 2016:101–12, Sundquist and Hultgård 2004, Guðmundsdóttir 2007:280–2, Pluskowski 2015:90, Tuczay 2015:65, Ginzburg and Lincoln 2020:51–2. For berserkers in action, see especially *Gisli Sursson's Saga* 2–3, *Grettir's Saga* 2, 19, 22, 40, *Egil's Saga* 64, *Hrolf's Saga* 24. At *Kormak's Saga* 12 (later 13th c. A D) Steinar dresses in a bearskin coat and mask to challenge Holmanga-Bersi to a fight.

Did the Homeric world know of a wolf-themed equivalent to berserkers? Homer applies the term *lyssa*, derivative of *lykos* (see Chapter 2), to battle rage at *Iliad* 9.239, 305, and 21.542; cf. Lincoln 1975 and Bouvier 2015. Pàroli 1986 esp. 300–17 goes so far as to contend that Petronius' own soldier-werewolf ('as brave as Orcus') reflects the Romans' familiarity with the equivalent of berserker culture in the Germanic societies with which they were in contact, notably those of the Suebi and the Chatti.

[15] For a full translation see Hollander 1936.

Odin knew what to do so that his enemies were rendered blind, deaf or panic-stricken in battle, and their weapons bit no more than twigs would have done. In the meantime, his men made their way without mail corslets and were as mad as dogs or wolves, bit on their shields, and were as strong as bears or bulls. They slew people, but neither fire nor iron had any effect upon them. This was what they called 'going berserk' [berserksgangr].

> Snorri Sturluson Heimskringla Ynglinga saga 6 (c. AD 1225; Ogden trans.)[16]

Rögnvald of Möre and many other great chieftains stood with him [Harald Fairhair], and so too berserkers, who were called wolfskins [úlfheðnar]; they wore wolf pelts instead of chainmail and defended the bow of the king's ship.

> Vatnsdæla saga 9 (mid-13th c. AD; Ogden trans.)[17]

Then the king [Harald Shaggy-Hair, lúfa] called upon his berserkers to advance. They were called 'wolfskins' [úlfheðnar] and could be bitten by no iron.

> Grettir's Saga 2 (c. AD 1310–20; Ogden trans.)[18]

Both Snorri and the Vatnsdæla saga imply the 'bare' (folk) etymology here. Just such a berserker wearing a wolfskin may be illustrated on a matrix for stamping helmet plates of c. AD 600 from Torslunda on the island of Öland.[19] Indeed, lupine berserkers may be attested as early as the fifth century AD. Their culture may be expressed in the names found on some remarkable runestones from Listerlandet in Blekinge, Sweden, of c. AD 550–650: Hathuwulfr ('Battle-wolf'), Hariwulfr ('Army-wolf'), and Heruwulfir ('Sword-wolf'). Of these Hariwulfr is already attested in Latinized form, Hariulfus, in a fifth-century AD inscription from Trier.[20]

An exceptional example of the soul-projecting model of were-bearism is found in the description of Bodvar Bjarki's final fight in the c. AD 1400 Hrolf's Saga (Hrólfs saga kraka).[21] This text as a whole exhibits many intriguing parallels with

---

[16]   For a full translation see Finlay and Faulkes 2011.
[17]   For a full translation see Wawn 2000.   [18]   For a full translation see Byock 2009.
[19]   Höfler 1976:300, Gunnell 1994:70; Sundquist and Hultgård 2004:9, Tuczay 2015:65–6 (with drawn illustration), Pluskowski 2015:87–92. In the view of Pluskowski, the warrior figure accompanying the wolf-man here only has one eye and accordingly represents Odin. Having examined good images of the artefact, I remain unconvinced that this is true (and there is certainly no indication of it in the drawing reproduced by Tuczay).
[20]   Sundquist and Hultgård 2004:1–4, with details of the runestones and some interesting observations on early Germanic onomastics. CIL xiii.3682 (Rheinisches Landesmuseum Trier no. 186).
[21]   The text is listed in the AD 1461 catalogue of the Möðruvellir monastery. For discussion of Bodvar Bjarki see Caldwell 1940, Jones 1972:123143, Davidson 1986:143–7, Schjødt 2003 (for the narrative as reflecting the initiation rites of the berserker), Guðmundsdóttir 2007:282–4, Tolley 2007 (comparing an interesting Sami folktale recorded in the eighteenth century), McGlynn 2009 (passim, esp. 163–4 for the shamanistic aspects of the tale), Tuczay 2015:71–2, 76. Cf. Ward 1975 for the folktale of the 'Bear's son'. For shamanism in Old Norse literature more generally see Buchholz 1968, Biering 2006.

our own *c.* AD 685 to *c.* 725 Anglo-Saxon *Beowulf*, and it is indeed the figure of Bodvar Bjarki himself that corresponds to that of Beowulf, whose name may be construable as 'Bear-wolf' (after *beorn*, 'bear'; otherwise 'Bee-wolf').

According to this text, Bjorn ('Bear'), the son of King Hring of Norway, falls in love with the freeman's daughter Bera ('She-bear'). When he refuses the advances of his stepmother Hvit ('White'), a wicked witch, she slaps him with wolfskin (NB) gloves and by this action curses him to be a cave bear by day and a man by night. In his bear form he cannot help but do the work of a savage marauder, with a devastating effect on his father's cattle. For shame he hides away even in his human form, and Hring knows not what has become of his son. Upon re-encountering Bera in his bear form, Bjorn becomes tame again and leads her back to his cave, where he returns to human form as night comes on. They make love and Bera conceives three sons from him. At Hvit's behest, the unwitting Hring has the marauding bear hunted down and killed, and she compels the pregnant Bera to taste its flesh on pain of torture or death. In due course she gives birth to three strong sons, Elgfrodi (Elk-Frodi), an elk-centaur in form, Thorir Hundsfótr (Houndsfoot), the tips of whose feet are caniform (NB), and finally the great Bodvar Bjarki ('Battle Bear-cub'), who is (outwardly) fully human in form. After many adventures, including the avenging of his father by the strangling of his stepmother in a leather bag, and the drinking of a little blood from the (elk) calf of his brother Elkfrodi, Bodvar finds himself beside King Hrolf of Denmark as his most trusted champion.[22]

The narrative culminates with an ambush assault on Hrolf's hall at Hleidargard (Lejre) by Hjorvard and Skuld, vassal king and vassal queen of Sweden. Skuld is Hrolf's half-sister, an elf and another wicked witch. Hrolf and his champions go out to meet their vast army, all except Bodvar, who remains in the hall. A great, invincible bear, more powerful than any warrior, is seen fighting beside Hrolf in the battle-line. Bodvar's closest friend, Hjalti, noticing that he is not in the battle, remarks upon the fact to Hrolf, who tells him that Bodvar will be where he can serve them best. Returning to the hall, Hjalti finds Bodvar sitting idly or asleep. Hjalti rouses him and reproaches him for not lending his strength—a bear's!—to the battle. Bodvar sadly tells him that, in disturbing him, he has not been as help-ful to King Hrolf as he thinks he has. Bodvar duly goes out to join the battle, alongside Hjalti, but the great bear has disappeared. And so now the battle turns

---

[22] *Hrolf's Saga* 18–23. Let us note here the role of ingestion: Bera evidently transmits animalian qualities to her children by eating the flesh of ursiform Bjorn, and bear qualities in particular to her finest son, Bodvar. And Bodvar doubtless reinforces his own animalian qualities by drinking the blood of his most outwardly animalian brother, Elk-Frodi. Similarly, at *Landnámabók* 3.5 (13th c. AD), Odd Arngeirsson kills a polar bear that has killed his father and brother, and eats it; by so doing he becomes a shape-shifter, acquires the bear's outstanding strength, and can cover vast distances in short times. Cf. Tuczay 2015:64, 68. More broadly, Byock 1998:84 n.59 compares the famous episode in *Völsunga saga* (19) in which Sigurd drinks the blood of the dragon Fafnir, to acquire the prophetic ability to understand the language of the birds.

fatally against Hrolf and his men. Skuld is able to deploy her magical skills to aid her troops, which she had not been able to do in the presence of the bear. To devastating effect, she magics up a great boar, the size of a bull, with arrows for bristles and of the colour of a grey wolf; and as her own troops are killed, she restores them to life as dreadful revenants.[23] Evidently, Bodvar is here projecting forth his soul, his true bearish self (thanks to his father Bjorn and the blood of Elk-Frodi). The tradition that he did so was probably an old one, and probably already underlay the now lost mid-tenth-century poem *Bjarkamál*, 'Lay of Bjarki'.[24] It is a curiosity that Bodvar is not described as a berserker in all this (and earlier in the saga he is actually differentiated strongly from Hrolf's berserkers); perhaps the author found their disruptive, thuggish, and uncouth nature unfitting for a noble warrior in an age of chivalry.[25]

The only other account of Bodvar to suggest his use of a similar bear projection is the Icelandic poem *Bjarkarímur*, 'Bjarki rhymes'. This poem derives from the fifteenth century, but it is thought to have been based upon a lost saga of *c.* AD 1200, *Skjöldunga saga*.[26] In the poem's description of Bodvar's battle with the berserker Agnar,[27] a white bear (*hvítabjörn*) jumps between the two engaged warriors and becomes Bodvar's hands. Agnar strikes it on the head with his sword, but ineffectually. Bodvar is then able to run him through with his own sword in turn, Laufi.[28] Bodvar may be projecting, but he is evidently not sleeping

---

[23] *Hrolf's Saga* 33.

[24] Only a few stanzas of the tenth-century *Bjarkamál* survive, principally as quotations in Snorri Sturluson's *c.* AD 1220 *Prose Edda* and his *Heimskringla* Olafs saga helga (the fragments are collated at Heusler and Ranisch 1903:31–2). It is possible that the rousing of Bodvar is referred to in the passage quoted at *Prose Edda* Skáldskaparmál 99 (190), as Pálsson and Faulkes 2012:168 conjecture. *Bjarkamál*'s description of the final battle at Hleidargard formed the basis of Saxo Grammaticus' account of the same in his *c.* AD 1200–20 *Gesta Danorum*, 2.52–62. While there is no explicit indication of soul projection on Bodvar's part here, Hjalti is made to speak to him no less than three times in order to rouse him from a deep sleep so as to participate in the battle. This seemingly indicates that the soul-projection theme was already present in the traditions behind *Bjarkamál* itself, even if not fully expressed there; see Davidson and Fisher 1980:ii, 48 n.63. We should note also Saxo's prior episode in which Bodvar kills an actual bear and presses Hjalti to drink its blood, to strengthen himself (2.51; this broadly corresponds with the dragon episode in *Hrolf's Saga*, 23).

[25] *Hrolfs Saga* 24. But he is securely listed as the first of Hrolf's berserkers at Snorri Sturluson *Prose Edda* Skáldskaparmál 43. See Ramos 2014:15, 17, 23, 41.

[26] Our best access to the contents of the lost *Skjöldunga saga* is now by means of a Latin summary of it made by Arngrímur Jónsson in the late sixteenth century (for the text of this see Benediktsson 1950–7 and Guðnason 1982; for an English translation see Miller 2007, accompanied by a useful introduction and notes by Acker and Guðnason). This summary (ch. 12) indicates that the *Skjöldunga saga*'s narrative ran quite closely parallel with that of *Hrolf's Saga* for the period of Bodvar's service with Hrolf, but it does not supply any details for Bodvar's battle with Agnar (a mere mention of it only) and it does not even mention Bodvar's actions in the final battle at Hleidargard, though we are told, intriguingly, of Hrolf himself being overcome by a mysterious lethargy in the course of the battle, which allows his enemies to prevail; Miller 2007:29 n.45 appropriately wonders whether this detail corresponds to Bodvar's trance.

[27] This battle is referred to in passing only at *Hrolf's Saga* 33.

[28] *Bjarkarímur* 7–9; for a translation, see Ramos 2014.

here.[29] Unfortunately the ending of the *Bjarkarímur* poem, in which the battle at Hleidargard would have been described, is also lost.

We do find another bear projected from sleep, however, in the (thirteenth-century) *Book of Settlements* (*Landnámabók*). This reports that, when Storolf and Dufthak were disputing grazing rights at Storolfvöllr, a man with second sight observed a great bear and a great bull emerge by night from their respective homes and fight on the contested wold. Both men were found hurt the following morning. Evidently the animals had been projected avatars.[30]

These projected bears should (also) be understood in terms of notion of the *fylgja* (pl. *fylgjur*).[31] This was a tutelary soul that could be projected in the form of an animal (or sometimes a woman) during sleep. In English the term is some-times rendered with a word derived from Irish folklore, 'fetch'. Just as these ava-tars are normally projected while their possessor is asleep, so they most typically manifest themselves also in the dreams of others, though they can also appear as waking visions too. *Fylgjur* can draw upon the full range of animal forms. In *Ynglinga saga* Snorri Sturluson even speaks of Odin's body lying asleep or dead while he visited remote lands in the form of a bird, animal, fish, or serpent.[32]

On occasion *fylgjur* can take the form of wolves. At the opening of the (thirteenth-century) *Egil's Saga*, thought to have been written by Snorri Sturluson, we are introduced to Ulf ('Wolf') the son of Bjalfi:

> However, every day, as evening came on, he would become so withdrawn that few men could share words with him. He was an evening-sleeper. The talk of men was that he was in fact a shape-shifter [*hamramr*]. He was called 'Evening-Wolf' [Kveld-Úlfr].   *Egil's Saga* 1 (Ogden trans.)[33]

This suggests an underlying notion that Ulf projects a wolf as he sleeps in the evening.[34] And we hear too of wolf-*fylgiur* being perceived in dreams. In (the later thirteenth-century) *Njal's Saga* Gunnar dreams that he sees the *fylgiur* of his enemies massing in the woods as a pack of wolves, ready for the attack.[35] In (the earlier fourteenth-century) *Howard the Halt's Saga* (*Hárvarðar saga ísfirðings*) Atli similarly dreams that he sees his enemies and the witch that presides over them in the form of a pack of eighteen wolf-*fylgjur* led by a vixen-*fylgia*.[36]

---

[29]   As Ramos 2014:14 notes.

[30]   *Landnámabók* 5.5; cf. Davidson 1986:147–8.

[31]   For *fylgjur* see Davidson 1986:153–6, Lecouteux 2003:45-7103-5, McGlynn 2009:161–3, 168–9, Pluskowski 2015:86, Tuczay 2015:61–4 (the last with a review of scholarship).

[32]   Snorri Sturluson *Heimskringla* Ynglinga saga 18; cf. Tuczay 2015:73–4, Pluskowski 2015:92 (the 'shamanic' aspects of Odin).

[33]   For a full translation see Scudder 2004. Discussion at Holtsmark 1968, Davidson 1986:150–1, Tuczay 2015:66–7.

[34]   Cf. Ramos 2014:32.   [35]   *Njal's Saga* 61.   [36]   *Hárvarðar saga Ísfirðings* 20.

The Early Modern Period (i): Western Europe

In their famous *Malleus maleficarum* ('Hammer of Witches') of AD 1487, Kramer and Sprenger provide their own version of Guillaume d'Auvergne's tale, quoted above:

> William tells about a certain man, who thought that he changed himself into a wolf at certain times, during which he was actually lying hidden in a cave. For he went there at a certain time, and although he remained fast there in the meantime, it seemed to him that he became a wolf and was going around devouring children. Although this was really just being done by a demon that was possessing a certain wolf, he wrongly believed, dreaming as he was, that he was going abroad. He was demented in this way for a long time, until eventually he was found, raving mad, lying in the wood.
>
> Kramer and Sprenger *Malleus maleficarum* part 1, question 10[37]

The archives of Modena record the 1518–19 trial of two men accused of witchcraft and more specifically werewolfism in the village of Bastia (Bastiglia), Pietro and Giacomo Garutti. Part of the evidence against Pietro was that his wife had once found him lying half-dead (*semimortuus*) on the ground and was so disturbed by this that she took ill and died. The transformation (that is, the projection) was initiated when one brother rolled up a belt, tied it with string, and gave it to the other one to keep. However, on one occasion, once the first had transformed, he was hunted down and killed by the local peasants before his brother could untie the belt. Matteo Duni sees the belt as equivalent to the wolfskin pelt one might don to transform. But given that we are not told that the belt was made of wolfskin, and that we are told that it was not donned but rather tied up, perhaps we should rather see the act of tying the belt up, of putting it temporarily beyond use, as symbolizing a rejection of *human* clothing, and as the equivalent to the doffing of the clothes and with them the human carapace.[38]

In his 1590 *Discours exécrable des sorciers* the jurist and demonologist Henri Boguet writes:

> So far as I can see, Satan sometimes puts the sorcerer to sleep behind a bush, whilst he goes off on his own and accomplishes the sorcerer's intentions, conferring upon himself the appearance of a wolf. In the meantime, he disrupts the

---

[37] For an edition and translation of the *Malleus maleficarum* see Mackay 2006 (translation also at Summers 1928). It is now disputed whether Sprenger was a genuine co-author. For this text in relation to werewolves see Summers 1933 index s.v. *Malleus*, Otten 1986:106–14, Oates 1989:319–20, Douglas 1992:161–3, Sconduto 2008:127–30, Pluskowski 2015:83–4, Dillinger 2015:145–9.

[38] Archivo di Stato di Modena, Inquisizione, busta 2, Processi 1489–1549, fascicle ii, *Contra Petrum et Jacobum strigos ad Bastiam*, 27 December 1518/19. See Duni 2015.

sorcerer's imagination to such an extent that it seems to him that he has been a wolf and that has run around and killed men and beasts alike ....When it comes about that they find themselves to have been wounded, it is Satan that passes onto them at once the blow that has been dealt to the body he has adopted.

Boguet 1590 ch. xlvii pp.188–9 (Ogden trans.)[39]

A few further examples of this line of thinking may be noted. In his *Compendium maleficarum* of 1608 Francesco Maria Guazzo claimed that the demon responsible for werewolfism forms the body of a wolf around itself from thin air.[40] In 1678 the Capuchin Jacques d'Autun spoke of sorcerers being thrown into a mesmeric trance or coma, while their familiar goes on the prowl as a wolf, causing the sorcerer to believe that he is himself living the life of a wolf.[41] In a 1728 essay in the *Hanau Breslauer Sammlung* Rhanaeus contended that dream-projection may be a phenomenon behind werewolfism generally.[42]

The Early Modern Period (ii): Livonia

Carlo Ginzburg has argued that the notion of werewolfism in the late Middle Ages was a hangover from an ancient 'shaman' ritual, this being part of a broader thesis that the key to the Witches' Sabbath lay in 'shamanism'.[43] His most striking evidence relates to Livonia (Estonia–Latvia). In the second edition of his work on divination, *Commentarius de praecipuis generibus divinationum* (1560), the German physician Kaspar Peucer describes the phenomenon of Livonian *lycaones* or *lycanthropoi*, men who believe that they turn into wolves, wander about the countryside, and kill cattle. For Peucer this is a deception brought about by the Devil, but he helpfully gives us much detail about it. The transformed fall to the ground suddenly and lie there senseless, lifeless, and corpselike. Their souls are drawn out of their bodies, as they believe, and sent into phantasms of wolf form. When they have done the Devil's bidding, their souls are returned to their bodies and they are restored to life. One of the individuals concerned claimed to have done battle in the form a wolf with witches in the form of butterflies.[44]

---

[39] Fuller translation at Ashwin and Summers 1929:146; cf. Summers 1933:120, Otten 1986:77–90, Oates 1989:323–4.

[40] Guazzo 1626 book 1 ch. 13; cf. Summers 1933:120.

[41] D'Autun 1678, discours xxx and xxxi; cf. Summers 1933:120–1.

[42] Rhanaeus in *Hanau Breslauer Sammlung. Supplement iii. Curieuser und nutzbarer Anmerkungen von Natur und Kunstgeschichten, gesammelt von Kanold*. 1728. *Non vidi*: I (perhaps unwisely!) depend for the reference on Baring-Gould 1865:50 (§§2–3).

[43] Ginzburg 1990 (1989).

[44] Peucer 1560 folios 141v–142v and 144v (the key phrase: *eductas e corporibus animas in efficta luporum forma φάσματα immitti*); cf. Ginzburg 1990:156–7; Milin 1993:71–3, 96–7, Duni 2015:133–4, Ginzburg and Lincoln 2020 esp. 201–3.

Ginzburg also cites a more particular Livonian case. For all that it does not include an explicit claim of soul flight, the assumption of it is rather demanded for intelligibility. In 1691 a supposed Latvian werewolf named Thiess, of 80 years of age, was interrogated in Jürgensburg. His (not entirely consistent) testimony may be summarized as follows. He had first become a werewolf when a werewolf from Marienburg had transferred his curse to him, and he hoped one day to be able to pass the curse on in turn to someone else. The curse was transferred in the following fashion: the existing werewolf would drink his victim's health, blow three times into the jug, and pass it to the victim while declaring, 'May what befell me befall you'; if the victim accepted the jug, the curse was passed over to him. On three nights of the year (those of St Lucy and St John and the Pentecost), the werewolves of Livonia would transform themselves either by donning wolf pelts or simply by divesting themselves of their human clothes in the forest, before tearing apart various items of livestock (but they would roast them, with their wolf paws, before eating them). They would then travel to Hell, which was in a cave under the earth and accessed through a door at the end of a lake called Puer Esser in a bog near Lemburg/Malpilis. The sorcerers would hide away the earth's goodness or fertility there—in the form of its livestock, fish, fruit, and grain—and the werewolves, as 'the Dogs of God', made it their task to retrieve these by doing battle with them. The sorcerers would resist them with iron goads and with broomsticks fitted with horse-tails. Success meant that the werewolves secured the fertility of their local fields and the sea for the year, and averted famine. On returning to the surface with the retrieved grain, they would throw it into the air and the land would be blessed. At the time of the investigation Thiess was sporting a wound on his nose that he claimed had been inflicted by the sorcerer Skeistan with his horse-tail broomstick, as he had attempted to prevent him from bringing back some wheat grain.[45]

One is struck here by the alignment between these latter claims and the beliefs and rituals of one of the more striking soul-projecting cultures of modern times, that of the Inuit. Rasmussen's anthropological reports on these, made in 1920, are already familiar to ancient historians via the helpful summary made by Walter Burkert:

---

[45] This account reflects the trial records published at von Bruiningk 1924:163–220, with the key portion now translated into English at Ginzburg and Lincoln 2020:13–32. For reconstructions and discussions see Höfler 1934:345–51 (partly translated at Ginzburg and Lincoln 2020:40–5), Ginzburg 1990:153–9, Metsvahi 2001, de Blécourt 2007b:49–51, Lincoln 2018:37–53. Further discussion of the extent to which Thiess's claims should be seen to document shamanism or shamanistic ideas at Douglas 1992:151–70 (cf. 26–7, 31–4, 37, 57, 66, 71–2, 89, 80–3, 224–5, 261), Milin 1993:97–102, Metsvahi 2015:214–15, 218–19, Lecouteux 2003 (1992):118–23, 168–76, de Blécourt 2007b (much scepticism), Duni 2015:131–6 (an important corrective to de Blécourt's scepticism), Ginzburg and Lincoln 2020 passim.

The most vivid examples comparable to our tale pattern come from the Eskimos of Greenland, who live mostly on seal hunting. They believe that seals belong to a mistress of animals, Sedna, the old woman 'down there.' If a tribe fails to find enough seals and is threatened by famine, it must be due to the wrath of Sedna; and this is the situation for the shaman to step in and help by appeasing Sedna. A festival is called, and the shaman, in a trance, sets out to travel to the deep sea; he meets Sedna and asks why she is angry. It is because of human sins, especially those of women, who have broken certain taboos; Sedna herself is covered in filth on account of their uncleanliness. The shaman has to tidy up Sedna, to ask her forgiveness. Of course he succeeds, finally, and comes back from his ecstatic travel bringing with him the animals. The hunters start real hunting immediately, their optimism renewed, and as a result will prove successful.

Burkert 1979:88–9[46]

Both adventures, we note, secure the variety of fertility relevant to their communities.

The Modern Period

In his 1854–6 book *Dogme et rituel de la haute magie* (*The Doctrine and Ritual of High Magic*),[47] the occultist Éliphas Lévi showed himself to be a good pupil of St Augustine (as will shortly become clear):

We may now boldly assert that the werewolf is nothing other than the sidereal body of a man. The wolf represents his wild and bloody instincts. Whilst his phantom disports itself in the countryside, he sleeps peaceably in his bed and dreams that he is a true wolf. What renders the werewolf visible is the almost somnambulistic over-excitement created by the fear of those that see him. Alternatively, it is rendered visible by the tendency, more peculiar to simple country people, to put oneself into direct communication with the astral light that is the common medium of visions and dreams. The blows experienced by the werewolf do actual harm to the sleeping person because of the odic and sympathetic pressure of the astral light, and by means of the correspondence between the immaterial body and the material one.

Lévi 1854–6:i, 278–9 (Ogden trans.)[48]

---

[46]   After Rasmussen 1926. For Sedna and her shamans, see now Laugrand and Oosten 2010.
[47]   Translated in 1896 (Waite) as *Transcendental Magic, its Doctrine and Ritual*.
[48]   Cf. Tupet 1976:76.

In his 1883 *Essai sur l'humanité posthume* (*Essay on the Human Afterlife*) Adolphe D'Assier tells of a miller that lived at Serisols some thirty years before:

> A miller by the name of Bigot had a certain renown for sorcery. One day his wife got up very early in the morning to go to wash some linen close to the house. He sought to dissuade her from doing it, repeatedly saying, over and over, 'Don't go there, you will have a scare.' 'But why should I have a scare?', his wife responded. 'I tell you that you will have a scare.' She took no notice of these warnings and went on her way. She had hardly started work at the washtub when she caught sight of a creature coming and going before her. Since it was not yet day, she could not make its shape out clearly, but she thought that she recognised a type of dog. Inconvenienced by these comings and goings, but unable to drive the creature off, she threw her beater at it, and this struck it in the eye. The creature disappeared at once. At the same time Bigot's children heard the man give out a cry of pain in his bed, adding 'The hussy! She has just taken out one of my eyes!' And indeed, from that day forward, he became one-eyed. Several people have told me about these events, including the very children of Bigot.
>
> D'Assier 1883:283–4 (Ogden trans.)[49]

In Algernon Blackwood's 1908 short story 'In the Camp of the Dog' ('case v' in his collection *John Silence, Physician Extraordinary*), a group of campers in Sweden are terrorized by a large dog, which turns out to be an ethereal projection from the sleeping body of one of the party, an embodiment of his desire for one of the women in the group. When the dog is shot, the camper is left psychically wounded, but these wounds are (one is relieved to discover) healed by the love of the woman in question.[50]

Finally, in her 1930 *Psychic Self-Defense*, the Welsh occultist Dion Fortune (Violet Firth) describes at some length the occasion on which she had contrived to extrude an ectoplasmic wolf from her solar plexus, to which it remained attached by a sort of umbilical cord. It was a product of her resentment at a personal slight and of her brooding upon Fenrir, the great eschatological wolf of Norse mythology, and the berserkers. It was 'grey and colourless' but had weight. As she asserted her mastery over the snarling beast, it morphed into a meeker Alsatian dog. With due concentration, she was able to reabsorb the creature by sucking it back down the ectoplasmic cord. Another in her household witnessed the creature, both sleeping and waking.[51]

---

[49] Cf. Summers 1933:238.   [50] Discussed at Frost 2002:93–5   [51] Fortune 1930 ch. 4.

Werewolves and Projected Souls in the Ancient World

Was the notion of soul-projection associated with werewolves already in antiquity?[52] I believe that it was, for two reasons. The first is that the notion already seems to underlie Augustine's treatment of the question of human–animal transformation in general. And the second is that ancient beliefs about werewolves and their clothing coincide in a significant fashion with ancient beliefs about the soul-projectors of the Pythagorean tradition, the so-called 'Greek shamans'.

The passage of Augustine in question is a protracted and difficult one from the *City of God* (AD 413–23).[53] Augustine's starting point is the myth in accordance with which Diomede's companions were transformed into birds after the fall of Troy. He relays at length Varro's defence of the truth of this story. In doing this he briefly mentions Homer's Circe changing Odysseus' companions into beasts (no particular creature is specified), and then speaks at some length about Arcadian werewolfism in connection with Zeus Lykaios, including the experiences in this context of the boxer Demaenetus, and indicates that Varro somehow connected these rites to those of the Roman Luperci (see Appendix C). He then passes on to Italian folk beliefs:

> For we too, when we were in Italy, used to hear such things about a particular district of those parts, where it was said that women that kept inns, imbued with these evil crafts, used to give things in cheese to such travellers as they wished, or as they were able to, as a result of which they were immediately turned into beasts of burden, made to carry whatever was demanded and returned to their own form again once they had performed their tasks. But their minds did not become those of beasts, but were preserved in their rational and human state, just as Apuleius told or pretended happened to himself [*sic*] in the books that he wrote under the title of *The Golden Ass* [= *Metamorphoses*], namely that after taking a drug he became an ass but retained his human mind.
>
> Augustine *City of God* 18.18

Augustine, clearly taking such reports of animal transformation seriously, goes on to offer his explanation of the mechanics of the phenomenon. In essence, animal transformations are the phantasms of sleeping individuals, which may of course appear real enough to the dreamers themselves, but they can also do so to others

---

[52] Baring-Gould 1865:113–22 was already suggesting, in an admittedly vague and unfocused way, that a belief in metempsychosis underlay a wide range of werewolf traditions, including even that of Lycaon's transformation into a wolf (114), which is frankly hard to justify.

[53] Augustine *City of God* 18.16–18. Discussion at Summers 1933:82–4, Kratz 1976:61–8, Tupet 1976:75, Harf-Lancner 1985:207–12, Lecouteux 2003 (1992):106–9, Sconduto 2008:15–25, Pluskowski 2015:95–6.

too. These phantasms are inevitably insubstantial. To the extent that they exercise physical force in the external world, this is the work of 'demons', by which Augustine denotes not ghosts but malign supernatural entities:

> If demons do indeed do the sort of things under discussion, they do not of course create things in essence. Rather, they just change the appearance of those things which have been created by the true God, so that they should seem to be what they are not. And so, the mind aside, I could not believe that even the body could be truly transformed into the shape or limbs of a beast by the craft or the power of demons. But when a man's bodily senses are asleep or overpowered, a figment of his imagination [*phantasticum*],[54] which changes itself into countless sorts of things even as he thinks or dreams and takes on forms that resemble bodies with remarkable agility, even though it is not a body itself, can be brought to the perception of others as if in corporeal form, in some fashion I am unable to express. This happens in such a way that a man's body may lie somewhere, quite alive, albeit with his senses much more strongly and emphatically confined than during sleep, whilst the figment of his imagination manifests itself to the senses of others as if embodied in the form of some animal, and the man even seems to himself to be transformed, just as he can seem to himself to be in sleep, and to carry burdens. These burdens, if they are truly substantial, are carried by demons, so that people are fooled as they see on the one hand the actual substances of the burdens and on the other the pretended bodies of the beasts of burden. A man called Praestantius told that this happened to his father, namely that he consumed that drug in some cheese in his own house, and lay on his bed as if asleep, although he could in no way be roused. He said that he returned to consciousness after a certain number of days and told the story of what he had experienced as if recounting dreams. He said that he had become a pack-horse indeed, and had, in the company of other beasts of burden, carried supplies for the soldiers of the 'Rhetian' legion, so called since it was being dispatched to Rhetia. It was discovered that this had happened, just has he recounted it, even though these things had seemed to be dreams to him. Another man told that during the night, in his own house, before he went to bed, he had seen come to him a certain philosopher that was very well known to him. This man had explained to him a number of points of Platonic philosophy which he had refused to do when previously asked. When that same philosopher had been

---

[54] In his dictionary of Christian Latin Blaise explains the key but tricky term *phantasticum* as follows: 'the phantom, the double of a man, capable of escaping from him as he sleeps and manifesting itself before others in a material form' (Blaise 1954 s.v., approved by Tupet 1976:75). This seems to me to be less an explanation of the term than a summary of the context in which Augustine deploys it here. The suite of Greek terms from which it is ultimately derived (φαντασικός, φαντάζω etc.; cf. LSJ s.vv.) emphatically express the creation of images in the mind. Moreau's explanation is better: '...the notion of the *phantasticum*, which is at once the representation the dreamer possesses of himself, and at the same time a kind of phantom' (1998:7).

asked why he had done that in the man's house, even though he had refused to do it in his own house when the man sought it from him, he replied, 'I didn't do it, but I dreamed that I did.' And so the thing that the one man saw in his sleep was shown to the other man whilst he was awake by means of a vision proceeding from a figment of the first man's of imagination.

Augustine City of God 18.18

Augustine then concludes his discussion with some ring composition, by affirming that this is what he believes to have been the mechanism underlying the Arcadian wolf transformations and Circe's transformations. Finally, returning to Diomede's companions, he declares, rather curiously, that these considerations do not bear upon their case after all, and that here the demons simply just substituted birds for the companions they had spirited away. Clearly, Augustine is not speaking exclusively about werewolfism here, though given that it forms the inner ring of his three principal examples of animal transformation in pagan culture (Diomede–Circe–Arcadia—Arcadia–Circe–Diomede), it does seem to be at the forefront of his mind. This argument as a whole has the appearance of being a Christian-theological rationalization of a notion that the animals seen in such cases were the projected souls of sleeping humans.

It is worthwhile turning again to the fragment on *strix*-witches attributed to the eighth-century AD John Damascene and quoted fully in Chapter 1: 'Somehow they enter houses, even though the doors have been locked, together with their body, or just by means of their bare soul…If they were to say that a witch enters the house just as a bare soul, with her body resting on a bed….'[55] Here again we find witches associated with soul-projection from a catatonic body, although in this case they are projecting their own souls rather than those of others. There is no explicit indication of animal transformation in this case, but we recall that a *strix* is, literally, a screech owl, and it is precisely into this creature that the *strix*-witch transforms herself, especially in the classical Latin tradition, in order to penetrate homes and devour and destroy babies. We recall too, for what it is worth, that *strix*-witches are also strongly associated with werewolfism in the classical Latin tradition (Chapter 1).

Pagan stories of soul-projection offer a plausible background to Augustine's and John Damascene's thinking. Soul-projection was the distinctive feat of the 'Greek shamans' of the Pythagorean tradition. The most famous example amongst these is Aristeas of Proconnesus, supposedly of the early seventh century BC, upon whom (second-century AD) Maximus of Tyre offers the following succinct note, while associating him with Pythagoras and his reincarnations:

---

[55] John Damascene *De draconibus et strygibus PG* 94, 1599–1604, at 1604.

The body of a man of Proconnesus would lie there breathing, albeit indistinctly and in a fashion close to death. His soul would escape from his body and wander through the ether like a bird, observing everything beneath, land, sea, rivers, cities, peoples, their experiences and the natural world. Then it would enter into his body again and set it back on its feet, as if it were making use of an instrument, and it would recount the various things it had seen and heard among the various peoples.   Maximus of Tyre 10.2

The elder Pliny records that Aristeas' soul could be observed flying out of his mouth in the form of a raven.[56] As with the *strix*-witch, a bird is, for obvious reasons, a form of choice for a projected soul to adopt, particularly one destined for an extended journey. Herodotus had already spoken of Aristeas, albeit in a slightly confused way. He seems to tell us that Aristeas once appeared to drop dead in a fuller's in Proconnesus, but in fact went into a catatonic state from which he projected his soul and sent it, in humanoid form, on a trip to Cyzicus, with a visitor to Proconnesus from Cyzicus encountering it on the road. He seems to tell us that Aristeas' disembodied but manifest soul could dematerialize. He seems to tell us that Aristeas, in a state of possession by the god Apollo (*Phoibolamptos*), sent his soul on a seven-year voyage to the never-never land of the Issedones, who supposedly lived somewhere north-east of the Scythians, from where he learned of the yet more marvellous peoples of the Arimaspians and the Hyperboreans (the last of whose lands, Pindar tells us, one could not reach by travelling by ship or on foot, that is, one could only do so by flying); these adventures he recorded in his lost poem the *Arimaspeia*. And Herodotus also seems to tell us that Aristeas could suspend his life, for he rematerialized 240 years after his original span of life in Italian Metapontum, where he established a cult of his favoured Apollo, and told that he had once attended the god in the form of a crow (the bird again representing Aristeas in projected-soul form).[57]

Another soul-projecting figure with similar Pythagorean and Apolline affiliations was Abaris. As we learn from Porphyry, Abaris was himself a Hyperborean and indeed a priest of Hyperborean Apollo, whom he conjectured to be manifest in Pythagoras, with his golden thigh, when he encountered him:

It is commonly spoken of that Pythagoras showed his golden thigh to Abaris the Hyperborean after the latter had conjectured that he was Hyperborean Apollo,

---

[56] Pliny *Natural History* 7.174.

[57] Herodotus 4.13–16; Pindar *Pythians* 10.29–30; cf. also Apollonius *Mirabilia* 2. For Aristeas and the 'Greek shamans' in general see above all Meuli 1935, Dodds 1951:140–7, Eliade 1964 (1951):387–94, Bolton 1962, Burkert 1962, 1972:140–65, 1979:88–94, Kindstrand 1981, Metzler 1982, Bremmer 1983:24–53, 2002:27–40, 2016:65–7, 2018, Zhmud 1997:108–16, Luck 1999:117–19, Ustinova 2002b, 2004a, 2004b, 2009 esp.47–51, Lecouteux 2003 (1992):153–7, West 2004, Ogden 2009:9–16, 300–1.

whose priest he was, thus confirming the truth of it .... Abaris acquired the title 'air-traveller', because he rode on an arrow given him by Hyperborean Apollo and crossed rivers and seas and inaccessible places, travelling somehow through the air. Some supposed that Pythagoras had exercised the same power when he conversed with his companions in both Metapontum and Tauromenium on the same day.[58]   Porphyry *Life of Pythagoras* 28–9

The golden (and doubtless feathered) arrow given to Abaris by Apollo with which to fly to and inevitably from inaccessible places bears obvious comparison with Aristeas' Apollo-possessed soul-flight and bird manifestation.

These soul-projecting abilities were eventually inherited by the so-called 'Neo-Pythagoreans'. As we have seen in Chapter 2 (where the passage is quoted), Philostratus' Apollonius of Tyana was able to travel instantaneously to Ephesus, seemingly from Smyrna, simply by saying 'Let us go'.[59]

But the most germane example of a Greek soul-projector for our purposes is in fact that of Hermotimus of Clazomenae (supposedly of the seventh century BC), of whom the (2nd c. BC) paradoxographer Apollonius recounts the following story, which should be compared closely with the passage of Bishop Patrick with which we opened the chapter:

The following sort of thing is reported of Hermotimus of Clazomenae. They say his soul would wander from his body and stay away for many years. Visiting places, it would predict what was going to happen, for example torrential rains or droughts, and in addition earthquakes and pestilences and the suchlike. His body would just lie there, and after an interval his soul would return to it, as if to its shell, and arouse it. He did this frequently, and whenever he was about to go on his travels he gave his wife the order that no one, citizen or anyone, should touch his body. But some people came into the house, prevailed upon his wife and observed Hermotimus lying on the floor naked and motionless. They brought fire and burned him, in the belief that, when the soul came back and no longer had anything to re-enter, he would be completely deprived of life. This is exactly what happened. The people of Clazomenae honour Hermotimus even to this day and have a temple to him. Women may not enter it for the reason above [i.e., the wife's betrayal].   Apollonius *Historiae Mirabiles* 3[60]

---

[58] Metapontum and Thurii, according to Philostratus *Life of Apollonius* 4.10.

[59] Philostratus *Life of Apollonius* 4.10.

[60] Cf. Clearchus of Soli *On Sleep* F7 Wehrli (3rd c. BC): 'Here is a proof that it is possible for the soul to leave the body and enter it again: the man in Clearchus who used a soul-drawing wand [*psuch-oulkos rhabdos*] on a sleeping lad and persuaded the great Aristotle, as Clearchus says in his books *On Sleep*, that the soul separates from the body and enters it again and treats it as a sort of hotel. For the man struck the boy with his wand and drew out his soul. Leading the soul some distance from the body with the stick, he demonstrated that the body remained motionless and was preserved unharmed and was unable to feel anything when pricked, as if it were dead. In the meantime the soul was at some

Now, the importance of the protection of the soul-projector's body while his soul is off on its flights, so that he can recover his physical form, finds a striking parallel in the importance attached to the protection of the werewolf's clothes, while he is off as a wolf, so that he can recover his human form. In both cases, a vital shell must be recovered (see Table 4.1). On the werewolf side, this is quite clear from some of the clothing-related passages reviewed already in Chapter 3:

- Petronius' soldier divests himself of his human clothes in the cemetery in order to become a wolf, keeping them safe by magically turning them to stone with a circle of urine (cf. also the Introduction, where the passage is quoted).[61]
- In Pliny's account of the Anthid rite at the Arcadian Lykaia, the Anthid men divest themselves of their clothes, hang them on a tree, swim across a pool, and become wolves, recovering their clothes and their human form in due course, if they have abstained from human flesh in the meantime (cf. also Chapter 6, where the passage is quoted).[62]
- Aesop's thief, pretending to be a werewolf, asks the innkeeper to keep his human clothes safe for him while he transforms, evidently so that he too can recover his human form in due course (the passage is quoted in Chapter 3).[63]

Table 4.1 Werewolf and soul-projector in the ancient world

	Werewolf (Petronius, Pliny, Aesop)	Soul-projectors (traditions of Aristeas and Hermotimus)
Human/mortal shell to be divested	Shell identified with clothing	Shell identified with physical body
Core projected	Wolf	Soul
Preservation of shell, to permit return of core	By turning to stone (Petronius); by hanging on tree (Pliny); by entrusting to a second person (Aesop)	By leaving in a discreet place (Aristeas); in the care of a second person (Hermotimus)
Frustration of core's return to its shell	By theft of clothes (implied possibility in Petronius and Aesop)	By burning of body (Hermotimus)

remove from the body. But, when the wand brought it back into association with the body and it re-entered it, the boy described everything in detail. As a result of this, Clearchus says, Aristotle and the other spectators of such scientific experiments came to believe that the soul was separable from the body. But the point I'm making, that the soul is able to leave the body and enter it again and make it breathe again after abandoning it, has long been demonstrated by the writings of the leaders of the Peripatos.'

---

[61] Petronius *Satyricon* 62.   [62] Pliny *Natural History* 8.81.
[63] Aesop *Fables* 419 Perry = 196 Halm = 301 Hausrath and Hunger.

An item of ancient (pure) wolf lore seems to harmonize with both the werewolf and the soul-projector themes here. It was held that wolves had an aversion to squills or sea onions, so that both animals and humans could use these to avert wolves from where they were not wanted. More particularly, mischievous foxes would secrete them in wolves' own lairs when they were away, so that they could not return to their homes.[64] Here again the lupine core is deprived of the opportunity to return to its shell by cunning action while it is off a-wandering.

Some of the medieval werewolf tales exhibit a strong parallelism with the central motif of the Hermotimus tale.[65] Just as Hermotimus' wife betrays him as he is on a soul flight by letting his enemies destroy his body, so the perfidious wives of the medieval werewolf tradition make off with their husband's clothes while he is in wolf form so that he cannot transform back. A strong example is provided by Marie de France's brief Anglo-Norman French lay *Bisclavret* (AD 1160–78). Here we are told that Bisclavret, a Breton knight, loves his wife and she him. But he disappears for three days a week and nobody knows what happens to him. One day his wife accuses him of having another lover, but he tells her he cannot tell her what his disappearances are about, for she will no longer love him, and he will lose his very self. She insists and he tells her he is a werewolf and that he runs into the woods to live on plunder. She asks him whether he takes his clothes off, and where he keeps them. He refuses to tell her, for if he lost them he would never be able to recover his human form, but she presses him until he does: in a hollow stone under a bush near a chapel (cf. Gervase of Tilbury's Chaucevaire, discussed in Chapter 3). The wife is horrified by what she has heard and terrified of her husband, whom she never wants to sleep with again. When Bisclavret is next off on his adventures, she sends for a knight who has long admired her, explains all, and sends him to get his clothing. So far as the community is concerned, Bisclavret has disappeared, and in due course his wife marries the knight. A year later, the king is out hunting with his dogs and corners Bisclavret, still, inevitably, in his wolf form, but Bisclavret runs over and kisses his foot, paying homage. The king immediately recognizes the wolf's intelligence and retains him as a favourite at court. Bisclavret accompanies him everywhere, faithfully. When the knight appears at court, he attacks him. The king calls him off. Since this is so out of character, the court concludes that the knight has wronged Bisclavret in some way. Some days later Bisclavret's wife comes to greet the king, when he is staying nearby. As soon as Bisclavret sees her, he leaps upon her and bites the

---

[64] Aelian *Nature of Animals* 1.36, Aristophanes of Byzantium (et al.) *Aristophanis historiae animalium epitome subjunctis Aeliani Timothei aliorumque eclogis* 2.241, *Geoponica* 15.1.7; cf., more generally, *Geoponica* 18.7.8, Ambrose *Hexaemeron* 6.4.29 (*PG* 14.252–3). Cf. Eckels 1937:23–4, Gordon 2015:30. Aelian further tells that there was an Egyptian plant named *lykoktonos* ('wolf-slayer') that would kill any wolf that stepped on it (9.18); nor could wolves set foot on the island of Crete or certain parts of Mt Olympus (3.32).

[65] See Small 2013 for the motifs of clothing and skin in all the texts discussed in the next two paragraphs.

nose off her face. The knights of the court are about to turn on Bisclavret when a wise man intervenes, again noting the uncharacteristic nature of the attack and pointing out that the woman is Bisclavret's wife. The woman is immediately held in suspicion and tortured, until she reveals all. The king forces the woman to bring Bisclavret's clothes back, and he gives them to him. But he is too ashamed to put them on in public, and is permitted to do so in the king's private chamber. In due course, the king returns to the chamber to find him sleeping there. The king is delighted by his reappearance, and returns his lands to him, with extra. Bisclavret's wife and her knight lover are banished from the realm. Several of the women descended from her are born noseless.[66] As in the Hermotimus tale, the consequences of the wife's treachery are visited upon the women of future generations. In an observation with a particular pertinence for our analysis of the classical material above, Claude Lecouteux observes that, in the Bisclavret story, 'Clothes are thus quite obviously a substitute for the body.'[67] In connection with this tale too I note Mauritz Schuster, Martin Smith, and Gareth Schmeling's interesting contention that Petronius' werewolf's technique of turning his clothes to stone with a circle of urine is a parody of an already traditional motif in accordance with which the werewolf hides his clothes under a stone.[68]

In the Picard French *Lai de Melion* (AD 1190–1204; summarized in Chapter 1), Melion tells his unfaithful wife to guard his clothing while he transforms into wolf in order to bring down a stag for her. It is implied, rather than directly stated, that she runs off with his clothes as she runs off with Melion's squire. The lay makes much also of the episode in which Melion is discreetly reclothed in association with his eventual transformation back into human form. However, there is some double determination here, for a magic ring is also needed to effect the transformation, in both directions. The motif of the faithless wife that exploits her husband's werewolf secret is also found in the Latin romance *Arthur and Gorlagon* (thirteenth–fourteenth century AD; also summarized in Chapter 1), although now without the original conjoined motif of the theft of the clothes. Indeed the theme of the unfaithful wife in itself fully pervades this text: not only is Gorlagon betrayed by his wife and so trapped as a wolf but also, in his wolf form, he detects

[66] Marie de France *Bisclavret* esp. ll.57–134, 261–314. For the text see Rychner 1966; for an English translation see, e.g., Otten 1986:256–61 (Mason). For discussion see Smith 1894:11–13; Summers 1933:219–20, Battaglia 1965:361–89, Bambeck 1973, Faure 1978, Suard 1980, Ménard 1984, Harf-Lancner 1985:217–24, Benkov 1988 (for the role of clothing in particular), Douglas 1992:112–16, Milin 1993:53–63, 76–81, Moreau 1998:9 ('Mélusinian'), Leshock 1999, Pluskowski 2006:177–9, Sconduto 2008:39–56, Crane 2013:42–68 (the last with care). *Bisclavret* was reworked and extended in *Biclarel*, a self-contained episode of *Le Roman de Renart le Contrefait* (AD 1322); for text and translation see Hopkins 2005:84–105. Here too the clothes and their preservation in secrecy are of fundamental importance (ll. 233–40, 256–68, 444–50). And even greater emphasis is laid upon the wife's infidelity she takes her lover even before learning of Biclarel's werewolfism (53–6) and even has the audacity to accuse Biclarel rather of being unfaithful to her (127).

[67] Lecouteux 2003 (1992):114.

[68] Schuster 1930:162, Smith 1975:173, and Schmeling 2011:257–8; scepticism at McDougall 1984:145.

and exposes the faithlessness of his brother Gargol's wife too; and, restored to human form, he proceeds to give the lesson of the general faithlessness of wives to Arthur—an admonition of the treatment the latter can expect to receive from Guinevere.[69]

The Petronius and Aesop tales clearly presume an alternative narrative, should the werewolf be unsuccessful in retrieving his clothes, and such a narrative seems to be manifest in the Bisclavret tale and to a certain extent the Melion tale. That the motif of the adulterous wife (actual or latent) who takes advantage of her husband's absence while he is on his supernatural outing itself existed already in antiquity is demonstrated by the Hermotimus story. I think, accordingly, it is highly likely that antiquity already knew a werewolf story in which a perfidious wife made off with her husband's clothes.

(Before moving on from Bisclavret and his fellow French-romance werewolves, let us note that its distinctive motif of the just werewolf is already present in antiquity too. The Homeric Circe's werewolves would seem to fit the bill,[70] as would the Arcadian werewolves that successfully abstain from human flesh during the period of their transformation.[71] But perhaps the clearest version of the just werewolf in antiquity comes in a quite anomalous version of the Lykaon tale offered by Timothy of Gaza (fl. in the reign of Anastasius, AD 491–518): 'And there was once a king Lykaon, who was Arcadian by birth and was devoted to justice. Even if he happened to have turned into a wolf, he did not transform his character at the same time, but remained just.'[72])

Werewolves and Innkeepers: a Kaleidoscoping of Werewolf-tale Motifs

Let us return to Petronius. In Chapter 3 we saw, in the context of our discussion of the identifying-wound motif, how Petronius' tale can incorporate shards from

---

[69] I cannot forbear to mention another text from the same orbit as the three mentioned here, which contains a deceitful wife of a rather different sort. In the 12th–13th-c. AD *Vita S. Ronani* (preserved in Bibliothèque National MS 5275, edited at de Smedt 1889–93:i, 438–58) the (7th- or 9th-c. AD) Irish saint Ronan performs miracles and gathers followers in the region of Cournaille. In particular, he exercises control over the local wolves, compelling them to restore the sheep they take. A peasant woman, Keban, jealous of the hold the saint has over her husband, conceals her daughter in a coffin and accuses him of being a werewolf and of having eaten her. Ronan is tried before king Grallon. Dogs are launched against him to test his lupine nature, but they spare him and he is exonerated. The Holy Spirit then reveals all to Ronan. The girl is retrieved from the coffin, where, however, she has died of suffocation. Ronan restores her to life. Unchastened, Keban now accuses the saint of trying to seduce her. Wearied of her attacks, the saint departs from Cournaille and takes up the life of a hermit. Discussion at Milin 1991.

[70] Homer *Odyssey* 10.203–19; cf. Chapter 1.   [71] Pliny *Natural History* 8.80–2; cf. Chapter 6.

[72] Timothy of Gaza at Aristophanes of Byzantium (et al.) *Aristophanis historiae animalium epitome subjunctis Aeliani Timothei aliorumque eclogis* 2.237. The text is quoted more fully in Chapter 6.

other traditional werewolf tales untold. Now, in light of the *Bisclavret* analogue discussed in the section above, two further embedded shards seem to present themselves to us:

1. Like the *Bisclavret* tale, Petronius' tale incorporates *the motif of the unfaithful wife*, this in the form of Melissa, the wife of the innkeeper Terentius, who is maintaining an extramarital relationship with the immediate narrator himself, Niceros.[73] These details, though expounded with some colour, play no significant role in the central action of the tale, and one has to wonder why they are there and what their broader significance might be. I suggest that the motif of the cheating wife is knowingly borrowed from another, partly congruent werewolf tale, one already well established in tradition and broadly resembling the *Bisclavret* tale. If we push this analogy further, we cast her innkeeper husband, Terentius, in the role of the cuckold werewolf.

2. Like the *Bisclavret* tale, Petronius' tale incorporates *the motif of a victim of robbery running off*, albeit in the context of metaphor: 'I ran off home like the robbed innkeeper' (*tamquam copo compilatus*). If we push this analogy further in turn, our thoughts cannot but return again to the tale's actual innkeeper, Terentius. Dare we imagine, then, that our partly congruent werewolf tale focused on *an innkeeper-werewolf who ran off after having his vital clothes stolen from him by his unfaitfhul wife?*

That the ancient world was familiar with tales in which the hero (or, better, anti-hero) was trapped in animal form and faced the central challenge of recovering his human form is well illustrated by the other great classical Latin novel to survive. This is precisely the plot of Apuleius' *Metamorphoses*, in which Lucius is magically transformed into an ass, as of course it was of its mysterious Greek antecedent, reflected in the epitome *Onos*, whether penned by Lucian, Lucius of Patras, or person unknown (for which see Chapter 1).

As to the robbed innkeeper, the justification of this metaphor conventional in the Petronius scholarship, as evidenced by the commentaries of Smith and Schmeling, is underwhelming. This justification makes appeal to the supposed notion that innkeepers were traditionally themselves thievish, so that a robbed innkeeper would experience as it were a double dose of consternation.[74] The evidence usually

---

[73] For the possibility that Melissa may be projected as or assimilated to a prostitute, see Smith 1975:170, Schmeling 2011:253–4. The *Code of Justinian* has clear views on women connected with taverns: the daughters of innkeepers are associated with prostitutes and actresses as women in a moral category unfit for senators to marry (2.5.7); female slaves are forbidden to prostitute themselves in taverns under the pretence of serving as barmaids (4.56.3); senators and prefects are forbidden to confer citizenship on the daughters of innkeepers, amongst such other women as public actresses and the daughters of procurers (5.27.1); a tavern is one of the places a husband is permitted to kill his wife upon finding her there *in flagrante delicto* (9.9.30).

[74] E.g. Smith 1975:174 (on §62) and Schmeling 2011:259 (on §62). Cf. also Citroni 1984.

adduced in support does not make the case and rather suggests, simply, that an inn-keeper was, proverbially, far more likely to be a victim of robbery than a perpetrator of it. So it is, for example, that in the *Commentariolum petitionis* Quintus Cicero abuses Gaius Antonius of 'robbing all the innkeepers' in one or more of the prov-inces while purportedly undertaking a free legation, when he should rather have been canvassing in Rome in support of his candidacy for the consulship.[75]

Petronianists would do better to support their claim with some texts passed over in silence by both Smith and Schmeling. First, in *On Divination* Cicero has a wonderful story of an Arcadian visitor to Megara who was murdered by his inn-keeper (for his money, we presume). Somehow or other his ghost proleptically contrived to warn a friend that the murder was about to happen while the man himself yet lived. Unfortunately, the friend dismissed the dream, but he did take notice of a second one in which the ghost of the now dead man told him where to find the body. This he was able to do, bringing the innkeeper to justice.[76] Secondly, Meroe, the most dreadful witch of Apuleius' *Metamorphoses*, who ensnares Socrates with erotic magic and reduces him to abject penury before jugulating and temporarily reanimating him as he tries to escape, is also an innkeeper by trade (cf. Chapter 1).[77] Apuleius may also imply that innkeepers had a more gen-eral reputation for stealing from their guests too.[78] Thirdly, Galen refers in pass-ing to what is evidently an urban myth (in our terms, rather than his):

It is possible to understand the similarity of pig flesh to human being from the fact that some people have eaten human flesh as if it were pig flesh without

---

[75] Quintus Cicero *Commentariolum petitionis* 2. The phraseology used (*caupones omnes compilare*) is quite similar to Petronius', while the general sense seems to be metaphorical, or at any rate heavily metonymic. The other loci adduced are:
- Theophrastus *Characters* 6.5, where it is observed that the victim of *aponoia* (folly) is likely to go in for innkeeping.
- Varro *Menippean Satires* F329 Astbury = Nonius Marcellus *Compendiosa doctrina* 25.1, which may mean, 'that an innkeeper cheated [*sc.* someone] of money [*aes defraudasse copo-nem*], smeared a good woman [or a snake, according to the MSS] with mud and had a quarrel [literally "drew the saw"] with a ferryman', but would more naturally be construed to mean, 'that he [or she, person unidentified] cheated an innkeeper of money, smeared... [etc.]'; cf. Kleberg 1957:83–4.
- Aesop *Fables* 419 Perry = 196 Halm = 301 Hausrath and Hunger, discussed in Chapter 3 (and see further below), which rather projects the innkeeper as the victim of theft rather than the perpetrator of it. Rogge 1927:1021–2 argued that the 'robbed innkeeper' of Petronius was a specific reference to this Aesopic tale, the innkeeper running in terror from the supposed werewolf. Lefèvre 2003 agrees and further argues that Niceros' tale and Trimalchio's responding witch tale (Petronius *Satyricon* 63) have a common conception, with both of them making significant reference to Aesopic fables, Trimalchio's tale refer-ring, with its 'ass on the roof-tiles', to Babrius 125 Perry.

The relevance of innkeeper figures in early Latin drama is unclear. Ennius had a comedy entitled *Caupuncula* ('Little Landlady'; Warmington 1935–40:i, 360–1 no. 381) while Novius wrote an Atellan farce entitled *Maccus Copo* ('Innkeeper-Clown'; Frassinetti 1955:59). Cf. Schmeling 2011:259.

[76] Cicero *On Divination* 1.57 (44 BC).

[77] Apuleius *Metamorphoses* 1.5–19, esp. 7 for the innkeeping.

[78] Apuleius *Metamorphoses* 1.17.

having any suspicion of it, either in relation to taste or in relation to smell. For this was revealed to have been done by wicked innkeepers and others.

Galen *De alimentorum facultatibus* p.333 Helmreich (*CMG*)[79]

Presumably the human flesh in question derived from fellow guests the innkeepers had murdered to rob (in a doubly profitable enterprise).

These texts also imply that innkeepers were perceived, more broadly, as sinister and dangerous threats. In this connection, we have cause to recall again Augustine's Italian innkeeping women who drug their guests with pieces of cheese in order to turn them into beasts of burden.[80] We may also note that Artemidorus tells that dreams of innkeepers presage death for the sick, because innkeepers and death alike welcome all.[81]

Why might the werewolf or our proto-Bisclavret tale have run off? If we cleave closely to the Bisclavret tale itself, we might suggest that he runs off into the woods (or further into the woods) in his wolf form because, having been robbed of his clothes, he is now trapped in that form. But it is also possible that he ran off upon initially perceiving that his clothes were under threat, in order, that is, to retrieve or protect them. We may adduce an analogue (regrettably recent, alas) for the motif of the werewolf that runs off after his clothes have been interfered with. This is to be found in a Flemish story published by T. P. A. Lansens in 1855, which I quote verbatim from Kirby Smith's English rendering:[82]

A Flemish shepherd received a wolfskin from the devil on condition that he would put it on nights and go about to frighten people. At last he grew weary of it; but there was only one way to escape the skin and its consequences, which was to burn it; but, until it was completely burned to ashes, the shepherd would feel as much agony as though the skin were actually upon him. One day his master sent him off to Ypres and when he judged that the shepherd had reached the city he took the skin out of the hollow tree where it had been hidden and threw it into the fire. Instantly, the shepherd, though far off in Ypres, began to feel all the pains of being burned alive and *rushed for home at the top of his speed* [my emphasis]. Just as he reached the house the skin was completely consumed and his torture at once ceased. He thanked his master dozens of times, delighted because he was at last free of the devil and could now sleep in peace.

Smith 1894:29[83]

[79] = p.182 Wilkins = vi p.663 Kühn.   [80] Augustine *City of God* 18,18.
[81] Artemidorus *Oneirocritica* 3,57; cf. Fedeli 1995: 49.   [82] Lansens 1855:170–1.
[83] Haxthausen 1856:i, 322 reports on Armenian werewolfism. After sinning, certain women are compelled to be werewolves for seven years. A spirit comes by night and compels them to don a wolf-skin and acquire a wolfish nature, devouring children, starting with her own. When day comes the werewolf conceals the skin and returns to her own form. A hunter once tracked a wolf that had stolen a child. He found the child's mangled body, from which a trail of blood led to a hole in the rocks where the wolfskin was concealed. He threw the skin into a fire, whereupon a woman appeared, screaming in agony and attempting to rescue the skin from the fire. When the skin was completely consumed, she too disappeared in a puff of smoke. Cf. Smith 1894:29–30.

The parallel is suggestive, even though it is by no means exact for a proto-Bisclavret story: the clothes in question here are not those that confer human shape, but those that confer wolf shape.

And then one wonders whether there might also be some significant wordplay in the term *compīlātus*. The compound *com-pīlō* (long *i*) means 'to rob', but the simple *pĭlō* (short *i*), is a contronym, its literal meaning, 'to hair', yielding the contradictory practical meanings of both 'to grow hairy' and 'to pluck of hair' (cf. English 'to dust', which can mean both 'to cover with dust' and 'to remove dust from'). Might a *cōpō compīlātus* be an 'innkeeper grown (completely) hairy' or indeed an 'innkeeper stripped of his hair'?[84] The 'innkeeper grown (completely) hairy' reading would suit a context in which a lupine werewolf was running to prevent the theft of his human clothes, or fleeing in the wake of such a theft; the 'innkeeper stripped of his hair' reading would suit a humanoid werewolf running to protect his wolfskin, under conditions perhaps similar to those of the Flemish tale.

That Niceros should be implicitly and indirectly comparing himself to a were-wolf as he runs off to escape one—or to find one?—might be a nice ironic touch for Petronius (and indeed we have already noted that Niceros compares himself to a ghost). Let us return once again to the slight awkwardness of Aesop's story (discussed in Chapter 3), the focus of which switches rather oddly and awkwardly from the pretend werewolf's anxiety about the potential theft of his clothes to his actual theft of the innkeeper's clothes. Perhaps here too we are dealing with a tale in which traditional motifs have become kaleidoscoped: the innkeeper must not, at any cost, have his cloak stolen, for he, again, is a (real) werewolf, and depends upon it for his human form—and if the thief were inadvertently to turn the into a werewolf by stripping him of his cloak, that is of his humanity, what, do we suppose, would happen to him next? That innkeepers should be associated with werewolfism chimes in well with their association with cannibalism, given the association that that activity had with werewolfism in its own right (see Chapter 3 again on this).

Conclusion

Building on the themes explored in Chapters 2 and 3, this chapter has argued that the soul-projection ideas so strongly associated with werewolfism in the medieval and early modern periods were already associated with it in the ancient world. This notion is more or less explicitly articulated by Augustine, but long before him there obtained a striking parallel between werewolf narratives (in which the werewolf off on his adventures leaves behind the human shell constituted by his clothes and must keep them secure, so that he can don them again to retrieve his

---

[84] See *OLD* s.vv. *compīlō*, *pĭlō*.

human form), and the 'Greek shaman' narratives (in which the soul-projector must keep his catatonic human body secure as he sends his soul off on his adventures, so that the soul can reanimate it again and he can continue his physical life in the world). Petronius' intriguingly complex werewolf narrative, when taken with other evidence, presupposes the existence already in antiquity of other werewolf narratives broadly along the lines of Marie de France's *Bisclavret*, in which a werewolf, perhaps an innkeeper, is stranded in lupine form when his clothes are stolen by his unfaithful wife.

5

The Demon in a Wolfskin:
a Werewolf at Temesa?

This chapter picks up the theme of the association between werewolves and ghosts, developed in Chapters 2 and 4, with a study of the intriguing but complex traditions bearing upon the Hero of Temesa.

The Sources

There are several sources for the battle between Euthymus, the boxer of (Epizephyrian) Locri who won Olympic victories in 484, 476, and 472 BC, and the Hero of Temesa.[1] The fullest and best known of these is Pausanias, who wrote in the later second century AD. He attaches his account—which Dunbabin compared to 'a page of *Beowulf*'—to his notes on the statue of Euthymus at Olympia.[2] It falls into two parts, which it is important to keep separate; for the convenience of the exposition ahead, we shall designate them as 'Pausanias-A' and 'Pausanias-B.' The first part is a narrative:

> When Euthymus returned to Italy he fought with the Hero [*Hērōs*]. This was the background. They say that, in the course of his wanderings after the sack of Troy, Odysseus was brought to shore by the winds to several cities in Italy and Sicily, and in particular they say that he put in with his ships at Temesa. Anyway, one of his sailors got drunk there and raped a virgin. In punishment for this wrong-doing he was stoned to death by the locals. Odysseus thought no more about his loss and sailed off. However, the demon [*daimōn*] of the man that had been stoned let no opportunity pass, but killed the Temesans indiscriminately and launched attacks on every age-group. It came to the point that the Temesans were preparing to abandon Italy altogether, but the Pythia forbade them to do so. Rather, she bade them propitiate the Hero, enclose a precinct for him, build

---

[1] For a collation of the sources, with Italian translations and notes, see Visintin 1992:9–39; cf. also Pfeiffer 1965 at Callimachus F99 and Mele 1983:858–67. For Euthymus' Olympic victories, see Moretti 1957 nos.191, 214, 227. The Hero of Temesa is the subject of a well-regarded Dutch novel with Freudian themes, Simon Vestdijk's *De held van Temesa* of 1962; the tale is narrated, unreliably, by one Plexippus, who becomes the Hero's final priest; cf. Bremmer 1997.

[2] Dunbabin 1948:372–3; cf. Radt 2002–11:vi, p.150.

him a temple, and give him the fairest of Temesa's virgins as bride each year. They carried out the god's behest and the demon stopped terrorizing them. Now Euthymus came to Temesa, and it happened that the custom was being carried out for the demon at that time. He inquired into the rites they were performing and conceived the wish to enter the temple, and having done so to take a look at the virgin. When he saw her, his first reaction was pity for her, his second desire. The girl swore that she would marry him if he saved her, so Euthymus equipped himself and waited for the demon to arrive. He defeated the Hero in a battle, and (since he had driven him from the land) he [the Hero] disappeared and dove into the sea. Thereupon Euthymus had a glorious marriage and the people of the place were delivered from the demon forevermore. I also heard a story of the following kind about Euthymus, to the effect that he lived to an extreme old age, escaped death, and rather departed from the world of men in an alternative way. I heard that Temesa is still inhabited in my own time from a man that had sailed there to trade.   Pausanias 6.6.7–11 ('Pausanias-A')[3]

Having told this story, Pausanias then passes on directly to describe an 'ancient' image he saw:

That is just what I heard, but I know what follows because I happened across a painting. It was a copy of an ancient [archaias] one. It showed a young man, Sybaris, and a river, Kalabros, and a spring, Lyka. There was also a hero-shrine and the city of Temesa, and in the midst of these things was the demon that Euthymus cast out. His skin was awfully black and he was utterly terrifying to

---

[3] ἐπανήκων δὲ ἐς Ἰταλίαν τότε δὴ ἐμαχέσατο πρὸς τὸν Ἥρω· τὰ δὲ ἐς αὐτὸν εἶχεν οὕτως. Ὀδυσσέα πλανώμενον μετὰ ἅλωσιν τὴν Ἰλίου κατενεχθῆναί φασιν ὑπὸ ἀνέμων ἔς τε ἄλλας τῶν ἐν Ἰταλίᾳ καὶ Σικελίᾳ πόλεων, ἀφικέσθαι δὲ καὶ ἐς Τεμέσαν ὁμοῦ ταῖς ναυσί· μεθυσθέντα οὖν ἐνταῦθα ἕνα τῶν ναυτῶν παρθένον βιάσασθαι καὶ ὑπὸ τῶν ἐπιχωρίων ἀντὶ τούτου καταλευσθῆναι (8.) τοῦ ἀδικήματος. Ὀδυσσέα μὲν δὴ ἐν οὐδενὶ λόγῳ θέμενον αὐτοῦ τὴν ἀπώλειαν ἀποπλέοντα οἴχεσθαι, τοῦ καταλευσθέντος δὲ ἀνθρώπου τὸν δαίμονα οὐδένα ἀνιέναι καιρὸν ἀποκτείνοντά τε ὁμοίως τοὺς ἐν τῇ Τεμέσῃ καὶ ἐπεξερχόμενον ἐπὶ πᾶσαν ἡλικίαν, ἐς ὃ ἡ Πυθία τὸ παράπαν ἐξ Ἰταλίας ὡρμημένους φεύγειν Τεμέσαν μὲν ἐκλιπεῖν οὐκ εἴα, τὸν Ἥρω σφᾶς ἐκέλευσεν ἱλάσκεσθαι τέμενός τε ἀποτεμομένους οἰκοδομήσασθαι ναόν, διδόναι δὲ κατὰ ἔτος αὐτῷ γυναῖκα (9.) τῶν ἐν Τεμέσῃ παρθένων τὴν καλλίστην. τοῖς μὲν δὴ τὰ ὑπὸ τοῦ θεοῦ προστεταγμένα ὑπουργοῦσι δεῖμα ἀπὸ τοῦ δαίμονος ἐς τἄλλα ἦν οὐδέν· Εὔθυμος δὲ—ἀφίκετο γὰρ ἐς τὴν Τεμέσαν, καί πως τηνικαῦτα τὸ ἔθος ἐποιεῖτο τῷ δαίμονι—πυνθάνεται τὰ παρόντα σφίσι, καὶ ἐσελθεῖν τε ἐπεθύμησεν ἐς τὸν ναὸν καὶ τὴν παρθένον ἐσελθὼν θεάσασθαι. ὡς δὲ εἶδε, τὰ μὲν πρῶτα ἐς οἶκτον, δεύτερα δὲ ἀφίκετο καὶ ἐς ἔρωτα αὐτῆς· καὶ ἡ παῖς τε συνοικήσειν κατώμνυτο αὐτὴν καὶ ὁ Εὔθυμος ἐνεσκευασμένος ἔμενε (10.) τὴν ἔφοδον τοῦ δαίμονος. ἐνίκα τε δὴ τῇ μάχῃ καὶ—ἐξηλαύνετο γὰρ ἐκ τῆς γῆς—ὁ Ἥρως ἀφανίζεταί τε καταδὺς ἐς θάλασσαν καὶ γάμος τε ἐπιφανὴς Εὐθύμῳ καὶ ἀνθρώποις τοῖς ἐνταῦθα ἐλευθερία τοῦ λοιποῦ σφισιν ἦν ἀπὸ τοῦ δαίμονος. ἤκουσα δὲ καὶ τοιόνδε ἔτι ἐς τὸν Εὔθυμον, ὡς γήρως τε ἐπὶ μακρότατον ἀφίκοιτο καὶ ὡς ἀποθανεῖν ἐκφυγὼν αὖθις ἕτερόν τινα ἐξ ἀνθρώπων [ἄλλον] ἀπέλθοι τρόπον· οἰκεῖσθαι δὲ τὴν Τεμέσαν καὶ ἐς ἐμὲ ἀνδρὸς ἤκουσα πλεύσαντος (11.) κατὰ ἐμπορίαν. Given the nature of the close readings attempted in this chapter, and also the textual difficulties that beset the passages in question, I adopt here the practice of supplying the original Greek and Latin more systematically than I do in other chapters.

see. He had a wolfskin for his clothing. The picture was inscribed, and gave him the name Lybas.   Pausanias 6.6.11 ('Pausanias-B')[4]

Where did Pausanias see the picture? Probably somewhere at Olympia too. Presumably not in Temesa, for the very existence of which he has just had to rely upon the verbal report of another. And what did Pausanias mean by 'ancient', *archaias*? The word can, on occasion, correspond to our use of the word 'Archaic', but it can also, on occasion, signify nothing more specific than 'pre-Roman'.[5] Paola Zancani Montuoro guessed that the painting derived from the sixth century BC; Agnès Rouveret guessed that it belonged to the second half of the fifth century BC, a time at which personifications were in vogue with painters.[6]

Let us pass the remainder of the relevant sources in review in effectively chronological order. The Callimachean *Diegeseis* are little summaries of Callimachus' poems preserved in a first- or second-century AD papyrus discovered in Tebtunis.[7] Insofar as we may take them to represent the content of Callimachus' work accurately, they give us access to a tradition current by the early third century BC. The relevant *diegesis* reads as follows:

[Summary of the poem beginning with the line] *Of Euthymus*,[8] *everything in the house of the Zeus to whom Pisa belongs*...: Callimachus tells that in Temesa a hero [*hērōs*] left behind from Odysseus' ship exacted tribute from the locals and the neighbouring peoples. They would bring along a bed and a girl of marriageable age for him, leave them and depart without turning backwards.[9] In the morning, her parents would take her back again, a woman instead of a virgin. The boxer Euthymus liberated them from this tribute...

Diegeseis, *P. Milano Vogliano* i.18, col. iv, ll. 5–15
= Callimachus *Aitia* 4 F98 Pf.[10]

---

[4] Τό δε μὲν ἤκουσα, γραφῇ δὲ τοιάδε ἐπιτυχὼν οἶδα· ἦν δὲ αὕτη γραφῆς μίμημα ἀρχαίας. νεανίσκος Σύβαρις καὶ Κάλαβρός τε ποταμὸς καὶ Λύκα πηγή, πρὸς δὲ ἡρῷόν τε καὶ Τεμέσα ἦν ἡ πόλις, ἐν δέ σφισι καὶ δαίμων ὄντινα ἐξέβαλεν ὁ Εὔθυμος, χρόαν τε δεινῶς μέλας καὶ τὸ εἶδος ἅπαν ἐς τὰ μάλιστα φοβερός, λύκου δὲ ἀμπίσχετο δέρμα ἐσθῆτα· ἐτίθετο δὲ καὶ ὄνομα Λύβαν τὰ ἐπὶ τῇ γραφῇ γράμματα.

[5] Pausanias' use of the word *archaios*: Pirenne-Delforge 2008:41–3, Hedreen 2016:111; cf., more generally, Casevitz 2004.

[6] Zancani Montuoro 1968–9:13–19 (also suggesting Olympia as the location), endorsed by Mele 1983:866–7; Rouveret 1990:330–9, seemingly endorsed by Casevitz et al. 2002:137 (*ad loc.*). Papachatzis 1963–9 *ad loc.* has no relevant comment.

[7] Falivene 2011 offers a most helpful and interesting history and analysis of the papyrus.

[8] The universally accepted emendation of the papyrus' 'Eudemus' (Εὔδημου); cf. Pfeiffer 1965 *ad loc.* and Visintin 1992:16.

[9] Presumably because there must be no show of regret in those making the offering.

[10] Εὐθύμου τὰ μὲν ὅσσα παραὶ Διὶ Πῖσαν ἔχοντι. Ὅτι ἐν Τεμέσῃ ἥρως περίλοιπος τῆς Ὀδυσσέως νεὼς ἐδασμοφόρει ἐπιχωρίους τε καὶ ὁμόρους, οὓς κομίζοντας αὐτῷ κλίνην καὶ κόρην ἐπίγαμον ἐάσαντας ἀπέρχεσθαι ἀμεταστρεπτεί, ἕωθεν δὲ τοὺς γονεῖς ἀντὶ παρθένου γυναῖκα κομίζεσθαι. τὸν δὲ δασμὸν τοῦτον ἀπέλυσεν Εὔθυμος πύκτης...λέξας τὰς τῷ ἥρῳ...(I do not indicate here minor editorial restorations.)

A second fragment of Callimachus, refracted in Pliny's *Natural History*, also bears upon Euthymus. The passage of Pliny in question is corrupt, as are so many of the texts we must deal with in this chapter, but its gist remains clear:

> At the behest of the same [*sc.* Delphic] oracle, and with the endorsement of Zeus, the highest of the gods, Euthymus the boxer, ever the victor at Olympia save for a single defeat, was sanctified during his own lifetime and with his own knowledge of it. His homeland was Locri in Italy. I see that Callimachus tells that his statue at Locri and a second one at Olympia were both struck by a thunderbolt on the same day, that this was a unique marvel[?], that the command was given to make sacrifice to him[?], that this custom was maintained during his lifetime as well as after his death, and that the most surprising aspect of all this was the fact that it was the will of the gods.
>
> Pliny *Natural History* 7.152 = Callimachus *Aitia* 4 F99 Pf.[11]

Strabo, writing under the emperor Tiberius, offers rather different details in relation to the Hero:

> Near Temesa there is a heroon of Polites,[12] one of Odysseus' companions, beneath a canopy of wild olives [*agrielaiois*]. He was deceitfully killed by the barbarians and so became deeply wrathful, with the results that those that dwelled in the region collected tribute for him in accordance with some oracle, and that a proverb came about applicable to the [...?],[13] people saying of them that the Hero in Temesa had fallen upon them. They tell the story that when the Epizephyrian Locrians captured the city, the boxer Euthymus entered a bout [*katabanta*] with him and defeated him in a battle. He compelled him to release the locals from their tribute.   Strabo C255[14]

---

[11] The version of the text printed by Pfeiffer (1965) reads as follows. *Consecratus est vivus sentiensque eiusdem oraculi iussi et Iovis deorum summi adstipulatu Euthymus pycta, semper Olympiae victor et semel victus. patria ei Locri in Italia; ibi imaginem eius et Olympiae alteram eodem die tactam fulmine Callimachum ut nihil aliud miratum video †ad eumque† iussisse sacrificare, quod et vivo factitatum et mortuo, nihilque de eo mirum aliud quam hoc placuisse dis.* Cf. Visintin 1992:29–30.

[12] For Odysseus' crewman Polites in the *Odyssey*, see 10.224. Visintin 1992:21 considers the possibility that the cult may have originally been a 'citizen hero' (i.e. *hērōs politēs*), with its recipient in due course becoming identified with Odysseus' companion.

[13] The manuscripts are corrupt, offering the nonsensical πρὸς αὐτοὺς μηδείς. We need a word or phrase equivalent in meaning to Eustathius' 'those that lose their temper at the wrong time' (τῶν ἀγριαινόντων ἔξω καιροῦ), for which see below. Of the numerous conjectures recorded by Radt, the best are Piccolo's πρὸς τοὺς ἄγαν θυμώδεις ('to those excessively hot-headed') and Holwerda's πρὸς ἀλύτους μήνεις ('to unresolved bouts of wrath'), the latter being Radt's favourite for reasons of both palaeography and meaning. See the apparatus and commentary of Radt 2002–11 *ad loc.* (ii. p.136; vi, pp.148–50); cf. also Visintin 1992:18.

[14] ἔστι δὲ πλησίον τῆς Τεμέσης ἡρῷον ἀγριελαίοις συνηρεφὲς Πολίτου, τῶν Ὀδυσσέως ἑταίρων, ὃν δολοφονηθέντα ὑπὸ τῶν βαρβάρων γενέσθαι βαρύμηνιν, ὥστε τοὺς περιοίκους δασμολογεῖν αὐτῷ κατά τι λόγιον καὶ παροιμίαν εἶναι πρὸς †αὐτοὺς μηδείς†, τὸν ἥρωα τὸν ἐν Τεμέσῃ λεγόντων ἐπικεῖσθαι αὐτοῖς. Λοκρῶν δὲ τῶν Ἐπιζεφυρίων ἑλόντων τὴν πόλιν, Εὔθυμον μυθεύουσι τὸν πύκτην καταβάντα ἐπ' αὐτὸν κρατῆσαι τῇ μάχῃ, καὶ βιάσασθαι παραλῦσαι τοῦ δασμοῦ τοὺς ἐπιχωρίους.

Strabo's words on the proverb are corrupt too. However, Eustathius cites him for it, paraphrasing the current passage, and declares that the proverb applies to 'those that lose their temper at the wrong time'.[15] The pseudo-Plutarchian *Proverbs* of the first or second century AD explains it as follows:

> *The Hero in Temesa*: Whenever someone demands payment only to be found owing himself, he has become the Hero in Temesa [or: the Hero in Temesa has come about].   pseudo-Plutarch *Proverbs* 2.31 (at p.342 *CPG*)[16]

Aelian, writing in the early third century AD, writes on the proverb too, while also explaining for us Pausanias' mysterious words on the nature of Euthymus' death:

> Euthymus the Locrian – one of the Locrians in Italy – was a good boxer. He is believed to have been most amazing for the strength of his body. For the Locrians point to a stone of the greatest size, which he carried and placed before his doors. And he put an end to the Hero in Temesa, when he was exacting tribute from those that lived nearby. For he came to his temple, which was forbidden to most, and entered a contest [*diēgōnisato*] with him. He compelled him to pay back more than he had plundered. This was the origin of the proverb said of those who make a loss in their profits, 'The Hero of Temesa will come.' They say that this same Euthymus [*ton auton Euthymon*] descended into [*katabanta*] the river Kaikinos, which flows past the city of the Locrians, and disappeared [*aphanisthēnai*].   Aelian *Varia historia* 8.18[17]

Aelian perhaps depends in part on Strabo or a kindred source here: like Strabo, he projects Euthymus' battle against the Hero metaphorically as a further athletic contest for him.[18] Bruno Currie interestingly compares Aelian's words on Euthymus' disappearance with the *Alexander Romance*'s account of the dying Alexander's attempt to throw himself into the river Euphrates so that he might be considered a god.[19]

---

[15] Eustathius on Homer *Odyssey* 1.185: τῶν ἀγριαινόντων ἔξω καιροῦ. Cf. also Eustathius on Homer *Odyssey* prooimion, where he refers in passing to 'the deeply wrathful Temesan Hero of the proverbs (ὁ ἐν παροιμίαις Τεμέσιος ἥρως ὁ βαρύμηνις)'.

[16] Ἐν Τεμέσῃ ἥρως· ὅτ' ἀπαιτῶν τις αὐτὸς προσοφείλων εὑρεθῇ, ὁ ἐν Τεμέσῃ γέγονεν ἥρως.

[17] Εὔθυμος ὁ Λοκρὸς τῶν ἐν Ἰταλίᾳ πύκτης ἀγαθὸς ἦν, ῥώμῃ τε σώματος πεπίστευται θαυμασιώτατος γενέσθαι· λίθον γὰρ μεγέθει μέγιστον δεικνύουσι Λοκροί, ὃν ἐκόμισε καὶ ἔθηκε πρὸ τῶν θυρῶν. καὶ τὸν ἐν Τεμέσῃ ἥρωα φόρους πραττόμενον παρὰ τῶν προσοίκων ἔπαυσεν· ἀφικόμενος γὰρ ἐς τὸ ἱερὸν αὐτοῦ, ὅπερ ἄβατον ἦν τοῖς πολλοῖς, διηγωνίσατο πρὸς αὐτόν, καὶ ἠνάγκασεν ὧνπερ ἐσύλησεν ἀποτῖσαι πλείω. ἐντεῦθέν τοι καὶ διέρρευσεν ἡ παροιμία ἡ λέγουσα ἐπὶ τῶν ἀλυσιτελῶς τι κερδαινόντων ὅτι αὐτοῖς ἀφίξεται ὁ ἐν Τεμέσῃ ἥρως. Λέγουσι δὲ τὸν αὐτὸν Εὔθυμον καταβάντα ἐπὶ τὸν Καικῖνον ποταμὸν ὅς ἐστι πρὸ τῆς τῶν Λοκρῶν πόλεως ἀφανισθῆναι.

[18] On this imagery, cf. Fontenrose 1968:80.

[19] Currie 2002:41; *Alexander Romance* (A) 3.32.4–7 ≈ (Arm.) §268 Wolohojian; the tale is attested prior to this at *Liber de morte* 101–2 (text at Thomas 1960 and Heckel 1988) and Arrian *Anabasis* 7.27.3. Cf. Arrian *Anabasis* 7.27.3; discussion at Ogden 2011:128–9 and Baynham 2018.

Key parts of the tenth-century AD *Suda*'s material on Euthymus and the Hero would seem to be derivative of all three of Pausanias, Strabo, and pseudo-Plutarch:

Euthymus. Euthymus was a citizen of Epizephyrian Locri, and he competed in boxing against Theogenes of Thasos. Theogenes beat him and treated him with contempt, but he was not then able to win the wild olive [*kotinos*], because he had been exhausted by Euthymus. Euthymus prevailed in the three successive Olympiads and was crowned, because he faced not the Thasian as his opponent in the boxing, but others. This Euthymus also competed [*ēgōnisato*] against the Hero in Temesa, Alybas [*ton en Temesēi hērōa Alybanta*]. Temesa is in Italy, but Odysseus came to it in the course of his wanderings around Sicily. One of his sailors got drunk there and raped a maiden; he was stoned to death by the locals. Setting no store by the loss, Odysseus sailed on, but the demon [*daimōn*] of the dead man would not leave the people of Temesa be, attacking them and murdering them, with the result that they planned to abandon the city and escape, and would have done so had not the Pythia held them back. She told them to propitiate the Hero by constructing a precinct for him and giving over to him every year the most beautiful maiden they had, to be his wife. Euthymus learned that these rites had been performed for many years, entered the precinct, saw the maiden and felt pity for her. He also felt desire for her. So he equipped himself to make war on the demon, and as the demon approached by night he defeated him and drove him out, with the result that he no longer appeared there [*phanēnai*]. Euthymus took the maiden as his wife.   *Suda* s.v. Εὔθυμος[20]

The Hero in Temesa. Whenever someone demands payment only to find themselves owing more, the saying is, 'The Hero in Temesa.'

Suda s.v. Ὁ ἐν Τεμέσῃ ἥρως[21]

---

[20] Εὔθυμος, Λοκρὸς τῶν Ἐπιζεφυρίων, ὃς ἠγωνίσατο πὺξ πρὸς Θεαγένην τὸν Θάσιον. καὶ ὑπερεβάλετο μὲν ὁ Θεαγένης, ἐπηρεάσας τὸν Εὔθυμον, οὐ μέντοι ἐν παγκρατίῳ λαβεῖν ἠδυνήθη τὸν κότινον, προκατειργασμένος ὑπὸ Εὐθύμου. ἐνίκησε δὲ Εὔθυμος τὰς ἐφεξῆς Ὀλυμπιάδας τρεῖς καὶ ἐστεφανώθη, τοῦ Θασίου μὴ καταστάντος οἱ ἐς πυγμήν, ἀλλ' ἑτέρων. οὗτος ὁ Εὔθυμος ἠγωνίσατο καὶ πρὸς τὸν ἐν Τεμέσῃ ἥρωα Ἀλύβαντα. ἡ δὲ Τέμεσα τῆς Ἰταλίας ἐστίν, ἐς ἣν Ὀδυσσεὺς πλανώμενος περὶ Σικελίαν ἦλθεν. ἔνθα εἷς τῶν ναυτῶν μεθύσας καὶ παρθένον βιασάμενος κατελεύσθη ὑπὸ τῶν ἐγχωρίων. καὶ Ὀδυσσεὺς μὲν ἐν οὐδενὶ τὴν ἀπώλειαν θέμενος ἔπλει, τοῦ δὲ τελευτήσαντος ὁ δαίμων οὐκ ἀνίει τοὺς ἐν Τεμέσῃ ἀνθρώπους ἐπερχόμενος καὶ φονεύων, ὥστε καὶ ὥρμησαν φυγεῖν καταλιπόντες τὴν πόλιν, εἰ μὴ ἡ Πυθία σφᾶς ἐπέσχε, τὸν ἥρωα ἱλάσκεσθαι τέμενος ἐργασαμένους καὶ κατ' ἐνιαυτὸν τὴν καλλίστην οὖσαν παρθένον ἐς γυναῖκα ἐπιδιδόντας. ταῦτα πολλοῖς ἔτεσι τελούμενα πυθόμενος ὁ Εὔθυμος ἐσῆλθεν εἰς τὸ τέμενος καὶ τὴν παρθένον ἰδὼν καὶ οἰκτείρας, πρὸς δὲ καὶ ἐς ἔρωτα ἐλθὼν ἐνεσκευάσατο ὡς πολεμήσων τῷ δαίμονι, καὶ αὐτὸν μὲν νύκτωρ ἐπελθόντα ἐνίκησε καὶ ἐξήλασεν, ὡς μηκέτι αὐτόθι φανῆναι, τὴνδὲ παρθένον γαμετὴν ἠγάγετο.

[21] Ὁ ἐν Τεμέσῃ ἥρως· ὅταν τις ἀπαιτῇ τι μᾶλλον προσοφείλων εὑρεθῇ, τότε λέγεται ὁ ἐν Τεμέσῃ ἥρως. I can find no merit in the translation currently offered by the *Suda Online* website: 'Whenever someone is found making a request [*sc.* for exemption] but still owing, then "the Hero at Temesa" is said.'

The bulk of the *Suda*'s narrative (s.v. *Εὔθυμος*) would seem to derive from Pausanias, while the conceit of projecting Euthymus' battle against the Hero metaphorically as a further athletic contest for him again looks Strabonian, and the wording in which the *Suda* explains the proverb (s.v. *Ὁ ἐν Τεμέσῃ ἥρως*) closely resembles that of pseudo-Plutarch (while not necessarily offering exactly the same interpretation).

The Proverb

The most lucid unpacking of the proverb is Aelian's, who maps the person to whom the proverb is applied, the one losing money as he attempts to make it, onto the Hero. But this is unsatisfactory: it is not at all clear how Euthymus compelled the Hero to pay back more than he took, whether he killed him (again!) or merely banished him. Aelian's mapping may, however, be shared by pseudo-Plutarch (if we take the first and perhaps slightly easier reading suggested above), and by the *Suda* (if only because the latter borrows pseudo-Plutarch's phraseology).

However, the one losing money as he attempts to make it should surely be mapped, rather, onto the people of Temesa in their initial misfortune: it is they that demand recompense from Polites, the Hero, for the rape of the girl, only to find themselves owing to him instead the licence to rape—or even murder—further girls, *sine die*: that is the effect of the Hero 'falling upon them', in Strabo's words. It is after all possible that pseudo-Plutarch offers this interpretation (if we take the second and slightly less easy reading suggested above), and so too the *Suda* (again because the latter borrows pseudo-Plutarch's phraseology). And it is also probable that Eustathius read both the proverb and Strabo in this way. As we have seen, for him the proverb is applicable to people who lose their temper at the wrong time: these people surely map onto the Temesans, who inadvisedly stone Polites to death in their rage at his initial act of rape.[22]

Some Scholarship on Euthymus and the Hero

A breathtaking amount of scholarship has been published on Euthymus and the Hero of Temesa. We cannot take account of all of it here.[23] Amongst older contributions let us pick out just Giulio Giannelli's 1924 book, in which he found the

---

[22] Discussion of the proverb also at Visintin 1992:22–8.

[23] For the doxography up until 1992, see Visintin 1992:41–58. Among the more important general discussions of Euthymus and the Hero are: Frazer 1898:iv, 23–4, Pais 1908, 1909, de Sanctis 1909–10, Giannelli 1924:261–71, Gernet 1981 (1936), Fontenrose 1968, Bohringer 1979, Mele 1983, Arias 1987, Visintin 1992, Casevitz et al. 2002:133–8, Currie 2002.

imagery of sacred prostitution of the sort famously discussed by Herodotus to underlie the traditions of the Hero.[24] Amongst more recent contributions let us note Monica Visintin's book-length study of 1992, *La vergine e l'eroe: Temesa e la leggenda di Euthymos di Locri*, which offers a useful systematic collation and presentation of the evidence and doxography for the legend and its thematic hinterlands, together with a less useful Proppian analysis of it;[25] and Bruno Currie's article of 2002, 'Euthymos of Locri: A case study in heroization in the Classical period', which remains the place of first resort for the subject.

Currie's key contribution has been to integrate into the debate the striking inscriptional evidence that tells us that Euthymus was worshipped as a river god. Herms of the later fourth century BC from the Cave of the Nymphs at Euthymus' own Locri Epizephyrii, the Grotta Caruso, are inscribed with the phrase 'sacred to Euthymus' and carry an image of him in typical river-god guise as a human-headed bull, à la Achelous. This surely does give a crisp context to Aelian's claim that Euthymus disappeared into the river Kaikinos: it was by this act, we can now see, that Euthymus actually became the river Kaikinos, or at any rate merged with it. On the basis of this Currie proceeds to argue that the Hero too had been a river god; that the historical Euthymus somehow contrived to challenge him to a fight, on the model of Heracles' challenge to Achelous; and that Euthymus prevailed in this and accordingly took over the Hero's role as a river god and his accompanying honours.[26]

However, one may regret four aspects of Currie's analysis. First, the direct evidence that the Hero was ever himself a river god or thought of as a river god is lacking. The best circumstantial indication that he may have been, and it is quite a remote one, comes in the tenth letter of the collection ascribed to Aeschines, perhaps composed in the first or second century AD, which, like the Callimachean material, speaks of a supernatural *droit de seigneur*. Here we are told that the girls of Troy took a ritual bath in the river Scamander while uttering a sacred phrase in which they requested him to take their virginity (*labe mou, Skamandre, tēn parthenian*). One Cimon had exploited the rite: he had disguised himself as the river in humanoid manifestation by garlanding himself with reeds, and as

---

[24] Gianelli 1924:261–71; cf. Phillips 1953:57, Currie 1992:30–1. Herodotus 1.197–200 (on the temple of Mylitta in Babylon). On this model, the girl's defloration did not obstruct her marriageability, but rather enabled it. For the tradition of sacred prostitution (intriguingly) in Euthymus' home city of Locri Epizephyrii, see Clearchus of Soli F43a Wehrli at Athenaeus 516a and Justin 21.3; Cordiano 2000 denies any connection between this tradition and the Temesan rite. For temple prostitution in the ancient world generally see Budin 2008 and Scheer 2009.

[25] Visintin 1992, with 155–66 for the curious, algebraic, Proppian analysis of the tale.

[26] Currie 2002 esp. 29–31, 35. For the herms see Arias 1987 plates i–v. Bohringer 1979:16–17 had previously argued that Euthymus took over the Hero's role in a rather different way—becoming a werewolf in his place!

the fair but naive Callirhoe made her call he had leaped out from a riverside bush in order to oblige.[27]

Secondly, Currie is too ready to infer that Pausanias' tale is talking about the same sort of sacred marriage ritual as the *Diegeseis* does and so, in effect, to merge the two sets of data;[28] in this he is in good company with Visintin, who contends that Pausanias actually derives his material directly from Callimachus.[29] Thirdly, and relatedly, he is too ready to historicize the tale (or tales) of Pausanias and the *Diegeseis* and to find in them an account of a historical cult succession.[30] As to this point, one is readily reminded of Sourvinou-Inwood's bromides in relation to the myths of the Delphic oracle: the myth of Apollo's defeat of Python does not represent at any level a historical account of change of owner for the oracle.[31] Fourthly, he has little or no interest in the lupine imagery associated with the Hero in Pausanias' picture and has no proper account to offer of it.

In the following two sections I give myself the task of establishing the importance of making a three-way differentiation between the accounts of the Hero given by Callimachus, by Pausanias' narrative (Pausanias-A), and by Pausanias' picture (Pausanias-B).

Differentiation (i): Pausanias' Narrative vs Callimachus—Death and the Maiden

If Pausanias' narrative (Pausanias-A) is read without reference to the *Diegeseis*, and with an open mind, it tells us a rather different story. Yes, the girl offered up is to be a 'bride' of the demon, as in the *Diegeseis*, but there is of course no mention

---

[27] Currie 2002:32–3. [Aeschines] *Letters* 10.3–6: 'In the Troad it is the custom for marrying virgins to go to the river Scamander, bathe themselves in it and pronounce this phrase in the manner of a sacred utterance: "Scamander, take my virginity." Amongst the others Callirhoe came to the river to bathe, a virgin of great repute, although her father was not amongst the distinguished. I too went to watch the festival and the bathing of the girls (it is lawful to do so from a certain distance), alongside their relatives and rest of the crowds that had come from afar. But my fine fellow Cimon hid himself in the bushes on the banks of the Scamander, and garlanded himself with reeds. This was his plan, obviously: a well-prepared daylight ambush for Callirhoe. As she was bathing and pronouncing the customary phrase, "Scamander, take my virginity" (I learned this after the event), Cimon leaped out of the Scamander's bushes and said, "I am Scamander: I gladly accept and take Callirhoe, and I will do many good things for you." Saying this, he seized the girl and then disappeared [*aphanēs gignetai*]. Not that the affair "disappeared", however. For, four days later there was a procession for Aphrodite, and the recently married girls were processing. I was watching the procession. The young bride saw Cimon watching the procession by my side, just as if he had done nothing wrong. She ran up to him and kissed him. She turned back to her nurse and said, "Nurse, can you see Scamander here, who took my virginity?" On hearing this the nurse cried aloud and the affair was revealed.' The motif of the river god *disappearing*, of which play is actually made, intrigues, however.

[28] Currie 2002 esp. 27, 30–1.

[29] Visintin 1992:17,131, chastising scholars for paying insufficient attention to Callimachus and thereby supposedly drawing the false inference that Pausanias' story of the Hero entails human sacrifice as opposed to sacred marriage. Alas, that is the inference I continue to draw.

[30] Cf. also, in this regard, Mele 1983:872–88.   [31] Sourvinou-Inwood 1987.

of the girl being taken back home the next day by her parents, and the whole tenor of the tale rather suggests that the girl's 'marriage' to the demon will entail her death. He will take her back to the underworld with him. Euthymus is to save her not from a fate worse than death, but from death itself.[32] I make this claim primarily on the basis of the strong alignment of themes and motifs between Pausanias' narrative and four other tales, the first of which is well known. This alignment is tabulated in Table 5.1:[33]

1. The tale of Perseus and Andromeda. Ethiopia (or Joppa) is ravaged by a sea monster sent by Poseidon, to avenge the Nereids whom the queen of the land, Cassiopeia, has insulted. Ammon tells the king, Cepheus, that he can save the land by pinning out his daughter Andromeda on the coast for the sea monster to devour, in a one-off sacrifice. This is duly done. Perseus, flying past after decapitating the Gorgon, espies her in her vulnerable state, falls in love with her, enquires into the circumstances, and does a deal with both the girl herself and her father to deliver her from the sea monster on condition that she marry him afterwards. He duly slays the sea monster (by attacking it from within, according to one account) or petrifies it, and takes the girl.[34]

2. The tale of Heracles and Hesione. In a very similar tale, Poseidon punishes Laomedon for cheating him of his wages for building the walls of Troy by sending a sea monster to ravage the Trojan land. Ammon (again) tells the king that he can control the sea monster by means of the annual sacrifice of a virgin girl to it, chosen by lot. When the lot falls upon a daughter of the noble Phoenodamas, he shames Laomedon into offering his own daughter, Hesione, instead. In the course of the Argonautic mission Heracles happens past as she is pinned out, takes pity on her, and he does a deal with her father that he will deliver her in return for his immortal horses. Heracles substitutes himself for the girl and thus gets himself inside its belly (according to some sources even donning the girl's dress in the process). He then destroys the monster from within by hacking away at its liver. Laomedon,

---

[32] For the notion that the girl might become a 'bride of Hades' see Visintin 1992:148, 152–3; she compares Euripides *Iphigenia at Aulis* 460–1, where we are told that Hades will marry Iphigenia at her sacrifice. Cf. also Casevitz et al. 2002:137.

[33] For the comparison of one or more of the following four tales with the Euthymus story in previous scholarship, see Frazer 1898:iv, 23–4 (on Pausanias 6.6.7–11), v, 143–5 (on Pausanias 9.26.7), Pais 1908:46–7, 1909, Gernet 1981 (1936):132, Fontenrose 1959:101–3, 119–20, 1968:80–3, Mele 1983:868–71, 884, Visintin 1992: 61, 119, 132, 141–7, Felton 1999:26–7, Casevitz et al. 2002:136, Hansen 2002:127–8.

[34] See, e.g., Euripides *Andromeda* FF114-56 *TrGF*; Aristophanes *Thesmophoriazusae* 1009–135; Lycophron *Alexandra* 834–42; Ovid *Metamorphoses* 4.663–5.268; Manilius 5.504–634, 834–46; Apollodorus *Bibliotheca* 2.4.3; Hyginus *Fabulae* 64, *Astronomica* 2.9–11, 31; Lucian *Dialogues in the Sea* 14; *LIMC* Andromeda i, Perseus. A fuller list of sources at Ogden 2013a:123–4 n.30, with discussion at 123–9; the principal sources are translated at Ogden 2013b:103–7.

Table 5.1 The Hero of Temesa and comparative narratives

	Hero of Temesa (narrative): Pausanias 6.6.7–11 (Pausanias-A)	Hero of Temesa (picture): Pausanias 6.6.11 (Pausanias-B)	Lamia-Sybaris: Antoninus Liberalis *Metamorphoses* 8	Dragon of Thespiae: Pausanias 9.36.7-8	Ketos of Ethiopia/Joppa: various sources	Ketos of Troy: various sources
Nature of monster	Hero, demon	Demon, black, wearing wolfskin: Lybas (Alybas, Alibas, Lykas?)	Lamia-Sybaris (partly humanoid, partly serpentine?)	Dragon	Sea monster	Sea monster
Initial indiscriminate marauding of monster	Hero kills indiscriminately	—	Beast snatches flocks and people on daily basis	Dragon devastates Thespiae	Indiscriminate marauding, together with flooding	Sea monster destroys people and crops, together with flooding
Oracle's intervention	Delphic Apollo's advice, when the Temesans plan to relocate	—	Delphic Apollo's advice, when the Delphians plan to relocate	'The god's' advice	Ammon's advice	Ammon's advice
Victim	Annual sacrifice: beautiful virgin girl	[CONJECTURE: The youth (*neaniskos*) Sybaris]	One-off sacrifice of a citizen lad (*kouros*, *pais*); in this case, Alcyoneus, fair in looks and character	Annual sacrifice of ephebe (*ephebos*); in this case, Cleostratus, a love object	One-off sacrifice: the beautiful virgin Andromeda	Repeated sacrifices of virgin girls; in this case, the beautiful virgin Hesione
Selection of victim	The most beautiful girl of the year	—	By lot	By lot	By Ammon's oracle	By lot; Laomedon shamed into offering own daughter Hesione by noble Phoenodamas

Continued

Table 5.1 Continued

	Hero of Temesa (narrative): Pausanias 6.6.7–11 (Pausanias-A)	Hero of Temesa (picture): Pausanias 6.6.11 (Pausanias-B)	Lamia-Sybaris: Antoninus Liberalis *Metamorphoses* 8	Dragon of Thespiae: Pausanias 9.36.7-8	Ketos of Ethiopia/Joppa: various sources	Ketos of Troy: various sources
Victim as bride	Given to demon as wife (*gynaika*); becomes bride of Euthymus	[n/a]	[n/a]	[n/a]	Andromeda betrothed to Phineus; becomes bride of Perseus	Heracles ultimately gives Hesione to his companion Telamon to marry
Saviour	Euthymus ('Courageous')	[CONJECTURE: Kalabros]	Eurybatus, son of Euphemios	Menestratus ('Stands fast in/against the rank')	Perseus	Heracles
Saviour's riverine connection	Euthymus' mysterious death [Aelian *VH* 8.18: Euthymus disappears into river Kaikinos, *sc.* to become a river god]	[CONJECTURE: Kalabros is a river]	Eurybatus is a descendant of the river Axios	—	—	—
Saviour's business	[Strabo C255: context of the Western Locrian conquest of Temesa]	—	Returning from Curetis	Existing lover	Returning from the land of the Gorgons	The episode is an intermezzo in the Argonaut mission
Saviour's response to victim	Pity and desire	—	Desire	Established love	Love	Pity
Saviour makes deal	With victim, to marry her	—	—	—	With victim and her father Cepheus, to marry her	With the victim's father Laomedon for his immortal horses

Saviour substitutes self for victim	Lycophron *Alexandra* 31–6, 470–8, Schol. Homer *Iliad* 20.147: Heracles puts on Hesione's dress and feeds self to sea monster	Lycophron *Alexandra* 834–46: Perseus allows sea monster to eat him in Andromeda's place	Menestratus hands himself to the dragon (in fish-hook armour)	Eurybatus takes on Alcyoneus' sacrificial garlands	—	[Possibly, if Pausanias' *eneskeuasmenos* refers to transvestism rather than arming]
Saviour enters unenterable place	The sea monster's maw	The sea monster's maw	The dragon's maw	Cave of Lamia-Sybaris	—	Unenterable temple of Hero [cf. Aelian, *abaton*]
Fate of monster	Slain	Slain/petrified into rock	Killed from within by fish-hook armour	Cast down and disappears to become the spring Sybaris	[CONJECTURE: Becomes spring Lyka]	Cast down and disappears into the sea [cf. Aelian *VH* 8.18 on Euthymus' own fate: goes down into river Kaikinos and disappears]
Role of name 'Sybaris'	—	—		Sybaris is the alternative name of the monster	Sybaris is the name of the youth[-victim?]	—
Epizephyrian Locrian connection	—	—		Sybaris gives her name to the city founded by the [sc. Epizephryian?] Locrians		Euthymus an Epizephyrian Locrian [Strabo C255: Western Locrian conquest of Temesa]

up to his old tricks, then cheats Heracles too of his rewards by palming him off with mere mortal horses. In revenge Heracles seizes the girl and gives her to his companion Telamon to marry.[35] Visintin and Currie have suggested that Pausanias' deployment of the term *eneskeuasmenos* in his Euthymus story signifies that Euthymus' 'equipping' of himself similarly entailed him dressing himself up as the girl and replacing her, so as to be able to deceive the monster (though they both miss the trick of making specific comparison with the Hesione episode in this regard).[36]

3. The tale of Menestratus' defeat of the Dragon of Thespiae, uniquely preserved by Pausanias himself:

> In the city at Thespiae there is a bronze statue of Zeus the Saviour. They explain that a dragon [drakōn] was once devastating the city, and the god gave the command that the ephebe [young adult, 18–20 years of age] chosen by lot each year should be given to the beast. They say that they do not remember the names of those that were killed. But they tell that when the lot fell upon Cleostratus, his lover Menestratus devised a plan. He had a bronze breastplate made with a fish hook pointing upwards on each of its little segments. He put this breastplate on and handed himself over willingly to the dragon. His purpose was, in handing himself over and being killed, in turn to kill the beast. In return for this Zeus has acquired the epithet 'Saviour'.   Pausanias 9.26.7–8

4. The tale of Eurybatus and Lamia-Sybaris, originally told in the lost *Heteroioumena* of Nicander (2nd c. BC), and uniquely preserved for us by Antoninus Liberalis:

> *Lamia or Sybaris.* Nicander tells the story in the fourth book of his *Metamorphoses* [*Heteroioumena*]. Beside the foothills of Mt Parnassus, on the south side, there is a mountain which is called Cirphis, near Crisa. On it there is still now a gigantic cave in which a huge and overweening beast used to live. Some called it Lamia, others Sybaris. This beast would venture abroad on a daily basis and snatch up flocks and people from the fields. The Delphians had been deliberating about moving their city and consulted the oracle as to what land they should turn to. The god indicated that they would be delivered from their misfortune if they had the heart to stay where they were and expose beside the cave a citizen lad [*kouros*]. They did just as the god said. Lots were drawn, and it fell upon Alcyoneus, the son of

---

[35] See, e.g., Palaephatus 37, Lycophron *Alexandra* 31–6, 470–8, Diodorus 4. 32, 42, Ovid *Metamorphoses* 11. 199–215, Valerius Flaccus *Argonautica* 2.451–578 (the most expansive account), Apollodorus *Bibliotheca* 2. 5. 9, 2. 6. 4, Hyginus *Fabulae* 31, 89, Philostratus *Imagines* 12; *LIMC* Hesione, Ketos. Fuller sources at Ogden 2013a:119 n.15, with discussion at 118–23; the principal sources are translated at Ogden 2013b:108–18.

[36] Visintin 1992:144, Currie 2002:38.

Diomus and Meganira. He was his father's only child, and fair both to look at and in the nature of his personality. The priests garlanded Alcyoneus and took him off to the cave of Sybaris. As a god would have it, Eurybatus, the son of Euphemius and descended from the river Axius, a young but noble-minded man, on his return from Curetis, happened upon the boy as he was being led off. He was smitten with love and asked the purpose of their journey. He thought it terrible that they should not resist the beast by force, but should stand by and watch the boy [*pais*] be slain in pitiful fashion. He took the garlands from Alcyoneus' head, put them on his own and bade them take him off in the boy's place. When the priests had taken him off, he ran up and snatched Sybaris from her lair. He brought her forth to where all could see and hurled her from the rocks. As she was carried down she struck her head against the foothills of Crisa. The creature herself, thus wounded, disappeared from view, but a spring emerged from that rock, and the locals call it Sybaris. And it was in the name of this spring that the Locrians too founded the city of Sybaris in Italy.   Antoninus Liberalis *Metamorphoses* 8[37]

The alignment between the Antoninus tale and Pausanias' narrative (Pausanias-A) is particularly strong. Without grinding through every single point of similarity between the two (most of which are self-evident, and are in any case tabulated), let us highlight here a few of the more curious points of contact:

- **The saviour's riverine affinities.** One of the most striking correspondences between Antoninus' tale and Pausanias' narrative relates to the saviour figure: Pausanias' Euthymus is or becomes a river (admittedly this is only alluded to obscurely by Pausanias, whereas it is explicitly stated by Aelian); Antoninus's Eurybatus is the descendant of the river Axius. There is, furthermore, a vague assonance between the name of Euthymus and that of Eurybatus, and a stronger one between that of Euthymus and that of Eurybatus' father, Euphemius.
- **Epizephyrian Locri.** Both accounts exhibit an association with Epizephyrian Locri. In Pausanias' narrative Euthymus is a citizen of the city; in Antoninus's tale it is asserted that the city ultimately named after the spring of Sybaris is founded by (*sc.* Epizephyrian) Locrians. This is, however, a maverick claim, with other sources crediting the foundation of the city of Sybaris rather to Achaeans and Troezenians.[38]
- **Entering the forbidden place.** Pausanias makes much of Euthymus entering the unenterable temple of the Hero; Antoninus's Eurybatus shows similar daring in entering the cave of Lamia-Sybaris, to drag her out. The degree of

---

[37] For general discussion see Papathomopoulos 1968:86–7.
[38] Aristotle *Politics* 1303a; Strabo C263.

daring here is perhaps exposed by the further parallel tales of Perseus and especially Heracles, who actually enter into the mouths of their respective sea monsters to save their girls.

- **The disappearance of the monster.** Attention is drawn in both cases to the monster's downward disappearance. Pausanias has the Hero disappear after diving down into the sea (*ho Hērōs aphanizetai te katadys es thalassan*);[39] Antoninus has Lamia-Sybaris cast down and disappear to become the spring named for her (*kata tōn petrōn erripsen... aphanēs egeneto*).[40] But here it is noteworthy and suggestive that Aelian articulates Euthymus' own eventual fate in the same terms: he goes down into the river Kaikinos and disappears (*katabanta epi ton Kaikinon potamon... aphanisthēnai*).[41] There is a curious assimilation between victor and vanquished, as one disappears into a river, the other into the sea.[42]

To conclude, the story type as conveyed by Pausanias' narrative (Pausanias-A) presses us to assume that the fate of the annual bride given to the Hero is death, and that Pausanias' narrative is therefore incompatible with Callimachus' account of the rite. There is, of course, also a striking correspondence between Antoninus' narrative and Pausanias' picture (Pausanias-B), in that both deploy the name Sybaris. For Antoninus Sybaris is the name of the monster and of the spring into which she is transformed, whereas in the picture it is the name of a young man— the monster's victim, we shall contend below.

Furthermore, we probably should indeed expect the bride of a ghost to die. Ancient ghost stories were not entirely consistent on the point, but there was a general belief that ghosts carried with them the contagion of death. The point is made clearly with reference to antiquity's favourite ghost-tale story type, that of the haunted house (discussed in Chapter 4). In Plautus' adaptation of the story type, Theopropides is terrified by the implications of merely having knocked on the door of a house he believes to be haunted by a ghost.[43] In Pliny's account of the same story type, the reader is led to believe that when the ghost beckons the philosopher Athenodorus with its finger, it is beckoning him down to the

---

[39] The means by which the demon is disposed of is a technique of *pharmakeia*, scapegoating. Scapegoats, *pharmakoi*, were normally expelled from a community, together with their pollution, by being whipped or pelted with rocks and driven over the border or into the sea. See, e.g., Istros *FGrH/BNJ* 334 F50, Helladius *apud* Photius *Bibliotheca* cod. 279 p.534a Bekker, Photius *Lexicon* s.v. περίψημα. Further sources and discussion at Ogden 1997:15–23 and Bremmer 2008:169–214, esp. 175–96 (the culmination of his earlier publications on the subject); see further Chapter 6.

[40] Complementarily, the spring into which she is transformed 'appears up' (*anephanē pēgē*).

[41] And in this last connection it is interesting too that ps.-Aeschines' account of Cimon's impersonation of the river Scamander ends with his disappearance: **aphanēs** *gignetai*. The word is not used casually; indeed, attention is drawn to it as ps.-Aeschines proceeds directly to his account of the subsequent revelation of the impersonation: *ou mēn kai to pragma* **aphanes** *gignetai....*

[42] Cf. Fontenrose 1968:81.   [43] Plautus *Mostellaria* 446–531.

underworld with itself.[44] A more graphic example is provided by the ghost of the old woman sent by a witch to kill the miller in Apuleius' *Metamorphoses*: she takes him by the hand and leads him into his office; when the locked door is broken down, the miller's hanging body is found, but of the old woman there is no sign.[45] More germanely, we may point to the case of Protesilaus, the first man to die at Troy, and his widow Laodamia. The gods took pity on Laodamia, who missed her husband so badly that she had a wax image of him made for herself to embrace, and so Hermes restored him to her from the underworld for a few hours. But when he took him back, she killed herself for grief.[46] We may point also to Phlegon of Tralles' account of the originally Hellenistic tale of Philinnion. Here the ghost of a young bride returns and spends three nights sleeping with the new lodger, Machates, in her parents' house (in her childhood bedroom, perhaps?). Discovered by the household maid and then by her parents, the ghost disappears forever and Machates' suicide follows shortly after.[47] In both of these last tales two logics keep pace with each other: the living lover's death is determined both in a rational way, as it were, by their grief at being deprived of their beloved, and, at the same time, in a non-rational way, by the contagion of death. An intriguing case too is provided by the story the heroine Anthia tells in Xenophon of Ephesus' second-century AD *Ephesiaca*, to explain the origin of the epilepsy she feigns:

> When I was still a girl, I wandered away from my family during an all-night festival. I came to the tomb of a man who had just recently died. And then a man appeared before me, jumping up out of the grave, and he tried to hold on to [*or* to possess – *katechein*] me, but I tried to run off and kept screaming. The man was fearful to look at, but his voice was more terrible by far. Finally, when it became day, he let me go but he struck me in the chest and said he had cast this disease into me. And from that point I have been subject to various forms of attack from the disease over the years.   Xenophon of Ephesus *Ephesiaca* 5.7.7–9

If the ghost had been able to hold on to Anthia and take him back with her, we can only infer that she would have joined him in death. Her degree of contact with the ghost was insufficient to achieve this, but it did leave her with the mini-deaths of epilepsy.[48]

[44] Pliny the Younger *Letters* 7.27.5–11.   [45] Apuleius *Metamorphoses* 9.29–31.

[46] See, e.g., Euripides *Protesilaus* FF646-57 *TrGF*; Propertius 1.19.7–10; Ovid *Heroides* 13; Apollodorus *Epitome* 3.30; Hyginus *Fabulae* 103–4; Lucian *Dialogues of the Dead* 23, Servius on Virgil *Aeneid* 6.447; First Vatican Mythographer 2.56; Eustathius on Homer *Iliad* 2.701, schol. Aristides vol. iii p.671 Dindorf; Tzetzes *Chiliades* 2 historia 52.

[47] Phlegon of Tralles *Mirabilia* 1; Proclus supplies the details missing from the beginning of the story: *Commentary on Plato's Republic* pp.115–16 Kroll. For commentaries on this text, see Hansen 1996, Stramaglia 1999:217–57.

[48] As I note at Ogden 2009 no. 319, the explanation Anthia gives also seems to feint towards accounting for the epilepsy as resulting from direct possession by the ghost, with the word used to

There are counterexamples, of course. No ill seems to befall Herodotus' mother of Demaratus when the hero Astrabacus visits her from his local heroon in the guise of her husband, Ariston, to sire Demaratus upon her, leaving with her a garland from his heroon as a token of his visit: at any rate, she had to live to give birth.[49] However, we may think that this particular hero's modus operandi is more divine than ghostly. It is strongly reminiscent of Zeus' visit to Alcmene in the guise of her Amphitryon in order to sire Heracles leaving with her a cup he had supposedly taken from the Teleboans.[50] Nor does Herodotus' Periander appear to have suffered any fatal consequences from having sex with the corpse of his wife, Melissa (her ghost was presumably present, since it knew about it).[51]

We have differentiated the Pausanian rite from the Callimachean one—but what are we to do with this differentiation? The Hero and his rite, if they had ever existed, were both already long in the past by the time that Callimachus wrote, let alone Pausanias, and there is no reason that contradictory and fantastical traditions about the rite should not have developed about its nature over time. If, nonetheless, it is felt that it is inconceivable that Pausanias' rite (in which the girl is killed by supernatural means) was historical,[52] whereas Callimachus' rite (in which she is merely deflowered—and that too perhaps only in an imaginary or symbolic way) may well indeed have been historical, then a model may be proposed for the coexistence of the two accounts. This model is to be constructed from the confusing and initially contradictory evidence for the rite of the (Eastern) Locrian Maidens. The evidence for it gives us:

1. **In remote mythical time an original outrage**, the rape of Cassandra by Ajax the Less in Athena's temple at Troy.[53]
2. **A description of a horrid rite of expiation**, in which Ajax's people, the Eastern Locrians, must send two virgin girls all the way to Troy every year to serve as slaves, ragged, barefoot, and shorn, sweeping the precinct of Athena until the day they die, whereupon their bodies are disposed of as polluted material.[54]

describe the ghost's attempt to hold on to Anthia, *katechein*, being the normal term for demonic possession. The episode is discussed by Puiggali 1986 and Susanetti 1999:157–66.

[49] Herodotus 6.69.
[50] Hesiod *Shield* 27–56, Pherecydes F13a–c Fowler (F13a = Herodorus F16 Fowler, *apud* Athenaeus 474f), Plautus *Amphitruo passim*, Diodorus 4.9, Apollodorus *Bibliotheca* 2.4.8; further sources at Gantz 1993:374–8.
[51] Herodotus 5.92.
[52] And in any case human sacrifice was almost certainly never a normal historical practice in ancient Greece: see Chapter 6, n. 90.
[53] Arctinus *Sack of Troy* (as summarized in Proclus' *Chrestomathia*), Lycophron *Alexandra* 1150–1, Apollodorus *Epitome* 5.22, Pausanias 1.5.2, 5.11.6, 5.19.5, 10.26.3, 10.31.2, Quintus Smyrnaeus 13.420–9, etc.
[54] Aeneas Tacticus 31.24, Timaeus *FGrH/BNJ* 566 FF146a–b, Lycophron *Alexandra* 1141–71, Euphorion F187 Lightfoot, Apollodorus *Epitome* 6.20–22, Plutarch *Moralia* 557d.

3. **A description of a more civilized rite of expiation**, the historicity of which is partly guaranteed by an inscription, in which an annually rotating pair of girls serves in a precinct of Athena, not even at Troy (Ilium), but nearer home at the temple of Athena *Ilias* in Ozolian Locris, before returning home to marry and resume a normal life.[55]

To finesse the now standard way of approaching this set of data, it could be said that the horrid version of the expiation rite represents an imaginary past version of the more civilized, historical version of it, indeed that it constitutes a further myth in itself, one with an intermediate role. The function of this intermediate myth is to provide an apologetic aetiology for, a mitigation of, the more civilized—but still distinctly unpleasant—actual rite practised, which was perhaps a rite of passage performed on behalf of all the girls of Eastern Locris of the same age-year: 'You may think you have it bad now—but look how much worse this rite used to be, or could be again.'[56]

So too in the Temesan case it could be thought that we have:

1. **In remote mythical time an original outrage**, in which the Temesans stone Polites to death (Strabo). We have the theme of rape in this starting-point story too, of course, but in this case the rape, a non-sacrilegious one, does not constitute the relevant outrage.
2. **A description of a horrid rite of expiation**, in which the Hero kills the girl given to him every year (Pausanias).
3. **A description of a more civilized rite of expiation**, in which every year a girl spends a single night in the Hero's shrine, from which she emerges (supposedly) no longer a virgin, but nonetheless returns to normal life (Callimachus).

Again, the intermediate historicizing myth of a once horrid rite of expiation could be seen as an apology for a more civilized though still unpleasant rite actually performed, unpleasant enough even if only imaginary defloration by some ethereal entity is in question. Again the girl perhaps performs a rite of passage on behalf of all the girls of Temesa in their age-year.

When it came to developing a retrospective story—a myth again, of course—about the closing down of the rites for the Hero of Temesa, it could be that the distinction between the details of the actual rite (the Callimachean one) and its mythical forebear (the Pausanian one) dissolved, not inappropriately, leaving us with the contrasting accounts of Euthymus and his girl that remain to us.

---

[55] *IG* ix.1² 706 (earlier 3rd c. BC), Callimachus F35 Pf., Strabo C600, Aelian F50 Domingo-Forasté, Servius on Virgil *Aeneid* 1.41. It is not clear which of the two rites is referred to by Polybius 12.5.7.
[56] Cf. Graf 2000, Hornblower 2015:405–19.

Differentiation (ii): Pausanias' Narrative (Pausanias-A) vs Pausanias' Picture (Pausanias-B)—the Other Tale of the Hero of Temesa

As Currie has importantly noted, we thank Pausanias for in effect preserving not one but two strikingly different traditions, namely that of the tale he narrates (Pausanias-A) and that of the picture he describes (Pausanias-B), which, whatever the action it implied, apparently worked with a rather different cast list, animate and inanimate alike.[57] Pausanias does not in fact formally tell us that Euthymus was included in the picture. It is just possible that he imagines that he conveys his inclusion in an elegant and indirect way by means of the relative phrase 'that Euthymus cast out', but I think it unlikely, and I assume that he was indeed not in the picture. None of the other sources mention the youth Sybaris, the river Kalabros, or the spring Lyka.[58]

When we align the motifs, actual or potential, in or implied by Pausanias' description of his picture with those of his Euthymus narrative, and also with those of Antoninus' Lamia-Sybaris tale especially, we uncover an underlying tale parallel to that of Pausanias' narrative, despite its different cast list (see Table 5.1 again):

- The saviour figure in the picture (Pausanias-B) is no longer here the river-god-in-training Euthymus, but the river-god-pure-and-simple Kalabros. We may note, however, the broad assonance and structural similarity between the names of Kalabros and the river with which Euthymus was to merge, Kaikinos. The Kalabros, evidently though oddly the supposed eponym of Calabria, is not a river currently recognized by historical geographers.[59] The *Barrington Atlas* tentatively identifies a river at the very toe of Italy as the Kaikinos.[60]
- The sexually desirable victim offered up to the monster in the picture is no longer the nameless girl of the narrative but the named youth, Sybaris the young man (*neaniskos*), counterpart of the lad (*kouros*) and boy (*pais*) Alcyoneus offered up to the Dragon of Thespiae and of Cleostratus, the

---

[57] Currie 2002:28.

[58] De Sanctis 1909–10 rightly saw that Pausanias did not specify Euthymus' actual inclusion in the picture (before promptly reincorporating him into it), and Lawson 1926b:118 took it for granted that Euthymus did not feature in it. But scholars have typically taken Euthymus' presence in it to be implied (whether by the picture itself or by Pausanias): thus Currie 2002:30–1, who regards the picture as associating Euthymus with the river Kalabros, as well as with Sybaris, whom he takes to represent another river.

[59] Or should we take 'Kalabros' to be a corrupt form of 'Kalauros'? See Mele 1983:882–3.

[60] Talbert 2000 Map 46, C5. Further speculation on the tale's rivers at Zancani Montuoro 1968:7–12.

ephebe (*ephēbos*) offered up to Lamia-Sybaris.[61] The Hero could not marry the youth, and so presumably all he could do was kill him, much as the Dragon and Lamia-Sybaris would have killed their boys. The Dragon and Lamia-Sybaris killed by devouring, and perhaps that too was the method of the lupine Hero: after all, man-eating is what wolves do.[62]

- In both Pausanias' picture and the Lamia-Sybaris tale, we are probably dealing with a monster that is mixanthropic: partly humanoid and partly animal, a wolf-man and a snake-woman respectively (we will discuss the latter in the next section).

- The Hero is no longer chased into the sea to disappear but turned into a spring (*Lýka*), just like the Lamia-Sybaris defeated by Eurybatus—and perhaps similarly after being hurled *down* over a cliff. The monster and the spring into which he is transformed are shown together in the painting in an act of narrative compression of a sort familiar in Greek art. Just as Eurybatus' spring expresses its continuity with the monster by sharing its name, Sybaris, so the Temesan spring expresses its continuity by—as a minimum—reflecting in its name the wolfskin the monster had been sporting (*lýkou... derma*). Just as we observed an odd affinity between the monster and the champion in Pausanias' narrative, with the champion disappearing into the river and the monster into the sea, here in Pausanias' picture we have another odd watery affinity, with the champion embodied in a river and the monster embodied in a spring.

According to this interpretation, the tale implied by Pausanias' picture (Pausanias-B) in fact sits squarely between the specific narrative type of Pausanias' Euthymus narrative (Pausanias-A) and that of the Lamia-Sybaris narrative.

What did the legend on the picture call the Polites–Hero figure? The manuscripts of Pausanias have given rise to lively dispute. As they actually stand, the difference between them comes down to just a spacing and a grave accent (*Lýban tà* vs. *Lýbanta*).[63] Either way, they all alike tell us that the legend gave the figure

---

[61] My suggestion that Sybaris is the intended victim is anticipated in a roundabout way by Pais 1908:45 and in a dismissive way by Currie 2002:28. Pais, in his attempt to assimilate Pausanias' picture to Pausanias' narrative, proposed emending the text of his description of the picture slightly to have him tell us that the painting included not 'a youth Sybaris' (νεανίσκος Σύβαρις) but 'a youth [i.e. Euthymus] *and* [the maiden] Sybaris'. Giannelli 1924:261–71 thought rather that 'the youth Sybaris' was an alternate saviour figure to Euthymus, and that the painting accordingly spoke metaphorically of the city of Sybaris' delivery of the city of Temesa from the paying of tribute; cf. also Phillips 1953:57, Peronaci 1974:271–2, Mele 1983:865, Visintin 1992:45, 53, 58, asevitz et al. 2002:137. But the corollary notion (Mele, Casevitz et al.) that Sybaris therefore represents the river Sybaris, to match Euthymus' riverine affinities, won't stand: why, in that case, would Pausanias designate the adjacent Kalabros a river, but not Sybaris?

[62] For the Hero's lupine associations see Visintin 1992:109–29, esp.110–15 on the wolf as a raw-flesh-eating creature (Aesop no. 97 Perry, Aelian *Nature of Animals* 7.20 etc.).

[63] ἐτίθετο δὲ καὶ ὄνομα **Λύβαν τὰ** ἐπὶ τῇ γραφῇ γράμματα or ἐτίθετο δὲ καὶ ὄνομα **Λύβαντα** ἐπὶ τῇ γραφῇ γράμματα.

the name *Lybas* in its nominative form, and they vary only in the grammatical declension to which they ascribe it (first or third).

This reading is perfectly acceptable, and even if the name signifies nothing in itself, it can still be seen to be meaningful in context. As we have just seen, the picture asserted a significant link between the name of the spring, *Lýka*, and the wolfskin, *lýkou... dérma*, worn by the Hero figure. Given the generosity of the ancient mind in its approach to folk etymology, it is quite possible that the name *Lýbas* was felt good enough to form a significant triad with these other two terms: at least it shared the opening syllable *lý-*. It is also conceivable, though I shall build nothing on this, that *Lybas* did in a sense form a proper etymological triad with the other two terms, if it derived from an Italic word signifying 'wolf'. The basic Proto-Indo-European word for 'wolf' was **ulkʷos*, in which the origins of our own word can be seen. But both Greek and the Italic languages built their derived words on a metathesized version of this form, **lukʷos*. The reflex of the Greek *lykos* from this version was then simple and direct, and the Latin reflex should have been equally so, **lucus*. Perhaps such a form remains visible in the place name *Lucania*, if this does indeed signify 'Wolf-land' (but this is just one of many hypotheses as to the toponym's origin). The actually attested Latin word for 'wolf', *lupus*, however, has resolved the original labiovelar *kʷ* into the labial *p* as opposed to the anticipated velar *c*. This type of resolution is a trait of the Sabellic branch of the Italic languages, and so tells us that *lupus* must have been borrowed into Latin from this subfamily. This allows us in turn to reconstruct with confidence the unattested word for 'wolf' in the Sabellic language Oscan, the language of the indigenous Italians in the region of Temesa: with the final syncopation also characteristic of that language, it would have been **lups*.[64]

Nonetheless, emendations have been proposed, falling into two groups.[65] The first group brings the Hero figure's name more closely into line with the spring and the wolfskin by emending it to *Lýkas* (Λύκας).[66] One point of interest in this hypothesis is that it would bring the tale in turn more closely (albeit not perfectly) into line with the Lamia-Sybaris tale of Antoninus, wherein the monster and the spring created from it bear the same name.

---

[64] See Marcinkowski 2001:1–3, Moreau 1997:70–1, de Vaan 2008 s.v. *lupus*. The last, however, expresses some reservations both in relation to the metathesis of the root and to Latin's borrowing of the Sabellic form (though he has no better solution to offer).

[65] Discussion at Maass 1907:42, Pais 1909:387–8, Lawson 1926a, 1926b, Gernet 1981 (1936):132 and 138 n.81, Mele 1983:864, 886, Moreau 1990a:38–40, Visintin 1992:15, 46–9, 59–73, Casevitz et al. 2002:138.

[66] See Gernet 1981 (1936):138 n.81 and Visintin 1992:63 for the further speculation that Pausanias' phrase Λύκα πηγή should not be construed as a pair of nominatives in apposition, 'a spring, Lyka', but as a nominative πηγή preceded by a Doric genitive, 'Lykas' spring'. We need not be detained by the contention of Biraschi 1996 ('Καλύκα πηγή in Paus. VI 6, 11?') that the key to this passage somehow lies in a ps.-Stesichoran reference to a tragic girl Kalyke (F100 *PMG* = F277 Campbell = F326 Davies-Finglass).

The second group adds an alpha to the front of the name. The fairly worthy justification for this is that *Alýbas* (*Ἀλύβαντα*) is the form of the name given to the Hero by the *Suda*'s entry on Euthymus (there seems to be no reason to doubt the reading here),[67] which evidently depends upon Pausanias in part. Of course, we cannot be sure that the lexicographer was not himself struggling to make sense of the same text of Pausanias that we have. Nonetheless, this name has been seized upon and compared with a Greek world *alíbas* (*ἀλίβας, -αντος*) signifying 'corpse' and found, for example, in Plato and Hesychius.[68] This comparison may or may not prompt the further emendation of the name's upsilon to an iota (*Ἀλίβαντα*), to match the word fully: the *ι/υ* variation is contended to be a relatively trivial matter. Given that it is the fate of the Hero, in Pausanias' narrative (Pausanias-A) at any rate, to be driven into the sea, the *Etymologicum Magnum*'s gloss on (the accusative plural form) *alíbantas* becomes particularly suggestive: 'Those that die in the sea; or the dried out; others apply the term to those that remain unburied because of poverty.'[69] If *Alýbas* were Pausanias' original reading, one could, just about, still imagine a folk etymology attempting to tie the name to the *lyk-* root; but *Alíbas* is surely too remote to have licensed ancient speculation of this kind.[70]

---

[67] The only variant in the MSS is *Ἀλύβαντε* (V); see Adler 1971 *ad loc.*

[68] LSJ s.v. *ἀλίβας, -αντος*. Plato *Republic* 387c: *ἔνεροι καὶ ἀλίβαντες*, 'those below and the corpses'. A derived term is strikingly deployed at Lucian *Menippus* 20 to make a parodic name for a dead man in the underworld: *Κρανίων Σκελτίωνος Νεκυσιεὺς φυλῆς Ἀλιβαντίδος*, 'Skully, son of Skeleton, of the deme of Corpsetown and of the Cadaver [*Alibantis*] tribe'. Ancient etymologists considered that the word had come to signify 'corpse' on the basis that it literally signified 'lacking moisture' (i.e. *ἀ*-privative + *λιβάς, -άδος*, 'spring', 'fount' or 'stream'—LSJ s.v.). Thus: Plutarch *Aquane an ignis sit utilior, Moralia* 956a, *ἀμέλει τοὺς ἀποθανόντας ἀλίβαντας καλοῦσιν ὡς ἐνδεεῖς λιβάδος, τουτέστιν ὑγρότητος, καὶ παρὰ τοῦτο στερουμένους τοῦ ζῆν* ('anyway, they call the dead *alíbantes* because they are without *libás*, which is to say moisture, and thereby deprived of life'); Hesychius s.v. *ἀλίβας· νεκρός ἢ βροῦχος. ἢ ποταμός. ἢ ὄξος* ('*alíbas*: corpse or ??? or river or vinegar'); Hesychius s.v. *ἀλίβαντες· οἱ νεκροί. διὰ τὸ ξηροὶ εἶναι, καὶ οἷον ὑγρασίαν τινὰ μὴ ἔχειν* ('*alíbantes*: corpses, on account of them being dry and as it were not having any moisture'); Hesychius s.v. *διερόν· ὑγρόν. χλωρόν. ζωόν. ἔναιμον· ὑγρὸς γὰρ ὁ ζῶν, ὁ δὲ νεκρὸς ἀλίβας* ('*dieros*: wet, fresh, live, filled with blood; for the living man is wet, but the corpse is *alíbas*'). Chantraine 2009 *ad loc.* suggests that the term *alíbas* may have been applied to vinegar on the basis that it was 'dead' wine. If *Alíbas* was indeed the original name of the demon in Pausanias' picture, then it might have been considered, in context, to signify 'not-spring', a pertinent speaking name for the Hero prior to his defeat and his transition into being, precisely, a spring. Another speculation relates the Hero's name to a toponym *Ἀλύβας* or *Ἀλύβη*, the supposed original name of Metapontum: Stephanus of Byzantium s.v. *Ἀλύβας* and Eustathius on Homer *Odyssey* 24.304; cf. Visintin 1992:68–70, with further sources and discussion.

[69] *Etymologicum Magnum* s.v. *Ἀλίβαντας· τοὺς ἐν θαλάσσῃ τελευτήσαντας. ἢ τοὺς ξηρούς. ἄλλοι τοὺς διὰ πενίαν ἀτάφους*. Cf. Lawson 1926a:54, 1926b:120. For the significance of dryness here, see n. 68.

[70] Currie 2002:34, ever keen to identify the Hero as a river god, notes that the river that flows past what some consider to have been the site of the Hero's sanctuary is currently called Oliva, and speculates as to whether this name might derive from an ancient name *Alýbas*; cf. La Torre 1997:368. But the site of Temesa itself, let alone the tomb, is hardly settled: see Maddoli 1982, Mele 1983:848–57, Casevitz et al. 2002:135–6.

Does the wolfskin-wearing Hero of Pausanias' picture (Pausanias-B) devour the lad? Visintin points to the Lykaon myth, in which the devouring of a human sacrifice effects transformation into a wolf (for which see Chapter 6).[71]

Serpentine Monsters

It is self-evident that in the first three of the comparative tales for Pausanias' narrative (Pausanias-A) adduced above (those bearing upon the sea monster of Ethiopia or Joppa, the sea monster of Troy, and the Dragon of Thespiae), the featured monster is of a serpentine nature. As to the fourth comparative tale, no direct indication is given of the nature of Lamia-Sybaris' monstrous form.[72] However, the tight narrative alignment with the Thespiae story would suggest that she was some sort of serpent. More particularly, she may have been an anguipede, a creature with a humanoid upper half and a serpentine lower one, as female dragons tended to be in the ancient world. Such is the *lamia* sent against Argos by Apollo in Statius' wonderful tale of Coroebus of Argos, save that she also has a serpent head growing out of the top of her humanoid head.[73] Such are the *lamias* Dio Chrysostom tells us infest the Libyan desert, save that they have a terrible serpent head at the end of their serpent tail.[74] And the ostensibly humanoid *lamia* famously faced by Apollonius of Tyana in Corinth is declared by the sage to be an *ophis*, 'snake': does she conceal a serpentine lower half beneath her skirts? Or does she combine a humanoid element and a serpentine one in a different way (perhaps by shape-shifting between the two)?[75] We may conclude, accordingly, that the monsters in all four of these comparative cases are essentially serpentine in nature.

Could it be then that the Hero also boasted some sort of serpentine element that the tradition has failed to preserve for us? The extreme version of this hypothesis would contend that, whereas in the picture variant of the story (Pausanias-B) the Hero was a wolf-man tout court, in the narrative variant (Pausanias-A) he was rather a serpent-man tout court. For what it is worth, the affinity between the dead hero and the living serpent was well established in the Greek world.[76] But there are less radical alternatives, as we shall see.

---

[71] Visintin 1992:123, with 131–53 on human sacrifice more generally.
[72] On *lamias* and their form, see Ogden 2013a:86–92, 2013b:97–108 (nos. 68–74).
[73] Statius *Thebaid* 1.562–669. The creature in question is termed a *lamia* in the parallel narrative at First Vatican Mythographer, 2.66. A creature of just this type is illustrated on a lekythos in the Louvre, Musée du Louvre CA1915, wrongly identified by *LIMC*, the standard lexicon for the iconography of classical mythology, as depicting Python (*LIMC* Apollon 998).
[74] Dio Chrysostom *Orations* 5.   [75] Philostratus *Life of Apollonius* 4.25.
[76] I offer three examples:
  • On a marvellous Tyrrhenian amphora of *c.*575–550 BC, *LIMC* Erinys 84 = Alkmaion 3 (where illustrated) = Grabow 1998 K103, Amphiaraus rises from his barrow and over the dead body of Eriphyle in the form of a gigantic bearded serpent in order to threaten her son and murderer Alcmaeon with bared fangs, as he departs in a chariot. Note also *LIMC* Alkmaion 9.

The Hero in the Wolfskin: a Werewolf?

As we have seen, there is no compelling *need* to search for further explanations of the Hero's wolfskin in Pausanias' picture (Pausanias-B); a minimal explanation can be satisfactory. The Hero had become the spring Lyka: giving him a wolfskin to wear offered a graceful *aition* for the name of the spring. Perhaps, in a similar way, the Delphic monster had originally just been Lamia (or *a lamia*), but had been retrospectively given the additional name Sybaris to construct an *aition* for the name of the spring into which she was transformed. But the minimal explanation need not be the end of the investigation. Myth and folktale are polysemic and one may point to possible further patterns of significance lurking beneath the detail of the wolfskin.[77]

We may well, then, ask whether this Hero in a wolfskin salutes werewolfism in an ancient context, and a decent case can be made that he does. First, as we have seen, there was an established notion in the ancient world that the two constituent elements of a werewolf, the man and the wolf, variously corresponded to an inner core and an outer carapace or shell (Chapter 3): do we have here an inner man, in the form of the ghost, and an outer shell in the form of the wolfskin?

Furthermore, as we have also seen, there was a particular association in the ancient world between werewolves and ghosts or disembodied souls (Chapters 2 and 4 *passim*). It is, I think, particularly appropriate to conceptualize the Hero of Temesa as a 'ghost'. One may wonder, it is true, whether returning 'heroes' are always conceptualized in a way that might accurately be defined by this term. Astrabacus again is a case in point: his reported actions characterize him more as a demigod than as a dead man. However, in the case of the Hero the characterization of him as 'black' in the picture suggests that we are indeed in proper ghost territory.[78]

- From *c.* 540 BC we find serpents in the roles of avatars in hero reliefs. The finest example is also the earliest: the Laconian Chrysapha relief, Berlin Pergamon Museum no. 731 = Ogden 2013a:252 fig. 7.1, on which a great serpent arches over the back of the throne on which its hero is seated in humanoid form. For discussion of reliefs of this type see Salapata 2006.
- Diogenes Laertius 5.89–90 (= Heraclides of Pontus F16 Wehrli, incorporating in turn fragments of Demetrius of Magnesia (1st c. BC) and Hippobotus (*c.*200 BC)) tells that Heraclides of Pontus enjoined his intimates to replace his corpse on its bier surreptitiously with his pet serpent (*drakōn*), so that people would believe he had joined the gods in death. The association between anguification and heroization specifically seems particularly clear here.

See Ogden 2013a:147–54, where these examples are treated in more detail, and further ones supplied.

---

[77] For a study of the general significance of the wearing of animal skins in Greek culture (without reference to the Hero, however) see Harden 2017.

[78] For the blackness of classical ghosts, see Homer *Iliad* 3.360, *Odyssey* 11.606, Sappho 58d, Euripides *Hecuba* 71 and 704–5, Phlegon *Mirabilia* 2, Lucian *Philopseudes* 16, 31, 32, *PGM* VII 348–58; discussion at Winkler 1980:160–5. Cf. again too, now in the Christian realm, the black, fiery-eyed demon dog (of the 5th c. AD) at *Passio S. Tryphonis*, 1–2 (Chapter 2).

Another three-way association between wolf, ghost, and virgin sacrifice may be found in Euripides' *Hecuba*. Here Hecuba speaks of two parallel dreams she has had, which prefigure the sacrifice of her daughter Polyxena to the ghost of Achilles: first, a dream of a dappled deer being jugulated and dragged from her knees by the bloody paw of a wolf; and, secondly, a dream of the ghost of Achilles demanding the sacrifice of a Trojan girl at his tomb. The key portions of text may be interpolations and not genuinely Euripidean, but they presumably remain ancient.[79]

It is quite possible, too, that Pausanias' picture description refracts the lupine imagery of Aita, the Etruscan Hades, reviewed in Chapter 2.[80] The Etruscan zone proper extended as far south only as Campania, some 200 miles north of Temesa (this in the fifth and fourth centuries BC), but the whole of southern Italy remained susceptible to Etruscan influence in various ways.[81] The great attraction of identifying the Hero with Aita in his wolfskin (if only at the level of imagery) is that Aita's serpentine weapons allow us to bring the Hero's story more fully into line with the four analogues for Pausanias' narrative (Pausanias-A) discussed above, in which the monster is of a manifestly serpentine nature:

- On a *c.*350–325 BC red-figure stamnos from Vulci, Aita is shown with Persephone in his chariot (either her abduction or her return is depicted): two snakes project from Hades' hair over his forehead.[82]
- In the *c.*340–320 BC Orcus II tomb fresco at Corneto discussed in Chapter 2 a wolfskin-clad Aita holds up in his left hand a black snake and seems to be about to hurl it at Geryon, to whom he points with his right, in a pose that recalls that adopted by Zeus for hurling the thunderbolt. The accompanying Persephone's hair is bound in a diadem of snakes too.[83]
- On a late fourth-century volute crater from Orvieto Aita is shown in his chariot brandishing a serpent sceptre.[84]

---

[79] Euripides *Hecuba* 90–1 (deer) and 92–7 (Achilles); according to Diggle 1984 (the OCT) 90–1 are spurious, and 92–7 may well be too ('*haereo*'); so too Kovacs 1995 (Loeb). Visintin 1992:79–85 adduces this passage in elucidation of the Hero; cf. also Mainoldi 1984:134–5.

[80] Cf. Cook 1914–40:i, 99 (noting that the comparison between our 'Lykas' and Aita had been made explicitly by Roscher at *Abhandlungen der sächsischen Gesellschaft der Wissenschaften*, Philologisch-Historische Classe 1897 xvii.3, 44–5, 60–1; *non vidi*, alas), Gernet 1981 (1936):132–3 and Weber-Lehmann 1995:72–100, with pll. 21–4. Casevitz et al. 2002:138 compare the Hero's blackness with the *blueness* of demons and of Charun in Etruscan funerary art.

[81] Let us remark here that both Chantraine 2009 and Beekes 2010 in their etymological dictionaries (s.v. ἀλίβας) note, oddly without scorn, the conjecture that the term *alíbas* might have something in common with the Etruscan verb *lupu*, 'he died'. Cf. Rissanen 2012:130, where the idea is entertained that the influence of this same Etruscan word, in combination with the ancient Italian association of wolves with death, influenced the development of the Latin form *lupus*, with the unexpected –*p*-, in place of the anticipated form *lucus*. I consider the Sabellic explanation of *lupus* given above to be preferable (although the two explanations are not completely incompatible).

[82] Museo Gregoriano Etrusco Vaticano 14,963 = *LIMC* Aita/Calu 1.   [83] *LIMC* Aita/Calu 6.

[84] Orvieto, Museo Faina 20 (2646) = *LIMC* Aita/Calu 14. Nor can I forbear to mention the underworld scene depicted on a fourth-century Etruscan vase from Orvieto, in which Persephone's chariot

- On a *c.*300 BC relief sarcophagus also from Orvieto's Torre San Severo, an Aita brandishing a serpent sceptre and a Persephone with her serpent diadem attend the scene as Achilles slaughters Trojan captives before the tomb of Patroclus.[85]

We turn again to the superb wolf-man on the tondo of the Tityos Painter's (*c.*540–510 BC) Pontic Plate from Vulci and now in Rome's Museo Etrusco di Villa Giulia, referred to in Chapter 2 (Figure 5.1).[86] What does this running figure, with a wolf's head and a humanoid body covered in wolfskin, but no other immediate context, represent?[87] The only potential clue, if clue it be, lies in the frieze surrounding the image of the wolf-man, which shows the centaur Nessus

Figure 5.1 Tityos Painter (*c.*540–510 BC), Pontic Plate from Vulci, Osteria Necropolis, Tomb 177. Museo Etrusco di Villa Giulia, Rome.

is drawn by large birds of prey with serpent heads and tails [!], while the ground below is infested with serpents: Museo Faina, Orvieto 19 (2645) = *LIMC* Aita/Calu 9.

---

[85] Illustrated at Messerschmidt 1930:67, fig. 3.

[86] Found in Vulci's Osteria Necropolis, Tomb 177.

[87] Elliot 1995:27 relates the figure to the monster named Olta mentioned at Pliny *Natural History* 2.140 (for whom again see Chapter 2), but wholly without warrant: Pliny gives no indication that this marauder has any lupine affinity whatsoever; cf. Chierici 1994, Rupp 2007:72, Rissanen 2012:131–4.

pursuing Deianeira, and Heracles in turn pursuing the centaur with a massive club. Some explanations have indeed honoured the frieze and tried to construct a thematic bond with it for the wolf-man. Luca Cerchiai accordingly identifies him as Faunus, pointing to the burlesque story of Faunus' attempted rape of Heracles' lover Omphale in Ovid's *Fasti*.[88] Wayne Rupp suggests that the figure may be a generalized death demon (à la Aita), saluting the death that shortly awaits both Nessus and Heracles alike.[89] With wild speculation, we might suggest a further possibility that falls between these two: that the thematic bond between frieze and the tondo consists in both subjects being mixanthropic (part animal, part man) rapists. In this case the wolf-man might be a figure quite similar to our Hero—if, that is, we could be sure that the Hero of Pausanias' narrative (Pausanias-A) did indeed share the lupine affinities of the Hero of his picture (Pausanias-B).[90]

Conclusion

This chapter has returned to the theme of the association between werewolves and ghosts initiated in Chapter 2 with an investigation into the case of the wolfskin-wearing Hero of Temesa, the vengeful ghost-demon of Odysseus' crewman Polites. It has been argued that the figure should be viewed as a werewolf amongst other ancient werewolves. It is important to disaggregate the various accounts of the Hero and to differentiate between them, including the two offered side by side by Pausanias. These last two accounts, that of the periegete's substantive narrative (Pausanias-A) and that implied by his description of the picture (Pausanias-B—it is in this context that the Hero is explicitly said to wear his wolfskin), both align in an informative way with a productive story type in which champions deliver victims from a usually serpentine monster. Careful analysis of Pausanias' description of the picture in the light of the story type exposes the fact that it plays with a rather different cast list from that of Pausanias' narrative, one in which the role of the athlete-champion Euthymus is actually taken by the river Kalabros and the role of the victim is taken not by a girl, but by the youth Sybaris. So far as the comparative examples of this story type are concerned, the picture description aligns particularly well with Antoninus Liberalis' tale of the delivery of the youth Alcyoneus from the Lamia-Sybaris monster of Delphi by Eurybatus, descendant of the river Axius. In both cases the monster is seemingly transformed into a

---

[88] Ovid *Fasti* 2.303–58 (as Faunus attempts to rape the person he thinks is Omphale, he is embarrassed to discover that she has exchanged her clothes with Heracles); Cerchiai 2000.

[89] Rupp 2007:72.

[90] I note that, without knowing this plate, Gernet 1981 (1936):133 was moved to compare, in an indirect way, Euthymus' delivery of the girl from the Hero with Heracles' delivery of Deianeira from Nessus.

spring after its demise. The story type comparanda further press us to look for possible serpentine affinities for the Hero in Pausanias' two accounts, and we may just about be able to find them, not least with the help of the Etruscan Aita. We will return to the association between athlete-champions, wolves, and werewolves in the following chapter.

6

The Werewolves of Arcadia

At last, and finally, we turn to the subject that has hitherto dominated the study of the werewolf in a classical context: the myths and rites associated with the Arcadian Lykaia festival.[1] I have postponed treatment of this material to the end of the book precisely because of the need to decentre it from the study of the topic and to give proper focus, space, attention, and respect to the folkloric origins of the ancient werewolf, as we have done hitherto. The Anthid rite that lies at the heart of the Lykaia traditions is not, despite the drift of much recent scholarship, the key to the ancient werewolf; rather, it is a metaphorical derivative of the ancient folkloric traditions that are indeed the key. However, once the complex traditions relating to the Lykaia are disentangled, the traces of another folkloric werewolf tale—this above and beyond the aetiological myth of Lykaon himself—can be seen to emerge from them.

The extant ancient data bearing upon Arcadia is best understood as pertaining to three fields:

1. Historical (or historicizing) evidence for a rite of passage (or maturation or initiation) associated with the Lykaia sacrifices on Mount Lykaion, the modern Mount St Elias, in which a young man of the Anthid clan symbolically took on the lifestyle of a wolf for a fixed period, probably a brief one, in broad alignment with the ritual marginalizations of youth found in the Athenian practice of the *ephebeia* and the Spartan practice of the *krypteia*.
2. A suite of closely related myths of an original, primordial, and aetiological transformation into a wolf, this by the eponymous Lykaon, and occasioned

---

[1] For Lykaon and the Lykaia specifically see: Böttiger 1837:135–58, Hertz 1862:34–40, Immerwahr 1891:i, 1–24 (including fullish reproduction of source texts); Drexler 1894–7; Farnell 1896–1909:i, 41–2, 144–6; Smith 1894:13–19; Cook 1914–40:i, 63–99, esp. 81–8; Meyer 1927; Halliday 1928:168–73 (on Q39); Schuster 1930:151–2; Summers 1933:134–45; Eckels 1937:49–60; Kroll 1937; Jeanmaire 1939:540–69, Lévêque 1961:98–100, Nilsson 1967:397–401; Piccaluga 1968; Gernet 1981 [1936]; Vidal-Naquet 1981a, Burkert 1983a:84–93 (esp. 90–3); Mainoldi 1984:11–18, Jost 1985:249–69, 1989, 2002, 2005:1–19, 2016; Wathelet 1986, Buxton 1987:68–74, 2009:135–7; Bourgeaud 1988:23–44; Sourvinou-Inwood 1988a:174–7; Detienne and Svenbro 1989:156–7; Forbes-Irving 1990:50–7, 90–5, 216–18; Moreau 1997:72–9; Gershenson 1991:75–6, 99–103; Hughes 1991:96–107; Douglas 1992:44–54; Halm-Tisserant 1993:128–38; Bonnechere 1994:85–96; Bynum 2001: 166–70; Veenstra 2002:142–3; Pinotti 2003:96–101; Romano 2005, 2008; Zolotnikova 2005; Bremmer 2007b:65–78, 2019:358–70; Pirenne-Delforge 2008:67–72, 333–7; Aston 2011 esp. 102–6, 111–13, 119, 208–13, 249–50, 273–4, 342; Romano and Voyatzis 2010 (a popular but well-illustrated account of the Lykaion site); Metzger 2011:180–216 (esp. 207–10), 2012:146–50; Gordon 2015:34–44. Eidinow 2019.

by a sacrilegious act of human sacrifice and cannibalism or at any rate attempted cannibalism.

3. Another tale, now partly obscured from view, in which a supposedly historical individual, one Damarchus or Demaenetus, was transformed into a wolf for nine years at the Lykaia festival after eating part of a human sacrifice. The evidence for this story is badly concatenated with the evidence for the Anthid rite.

We shall lay all this data out in translation, considering the more easily separable material relating to category (2) here first. The material relating to categories (1) and (3) will initially have to be considered together because, as said, it is heavily concatenated, and indeed it will be one of this chapter's principal tasks to disentangle it. The material bearing on Lykaon extends to some length and is (despite its many variations) somewhat repetitive. It is laid out in full here for the sake of completeness and to support the volume's aim of incorporating a comprehensive sourcebook for werewolfism in the ancient world.

The 'Primary' (or Primordial) Aetiological Myths Focusing on Lykaon

According to the aetiological myth proper of the Lykaia, Lykaon or his sons are said to have been transformed into a wolf or wolves by Zeus after engineering a banquet of human flesh for the god. The story, in some version, was evidently known to the writer of a poem that later Greeks at any rate could regard as Hesiodic:[2]

> The commentators on Lycophron explain the 'transgression' [*paraibasia*] of Lykaon against Zeus, to put it as Hesiod does.
>
> Hesiod *Catalogue of Women* F164 MW = 114 Most (earlier 6th c. BC)[3]
> (= Eustathius on Homer *Iliad* 2.608, i. p. 468.13–14 van der Valk)[4]

---

[2] For the myth of Lykaon see Drexler 1894–7, Smith 1894:14–20, Cook 1914–40:i, 63–99, esp. 77–81, Meyer 1927, Jeanmaire 1939:540–69, Nilsson 1967:397–401, Piccaluga 1968 esp. 31–98, Burkert 1983a:98–108, Mainoldi 1984:16–17, Borgeaud 1988:23–44, Barkan 1986:24–7 (with care); Borgeaud 1988:23–44; Forbes Irving 1990:216–18, Gantz 1993:725–9, Jost 1985:261–3, 2005, 2016, Detienne 2003, Gourmelen 2003, 2004:275–80, Pirenne-Delforge 2008:67–72, 333–7. Given the frequency of metamorphosis in Greek myth, transformation into wolves is surprisingly rare. Another example is found in the obscure myth of Theophane recorded at Hyginus *Fabulae* 188. Poseidon fell in love with her and carried her off to the island of Crumissa, where, to conceal her, he changed her into a ewe, himself into a ram, and all the citizens of Crumissa into sheep also. When Theophane's suitors arrived on the island in pursuit, they started slaughtering the citizen-sheep to eat, and so Poseidon turned them into wolves. Sleeping with Theophane in ovine form, Poseidon sired the ram with the golden fleece that would carry Phrixus to Colchis and become the object of the Argonauts' mission.

[3] For the dating of the *Catalogue* see Most 2006–7:lv.

[4] Cf. also: [Hesiod] F163 MW (= 115 Most), quoted below, *apud* Apollodorus *Bibliotheca* 3.8.2, referring to Callisto, albeit in such a way that *may* indicate that Hesiod did not connect her with Lykaon; F165 MW (= 117 Most), where Arcas is referred to in passing as an 'ancestor'; and F354 (dubium).

The following sections chart, in (rough) chronological order of attestations, the several recorded variants of the Lykaon myth, with discussion following.[5]

Version (a): Lykaon attempts to feed Zeus the flesh of his (Zeus'), son, Arcas, eponym of Arcadia.

> *On Bootes and Arctophylax.* Concerning this it is said that Arcas was born of Callisto and Zeus, and that he lived in the region of Mt Lykaion after Zeus had raped her. Lykaon got hold of him and hosted Zeus, as Hesiod tells, and, chopping up the child, set him on the table [*trapeza*] for Zeus. So Zeus overturned the table, and that is how the city of Trapezus gets its name. He blasted his house with a thunderbolt, and turned Lykaon into a beast, making him a wolf. He put Arcas back together and made him perfect again. He was reared by a goatherd. It appears that, when he had become a youth [*neaniskos*], he ran to Mt Lykaion and had sex with his mother. The inhabitants of the place were on the point of sacrificing them both in accordance with the law, but Zeus drove them off and catasterised Callisto and Arcas because of their relationship to him.
>   [Hesiod] F163 MW= [Eratosthenes] *Catasterismi* 1.8 (2nd c. BC—3rd c. AD)[6]

> ...Lykaon's guilty altars...   Statius *Thebaid* 11.127 (*c.* AD 92)[7]

> It is said that Lykaon, when Jupiter came to him as a guest-friend, chopped Arcas up with other meat and put it before him for a meal. For he was keen to discover whether it was indeed a god that sought his hospitality. This done, he was punished commensurately. For at once Jupiter threw forth the table and struck his house with a thunderbolt. Lykaon himself he changed into the form [*figura*] of a wolf. He collected the boy's limbs and reconstituted them and gave him to one of the Aetolians to rear.   Hyginus *Astronomica* 2.4 (2nd c. AD)

> It is said that Jupiter came to Lykaon the son of Pelasgus as a guest-friend, and raped his daughter Callisto, from whom Arcas was born. He bestowed a name upon the land [*sc.* Arcadia] from his own. But the sons of Lykaon wished to make trial of Jupiter, to see whether he was a god. They mixed human flesh in with the rest of the meat, and gave it to him as part of the meal. When he realised this, he angrily overturned the table and killed Lykaon's sons with a thunderbolt. Arcas later built a walled city in that place, called Trapezus. Jupiter changed their father Lykaon into the form [*figura*] of a wolf.   Hyginus *Fabulae* 176 (2nd c. AD)

---

[5] Metzger 2011:188 offers a useful table of the motifs found across the set of variants.

[6] The association of this text with (any kind of) Hesiod is almost certainly spurious, and it is accordingly unsafe to date the material in this passage prior to the pseudo-Eratosthenic *Catasterismi*, a text that seemingly evolved between the age of Eratosthenes himself and the third century AD. See Fowler 2000–13:ii, 104–5, Jost 2016:24–5, 30–1. For this tricky Eratosthenic text more generally, see now Hard 2015 (an introduction and translation, also interleaving the relevant portions of Hyginus' astrology).

[7] This vague reference is in fact compatible with versions (a), (b), and (d).

The constellation of Bootes, also known as Arcturus, is said to be the guardian of the Wain because it follows the Wain, that is its seven constituent stars, and is as it were tucked underneath them. They say this is Arcas the son of Jupiter and Callisto, after whom Arcadia is named. Lykaon the son of Pelasgus, when he was hosting Jupiter as a guest-friend, hacked this infant up limb from limb, killing him, and set him before Jupiter as a meal, to see whether Jupiter was a god.... Arcas is said to have been born of Callisto and Jupiter and to have lived opposite Lykaon. He was cut up into little bits by this same Lykaon and set on a table, but he was then remade again and reared by a certain goatherd. 'Burned the house of Lykaon with a thunderbolt of Jupiter'—and in that place a city was built, which was called Trapezus. But he turned Lykaon into a wolf. He fitted Arcas' limbs back together and restored him to life, and gave him to a certain goatherd to rear....   Schol. Germanicus *Aratea* pp.123–4 Breysig (3rd c. AD)

Version (b): Lykaon attempts to feed Zeus the flesh of his own son, Nyctimus.

'...she-wolf-shaped [*lykainomorphōn*] butcherers of Nyctimus...': It is told that, when Zeus was being received as a guest-friend by Lykaon, he sacrificed the younger of his children to him and laid before him a certain boy called Nyctimus. Zeus became angry and sent thunderbolts against not only the one that had attempted this, but also many of the others, although it had just been from Lykaon and a few others that he had accepted the invitation [?—the meaning of the text is obscure at this point]. He overturned the whole table, after which he named the city of Trapezus in Arcadia. He changed many others into wolves, and for this reason the Arcadian mountain was called Lykaion.

The he-goat spoke incorrectly, for he should have said 'he-wolf-shaped' [*lykomorphōn*]. For the sons of Lykaon became not she-wolves but he-wolves, according to him. The story is as follows. Pelasgus was the son of Zeus and Niobe, and he had a son Lykaon from the girl Meliboea or from Cyllene, as others say in contradiction. He became king of the Arcadians and sired fifty children from many marriages. But his offspring were impious. Among these were Menarus, Thesprotus and Nyctimus, Caucon, Lycus, Phthius and Teleboas, Haemon, Mantinous, Stymphalus and Clitor, Orchomenus and others, all of whom, as I said, were exceptional in their impiety and arrogance. Zeus approached them in the guise of a workman for hire, and they invited him on the basis of guest-friendship, and slaughtered a child of the locals. They mixed up his entrails and laid before him on a table. Zeus was disgusted and overturned the table, whence that place in Arcadia is now called Trapezus. He blasted Lykaon and his sons with a thunderbolt, apart from the younger Nyctimus. After Nyctimus had taken over the kingdom the flood of the age of Deucalion occurred because of the impiety of the sons of Lykaon. Otherwise, Zeus was entertained by the Arcadian Lykaon and dined with him. His sons, testing whether he was a god, butchered Nyctimus, mixed up his flesh with the other flesh and placed it before Zeus. He became angry and overturned the table, which is why there is a city of Trapezusa [*sic*] in Arcadia. He destroyed the sons of Lykaon with a thunderbolt and continuously rained down thunderbolts upon Arcadia, until the Earth, calling upon Zeus, stretched out her hand to him, and that is why they say that the first truce was among the Arcadians. He changed some of the sons of Lykaon into wolves.... 'Butcherers of Nyctimus.' This is rubbish. For they did not butcher Nyctimus, but another child, a local one, as Apollodorus and others say.

> Lycophron *Alexandra* 481 (*c*. 190 BC), with schol. (Byzantine)[8]

Zeus himself shared a human table with the Ethiopians and an inhuman and unlawful one when dining with Lykaon the Arcadian. Despite himself, he filled himself with human flesh. For Zeus did not know that Lykaon the Arcadian, the host of his feast, had slaughtered his own son (Nyctimus was his name) and put him before him for his meat.

> Clement of Alexandria *Protrepticus* 2.36.5, p.31 Potter (2nd c. AD)

Do we say that ... Jupiter, invited to the table as a guest-friend, lunched in ignorance upon the offspring of Lykaon, instead of chitterlings?

> Arnobius *Adversus nationes* 4.24 (*c*. AD 300)

Others say that, because Lykaon put his own son before Jupiter to dine on, Jupiter destroyed Lykaon himself with a thunderbolt and made a flood in which men perished, apart from Pyrrha, daughter of Epimetheus, and Deucalion, son of Prometheus, who were kept safe from the flood by the height of Mt Parnassus, and reconstituted the human race, as was said above.

> Servius on Virgil *Eclogues* 6.41 (4th c. AD)

I used to hear how Lykaon received your father [Zeus] himself, together with the other blessed gods, and he chopped up his son Nyctimus with his hand and laid him before your father in his ignorance, and touched the same table as Zeus, ruler of all, beside the plain of Arcadia.   Nonnus *Dionysiaca* 18.20–4 (*c*. AD 400)

Version (c): Lykaon's sons attempt to feed Zeus the flesh of a local, and it is accordingly they (or again Lykaon himself) that are transformed into wolves.

That Lykaon, king of the Arcadians, the son of Pelasgus, maintained his father's precepts justly. In his own desire to deter the people he ruled from injustice, he used to claim that Zeus would visit him on each occasion in the guise of a guest-friend in order to scrutinise the just and the unjust. And once, as he himself said, he was making a sacrifice before receiving the god. He had fifty sons, as

---

[8] This variant in particular is reminiscent of the myth of Tantalus: see Douglas 1992:47.

they say, from many wives. Some of these, who were attending the sacrifice, wanted to know if they were really going to receive a god. So they sacrificed a child and mixed him in with the meat of the sacrifice, so that their actions would not escape detection, if a god was really visiting them. Great storms and thunderbolts broke forth from the deity, and they say that all of the child's killers were destroyed.

Nicolaus of Damascus *FGrH* 90 F38 (later 1st c. BC)

= *Suda* s.v. Λυκάων (10th c. AD)

To Pelasgus and Meliboea the daughter of Ocean, or, as others say, the nymph Cyllene, the son Lykaon was born. He ruled over the Arcadians and sired fifty sons from many wives... [these are named]. These sons surpassed all men in their arrogance and impiety. Zeus wanted to test their impiety and approached them in the guise of a labourer for hire. They invited him to receive the gifts of guest-friendship. They jugulated a child from amongst the locals, mixed his entrails in with the sacrifice and placed them before him, this at the suggestion of the elder brother Maenalus. Zeus was disgusted and overturned the table, whence the place is now called Trapezus, and he destroyed Lykaon and his sons with thunderbolts, except for Nyctimus, the youngest. For Earth grabbed Zeus' right hand and stopped him from his anger. When Nyctimus inherited the kingdom the flood of the time of Deucalion occurred. Some said that this happened on account of the impiety of the sons of Lykaon.

Apollodorus *Bibliotheca* 3.8.1–2 (*c.* AD 100)[9]

Version (d): Lykaon attempts to feed Zeus the flesh of a Molossian hostage.

'Not satisfied with that, Lykaon opened with a knife the throat of a hostage sent from the Molossian people. Some of his limbs, still only half dead, he softened in boiling water, others he roasted over fire. As soon as he had laid this meal on the table, I, Jupiter, with avenging thunderbolt, brought down the palace on top of the household gods that were deserving of such a master. Lykaon himself fled in terror. Making his way to the still of the countryside, he howled and tried in vain to make human utterance. His mouth filled with foam and, with its familiar desire for slaughter, turned its frenzied hunger against the flocks, once again rejoicing in blood. His clothes turned into tufts of hair, his arms into legs. He became a wolf but retained traces of his previous form: the same grey hair, the

---

[9] This version of the tale is also referred to at Hyginus *Fabulae* 176 and schol. Lycophron *Alexandra* 481, quoted above, under versions (a) and (b) respectively. Some of Lykaon's sons sport names shared by Giants. This may be an ancient connection, or it may be a relatively late one forged on the basis that, like the Giants, Lykaon's sons constitute a (mini-)race of enemies of the gods. See Elderkin 1940:231 (noting, albeit without references, that the name Harpalykos/Harpolykos is shared by one of Lykaon's sons at Apollodorus *Bibliotheca* 3.8.1 and a Giant in a gigantomachy scene on a 6th-c. BC Caeretan amphora, Louvre E732 = *LIMC* Gigantes 170), Vian 1952:238–46 esp. 240–1 (Aegaeon, Harpalycus, Pallas, Titanas), Piccaluga 1968: 31, 34, 65, Forbes Irving 1990:217.

same violent expression, the same flashing eyes, and the same wild mien...'
And now Jupiter was about to rain down thunderbolts on all the lands...He
decided on a different punishment: to obliterate the race of morals beneath
waves and send down rains from every part of the sky.

Ovid *Metamorphoses* 1.226-39, 253, 260–1[10]

You will repeat the disgusting banquet of Lykaon's table and attempt to cheat
Jupiter with deceitful food.

Scholium: Lykaon the king of Arcadia entertained Zeus and, wishing to test his
godhead, gave him a hostage he had from the Molossian region. Observing this
crime, Zeus turned him into a wolf and burned his house.

Ovid *Ibis* 431–2, with scholium

Version (e): Lykaon attempts to feed Zeus the flesh of an unnamed person.

Pelasgus' son Lykaon made cleverer discoveries than his father. Thus, he founded
the city of Lykosoura[11] on Mt Lykaion, called Zeus 'Lykaios' and founded the
'Lykaia' games. It is my opinion that the Athenians' Panathenaea festival was not
founded previously to this. The name of this festival was originally the Athenaea,
but they say that it acquired the name Panathenaea under Theseus, because at
that point it was established by the Athenians as a whole, all gathered together
into a single city. As to the competition at Olympia, I leave discussion of it out of
my present work, because people trace it back to before the human race and
claim that Cronus and Zeus wrestled there, whilst the Curetes were the first to
run a race. I at any rate believe that Cecrops the king of Athens and Lykaon were
of the same generation, but that they were not of equal wisdom in matters
divine. For Cecrops was the first to give Zeus the name of the Highest God, and
he thought it right to sacrifice nothing with a soul, but dedicated on his altar the
local cakes that the Athenians still call *pelanoi* even in our own day. Lykaon, by
contrast, brought the child of a human to the altar of Lykaian Zeus, sacrificed
the child and libated its blood over the altar. They say that he became a wolf
instead of a man immediately after the sacrifice. I for one believe this story. It
has been told by the Arcadians from of old, and it is, furthermore, likely. For in
those days men were guest-friends of the gods and shared tables with them,
because of their justice and piety. The honour of the gods was bestowed openly
upon the good, and the unjust received their anger in the same fashion, since
some gods came from men, and they are still worshipped in this day, such as
Aristaeus, the Cretan woman Britomartis, Heracles the son of Alcmene and

---

[10] Gordon 2015:34–5 contextualizes Ovid's account. He considers that the Lykaon myth has been
so successful in subsequent Western culture precisely because it had the good fortune to feature in the
earliest lines of this much-loved text.

[11] For Lykosoura and its site see Jost 1985:172–8 and Guimier Sorbets, Jost and Morizot 2008.

Amphiaraus the son of Oecles, and on top of these Castor and Polydeuces. In this way one could believe that Lykaon became a beast and Niobe the daughter of Tantalus a stone. But in my age—for wickedness has increased to its maximum degree and spreads over every land and all cities—no god is made from a man, with the exception of words and flattery directed towards the prominent, and the wrath of the gods is kept in store for the wicked for a later time, when they have departed this world. In every age, people that found lies on the basis of the truth have rendered many things that happened long ago, and even some that happen still now, incredible for most people...[12]

A little higher up Mt Lykaion is the circuit-wall of Lykosoura. It contains just a few inhabitants. Of all the cities the earth has ever produced, be it on the mainland or on the islands, Lykosoura is the oldest, and this was the first one upon which the sun looked. It was from this city that other men learned how to make them.   Pausanias 8.2.1–6, 8.38.1 (late 2nd c. AD)

For example Lykaon, who received guest-friends only to kill them. When he received Zeus and placed a feast of human meat before him, he was turned into a wolf and so demonstrated that the laws of hospitality should not be violated.
Servius on Virgil Aeneid 1.731 (4th c. AD)

Lykaon the king was transformed into a wolf because he put human flesh on the table before Zeus when he was being hosted by him.
Anonymus Paradoxographus De transformationibus
p.222, 3–5 Westermann (undated: Byzantine?)

Jupiter, impatient of human wickedness, assumed the guise of a man and came to Lykaon, king of Arcadia, who, plotting death for him as if for a mortal, set human limbs before him to eat. Once Jupiter had realised this, he did not just destroy him then and there but, so that he should not miss the significance of the punishment, he turned him into the shape of a wolf. The wolf retains Lykaon's ways in its hunger and his name in its appellation.
First Vatican Mythographer 1.17 (9th–11th c. AD)

Version (f): A late revisionist perspective on Lykaon.

There are many kinds of wolf. There is the 'kite', the 'falcon', the 'archer'. There is another variety that is the king of wolves and is so called. This one is not by nature oppressive towards sheep, but if ever it does snatch one, yielding to its hunger, it divides the spoils with the shepherd, devouring half the sheep itself but leaving the other half of it for him. And there was once a king Lykaon, who was Arcadian by birth and was devoted to justice. Even if he happened to have

---

[12] Gordon 2015:36–7 contextualizes Pausanias' account.

turned into a wolf, he did not transform his character at the same time, but remained just.

Timothy of Gaza (*fl.* in the reign of Anastasius, AD 491–518)
at Aristophanes of Byzantium (et al.) *Aristophanis historiae animalium*
epitome subjunctis Aeliani Timothei aliorumque eclogis 2.237

The Lykaon Myth: Discussion

'Lykaon est un loup—l'animal dont il porte le nom—, pas un loup-garou.'

Jost 2005:14

Jost might well be thought to have a point: it could indeed be said that Lykaon is at first a man, and then a wolf, and at no point a werewolf—if one were to insist either that to qualify as a werewolf one must change back at least once, or have the capacity to do so, or that one must somehow embody the qualities of human and wolf at the same time. This might be a superficially appealing definition of a werewolf, but it is ultimately an arbitrary one. And it could in any case be argued that Lykaon had a latent lupine quality before his transformation, given his actions. Nonetheless, given Lykaon's aetiological relationship with the Anthid rite, we cannot avoid discussion of him, partly unsatisfactory a figure though he may be as werewolves go.

As Cook noted, 'These rillets of [Lykaon's] tradition cross and recross one another with such complexity that it is difficult to map them or make out which after all is the main stream.'[13] The myth in its many versions is indeed well attested, but the lateness of all these attestations, the Hesiodic *Catalogue's* passing and unenlightening reference to Lykaon's 'transgression' aside, is remarkable.[14] Hesiod apart, the tradition begins with Lycophron's brief allusion. The pseudo-Eratosthenic *Catasterimsi* may be next, if they really are, in effect, as early as the second century BC. Otherwise we must turn to the late-first-century BC Nicolaus of Damascus and then to the Augustan Ovid.

In the first instance, the myth is ostensibly a specific aetiology of the sacrifices and associated rites on Mount Lykaion, but also, more abstractly, of the sacrificial relationship between man and god more generally. An additional specific aetiology is claimed from the fact that Zeus overturned the table (*trapeza*) upon which he was being fed in disgust, and this gave its name to the city of Trapezus.[15]

---

[13] Cook 1914–40:i, 79.
[14] For discussion of how much Hesiod knew about Lykaon, see Sale 1962.
[15] [Hesiod] F163 MW = [Eratosthenes] *Catasterismi* 1.8; schol. Lycophron *Alexandra* 481; Apollodorus *Bibliotheca* 3.8.1–2, all quoted above.

Modern interpreters of the myth (who tend to focus particularly on Pausanias' account of it) broadly agree that it is primarily concerned with man's place in the order of things, that is his relationship with the gods above and the animals below, and with the boundaries, good or bad, that separate him from both.[16] In the primordial age at the start of the tale man is found in a blessed state in which the boundary between himself and the gods is porous or even non-existent, insofar as Lykaon and Zeus share a table. The events of the myth then account for the act of separation that leaves man in a miserable condition: Zeus' overthrowing of the table signifies the end of the commensality between men and gods, while the distance that must now obtain between them, in terms of both space and power, is articulated in the awesome and devastating thunderbolt (the thunderbolt that was in fact central to the iconography of Zeus Lykaios).[17]

The cause of the fall is man's violation of the boundary below: Lykaon does this by treating a human as an animal in sacrificing him, and this violation of the boundary is then expressed in the transformation of his own body, as he passes from human to animal. The challenge and struggle for mankind henceforth is to try to reconstruct and maintain the boundary with the animals that Lykaon had violated, and the key to this lies in the life of civilization. This key too was given to mankind by Lykaon, insofar as, brutal though he was, he was also a culture hero, as Pausanias makes emphatically clear in strikingly poetic terms: he was the founder of Lykosoura, the first city upon which the sun ever looked, the construction of which conferred knowledge and understanding on the rest of mankind, and which was the model for all the other cities of the world. Pausanias makes it clear too that he was also the first *human* founder of a games festival, the Lykaia, and indeed the inventor of the all-important blood sacrifice, even if getting it wrong himself. Man's commitment to the life of the city is an attempt to maintain his separation from the animals, with the distance between them now marked clearly in terms of space and in terms of culture. The consequences of violating the boundary are evidently terrible for victims and perpetrators alike. As Emma Aston has observed, 'Inherent in the Lykaon myth, and explicit in Pausanias' narration of it, is regret at the lost closeness of man with god, but the accompanying closeness with the animal world and its perceived character is treated as purely malign.'

The Lykaon myth accordingly has much in common in its function with that of the famous myth of Prometheus' sacrifice at Mecone, as recounted by Hesiod: here too another culture hero, Prometheus, the bringer of fire to man, contrives to

---

[16] For useful articulations of the sort of approach laid out in this and the next two paragraphs (some of the nuances here are my own), see Buxton 1987:60–4, esp. 73, Forbes-Irving 1990:90–5, Gourmelen 2003, 2004:275–80 and Aston 2011:102, 209–12 (210, cit.). Cf. also, more broadly, Barkan 1986:25, Borgeaud 1988:23–31, Fowler 2000–13:ii, 104–5, Detienne 2003, Bynum 2001:166–72 (focusing principally on the account in Ovid), Jost 1985:262–3, 2005:15–18, Gilhus 2006:79 and Gordon 2015:36, 43.

[17] For the iconography of Zeus Lykaios and his thunderbolt, see Jost 1985:252–4.

separate man from the gods by presenting Zeus with another foundational but deceitful sacrifice. In a shared meal he fobs Zeus off with the animal's bones, disguised in the glistening fat, while retaining the good meat for himself and mankind, this constituting an aetiology of sacrifice in general. In revenge, Zeus inflicts upon Prometheus and mankind all the ills of Pandora's box.[18]

A different approach was taken by the author of the only monograph devoted to Lykaon, Giulia Piccaluga.[19] She argued that the myth of Lykaon was essentially a genesis myth, and that the myth and so too the cult activities on Mount Lykaion were addressed principally to the opposition between water and drought Her starting point for this is Pausanias' note on the spring of Hagno on Mount Lykaion: in times of drought the priest of Zeus Lykaios would bring forth a mist from the waters of the spring by lowering an oak branch to just below its surface and stirring it; the mist would rise into a cloud, attract other clouds, and bring rain.[20] As for Lykaon, he is a representative of the pre-civilized world prior to the primordial deluge. Nonetheless, his sacrilegious sacrifice has the ultimately positive effect of bringing down thunderbolts from heaven, and with them the all-important deluge, which fertilizes the earth and permits the grain to grow. Lykaon's punitive transformation into a wolf marks the origin point of all animal species, a wolf being chosen to stand for the whole because it was an animal of particular import-ance in Arcadia, and iconically ferocious. The Anthid rite of the Lykaia is merely a re-enactment of Lykaon's fate. This line of thought has not found favour. Madeleine Jost and others have noted that the motif of the deluge looks like a relatively late intrusion into the myth and that it may even originate in a novelty artificially introduced by Ovid in order to enable him to link the story of Lykaon to the following story in his ultimately random chain of tales in the *Metamorphoses*, that of Deucalion, the Greek Noah. Piccaluga's dismissive attitude to the werewolf imagery has also been considered unsatisfactory.[21]

Needless to say, the myth emphatically presents Lykaon—and thereby similarly Lykaios, Lykaion, Lykaia, and Lykosoura—as a speaking name expressive of 'wolf' (*lykos*). The metaphorical wolves of the Anthid rite, of which more anon, point the same way. There has been considerable debate amongst scholars as to whether this verbal relationship expresses a true etymology or a confected ('folk') one. For morphological reasons, it may be preferable to derive all these names, Lykosoura aside, from the vestigially attested term *lykē*, 'light' (cf. Latin *lux* and, indeed,

---

[18] For Prometheus at Mecone see Hesiod *Theogony* 535–616 and *Works and Days* 42–105, with the important analysis of Vernant 1981 and 1989.
[19] Piccaluga 1968, esp. 99–146.   [20] Pausanias 8.38.3–4; for this rite see Jost 1985:251–2.
[21] Piccaluga's approach receives short shrift from Jost 1985:263 n.2, 265, Buxton 1987:78 n.48, and Forbes-Irving 1990:91 n.114; cf. also Merkelbach 1970; Gordon 2015:43 shows uncharacteristic restraint. Ovid on Deucalion and the flood: *Metamorphoses* 1.253–437. The motif of the flood is sub-sequently incorporated by Apollodorus *Bibliotheca* 3.8.1–2 (though one wonders whether this text is really likely to have taken the detail from Ovid), schol. Lycophron *Alexandra* 481 and Servius on Virgil *Eclogues* 6.41.

English 'light').[22] The simple form is supplied (perhaps invented) by Macrobius, but it is found compounded in the adjective *amphilykē* ('around-light'), which Homer attaches to 'night' to mean 'twilight'.[23] Aspects of the Lykaon myth and the Lykaion sanctuary and its practices may offer some support to the 'light' reading: the son named Nyctimus ('Of night'); the fact that one did not, supposedly, cast a shadow in the Lykaion sanctuary;[24] the fact that before the altar of Zeus there had once stood two pillars oriented towards the rising sun, topped with golden eagles.[25] Of course all these features too may merely be the expressions of a bogus etymology.

The themes of the Lykaon myth are found elsewhere in Arcadian myth and cult. As to the theme of child-eating, when the 'acorn-eating' Phigalians once neglected their cult of Demeter Melaina, the Pythia threatened them:

> Soon she [Deo, Demeter Melaina] will make you eaters of each other and diners upon children, / if you do not propitiate her anger with libations on behalf of all the people / and decorate the recess of her cave with divine honours.
>
> Pausanias 8.42.6[26]

And the man–animal boundary was also violated at Lykosoura in the form of the animal-headed but otherwise humanoid dancing figures that decorated the veil of Despoina's cult statue.[27]

Lykaon 'the wolf' lives on today: a genetically distinct species of wolf resident in northern Canada now rejoices in the Latin nomenclature *Canis lycaon*.[28]

---

[22] For the 'light' hypothesis and others see Cook 1914–40:i, 63–8, 81, Gernet 1981 [1936]:134 n.17, Eckels 1937:54–5, Jost 1985:250–3, Buxton 1987:72, 78 n.49, Gershenson 1991:17–19, 131–3, Hughes 1991:102, Zolotnikova 2005, Bremmer 2007b:77 and most recently Gordon 2015:42 and Heinrichs 2015:35 (the last with approval). It is possible to read Lykosoura as signifying 'Wolf-tail' (*lykos* + *oura*; Pape and Benseler 1911 s.v.). However, it would be anomalous to build a compound onto a nominative form in this way, as opposed to onto the root with a linking 'o' or onto the genitive, as in Kynos-oura, 'Dog's tail' (where the first-glance direct parallelism with Lykosoura is illusory: *kynos* is the genitive form of *kyōn*); Chantraine 2009 s.v. λύκος argues plausibly that Lykosoura is actually a calque on the prior Kynosoura. Pausanias 10.6.2 tells that the city of Lykoreia was founded on the top of Parnassus when its settlers were led there by howlings of wolves; cf. Gernet 1981:127.

[23] Macrobius *Saturnalia* 1.17.37; Homer *Iliad* 7.433. But this then raises the question of the status of *lykophōs*—'twilight'.

[24] Polybius 16.12.7 (incorporating Theopompus *FGrH* 115 F343), Plutarch *Greek Questions* 39, Pausanias 8.38.6. Plutarch denies the truth of this claim, but suggests that, were it true, the explanation might lie in the facts that those that entered the sanctuary were condemned to death, and the souls of the dead, according to the Pythagoreans, cast no shadows. See Frazer 1898 on Pausanias *ad loc.*, Cook 1914–40:i, 6, Halliday 1928 on Plutarch *ad loc.*, (pp.172–3), Jost 1985:255–8.

[25] Pausanias 8.38.7.

[26] For the associations between the cults of Zeus Lykaios and Demeter Melaina, see Aston 2011:102–6. Aston, building on Bruit 1986, suggests that the aetiological myths of the Phigalians and of Lykaon alike articulate a progression from primitive, wild food (acorns in the case of Phigalia) to civilized food.

[27] Aston 2011: 239–44 (with fig. 30), 299–301; cf. also 102–3.

[28] Musiani et al. 2010b:3, Wayne 2010:31–2.

Lad Sacrifice, the Anthid Maturation Rite and the Tale of Demaenetus/Damarchus: the Sources

We pass on now to the data bearing upon categories (1) and (3) above, which is to be gleaned from the following series of texts:

'Is it not clear, that whenever a tyrant is produced, he develops out of being a champion of the people and out of nothing else?'

'Very clear.'

'What is the beginning of this transformation from champion of the people to tyrant? Is it not clear that it falls at the point at which the champion begins to do the same thing as the man in the myth which is told in connection with the sanctuary of Lykaian Zeus in Arcadia?'

'What myth is that?', he said.

'The myth tells that the man who has tasted human entrails, one set of these having been cut into the entrails of the other sacrificial victims, must by all means become a wolf.[29] Or haven't you heard that story?'

'I have.'

'So is it not the same when a champion of the people, with a mob all too ready to obey him, fails to hold back from shedding the blood of his own people, but makes unjust accusations, of the sort they are wont to do, and brings men into court and murders them, depriving people of their lives, tasting the gore of his kin with his tongue and unholy mouth, drives men into exile, kills them, and moots the cancellation of debts and the redistribution of land? Is it not inevitable that the sort of man who does this is, as a consequence, either fated to be killed by his enemies or to be a tyrant and to be transformed into a wolf from having been a man?'

'Highly inevitable,' he said.   Plato *Republic* 565d–566a (*c.*370 B C)

But this at any rate, Socrates, is not a hard thing to understand, namely that people do not all use the same laws, but different people use different ones. For example, it is illegal for us to sacrifice humans, and actually unholy, but the Carthaginians make such sacrifices on the basis that they are holy and legal for them. And indeed some of them actually sacrifice their own sons to Cronus, as you have probably heard. And it is not just barbarian men that use alternative laws: even men in the Lykaian festival and the descendants of Athamas[30] make this kind of sacrifice even though they are Greek.

[Plato] *Minos* 315b–c (4th c. B C)

---

[29] Ὡς ἄρα ὁ γευσάμενος τοῦ ἀνθρωπίνου σπλάγχνου, ἐν ἄλλοις ἄλλων ἱερείων ἑνὸς ἐγκατατετμημένου, ἀνάγκη δὴ τούτῳ λύκῳ γενέσθαι.

[30] For these sacrifices, see Herodotus 7.197; cf. Hughes 1991:92–6.

[…says Theophrastus…] Accordingly, even in this day, it is not just in Arcadia, at the Lykaia, nor just at Carthage, that everybody makes human sacrifice together [κοινῇ πάντες ἀνθρωποθυτοῦσιν], the latter sacrifices being made to Cronus, but periodically people wet their altars with kindred blood to preserve the memory of the custom.

Theophrastus *On Piety* F584a Fortenbaugh (later 4th c. BC)

apud Porphyry *On Abstinence* 2.27.2 (later 3rd c. AD)

= Eusebius *Praeparatio evangelica* 4.16.10 (early 4th c. AD)

And just as if he [Philip V] had tasted human blood and acquired the taste for slaughter and for breaking oaths taken with his allies, be became—not a wolf from having been a man, as in the Arcadian myth [κατὰ τὸν Ἀρκαδικὸν μῦθον], as Plato mentions—but a bitter tyrant from having been a king.

Polybius 7.13.6 (2nd c. BC)

We should be confident in the belief that it is untrue that men are turned into wolves and restored again to their own form. Otherwise, we should believe everything that we have learned to be fabulous over all these centuries. All the same, we will indicate the origin of the popular superstition that skin-shifters/ werewolves [*versipelles*] are among those subject to a curse [*maledictis*]. Euanthes [Anon., Testimonium de Arcadia, *FGrH* 320 F1], by no means the most despicable of Greek writers, reports the Arcadian tradition that a man chosen by lot from the family of one Anthus is escorted to some pool [*stagnum*] in the area. He hangs his clothes on an oak tree, swims across the pool, goes off into the wilderness, is transformed into a wolf, and joins a pack with others of the same kind for nine years. If he has held himself back from a human [*si homine se abstinuerit*] in that time,[31] he returns to the same pool, swims back across it, and recovers his form, with nine years' aging added to his erstwhile guise. Euanthes adds the rather fantastical detail that he recovers the same clothes. The extent of Greek gullibility is amazing. No lie is so outrageous as to want witness. Similarly, Euagropas, recorder of the Olympic victors, reports that Demaenetus of Parrhasia, at the human sacrifice that the Arcadians were still then making to Zeus Lykaios, tasted the entrails of the slaughtered boy and turned himself into a wolf. The same man was restored to human form in the tenth year afterward, underwent athletic training in boxing and returned from Olympia a victor.

Pliny *Natural History* 8.80–2 (before AD 79)

As for the boxer, the Arcadian from Parrhasia named Damarchus, all the things the charlatans say about him are unbelievable to me, except, that is, for his victory at Olympia. They say that he changed from a man into the form/appearance

---

[31] A slightly vague phrase (see Gordon 2015:39), but it must surely carry the connotation of abstaining from devouring human flesh, and comparison with Pausanias 8.2.6, quoted next, confirms that.

[*eidos*] of a wolf at the sacrifice to Lykaian Zeus and that after this he became a man again in the tenth year. Nor does it seem to me that the Arcadians say this about him, for if so it would be stipulated by the inscription at Olympia. It says this: 'Damarchus son of Dinytas, a man of Parrhasia in Arcadia by birth, dedicated this statue.' This is as far as it goes.   Pausanias 6.8.2 (later 2nd c. AD)

For they say that since the time of Lykaon someone ever becomes a wolf from being a man at the sacrifice of Lykaian Zeus, but not for the whole of his life. Whenever he is a wolf, if he abstains from human flesh, they say he becomes a man again from being a wolf, but that if he has tasted it he remains a beast forever.   Pausanias 8.2.6[32]

On the highest summit of the mountain [Mt Lykaion] is a pile of earth, the altar of Zeus Lykaios, and the bulk of the Peloponnese can be seen from it. Before the altar stand two pillars, on the eastern side, and in olden times gilded eagles had been made to stand on top of them. They sacrifice to Zeus Lykaios on this altar in secret fashion. I would prefer not to push my nose into the details of the sacrifice. Let it be as it is and as it was from the beginning.   Pausanias 8.38.7

... Varro mentions other things, these no easier to believe, in connection with that most famous woman mage [*maga*] Circe, the one who also transformed Odysseus' companions into beasts, and in connection with the Arcadians. These, chosen by lot, would swim across a certain pool [*stagnum*], and they were changed into wolves there. They would make their lives in the desolate parts of that region alongside similar wild animals. If, however, they did not feed on human flesh, then after nine years they would swim back across that same pool and resume their human form. Finally he [Varro] also declares that a certain Demaenetus—he supplies the name—tasted some of the sacrifice that the Arcadians used to make to their god Lykaios by means of slaughtering a boy, and was turned into a wolf; in the tenth year he was restored to his own form, trained himself in boxing and prevailed in an Olympic competition. This same historian, Varro, holds that there was no other reason for the application of this epithet 'Lykaios' to Pan and Zeus in Arcadia other than this transformation of men into wolves. This was because they thought that the transformation could not be made to happen except by the power of a god. For a wolf is called *lykos* in Greek, and it is obvious that the name Lykaios is derived from it. He also says that the Luperci of the Romans arose, as it were, from the seeds of these mystery rites.
    Augustine *City of God* 18.17 (AD 413–23)

---

[32] This passage follows on directly from the first part of the one quoted under version (e) of the Lykaon myth, above. On the basis of this text it must be admitted that Burkert 1983a:88 is wrong to assert that the Anthid rite is not linked with the Lykaia: the motif of the abstinence from human flesh clearly belongs with the rite, as comparison with the Pliny and Augustine passages shows.

There is talk also of the sacrifice that the Arcadians used to make to their god Lykaios. Any people that took meat from it were changed into the shapes of animals.

Isidore of Seville *Etymologies* 8.9.5 (*c.* AD 600)

Some Initial Observations on the Sources

A number of the sources printed here can be sorted into subordinate traditions. The pseudo-Platonic *Minos* seems to take inspiration *in part* from the genuine Platonic texts, the *Republic* and the *Laws*. In turn it seems to be the (sole) model for the fragment of Theophrastus preserved by both Porphyry and Eusebius.[33] Polybius would seem to have revisited the well of the *Republic* directly.

Augustine's material aligns strongly with that of Pliny, but he does us the great service of attributing it to Rome's great antiquarian Varro. We can confidently assume that Pliny depends on the same passage of Varro, which seems to lie very close beneath the surface of both texts, and also that Varro himself had cited 'Euanthes' and 'Euagropas', who retain their credits in Pliny, but not in Augustine. Isidore need only depend on Augustine.[34] The alignment of the Pliny and Augustine texts sheds light, incidentally, on the methods and agendas of each. Pliny cites the original Greek sources for his material, while eliminating the intermediary Varro, presumably to take credit for the research and to lend his words maximum authority, while also trying to escape the shadow of his titanic predecessor in Latin letters. But by the time of Augustine such sensitivities are past, and no appeal beyond the great Varro is necessary. As a unitary source for all this material, Varro also offers Augustine a better purchase for sustained personal engagement.[35]

'Euanthes' and 'Euagropas' both invite comment. Euanthes is otherwise unknown, which led Karl Müller to emend the name to Euanoridas[36] and Felix Jacoby and others to emend it to Neanthes (*sc.* of Cyzicus).[37] However, one must wonder whether the shared element between the names 'Euanthes' ('Fair-flowering') and 'Anthus' (Flowering One') is significant: 'Euanthes' may indeed be

---

[33] Cf. Gordon 2015:39, 55 n.87.

[34] Cf. Smith 1894:17, Cook 1914–40:i, 71–3, Eckels 1937:33 n.4, Mainoldi 1984:14–15, Gordon 2015:55 n.89.

[35] For Pliny's attitude to his sources see Murphy 2004. Cf. also, more generally, Doody 2016 (I thank Dr Doody for these references).

[36] Müller at *FHG* iv p.407; cf. Cook 1914–40:i, 72–3. This on the basis that Pausanias cites Euanoridas of Elis' *Olympionikai* at 6.8.1, shortly before he conveys his (Olympic-victory-themed) Damarchus material.

[37] Jacoby at Neanthes *FGrH* 84 F41 (so too Baron at *BNJ* ad loc.), Hughes 1991:99, Bremmer 2007b:69, 2019:361 and Gordon 2015:56 n.91. For (the 4th–3rd-c. BC) biographer and historian Neanthes in general see the *FGrH* and *BNJ* entries and now also Schorn 2018:1–49. It must be conceded that Neanthes, one of whose works was entitled *Myths, City-by-City* (κατὰ πόλιν μυθικά), had an antiquarian interest in ritual, and even spoke of Pythagorean metempsychosis (see esp. FF1, 6–12, 14–16, 29a, 32–3, 36–9, 42). None of his forty-two fragments (excluding the Pliny text in question) mention Arcadia.

a corruption influenced by the adjacent 'Anthus'; or it could be that Euanthes was himself an appropriately named scion of the family of Anthus, in which case his testimony, historically reliable or otherwise, might have been of considerable interest.[38]

'Euagropas', the reading of the manuscripts at this point, is not a known or expected Greek name, and is rather more likely to be corrupt. The emendation of 'Scopas', adopted by Jacoby, seems arbitrary but has been influential.[39] The summary list of Pliny's citations (which occupies his Book 1) offers the surely also corrupt 'Agrippa' at the corresponding point, under 'external sources'. The most obvious restoration amongst familiar Greek names would seem to be Euagoras; for what it is worth, a historian of this name is vestigially attested, one Euagoras of Lindos (1st century BC–1st century AD); his testimonia and fragments, such as they are, do not offer a ready context for this material.[40]

It is self-evident that Demaenetus of Parrhasia (Pliny and Augustine—that is, Varro) and Damarchus of Parrhasia (Pausanias) are one and the same figure. In fact the prior element of both names, *Dēm-*, *Dam-*, is the same but for a dialectal variation. For convenience henceforth we will refer to this figure simply as 'Damarchus'.[41]

The Sources for Human Sacrifice, the Anthid Rite and the Tale of Damarchus: Centripetal and Centrifugal Approaches

Just as the Grand Old Duke of York marched his ten thousand men up to the top of the hill and marched them down again, I shall initially consider the possibility of a centripetal reading of the above sources, before urging instead that we should read them centrifugally. A maximally centripetal reading might proceed as follows:

> Every nine years a lad was sacrificed in some sort of association with Zeus Lykaios (Plato, [Plato], Theophrastus, Polybius, Pausanias). But he was not actually killed: rather he experienced merely a 'social death' and 'became a wolf' for nine years; this he did in the course of the Anthid rite, in which he undressed, hung his clothes on a tree, swam across the pool, and took up life in the wild, before eventually, all being well, returning across the pool, recovering his clothes, and rejoining human society (Varro *apud* Pliny and Augustine, Isidore).

---

[38]   Cf. Bremmer 2007b:69, 2019:361.

[39]   Jacoby on Skopas (?) *FGrH* 413 F1; he is followed by Bremmer 2007b:64, Metzger 2011:205, and Anderson at *BNJ ad loc.* There is more caution from Summers 1933:140 and Gordon 2015:55 n.89, the latter with discussion of other conjectures (nothing compels).

[40]   Euagoras of Lindos *FGrH/BNJ* 619.

[41]   This has been self-evident to scholars at least since Böttiger 1837:142, though it is no longer so to Jost 1985:259, who regards Damarchus and Demaenetus as two separate figures.

The most famous example of such a transformation was that of the boxer Damarchus, who, we are told, had spent nine years as a wolf and had transformed back 'in the tenth' ('Euagropas' *apud* Pliny, Pausanias).[42] The exclusion of youths to the wild margins for a certain period is a familiar rite of passage attested in other ancient Greek societies: at Athens in the form of the *ephebeia*, and at Sparta in the form of the *krypteia*; at Athens again girls in a premarital rite of passage ran wild as if they were 'bears' in dedication to Artemis. In a cyclical pattern, one individual was ever 'playing the wolf' on behalf of the Arcadians: as one man's period of service came to an end, another's would begin.[43]

Despite its superficial attractiveness, there are notable problems with such a reading:

1. A particularly important consideration: the story of Damarchus is presented as exceptional—he was not one werewolf among others but a man of unique experience. His story cannot be taken as any kind of evidence for a standard and recurring procedure; and a key part of this uniqueness was his (unexplained) consumption of the human flesh, which clearly was not normally eaten, even if a human sacrifice of some sort was normal.

2. Damarchus was transformed into a wolf when he ate human flesh, but he can hardly have eaten his own flesh, as the model above would rather entail. In this regard he differs importantly from the Anthid werewolves: the strong implication of the evidence in their case is that they are transformed not by the devouring of flesh, let alone by the act of being sacrificed themselves, but by the act of doffing their clothes and swimming across the pool.

3. Another important consideration: the period of nine years is far too long for any marginalization-of-youth rite of passage, of which more anon.

4. And in any case such a merging of data is careless of chronology. The historical Damarchus' floruit is likely to have fallen in the early fifth century BC (see below), but, given the problems that surround Pliny's Greek sources for it, we cannot be sure how long the Anthid rite was attested prior to the point at which Varro wrote, in the earlier first century BC.

It emerges strongly that it is important to disaggregate the material bearing upon the Anthid rite from the material bearing upon Damarchus.

---

[42] Burkert 1983a:90 notes that, given that Damarchus went on to win Olympic victories after nine years as a wolf, he must have been young at the time of his initial transformation: 'no older than 16'.

[43] This is broadly similar to the position towards which Heinrichs moves at 2015:46 (inspired by what he takes to be the dedication of the 'lad in every ninth year' in the Arcadian bronze tablet he publishes, for which see below); the phrase 'social death' is his. One thinks of Gerald of Wales's tale of the werewolves of Ossory in his *c.* AD 1188 *Topographia Hibernica*, §19. In this case the abbot Natalis had put the people of Ossory under a curse, so that every seven years two of them must put off human form, becoming wolves, and leave the dwellings of men. If they survived as wolves for seven years, they were restored to human form and then two other people of Ossory must take their place as wolves.

The Anthid Rite as a Maturation Rite

Many have found the Anthid rite described to be a rite of passage, initiation, or maturation of a sort common in ancient Greek cities, and characterized by a temporary period of ritual and spatial marginalization.[44] In Attica, as we learn from the Aristotelian *Constitution of Athens*, citizen men of 18 years of age passed into the *ephebeia*. After a year of training that culminated in a drill performance before the Assembly in the theatre, the ephebes ('cadets') were given a spear and a shield by the state, whereupon they were dispatched to patrol the frontiers of the country in their cloaks for two years, being stationed in guard posts the while.[45] Michael Jameson went so far as to contend that the ephebes had a special association with the Athenian cult of Apollo Lykeios, with the epithet to be read in this context as signifying 'of the wolves', but his case is a thin one.[46]

A scholiast to Plato has this to tell us of the equivalent phenomenon amongst the Spartans:

A young man was dispatched from the city on orders not be seen for a certain amount of time. He was compelled to roam over the mountains. He could not sleep securely, lest he be caught, nor could he make use of servants or bring food with him to maintain himself. This was another form of training for war. For they dispatched each of the young men unarmed and commanded them to wander around for a whole year outside in the mountains, to maintain themselves through theft and the suchlike, and to do it in such a way as to be seen by no one. The name *krypteia* ('Secret Service') was given to this. If they were seen at any time whatsoever, they were punished.   Schol. Plato *Laws* 633b

Plato himself, in the passage expanded upon here, had spoken of the boys being (brutally) trained in the *krypteia* as going barefoot and sleeping without attendants. The *Constitution of the Spartans* ascribed to Heraclides Ponticus and Plutarch

---

[44] For the association of the Anthid rite with a rite of passage see Jeanmaire 1939:550–69, Nilsson 1967:397–401, Piccaluga 1968:24–6, 60, Vidal-Naquet 1981a, Burkert 1983a:88–93, Mainoldi 1984:15, Wathelet 1986, Buxton 1987:68–74, Cheilik 1987:266–70, Sourvinou-Inwood 1988a:174–7, Forbes-Irving 1990:50–7, Hughes 1991:103–7, Veenstra 1994:85–96, Veenstra 2002:142–3, Jost 1985:259–67 (esp. 265–7), 2005:353–5, Moreau 1990a:34–7, 1997:72–9, Bremmer 2007b:71–5, Weiler 2007:49–51, Metzger 2011:207–10, Gordon 2015:41–4. The Anthids' crossing of the pool might also be seen as an initiatory gesture in itself given that, as Buxton 1987:70 observes, 'Washing or bathing in water from a spring is an element in several important Greek *rites de passage*'; so too Moreau 1997:76–7, Bremmer 2007b:70. For rites of passage in the ancient world in general, see van Gennep 1909, Jeanmaire 1939 *passim*, Turner 1967:93–111, Brelich 1969 *passim*, Bremmer 1978, Calame 2003, Dodd and Faraone 2003, Moreau 2004. Oddly, the Lykaia goes unmentioned in the last item here, and is mentioned by the penultimate one only in passing (46).

[45] For the *ephebeia* see [Aristotle] *Constitution of* Athens 42 (περιπολοῦσι τὴν χώραν); cf. Aeschines *Embassy* 167. Discussion at Pélékidis 1962 *passim*, Brelich 1969:216–28, Rhodes 1981:493–510; Vidal-Naquet 1981a, 1981b:174–80, Burkert 1985:260–4, Ma 2008.

[46] Jameson 1980:229–35.

further tell that the boys hid themselves away by day but stalked the land by night. Equipped with daggers, they were charged with killing every helot (serf) they came across on the roads or in the fields where they worked, and would seek out the strongest ones to attack.[47]

Both the ephebes and the lads of the *krypteia* are light-armed soldiers, significantly contrasting with heavy-armed hoplites in this regard, and sent out to patrol the wild and remote regions. That the Arcadians were familiar with a similar institution of some kind at any rate may be indicated by Pausanias' observation (after the mid-third-century BC Myron of Priene?) that during the (legendary) First Messenian War Aristodemus of Messene counted amongst his allies the 'mountain men' (*oreinoi*) of the Arcadians, and that they wore the hides of wolves and bears in lieu of wearing breastplates and carrying shields.[48]

Some have claimed to find traces of werewolf-themed initiation rituals elsewhere in Greek culture too:

1. It has been suggested that a rite of passage may underlie the Neuri's werewolfism, or at any rate Herodotus' conceptualization of it (for which see Chapters 1 and 2).[49]
2. The details of what seems to be an initiation rite at Delphi have also been found suggestive. Plutarch describes the rites that take place at its Septerion festival, which he holds to re-enact Apollo's slaying of the great serpent Python there:

> For the hut which is set up there around the threshing-floor every eight years is not the serpent's hole or its lair, but a representation of the house of a tyrant or a king. The approach to the hut is made in silence along the so-called the Dolonian Way. This is the route along which the Labyadae escort with lit torches the lad [*koros*] that flourishes on both sides [*amphithalēs*].[50] They throw the fire into the hut, overturn the table and then flee through the doors of the sanctuary without turning back. Finally, the wanderings of the boy, his period of service and the purifications that are performed at Tempe hint at some great curse and outrageous deed.   Plutarch *Failure of Oracles* 15, *Moralia* 418a–b

---

[47] For the *krypteia* see Plato *Laws* 633b–c with schol.; [Heraclides Ponticus] *FHG* ii p.210, Plutarch *Lycurgus* 28, *Cleomenes* 28, Justin 3.3.6. Discussion at Jeanmaire 1913, 1939:540–69; Chrimes 1949:374–5; Brelich 1969:155–7 (with the more important sources reproduced at n.133); Vidal-Naquet 1981a:153–5, 1981b:180–4; Ducat 1997; Dodd and Faraone 2003 (index s.v. *kypteia*). For its relevance to the Lykaia in particular, see Borgeaud 1988:41, Forbes Irving 1990:54, 56. Note also the inscriptions Petrakos 1999 nos. 6 and 19, for the mysterious Hellenistic Athenian *kryptoi*; cf. Ma 2008:194–5.

[48] Pausanias 4.11.3; cf. Burkert 1983a:91, Buxton 1987:71, Bremmer 2007b:71. But it may be less relevant if Pausanias is speaking here of a regular Arcadian army, populated by established adults and not by youths in transition. For Myron see *FGrH/BNJ* 106 esp. T1 and F3 (the latter indicating that Myron spoke of Aristodemus) and Ogden 2004:183–8.

[49] Cf. Buxton 1987:68.   [50] I.e., who has both his parents still living.

The account is confusing, but some of these details would appear to exhibit a kaleidoscopic relationship with the Anthid rite and the Lykaon myth: the Delphic rite focuses on a specific clan within the city; a lad is featured; a table is overturned; the lad wanders in exile before being able to return and reintegrate; the rite is performed on an eight-year cycle, although this need not entail that the lad wanders for the substantial period of eight years.[51] The curious term 'Dolonian Way' leads Gernet to associate this rite with the werewolfism he finds to underpin the myth of Dolon (for which see Appendix C) and to speculate—and that has to be the word—that the lad progressed along it dressed, like Dolon, in a wolfskin.[52]

3. There have been attempts to find an association between the imagery of initiation and that of the wolf-man in ancient Corinth too, in the context of Herodotus' tale of Periander's son Lykophron, 'Wolf-mind'.[53] According to this tale, the archaic tyrant Periander has killed his wife, Melissa, mother of his two sons.[54] When they visit their maternal grandfather, Procles, ruler of Epidaurus, he asks them whether they know who killed their mother. The elder son pays little heed to the remark, but the younger, Lykophron, is stricken with horror and realizes that she was killed by their father. On returning to Corinth he refuses to speak to him, until Periander drives him from his house in anger. In due course Periander asks Lykophron's slow-witted and uncomprehending brother what it was that Procles had said, and the boy tells him. Periander now bans Lykophron from all households in Corinth. He then goes on to proclaim a fine for anyone who converses with Lykophron but, on finding him starving under a colonnade, eventually addresses him himself, whereupon Lykophron responds to him merely that he is liable for the fine he has proclaimed. Periander then banishes him to his possession of Corcyra, evidently in the role of governor. As Periander grows old he again relents and sends to Corcyra asking Lykophron to return to take over his throne (the elder brother being judged unfit), but he refuses. Periander's daughter also intercedes with Lykophron, but he declines to return to Corinth while Periander lives. So Periander offers to exchange places with him in Corcyra, to which Lykophron agrees. But the people of Corcyra, dreading the direct rule of Periander, kill Lykophron before this can happen. Christiane Sourvinou-Inwood argues that Lykophron's

---

[51] For the Septerion see, more fully, Plutarch *Failure of Oracles* 15 (=*Moralia* 417e–418d) and also *Greek Questions* no. 12 (= *Moralia* 293c), the latter for an even more decisive statement that the rite re-enacts Apollo's slaying of Python. Further sources are collected at Burkert 1983a:127 n.64. Discussion at Halliday 1928:65–73, Jeanmaire 1939:387–407, Brelich 1969:387–438, Burkert 1983a:127–30, Hughes 1991:104, Rutherford 2001:200–3.

[52] Gernet 1981 (1936):128–9; cf. Jeanmaire 1939:395–401, Mainoldi 1984:21.

[53] Herodotus 3.50–3; cf. Diogenes Laertius 1.94–5 and Nicolaus of Damascus *FGrH* 90 F59; for a literary discussion of Herodotus' Lykophron episode, see Stahl 1983:208–10.

[54] According to Diogenes Laertius 1.94 Periander killed Melissa in pregnancy with a kick.

experiences reflect the ritual exclusion of the transitional youth in a number of ways: first, he is socially excluded, during which time he wanders about without food and unwashed ('that is, in a state of abnormality that reminds us of the Spartan youths during the *krypteia*'); secondly, he is spatially excluded as he is expelled from Corinth; thirdly, his period of exclusion begins at the age of 17; fourthly, his name evokes 'the symbolic connections between the figure of the wolf and the Greek male initiand' and is 'a name-paradigm for an adolescent initiand, appropriate to a mythical prototype of ephebic initiation'; fifthly, he solves a riddle, apparently a feat associated with initiands. Like the figure of Hippolytus well known from Euripides' play of that name, he is 'a failed ephebe', a youth who never contrives to emerge from his marginal ephebic status into full-blown adulthood.[55]

4. It has been suggested that some wolf-named figures in myth should be seen as 'masters of initiation', presiding over the maturations of young men: Lykomedes ('wolf-minded') of Scyrus presides over Achilles' transvestite episode, as the latter is on the cusp of manhood (transvestism also being viewed as an established component of rituals of initiation or maturation);[56] Homer's Autolykos, 'Very-wolf' or 'Wolf-self' (cf. Chapter 3) presides over his grandson Odysseus' killing of a boar, presumably his first, which might be thought to enable or symbolize his entry into the ranks of the men.[57]

Beyond this, there has been much speculation about the initiatory role of supposed 'werewolf confraternities' in the context of a wide swathe of Indo-European cultures, the principal evidence for which is the Norse material considered in Chapters 2 and 4.[58] It has been supposed, for example, that the tale of Sigmund and Sinfjötli reflects a lupine-themed practice of warrior initiation.[59] But there is little to justify the projection of such a practice into the Indo-European register beyond the comparison, for what it is worth, of the Arcadian material under review.

If we do after all imagine that the Anthid's supposed lupine transformation was preceded by his false sacrifice (as in the 'centripetal' hypothesis laid out above),

---

[55] Sourvinou-Inwood 1988a:174-7. In making this contention she makes appeal to the works of Jeanmaire 1939, esp. 550-69, Vidal-Naquet 1981a, Jameson 1980: 229-35 and Burkert 1983a:84-93; she also compares (n.65) the Homeric Lykophron, who leaves his homeland after killing a man (*Iliad* 15.430-2).

[56] So Moreau 1989 (cf. also 1990a-b, 1997:76). *Cypria* F19 West = schol. Homer *Iliad* 19.326; Euripides *Skyrioi* test.ii.a (hypothesis) *TrGF*; Ovid *Metamorphoses* 13.62-70; Apollodorus *Bibliotheca* 3.13.8; Hyginus *Fabulae* 96; Phliostratus *Imagines* 1, etc.

[57] So Moreau 1990a:32-4 (cf. 1997:76). Homer *Odyssey* 19.386-475.

[58] See, e.g., Przyluski 1940, Gerstein 1974, Ridley 1976, Campanile 1977:80-2, Steindorf 1985, McCone 1987, Gershenson 1991:118-26, Ivančik 1993, Ustinova 2002a, Pinotti 2003, Sundquist and Hultgård 2004, Ginzburg and Lincoln 2020 esp. 50-1, 150-1; cf. Bremmer 1987:43 and n.73, Gordon 2015:41-2 with n. 105, both with further bibliography, and the latter dismissive. (Ivančik's contention that Polyaenus 7.2.1 speaks of Alyattes of Lydia bringing metaphorical 'dog'-warriors into battle against the Cimmerians, as opposed to actual dogs, does not survive even casual scrutiny.)

[59] McCone 1987:103, Moreau 1990a:37, Lionarons 1998:59-64, Tuczay 2015:75.

then we might wish to compare his series of experiences with those of Lykaon's grandson Arcas in his myth as reconstructed by Walter Burkert: after his sacrifice and dismemberment, he is restored to life by Zeus, whereupon he becomes an ephebe. This, slightly ambitiously, on the basis of pseudo-Eratosthenes: 'Lykaon got hold of [Arcas]...chopping up the child...Zeus put Arcas back together and made him perfect again...when he had become a youth [neaniskos]....'[60]

The circumstantial case for the lupine imagery in the Lykaia rite reflecting a rite of passage is enhanced by the myth of the transformation of Lykaon's daughter Callisto into a bear, given that bear imagery lay at the heart of a maturation rite for girls in classical Athens, that of the arkteia ('Bearhood') festival, in which a selection of girls 'played the bear for Artemis' prior to marriage.

Callisto ('Beautiful One'), Lykaon's daughter, was raped by Zeus and consequently gave birth to a son, Arcas ('Bear'). Thenceforth her tale is found in a number of variants. The pseudo-Eratosthenic Catasterisms tells, as we have seen, that Arcas was the boy Lykaon sacrificed to Zeus, presumably as an act of paternal revenge. Zeus, however, reassembled him and, when he had become a young man, he ran to Mount Lykaion and had sex with his mother. When the locals were about to sacrifice the pair in accordance with their laws of incest, Zeus intervened and catasterized them both, with Callisto now also at this point, it seems, being transformed into the bear that she is in the heavens. The scholia to Germanicus' Aratea seemingly follow this version. Apollodorus, citing a range of earlier Greek sources, including Eumelus and Pherecydes (though it is not clear who had said what), and followed by Libanius and the scholia to Lycophron, tells rather that Callisto was a virgin devotee of Artemis and served in her hunting band. Zeus adopted the form of Artemis to rape her and then turned her into a bear to evade the notice of Hera. In this form she was then shot by her mistress Artemis, either because Hera persuaded her to do so or because she was angered by her loss of virginity. Zeus again catasterized her upon her death. Pausanias broadly follows this version, while specifying rather that it was Hera herself that transformed Callisto before persuading Artemis to shoot her. Ovid, Hyginus (in the Fabulae), Servius, Lactantius Placidus, and the First Vatican Mythographer tell rather that Hera turned Callisto into a bear in revenge. When the 15-year-old Arcas was subsequently hunting, he failed to recognize his transformed mother and was on the point of killing her when Zeus catasterized them both; Hera then secured a favour from her foster mother Tethys that the constellations should never touch the Ocean. In the Astronomica Hyginus specifies that the hunting Arcas chased his mother as a bear into the sanctuary of Zeus Lykaios, and that it

---

[60] Burkert 1983a:86–7. [Eratosthenes] Catasterisms 1.8 = [Hesiod] F163 MW: [Lykaon] τὸ βρέφος κατακόψας...[Zeus] τὸν δὲ Ἀρκάδα πάλιν ἀναπλάσας ἔθηκεν ἄρτιον...[Arcas] νεανίσκος δ' ὢν...; the passage is translated fully above.

was for this reason that the locals were determined to kill them both before Zeus catasterized them.[61]

The literary sources for the Athenian *arkteia* are all scholiastic and lexico-graphical, late and contradictory.[62] This is not the place to go into their complexities, nor into those of the rituals they describe (and indeed to adduce this material in explication of the Lykaia may well be to attempt to explain the *obscurum per obscurius*). But the most lucid sources, for our purposes, are the tenth-century *Suda* and the scholia to Aristophanes:

I *was a bear at the Brauronia:* Women used to celebrate a festival for Artemis by 'playing the bear' [*arketuomenai*]. They were dressed in saffron clothing, and they were between the ages of ten and five years old. They did this to propitiate the goddess. For a wild bear had been in the habit of visiting the deme of Philauidai [i.e. Philaidai] and tarrying there. It became tame and lived alongside the locals. A certain virgin was teasing the bear but, when she went too far, she upset it and the bear mauled her. Angered by this, her brothers speared it, and as a result a pestilential disease fell upon the Athenians. They consulted the oracle and the god told them that they would have deliverance from their ills if they compelled their virgin girls to play the bear [*arkteuein*] in compensation for the bear that had been killed. And so the Athenians passed a decree that no virgin should commence married life with a man unless she had played the bear for the goddess.   *Suda s.v.* ἄρκτος ἢ Βραυρωνίοις

The scholia to Aristophanes repeat much of this, but specify that the girls that performed the ritual were not all the citizen girls, as the *Suda* asserts, but a selected group of them. They made sacrifices both to Artemis of Brauron and to Artemis of Munychia. The scholia also speak of the Athenians performing a mystery rite for Iphigenia at Brauron, this on the basis that Agamemnon had

---

[61] [Eratosthenes] *Catasterismi* 1.8 = [Hesiod] F163 MW; Ovid *Metamorphoses* 2.409–531; Apollodorus *Bibliotheca* 3.8.2 (incorporating Eumelus F31 West and Pherecydes *FGrH* 3 F157/Fowler); Hyginus *Fabulae* 155, 176–7, *Astronomica* 2.4; Pausanias 8.3.5–6 (cf. 1.25.1); Libanius *Narrationes* 6; Lactantius Placidus on Statius *Thebaid* 3.685, *Narrationes fabularum Ovidianarum* 2 fabb. 5–6; schol. Germanicus *Aratea* pp.123–4 Breysig; First Vatican Mythographer 1.17; schol. Lycophron *Alexandra* 481. Note that Lykaon is identified as the father of Callisto in a fourth-century BC elegiac inscription on the Arcadian plinth at Delphi (Καλλιστὼ...Λυκανίδα): *Fouilles de Delphes* (Bourguet 1929) iii.1 no.3 line 3. For Callisto's (meagre) iconography see McPhee 1990. For the Callisto myth's relationship with a rite of passage, see Brelich 1969:263 n.69, 288, Calame 1997:252–3, Arena 1979, Lloyd-Jones 1983:97–8, Borgeaud 1988:31–8, Dowden 1989:182–91, Forbes Irving 1990:51–3, Sourvinou-Inwood 1990:10, Jost 1985:406–10, 2005:28–30.

[62] For the *arkteia* in general see Jeanmaire 1939:257–64, Brelich 1969:240–79 (with a convenient reproduction of the more important sources at 248–9 n.44), Sale 1975, Vidal-Naquet 1981b:179–80, Lloyd-Jones 1983, Perlman 1983, 1989, Cole 1984:238–44, Brulé 1987:218–60, Sourvinou-Inwood 1988b (cf. 1990), Dowden 1989:9–47, Calame 1997:98–100, Cosi 2001, Gentili and Perusino 2002, Faraone 2003 (with convenient translations of the sources at 51–4, but an eccentric interpretation), Parker 2008:232–48, Cherubini 2009b:81–9.

attempted to sacrifice her there, not at Aulis, and that she had been replaced on the altar not by the familiar deer but by a bear.[63] A series of vase fragments from Brauron shows little girls, quite plausibly between the ages of 5 and 10, running about naked, and it is thought that these represent the *arkteia* rite in action.[64]

The relationships between the myth and the maturation rite in this Athenian material render it possible to imagine that a similar maturation rite for girls existed also in Arcadia, alongside and duly sustained by the myth of Callisto, and that this bear-themed myth-rite complex constituted a female parallel to the male, wolf-themed, myth-rite complex constituted by the Lykaon tale and the Anthid performance. The association in turn between bears and wolves in this regard is perhaps suggestive in the light of their seemingly alternate status in the traditions of the Norse berserkers (for which see Chapter 4).

Werewolfism would seem to have offered a convenient metaphor within the context of the ancient world for practices akin to those of the *ephebeia* and the *krypteia*, providing as it did a model of (usually) temporary transformation of state, and being signally characterized by the motif of disappearance into the woods or wilderness at the point of transformation (for which see Chapter 3).

The Problem of the Nine-year Period (and the Timings of Transformations)

The great difficulty, however, with associating the Anthid rite with the *ephebeia* or the *krypteia* is that nine years is far too long for a maturation rite. One would expect a maximum, rather, of two or at most three years, as with the Athenian *ephebeia*.[65] A period of nine years is far more suitable to a story of individual and *exceptional* werewolf transformation than it is to any such rite. Thus, as is clear from the twelfth-century texts *Bisclavret* and *Guillaume de Palerne*, it is in exceptional circumstances that the werewolves Bisclavret and Alphonse spend an extended number of years in their wolf state before finally securing their return to human form. Alphonse in particular is trapped in lupine form for the entire

---

[63] Schol. Aristophanes *Lysistrata* 644–5; cf. also Hesychius s.vv. ἀρκτεία and Βραυρωνίοις and Harpocration s.vv. ἀρκτεῦσαι and δεκατεῦσαι. Eustathius on *Iliad* 2.772 and Bekker *Anecdota Graeca* s.v. ἀρκτεῦσαι preserve a story in accordance with which the people of the Piraeus (home of Munychian Artemis) were subject to the depredations of a marauding bear. The locals killed it but were then subject to a plague. Apollo told them they could be delivered from it if they sacrificed a girl to Munychian Artemis in compensation for the bear. One Embaros agreed to take care of the task if he were granted the priesthood of the goddess for life; he then pretended to sacrifice his own daughter, but actually concealed her in the shrine while sacrificing a goat dressed up as her. Apollo subsequently confirmed that all sacrifices to the goddess should be performed in this way in future.

[64] For the iconography of the *arkteia*, see Kahil 1977, 1983, Sourvinou-Inwood 1988b and Reeder 1995:321–8.

[65] A problem articulated well by Buxton 1987:72 and acknowledged by Hughes 1991:105–6, Bremmer 2007b:71, 73–4, and Gordon 2015:42–3, but not seen at all by Jeanmaire 1939:540–69 (comparing African 'leopard men'), Burkert 1983a:90–1, or Gershenson 1991:102.

adolescence of the titular Guillaume, protecting him throughout his life from baby to young lover.[66] No specific number of years is given for Bisclavret's period of transformation, though we may note that Mallory's (1485) allusive refraction of him is trapped as a wolf for seven years: 'Sir Marrok, the good knight that was betrayed with his wife, for she made him seven year a wer-wolf.'[67] Likewise the twelfth-century Gerald of Wales's exceptional (if slightly less so) werewolf pairs of Ossory serve for seven years at a time.[68]

We should note here that there is no general pattern in the ancient evidence for the frequency or duration of werewolf transformations. We have the following cases:

- A permanent transformation: Circe's wolves;[69] Lykaon himself (evidence above).
- A one-off transformation for nine (or ten) years: Damarchus of Parrhasia (or the Anthid rite), as discussed here.[70]
- Every year at a fixed point, for a few days: the Neuri.[71]
- Briefly overnight, perhaps at every full moon: Niceros' werewolf.[72]
- Often, presumably for a few hours at a time: Moeris.[73]
- Daily, as evening comes on: Marcellus Sidetes' medical lycanthropes.[74]

Let us say a little more of the Petronius text here. One question that will be of immediate interest to the reader who comes to this book from the movies is that of the role of the (full) moon in ancient werewolfism.[75] The modern expert on the comparative study of the werewolf, de Blécourt, makes the surprising claim that 'the motif of the full moon is a modern invention, since historical sources do not mention it as an instigator of metamorphosis'.[76] Is this really true? 'The moon was shining like the midday sun': admittedly Petronius does not specify explicitly that his (presumably) full moon has a causative effect in his werewolf's transformation, but one is left with the feeling that the detail of it is not merely decorative, or a mechanism to account for Niceros' ability to witness his colleague's night-time transformation clearly.[77] We do find the moon in the offing in some of the

---

[66] *Guillaume de Palerne*, passim. In Marie de France's *Bisclavret* the titular hero, whose normal transformations endure for three days in each week (ll. 25–6), after his wife's betrayal spends a year living as a wolf in the forest before he is found by the king; thereafter he spends an unspecified, but seemingly substantial, number of years living at his court as his wolf favourite, until all is revealed and he is eventually able to transform back (ll.135–314).

[67] Thomas Mallory *Le Morte Darthur* xix.11.

[68] Gerald of Wales *Topographia Hibernica* 19.   [69] Homer *Odyssey* 10.203–19.

[70] Pliny *Natural History* 8.80–2; Pausanias 6.8.2; Varro at Augustine *City of God* 18.17.

[71] Herodotus 4.105; Pomponius Mela 2.1.14; Solinus 15.   [72] Petronius *Satyricon* 61.

[73] Virgil *Eclogues* 8.94–100.   [74] Aëtius of Amida *Libri medicinales* 6.11.

[75] Incidentally, the modern notion that wolves howl at the moon is ill-founded. They are, however, crepuscular creatures, and so may be generally active during a bright full moon. See Lopez 1978: 38.

[76] De Blécourt 2015b:2–3; cf. 2013a:205–6; *pace* Roberts 1999:578.

[77] Niceros also tells that the time of the werewolf's transformation was around the time of dawn. Borghini 1991, followed by Schmeling 2011:256, contends that this timing is significant in light of the fact

other ancient werewolf texts. Propertius' drunken bawd-witch Acanthis is said to bewitch the moon adjacently to transforming herself into a wolf: 'She was bold enough to bewitch the moon and impose her orders on it, and to change her form into that of the nocturnal wolf ....'[78] Similarly, in his *Amores* Ovid associates his counterpart to Acanthis, Dipsas, with the moon in her transformation: 'The face of the moon was deep red with blood. I suspect that she shape-shifts and flits about among the shades of the night and that her old body is covered with feathers.'[79] The turning of the moon red is, it must be noted, a motif of the magical practice of the drawing-down of the moon: Ovid seemingly blends the phenomena here, presumably for wit. And in his *Metamorphoses* Ovid again makes a further impressionistic association between the moon and the werewolf in speaking of the ingredients Medea throws into her cauldron for her rejuvenation potion: 'She added frosts collected under the all-night moon, the notorious wings of the screech owl, together with its flesh, and the entrails of the shape-shifting wolf, which changes its wild-animal form into a man.'[80] More telling, perhaps, is the prescription of the ancient amulet handbook the *Cyranides*: dried wolf's liver is of succour to the 'the moonstruck and the mad' (*selēniakoi kai mainomenoi*), while the wolf's canine tooth, worn as an amulet, protects them from bad dreams.[81] As we move forward into medieval traditions, Gervase of Tilbury mentions men changing into wolves every lunar month (*per lunationes*) in his *Otia imperialia* (AD 1210–14); more particularly he tells of one Chaucevaire (Calcevayra, Claceveyra) of Ardèche, who parts company from all his friends when the moon is full, lays his clothes under a bush or a secluded rock, and then rolls naked in the sand for a long time until he takes on the shape and voracity of a wolf, gaping for prey with wide-open mouth and yawning jaws.[82] And as we reach the early modern period, we find that Jean Grenier told de Lancre that he ran (as a wolf) in the moonlight.[83]

The Traditions of the Anthid Maturation Rite and the Tale of Damarchus Disaggregated

The difficulty of the 'nine-year' Anthid rite goes away if we hypothesize that Varro misleadingly carried forward the detail of the 'nine year' period from Euagropus'

---

that the Greeks called the twilight *lykophōs* or *lykaugēs*, 'wolf-light', for which cf. also Gordon 2015:51 n.34. Further discussion of the role of the moon in Petronius' tale at McDougall 1984:112–18.

[78] Propertius 4.5.13–14.   [79] Ovid *Amores* 1.8.12–14.
[80] Ovid *Metamorphoses* 7.268–71.
[81] *Cyranides* 2.23, p.152 Kaimakis (the section contains a number of other interesting cures using wolf parts); cf. Gordon 2015:31.
[82] Gervase of Tilbury *Otia imperiala* 3.120 (pp.51–2 Liebrecht). Cf. Smith 1894:20–1, Summers 1933:6, 16–17, 185–7, Milin 1993:46–7, Sconduto 2008:37, Pluskowski 2015:97.
[83] De Lancre 1612 §4.2; cf. Dillinger 2015:154–5.

account of the Damarchus tale (where Pausanias would indicate that it belongs) and incorporated it into the material on the Anthid rite he was deriving from Euanthes. If this is right then the rite may, in both actual fact and in other traditions, have been of a very different duration, including the two years or so that the *ephebeia–krypteia* comparison advocates.

Once this false bond is severed between the data sets for the Anthid rite and the Damarchus tale, they can both be understood in their own distinctiveness. Table 6.1 disaggregates and reconfigures the material in the texts quoted above and sorts it into the two distinct traditions.[84]

Is Plato (eteo-Plato, in the *Republic*) referring to the Anthid rite or the Damarchus tale? The generalizing tone might at first sight suggest the former, but his references to 'the myth' indicate the latter: he has in mind *a specific story*. I would suggest that Plato adopts a generalizing tone not because he is describing a recurring rite, but because he is extrapolating a general principle from the particular story of the Damarchus figure.

Table 6.1 The Anthid rite and the tale of Damarchus disaggregated

Text	Anthid rite	Tale of Damarchus: the other Arcadian 'myth' of the Lykaia
Plato *Republic* 565d–566a		…the man in the myth which is told in connection with the sanctuary of Lykaian Zeus in Arcadia?…The myth tells that the man who has tasted human entrails, one set of these having been cut into the entrails of the other sacrificial victims, must by all means become a wolf.
[Plato] *Minos* 315b–c		…even men in the Lykaian festival and the descendants of Athamas make this kind of [human] sacrifice…
Theophrastus F584a Fort.		…it is not just in Arcadia, at the Lykaia…that everybody makes human sacrifice together….

Continued

---

[84] For an example of a slightly careless further merging of the ancient sources in modern scholarship, see Burkert 1983a:85–6, where Damarchus' eating of human flesh at the sacrifice is paired with the Anthids' (ideal) abstention from it in their wolf form.

Table 6.1 Continued

Text	Anthid rite	Tale of Damarchus: the other Arcadian 'myth' of the Lykaia
Polybius 7.13.6		…he became—not a wolf from having been a man, as in the Arcadian myth, as Plato mentions—but…
Pliny *Natural History* 8.80–2	…the Arcadian tradition that a man chosen by lot from the family of one Anthus is escorted to some pool in the area. He hangs his clothes on an oak tree, swims across the pool, goes off into the wilderness, is transformed into a wolf, and joins a pack with others of the same kind ~~for nine years~~. If he has held himself back from a human in that time, he returns to the same pool, swims back across it, and recovers his form, ~~with nine years' aging added to his erstwhile guise~~. Euanthes adds the rather fantastical detail that he recovers the same clothes.	Demaenetus of Parrhasia, at the human sacrifice that the Arcadians were still then making to Zeus Lykaios, tasted the entrails of the slaughtered boy and turned himself into a wolf. The same man was restored to human form in the tenth year afterward, underwent athletic training in boxing, and returned from Olympia a victor. <for nine years…with nine years' aging added to his erstwhile guise>
Pausanias 6.8.2, 8.2.6, 8.38.7	For they say that since the time of Lykaon someone ever becomes a wolf from being a man at the sacrifice of Lykaian Zeus, but not for the whole of his life. Whenever he is a wolf, if he abstains from human flesh, they say he becomes a man again from being a wolf, but that if he has tasted it he remains a beast forever.	They sacrifice to Zeus Lykaios on this altar in secret fashion…the boxer, the Arcadian from Parrhasia named Damarchus…the charlatans say…that he changed from a man into the form/appearance of a wolf at the sacrifice to Lykaian Zeus and that after this he became a man again in the tenth year.
Augustine *City of God* 18.17	…the Arcadians. These, chosen by lot, would swim across a certain marsh, and they were changed into wolves there. They would make their lives in the desolate parts of that region alongside similar wild animals. If, however, they did not feed on human flesh, then ~~after nine years~~ they would swim back across that same pool and resume their human form.	…[Varro] also declares that a certain Demaenetus—he supplies the name—tasted some of the sacrifice that the Arcadians used make to their god Lykaios by means of slaughtering a boy, and was turned into a wolf; in the tenth year he was restored to his own form, trained himself in boxing and prevailed in an Olympic competition. <after nine years>
Isidore of Seville *Etymologies* 8.9.5		There is talk also of the sacrifice that the Arcadians used to make to their god Lykaios. Any people that took meat from it were changed into the shapes of animals.

Reconstruction of the Anthid Rite and its Werewolf Imagery

So what are we left with here? The Anthid rite takes place at the Lykaian sacrifice, *which is not necessarily a human one*. In any case, the Anthid that is to be transformed into a wolf is not transformed by eating sacrificial human flesh but either by the choice of the lot or, more immediately, by the act of hanging his clothes on the tree and then swimming across the pond. He lives in the wild for a period that is now unspecified, and theoretically with other wolves. If he abstains from devouring human flesh in the meantime—which he presumably always does—he then returns to his clothes and his humanity. We need not be surprised, as Pliny was, that his clothes remain where he left them, particularly if the period in question was closer to the two years or so of the *krypteia* or the *ephebeia* and considerably shorter than the erroneous nine years. The notion that the man is transformed into a wolf is, of course, a mere conceit, a metaphor for his life as a light-armed (?) patroller of the wilderness. As Borgeaud has noted, it is possible to imagine, on the basis of the Varronian account reflected in Pliny and Augustine, that the transformation was only supposed to occur once the Anthid had crossed the pool and was decently beyond the sight of any spectating crowd. Varro does actually speak of the man being 'escorted to some pool in the area', quite possibly a remote one.[85] Indeed, this is likely to have been true if the spectating crowd was situated on Mount Lykaion, which is bereft of pools of standing water.[86]

'Which presumably he always does': one way of understanding the ostensible purpose of the rite (as opposed, that is, to its social function as marking or enacting maturation) might be as an expiation of Lykaon's original crime. That human had presided over the illegitimate eating of human flesh; the Anthid redresses the balance by abstaining from the same human flesh, even though, as a 'wolf', he might legitimately devour it.[87]

There is one good reason, and possibly there are two of them, as to why werewolf imagery should be appropriate to this rite of temporary marginalization, and this relates to some of the motifs discussed in Chapter 3. As we saw there, the articulation between an inner world of civilization and an outer world of wildness is fundamental to ancient, medieval, and indeed modern thinking about the werewolf, and this evidently constituted a significant frame of reference for the shaping of the rite. It is also possible that the motif of wolf transformation being effected by the crossing of water was already an established one in the ancient world, and that this too was a significant frame of reference for the rite. However, it is also possible that the broader comparative evidence for this motif, from

---

[85] Borgeaud 1988:40.
[86] A point well made at Jost 1985:260–1 and Hughes 1991:100, though the latter concedes that the pool (*stagnum*) in question might have been a very small one. Perhaps an artificial pool could have been formed from the (ritually significant) waters of Hagno, for which cf. Pausanias 8.38.4?
[87] This interpretation is almost given by Gordon 2015:40.

which one would normally expect to infer its deep and prior existence in folklore, may all in fact be the product of the influence, direct or indirect, of the very words in question of Pliny and Augustine on the rite itself.

Reconstruction of the Tale of Damarchus

As to the Damarchus tale, it now proceeds as follows. We find ourselves in a world in which there is a human sacrifice at the Lykaia festival but, unlike the accompanying animal sacrifices, the human one is, importantly, not eaten. However, one year, by some means, Damarchus contrives to taste the human flesh at the festival, the human flesh having become mixed in with the animal flesh. The circumstances in which this takes place remain frustratingly obscure: he may do it deliberately, being defiant of human and divine law like Lykaon, or he may do it accidentally, being tricked into it by an enemy or rival. Damarchus, accordingly, and seemingly uniquely and exceptionally, is transformed into a wolf by the act of tasting the human flesh in the sacrifice and by that act alone—not by being chosen by lot, not by hanging his clothes on a tree, and not by swimming across a pool. He remains in this state for nine or ten years, and then turns back. We are not told anything of what he does during the intervening period. Nor are we told by what mechanism he contrives to turn back into human form. The sketchy narratives on which we depend perhaps suggest, if only by default, that he simply reverts to human form after his destined term of service as a wolf expires (à la Ossory). After returning to human form he becomes a successful Olympic boxer. While there may be an implication that his period as a wolf has improved his physical agility,[88] it may be preferable, for reasons we shall see, rather to view his strange experience as an indication that he is (already) an exceptional individual, and so destined for success already on that basis. Ingestion plays a focal role in both data sets, that for the Anthid rite and that for Damarchus, but it is a different one: Damarchus is transformed by ingesting human flesh; the Anthids are transformed by other means, but trapped in their transformed state if they eat human flesh in it.

Arthur Cook took what now looks like a naively historicizing approach to the tale of Damarchus: he thought that it documented a remote time when there was indeed human sacrifice on Mount Lykaion, while the Anthid rite constituted a more modern and civilized rite that came, over time, to replace it.[89] If one were to be tempted by this sort of approach, one might suggest, rather, that the supposed Damarchus rite represented an intermediate myth (after that of Lykaon), a horrid

---

[88] Burkert 1983a:92 contends that Damarchus' period as a wolf serves as training and preparation for his future Olympic victory.
[89] Cook 1914–40:i, 73, followed by Burkert 1983a:88 (surprisingly); cf. Buxton 1987:71, Hughes 1991:100.

version of the actual Anthid rite projected back into history to mitigate it, along the lines proposed in Chapter 5 in relation to the competing accounts of the Locrian Maidens rite and indeed of the Temesa rite.

There has been a long debate about the reality or otherwise of human sacrifice in ancient Greece generally,[90] and much of the focus of this debate has understandably been upon this notorious case of the Lykaia.[91] In recent years a consensus has built against the reality of human sacrifice at the latter festival (at any stage in its history), not least after renewed, deeper, and ever more sophisticated investigations of the great ash altar atop Mount Lykaion have revealed no relevant traces of human material (it consists almost entirely of the residue from sheep and goat sacrifice).[92] Two exciting recent discoveries have briefly seemed to offer new challenges to the consensus, but their threats have melted away again.[93]

---

[90] For contributions to the wider debate about the reality or otherwise of human sacrifice in the ancient Greek world, see above all the two books published in the early 90s, Hughes 1991 and Bonnechere 1994 (cf. 2009), both of them strongly opposed to the reality; see also Brelich 1967 (a theoretical approach, giving consideration to societies beyond the classical world), Henrichs 1981, Gershenson 1991:102–13, Rives 1995 (barely mentioning Arcadia), Georgoudi 1999, Bremmer 2007b, Lanzillotta 2007, Weiler 2007. Relatedly, Arens 1979 (*The Man-eating Myth*) contends that there has never been credible documentation of a cannibal *society* anywhere in the world (although human sacrifice need not entail cannibalism, nor cannibalism human sacrifice).

[91] For the debate about the Lykaia in particular, see Cook 1914–40:i, 70–81, Piccaluga 1968:15–21, Burkert 1983a:84–93, Mainoldi 1984:11–18, Hughes 1991:96–107, Bonnechere 1994:85–96, Bremmer 2007b:65–78, Roy 2011:77–9. Madeleine Jost, the doyenne of the study of Arcadian religion, actually does advocate the reality of human sacrifice at the Lykaia: Jost 1985:258–9, 264–5, 2002, 2005, Jost et al. 2008.

[92] See the recent reports of Romano 2005, 2008, 2019, Voyatzis Romano and 2010, Mentzer et al. 2017; building on the long tradition of such reports in the past, see Cook 1914–40:i, 81–92, Burkert 1983a:89–90, Hughes 1991:105, Gordon 2015:42–4, Heinrichs 2015:8, 46. For the ash altar see Pausanias 8.38.7.

[93] First, in 2015 Heinrichs published the first edition (on the basis of photographs only) of a remarkable bronze tablet apparently found in a London flea market. Hailing from Arcadia, probably Mt Lykaion itself, and dating to c.500 BC, it records a complex sacred law. According to his decipherment of the sixth line (]ἆται κόρϝον ἐνϝότοι ϝέτει ἐξαγελ ἀσπίδα, ἀκόντιον, φοινικίς, ξίφος…) it seemed that its first four words prescribed the cyclical dedication (i.e. sacrifice?) of a lad (a *korwos*, i.e. a *kouros*) to a god whose name or epithet ended in -atas, but is otherwise lost: 'To -atas a boy in every ninth year.' Heinrichs held that a new provision commenced with the line's fifth word, *exagel*, which could not, as read, be construed as a meaningful or complete form. However, in 2016 Carbon and Clackson published a second edition of the text based on autopsy of the object and produced a relatively coherent decipherment of the line as a whole in which the prospect of this human sacrifice now disappears: ἆται κόρϝον ἐνϝότοι ϝέτει ἐξαγεν ἀσπίδα, ἀκόντιον, φοινικίς, ξίφος…, 'For -atas, a boy in every ninth year is to carry out a shield, a javelin, a red cloak, a sword…' (the change of case between the accusative *aspida* and the nominative *phoinikis* is curious without being deeply troubling; *akontion* and *xiphos*, as neuter nouns, could be either case).

Secondly, in 2016 the Hellenic Ministry of Culture, Education and Religious Affairs issued a press release (10 August) reporting the discovery of the grave of a boy, his skeleton intact, in the lower levels of the ash altar atop Mt Lykaion. The press release dated the grave to c.1100 BC, but the word on the scholarly grapevine is now that it may not even be ancient; see Bremmer 2019:370. But even accepting the c.1100 BC date, the significance of the discovery has been over-egged: we do not know that the boy was the victim of sacrifice or killing in any way; it seems unlikely that the body had been subject to butchery; whatever the significance of the grave, it seems to have been unique and so cannot serve as a document of any cyclical or recurring ritual practice; even if there is a remarkable continuity of cult on Mt Lykaion (even indeed, in some respects, from c.2,500 BC!), it is hard to believe that the memory of the grave and its significance persisted into the historical period in any meaningful way.

But what then of Pausanias' discretion about the Lykaia sacrifices of, seemingly, his own day: 'They sacrifice to Zeus Lykaios on this altar in secret fashion. I would prefer not to push my nose into the details of the sacrifice. Let it be as it is and as it was from the beginning.' Does this imply that a sinister human sacrifice continued to take place in the second century AD? By no means: when things were 'secret' in Greek religion, it was often because they did not exist. One thinks here of the reports of a series of great dragons (*drakontes*) maintained by priestesses at various points in the Greek world, upon which it was forbidden for any to look.[94] But, in any case, all relevant activities were presumably finished with and long in the past by the time of Pliny and Pausanias: Strabo, writing already in the Tiberian age, noted that the sanctuary of Zeus Lykaios was honoured only 'to a small extent' in his time.[95]

The Function of the Damarchus Tale: the Werewolf-athlete, Guilty or Otherwise

Whatever else it might be, the story told of Damarchus, with its supernatural elements, serves to express or articulate the exceptional nature of an outstanding athlete.[96] In this regard, it should be aligned with the remarkable traditions bearing upon a series of distinguished Olympic athletes that flourished at the turn of the classical age: the traditions of particular interest here relate to Euthymus of Locri, Theogenes of Thasos, Cleomedes of Astypalaea, Milo of Croton, and Taurosthenes of Aegina.[97]

We have already encountered Euthymus of Locri (with known Olympic victories in 484, 476, and 472 BC) in the previous chapter. As we saw there, this distinguished boxer was the rival of Theogenes of Thasos before going into battle with the Hero of Temesa, the *daimōn* in a wolfskin. He was associated with other

---

[94] The key examples are the *oikouros ophis* of the Athenian acropolis (Herodotus 8.41); the Zeus Sosipolis serpent (Pausanias 6.20.2–6); the serpent of Juno Sospita at Lanuvium (Propertius 4.8.2–14, Aelian *Nature of Animals* 11.16); and the serpent of Metelis (Aelian *Nature of Animals* 11.17). See Ogden 2013a:347–50.

[95] Strabo C388: τιμᾶται...ἐπὶ μικρόν.   [96] Cf. the brief observation at Gordon 2015:39.

[97] On such traditions see above all Fontenrose 1968 and Bohringer 1979. It is just possible that one Coroebus should also be included in this list. Pausanias 8.26.3–4 tells of the tomb of the athlete Coroebus on the boundary between Elis and Heraea, who was proclaimed to be one of the first victors in the Olympic Games. If—but it is a very big 'if', and *pace* Bohringer 1979:9—this Coroebus is to be identified, somehow or other, as Fontenrose 1968:82 contended, with the Coroebus that Pausanias 1.43.7–8 tells us was buried in the Megarian *agora*, then he was responsible for a truly remarkable extra-athletic feat: the slaying of the terrible child-slaughtering serpentine Lamia sent by Apollo against Argos after the death of his daughter Psamathe there: Callimachus Aitia FF26–31e Pf., with diegesis; Conon *FGrH* 26 F1.xix (Photius cod. 186); Ovid *Ibis* 573–6 with schol.; Statius *Thebaid* 1.557–668 with Lactantius Placidus on 1.570; Palatine *Anthology* 7.154 (*kēr*); Pausanias 1.43.7–8 (*poinē*), 2.19.8; First Vatican Mythographer 2.66 (*lamia*). For discussion of this episode see Ogden 2013a esp. 86–9.

marvels too: at Locri he carried an enormous boulder; statues of him at Locri and at Olympia were both struck by lightning on the same day, whereupon Delphi and Zeus alike declared that he should receive heroic sacrifice already in his own lifetime; and he disappeared into and merged with the river Kaikinos, to be worshipped as such.[98]

And this Theogenes of Thasos was himself the most famous of the outstanding athletes. He distinguished himself in a range of sports, winning some 1,400 crowns for boxing, pancratium, and running at the various meetings, with known Olympic victories in 480 and 476 BC.[99] Our most important source for his tradition is Pausanias (as indeed he is such for all the athletes we discuss here). Theogenes was sired by Heracles himself, who had taken on the guise of his mother's husband, Timosthenes, to seduce her (much as he himself had been sired by Zeus in the form of his mother Alcmene's husband Amphitryon, and much as the Spartan king Demaratus was sired by the hero Astrabacus in the guise of his mother's husband Ariston). As a nine-year-old child, he took a fancy to the bronze statue of a god in the marketplace as he was on the way home from school, picked it up, and carried it home on his shoulders; he was spared execution for sacrilege, but compelled to take it back in the same way. After his death an enemy attempted to whip Theogenes' own bronze statue, contriving to pull it down on himself and kill himself. The Thasians accordingly tried the statue for murder and, upon a guilty verdict, dumped it in the sea. A sterility consequently fell upon Thasos, to which, Delphi told them, they could only bring an end by restoring the 'exile' Theogenes; by good fortune, they were able to do this when some fisherman accidentally hauled the statue up again.[100] Lucian tells us that the restored statue went on to offer healing services.[101] Posidippus, in an epigram composed to grace Theogenes' statue, tells that he had a voracious appetite that the island of Thasos was unable to satisfy, and that he had once devoured a Maeonian bull to win a bet.[102]

---

[98] Callimachus *Aitia* 4 FF98-9 Pf.; Pausanias 6.6.7–11; Strabo C255; Aelian *Varia historia* 8.18; *Suda* s.v. Εὔθυμος.

[99] Moretti 1957 nos. 201, 215.

[100] Pausanias 6.11.2–9; see also Plutarch *Moralia* 811d–e, Dio Chrysostom 31.95–7, Eusebius *Praeparatio evangelica*, *Suda* s.v. Νίκων (despite the suppression of the name!). The standard work on Theogenes has long been Pouilloux 1954:i, 62–105 and we now have a new substantial treatment of him in Azoulay 2016; cf. also Launey 1941, Brelich 1958:319–20, Harris 1964:115–19, Fontenrose 1968:75–6, Poliakoff 1987:121–2, Ogden 1997:125–30. Pausanias and the other literary sources call Theogenes 'Theagenes, son of Timosthenes', Thasian inscriptions call him 'Theogenes/ Theugenes, son of Timoxenos: see Pouilloux at 63 n.4. Heracles, Amphitryon and Heracles: the tale is most famously recounted in Plautus' *Amphitruo*; amongst earlier sources, see Pherecydes F13a–c Fowler; cf. Gantz 1993:375–6 and Fowler 2000–13:ii, 263–4. Astrabacus, Ariston and Demaratus: Herodotus 6.69.

[101] Lucian *Assembly of the Gods* 12.

[102] Posidippus 120 Austin-Bastianini = *Hellenistic Epigrams* 3126–9 (Gow and Page 1965) *apud* Athenaeus 412d–e.

Remarkable too was the boxer Cleomedes of Astypalaea, with an Olympic victory in 492 BC.[103] Subsequently, as Pausanias tells, he accidentally killed an opponent during another Olympic boxing match, and so was deprived of his prize by the judges. Maddened by grief, he returned to his home town and pulled down the pillar that supported the roof of the city's school, bringing it down upon about sixty children. The citizens gave chase, pelting him with stones, until he took refuge in the sanctuary of Athene, hiding himself inside a chest. The Astypalaeans struggled to get the chest open, and eventually resorted to breaking its boards apart, only to find it empty. Delphi subsequently explained to them that Cleomedes was no longer a man: he was the last of the heroes, and they were to make sacrifices to him as such.[104]

An athlete with much in common with Theogenes and Cleomedes but of still greater interest to us is Milo of Croton, who won six consecutive victories in wrestling at Olympia between 540 and 516 BC.[105] Amongst the many particular feats of strength ascribed to him are the following: he single-handedly carried his own statue into the Altis at Olympia; when a pillar began to give way in a Pythagorean school, he shouldered the roof until all could escape; he took the lead in helping the Crotoniates in putting to flight a far superior Sybarite army, taking the field dressed as Heracles.[106] He also had a gargantuan appetite, and once ate an entire bull while reclining before the altar of Zeus at Olympia, having previously carried it around the racecourse on his shoulders.[107] Milo is noteworthy for us for the manner of his death, which is recounted by Strabo and (a little less lucidly) by Pausanias. One day in the region of Croton he came across a tree trunk that was in the process of being split, with wedges driven into it. In an attempt to prove his strength and complete the task himself, he thrust his hands into the crack, whereupon the wedges, dislodged, fell out, but left him trapped. Stranded in this vulnerable state, he was devoured by wolves. This tale has strong folkloric flavours.[108]

---

[103] Moretti 1957 no. 174.

[104] Pausanias 6.9.6–8; the same material is recycled, without significant addition to its content, at Eusebius *Praeparatio evangelica* 5.34. See Harris 1964:119–20, Fontenrose 1968:73–4, Poliakoff 1987:123–4.

[105] Moretti 1957 nos. 115, 122, 126, 129, 133, 139.

[106] Pausanias 6.14.5–9; see also Diodorus 12.9; Strabo C263; Athenaeus 412f; Philostratus *Apollonius* 4.28. Further sources and discussion at Harris 1964:110–13, Fontenrose 1968:88–9, Poliakoff 1987:117–19.

[107] Athenaeus 412f (incorporating a number of sources, including Phylarchus *FGrH* 81 F3); cf. Aristotle *Nicomachean Ethics* 1106b.

[108] Strabo C263; Pausanias 6.14.8; cf. also the indirect allusion at Diodorus 6.1.2. We are reminded, kaleidoscopically, of Grimm no. 8 ('Der wunderliche Spielmann'; cf. ATU nos. 151 and 1159), in which a fiddler, walking through the woods, attracts the attentions of a wolf with his music. The wolf asks to be taught how to play, but the fiddler is anxious to unburden himself of his dangerous companion. He pretends to begin the music lesson by telling the wolf to insert his paws into a crack in a tree and, as soon as he does this, he jams a stone in with them so that the wolf is trapped. The wolf eventually works himself free and (in the company of other misused animals) makes to attack the fiddler. But by this time the fiddler's music has attracted the companionship of an axe-wielding woodman, who frightens the animals off with his axe. We think also of the story from the *Völsunga saga* (5) discussed

Taurosthenes ('Bull-strong') of Aegina, as Pausanias tells us, was victorious in the wrestling at Olympia (in 444 BC),[109] whereupon, on the very same day, an apparition of him manifested itself on his home island to announce the news.[110] Aelian knows what is evidently a rationalized version of this tale in which Taurosthenes sent the news home by carrier pigeon: the intermediate term here is the notion of projected souls flitting around in the form of birds, the familiar phenomenon associated with the Greek shamans' with whom the miraculous athletes have something in common (see Chapter 4).[111]

The six athlete traditions in question are bound together into a syndrome by a number of recurring themes or motifs (their strings of victories aside), some of which are more immediately obvious than others. The more obvious ones include:

- Supernatural origin or destiny (Euthymus, Theogenes).
- An association with Heracles (Theogenes, Milo).
- Bulls: the devouring of whole bulls (Theogenes, Milo); bull strength (Taurosthenes); the single-handed carrying of bulls (Milo).
- The single-handed carrying of heavy objects: a bronze statue (Theogenes, Milo); a bull (Milo); a boulder (Euthymus).[112]
- Schools, especially collapsing ones (Theogenes, Cleomedes, Milo).
- Mysterious appearance or disappearance (Taurosthenes, Cleomedes, Euthymus).
- The same thing, at the same time, in remote places (Euthymus, Taurosthenes).
- Retention of active power after death (Theogenes, Cleomedes; cf. Euthymus).

Less obvious is the recurring imagery of the narrative schema associated with the portentous deformed baby, the *teras*, and with the adult scapegoat or *pharmakos*. According to this schema, an individual is expelled from his community, either beyond the borders or into the sea, by stoning or whipping, in order to carry away from it the pollution that brings sterility. Should the scapegoat somehow contrive to return, he makes himself master of the community that has expelled him.[113]

---

in Chapter 1, in which Siggeir's mother, in the form of a wolf, comes to devour Sigmund's brothers by night as they are trapped in stocks in the forest.

[109] Moretti 1957 no. 308.
[110] Pausanias 6.9.3; cf. Fontenrose 1968:90.
[111] Aelian *Varia historia* 9.2.
[112] Cf. also the statues of Euthymus struck by lightning. Statues feature also in the traditions of Oebotas of Dyme and Euthycles of Locri. Oebotas, Achaea's first Olympic victor (in 756 BC), went unhonoured by his countrymen, and so his spirit cursed them never to win again at the games until Apollo advised them to set up a statue to him: Pausanias 6.3.8, 7.17.6 and 7.17.13. Euthycles of Locri (early 5th c. BC?), after death, sent a famine on the Locrians when they mutilated his statue: Callimachus FF84-5 Pf., with *Diegesis* ad loc. Cf. Bohringer 1979:7–8.
[113] For scapegoats see Chapter 5 n. 39; for the scapegoat schema specifically see Ogden 1997 esp. 1–2, 9–23, 29–34 (building above all on the underappreciated work of Delcourt 1938) and, for the application of the schema to the athletes discussed here, 124–30.

Traces of the schema can be found in the tales of Theogenes and Cleomedes in particular. This is a schema into which aspects of the Damarchus narrative do fit too. It could be said that after his expulsion into the wilderness, and his return from it, he brings back with him the exceptional powers that allow him to prevail as an athlete.

But the recurring theme or motif in this material with the greatest interest for us, albeit integrated into its various tales with very different syntaxes, is that of the wolf. Damarchus, Euthymus, and Milo make for an intriguing trio: the first is a werewolf, the second destroys a werewolf, and the third is devoured by wolves. (It should be noted that the identification of this productive motif importantly strengthens the case for reading the Hero of Temesa's wolfskin as a significant object, and therefore for reading him as a werewolf.) One may mention here too the tomb of a supposed victor in the Olympic pentathlon whom Pausanias was unable to pin down. This barrow tomb was in Sicyonian territory, adjacent to the Corinthian border: it belonged to a Messenian Lykos, 'Wolf'.[114]

Let us return to the question of whether Damarchus' devouring of the human flesh was deliberate or accidental. While Pliny's observation that he 'turned himself into a wolf' (*in lupum se convertisse*) may initially appear suggestive of intention, it need not be so: once Damarchus had tasted the meat, by accident or design, the transformation was presumably forced upon him.

The comparative material bearing upon the other great athletes does not permit us to resolve the issue, but it does allow us to refine some possibilities. We might initially be tempted to think, given that the tale of the transformation sets Damarchus up to be an Olympic victor, that he ought, thereby, to have been a 'good guy' and accordingly to have been only an unwitting devourer of the human flesh. But while Euthymus would appear to have had an unqualifiedly admirable character, the same cannot be said for all the others: Theogenes was clearly a headstrong and barely controllable youth, and could be said to have been vindictive in death; Cleomedes was a mass killer of children. And it could well be that the theme of the gluttonous, voracious appetite associated with Theogenes and Milo also lurks in Damarchus' tale: was it his uncontrollable—and headstrong?— appetite that drove him to devour the human sacrifice alongside the animal ones, and so effect his own conversion?

On the other hand, the Theogenes story also provides a model for the great athletes being subject to the malicious actions of their envious rivals and enemies, and this could justify the supposition that Damarchus was rather tricked into eating the human flesh unwittingly. The motif, in Damarchus' tale, of the human flesh being mixed in with animal flesh is found in some of the versions of the Lykaon myth, and in this case it is clear that the mixing in of the human entrails is designed to deceive and cheat the unwitting consumer of the sacrifice (namely

---

[114] Pausanias 2.7.2; cf. Bohringer 1979:17.

Zeus). Indeed, it is possible that the motif of the surreptitious mixing-in of human entrails with animal flesh actually began with the Damarchus tale, and was then swapped 'back' into the Lykaon tradition: the motif is first associated with Damarchus in (I would contend) Plato's *Republic*; whereas it is not associated with Lykaon in the preserved record until the work of Nicolaus of Damascus. The remainder of the Lykaon tradition has Zeus simply being tricked with a meal of pure human flesh, and perhaps that was the original conceit of his myth.[115]

The Damarchus Tale: Priorities, Logical and Chronological

Within the system of the evidence reviewed in this chapter the folktale-type story of Damarchus might appear 'secondary' in more than one way:

- In the evidence that survives, the Lykaon myth is usually presumed to be attested before the Damarchus tale.
- The Damarchus tale could be seen as functioning as a second aetiology for the Anthid rite after the Lykaon episode, supposedly taking place in the historical era, whereas the former takes place in a primordial, antediluvian era, when relationships between men and gods were far different.
- Paradoxically, the Damarchus tale could also seem secondary to the Anthid rite in that, according to usual understandings at any rate, it functions as a mere example of what could happen in the course of these long-established practices.
- The Damarchus tale could be seen as effectively constructing a sort of bridge between the remote myth of Lykaon and Zeus on the one hand and the practices of the Lykaian sacrifices and the Anthid rite as known in more in historical times on the other.

But I would contend that, in important logical and even chronological ways, the Damarchus tale should rather be regarded as prior and as primary. From the logical perspective, as an example of a more or less traditional folktale-type werewolf tale, as a sustainer of belief or interest in werewolves and the culture thereof, it is this tale *or at any rate tales of this sort* that structure the Anthid rite and that give meaning to its metaphorical werewolves—and thereby too, it might be thought, the myth of Lykaon itself.[116]

---

[115] The motif of human entrails being mixed in with animal flesh is found in the context of the Lykaon myth at Nicolaus of Damascus *FGrH* 90 F38; Apollodorus *Bibliotheca* 3.8.1–2 (Version (c)); Hyginus *Astronomica* 2.4 and *Fabulae* 176 (Version (a)); schol. Lycophron *Alexandra* 481 (Version (b)). Burkert's speculations (1983a:89–90) about human entrails and animal flesh bubbling away together in a 'tripod kettle' for a game of lupine Russian roulette seem somewhat fanciful.

[116] Cf. Cook 1914–40:i, 79, who insists that the myth of Lykaon originated in 'folklore', though by this he would seem to mean something rather different to what I do here.

And what of the chronological perspective? Here too the case is not quite as clear-cut as might at first appear. Damarchus at any rate was presumably an actual figure, if we take Pausanias seriously on his Olympia inscription, and we have no reason not to do so. There must, accordingly, have been a point at which this particular tale became attached to him, although the tale type could have flourished and done its work since long before this point. When did Damarchus live and win? Luigi Moretti hesitantly assigns his victory to *c.*400 BC (Olympiad 95) on the thin bases of the style of the epigram and the fact that Pausanias locates his statue amongst those of other victors of that sort of era, and he is followed by Walter Burkert in this.[117] But the more appropriate company against which to contextualize him is surely that of the other outstanding athletes honoured with parallel supernatural narratives: according to this consideration, he belongs rather at the turn of the classical era, around which most of the victories to which we have referred cluster (at the extremes, Milo's earliest victory was 540 BC, Taurosthenes' single victory was in 444 BC). Walter Hyde's former guess that Damarchus' victory fell at some point before 480 BC (Olympiad 75) would seem ideal.[118]

It is a remarkable fact that, although we have to assume that a version of Lykaon's story was known prior to the Hesiodic *Catalogue of Women*, which alludes to his 'transgression,'[119] the earliest *extant* text that can actually be demonstrated to have knowledge of the wolf transformation is Lycophron's *Alexandra*, to be dated to *c.*190 BC.[120] Iconography offers no further help in establishing a chronology for the development of the myth: it is another remarkable fact that the myth of Lykaon himself (in contrast to those of Callisto and Arcas) has left no trace whatsoever in the iconographic record, and that too despite its visual potential.[121] The tale of Damarchus, on the other hand, seems to be known already to Plato (in the *Republic*), prior to the mysterious 'Euanthes' and 'Euagropas', whatever their dates (Hellenistic?).[122] For full tellings of the two tales we have to wait for Varro in the early first century BC for Damarchus, and for Nicolaus of Damascus in the later first century BC for Lykaon.

[117] Moretti 1957 no. 359; Burkert 1983a:85; note the scepticism of Anderson at Skopas (?) *BNJ* 413 F1.

[118] Hyde 1903:10 no. 74; cf. Hughes 1991:233 n.89, Bremmer 2007b:68.

[119] I am not given pause by Wathelet 1986's contention that the *Iliad* scene in which Achilles butchers Lykaon, son of Priam, with his sword (21.34–135) alludes to the (already established) myth of Arcadian Lykaon and indeed the sacrificial practices of Mt Lykaion.

[120] For the date of Lycophron see Hornblower 2015:36–9. Pherecydes *FGrH* 3 F156/Fowler gives us the name if nothing else. It is hard to believe that some version of the Lykaon story as known to us did not feature in the tragedies named for him written by Xenocles (*TrGF* 33 F1; age of Euripides) and Astydamas ii (*TrGF* 60 T6 and F4a—probably; active from the 370s to the 340s BC). And doubtless his full story featured in the original version of the Eratosthenic *Catasterisms* (2nd c. BC–3rd c. AD). He is also named, as we have seen, in a fourth-century BC inscription from Delphi, *Fouilles de Delphes* (Bourguet 1929) iii.1 no.3 line 3. See Forbes Irving 1990:216–17.

[121] The *LIMC* entries for Lykaon (i and ii) refer to other Lykaons.

[122] Burkert 1983a:86 conjectures that Pausanias found the story of Damarchus in 'a local Hellenistic history', but that the story itself went back beyond Plato.

Conclusion

We have separated the ancient data on the werewolves of Mount Lykaion into three categories: (1) that bearing on the elaborate complex of aetiological myths about Lykaon himself and his human sacrifice, the bulk of which is surprisingly late; (2) that bearing upon the historical Anthid rite associated with the Lykaia festival, a rite with affinities to rites of maturation known from other Greek cities; and (3) that bearing upon a traditional tale in which Damarchus was transformed into a wolf at the Lykaia festival. The data in the latter two categories is heavily and confusingly concatenated and must be disentangled. When the two data sets are appropriately disaggregated, both the rite and the traditional tale become easier to make sense of. We can now see that those performing the Anthid rite were (supposedly) transformed into wolves not by eating human flesh but simply by virtue of being chosen by lot or, more immediately, by the act of doffing their clothes and swimming across a pool. After a period doubtless equivalent to one or two years patrolling the wilderness (under light arms?), they return across the pool and recover their clothes, and with them their humanity. And we can now see that the Damarchus tale described not one performer of the Anthid rite amongst others but an avowedly exceptional set of events—events explicitly presented as another 'myth', indeed. It is probable that the full tale told that Damarchus was tricked by an enemy or rival into—exceptionally and anomalously—eating flesh from a human sacrifice (while the practice of making human sacrifice in itself, but not that of eating it, may have been presented by the tale as normal within the context of a Lykaia rite). This act in itself had the effect of transforming him into a wolf for nine years. He probably reverted to human form automatically when the destined term of his transformation expired. This story found its home amongst a distinctive suite of supernatural stories attaching to the outstanding athletes of archaic Greece, some others of which (including those attached to Euthymus of Locri, as discussed in Chapter 5) also incorporate the wolf motif. On this basis, it can be taken that Damarchus' werewolfism either directly occasioned his exceptional achievements as an athlete, or that it was at least symbolic of them. This barely preserved tale is a precious survival, and it is important to treasure it amongst the jejune suite of folkloric werewolf stories known from the ancient world. Tales of the Damarchus sort—if not the tale of Damarchus itself—should be understood as logically prior to the Anthid rite, which was essentially a metaphorical derivative of them.

Conclusion

The World of Ancient Werewolves and their Stories

A summary of this book's main contentions has been offered in the Introduction, and plain conclusions have been appended to each of the subsequent chapters; there is no need to regurgitate them here. Instead, I now build on them to address an important question: how did the people of the ancient world know what a werewolf was? It was not by learning any definition extracted from a survey of Greek or Latin literature such as has been offered here. It was by being surrounded by good stories about them. In the course of our discussions we have contrived to expand slightly, in number and content, the catalogue of such good stories about werewolves we can document, directly or indirectly, for the ancient world:

- **The myth of Lykaon.** A fundamentally simple tale, albeit one with many variants (Hesiod *Catalogue of Women* F164 MW etc.; first attested, vestigially, in the sixth century BC). Lykaon presents Zeus with a human sacrifice and is punished with transformation into a wolf. (See Chapter 6.)
- **Pausanias' tales of the Hero of Temesa** (6.6.7–11; formally attested by the late second century AD, but declared to be 'ancient' by that point). A demon—the ghost of Polites—in a wolfskin (Lybas, Alybas, Alibas, Lykas?) demands the annual sacrifice of a youth as the price of refraining from indiscriminate marauding at Temesa. On the occasion that the youth Sybaris is devoted to him, he is challenged by Kalabros, who is probably enamoured of the youth, and in defeat transformed into the spring Lyka. Variants of this story featuring Euthymus as the saviour and a girl as the victim (Callimachus *Aitia* 4 F98 Pf.; attested from the earlier third century BC) may also have featured a werewolf-like creature. (See Chapter 5.)
- **The legend of Aristomenes (?)** (Rhianus *FGrH* 265 F46/F53 Powell, etc.; attested from the second century BC). A champion of the Messenian resistance, and a veteran of lupine and canid stunts at Spartan expense, Aristomenes is eventually killed and cut open to reveal a hairy heart within. (See Chapter 3.)
- **Petronius' werewolf story** (*Satyricon* 61-2; attested *c.* AD 66). Niceros' travelling companion transforms himself into a wolf by moonlight and secures the safety of the clothes he will need to transform himself back into human shape by urinating around them. He is subsequently (re-)identified as a

werewolf when, having returned to human shape, he displays the wound that had been inflicted on him in his lupine form. (See Introduction.)

- **A tale with an affinity to the subsequent** *Bisclavret*. The existence of this is implied by stray details in Petronius' tale, *inter alia*. A werewolf (an inn-keeper?) is trapped in lupine form when his clothes are stolen by his unfaithful wife. (See Chapter 4.)
- **The tale of Damarchus** (as reconstructed on the basis of Pliny *Natural History* 8.80–2 and Pausanias 6.8.2; attested by AD 79). As we have reconstructed it, the tale of Damarchus probably ran in the following fashion. An enemy or rival secretly slipped flesh from the human sacrifice in with Damarchus' portion of the animal sacrifice at the Lykaia, and he was tricked into eating it. This triggered his transformation into a wolf for nine years, until he was transformed back into human shape, perhaps by virtue of having served out his destined time in wolf form. Having been so transformed, he was left with exceptional physical abilities as a human being, which permitted him to triumph in the Olympic Games (or, otherwise, his werewolf transformation was more simply symbolic of his exceptional nature, or his exceptional fate, and this too was demonstrated, in parallel, by his Olympic victories). (See Chapter 6.)
- **Philostratus' dog-demon of Ephesus** (Philostratus *Life of Apollonius* 4.10; attested after AD 217). Apollonius of Tyana identifies a beggar as the source of plague in Ephesus, and has the townspeople stone him to death. When the pile of stones is removed, the body of a gigantic hound is found in the beggar's place. The beggar may have transformed himself into the creature by eating bread from his wallet. (See Chapter 2.)
- **Aesop's pretended-werewolf tale** (Aesop *Fables* 419 Perry; attested in the Byzantine age). A thief terrifies an innkeeper by pretending that he is about to transform into a werewolf, and by doing so steals his cloak. (See Chapter 3.)
- **A further or extended narrative, implied by the Aesop tale** (?). The innkeeper himself is a real werewolf and, stripped of his human form by the theft of his cloak, accordingly turns into his lupine form—whereupon the thief gets his comeuppance? (See Chapter 4.)

We should note here also the strong recurring motif of the association of werewolfism with witches and sorcerers (Chapter 1), although it has not been possible to reconstruct a distinctive tale as such around the motif.

This last point leads us on to the question of the home or homes of werewolf lore in the ancient world. We have seen, in Chapters 1 and 2 in particular, that our ancient texts make strong associations between, on the one hand, werewolves, sorcerers, and witches and, on the other hand, werewolves and ghosts. These associations are both syntagmatic, as we might say, and contextual. By 'syntagmatic' I define an association in which a relationship of some sort is constructed between the werewolf and the other entity in question. Thus, we have sorcerers or witches turning themselves into wolves (as with Herodotus' Neuri, Virgil's Moeris, Propertius' Acanthis), turning others into wolves (as probably with Homer's Circe), and (more loosely) deploying werewolf parts in their magical spells (as with Ovid's Medea). And so too we have werewolves that raise ghosts (as again in the case of Virgil's Moeris), and ghosts that somehow take on the form of or become wolves or dogs (as with Pausanias' Hero of Temesa and Philostratus' demon of Ephesus). By 'contextual' I define an association whereby werewolves are found in the same narrative or broader text as the other entities in question, without the establishment of a direct connection with them. An example of this in the case of sorcerers and witches would be Petronius' baby-stealing witches, who star in the tale told by Trimalchio that is paired by Petronius with Niceros' werewolf tale. Examples of contextual associations in the case of ghosts would be Petronius' werewolf tale itself, in which the werewolf transforms in a cemetery while Niceros imagines ghosts all around him, and the Marcellus Sidetes discussion, in which the lycanthropic are said to pass the night in cemeteries.

It is fair to say, bearing in mind both the syntagmatic and the contextual relationships, that in antiquity werewolves inhabited the same conceptual space, the same story world, as sorcerers, witches, and ghosts, just as they do in the suite of the modern Hammer horror movies and their derivatives. My strong suspicion is that tales of this sort were typically exchanged at dinners and symposia, precisely as we see happening in the case of Petronius' paired tales of Niceros and Trimalchio. Here we should note that Trimalchio's remarks to Niceros entail that he has told—or performed—his werewolf story at least once before.[1] Thelyphron's marvellous tale of cruel witches and the ghosts summoned back from the underworld in Apuleius' *Metamorphoses* is another example. Thelyphron is presented as a practised teller of his tale, and indeed his host, Byrrhena, similarly makes it clear he has told it many times before.[2] We see a particularly fine example of this phenomenon in Lucian's *Philopseudes*, in which the guests at a dinner or a symposium exchange ten tales of sorcerers and ghosts (no werewolves, alas) between them.[3] We know that the Romans at any rate even had the practice of bringing professional storytellers, *aretalogi* (ἀρεταλόγοι), into their dinner parties and symposia. Suetonius tells that the emperor Augustus, no less, enlivened his dinners with

[1] Petronius *Satyricon* 61–3; cf. Sandy 1970:468–9, McDougall 1984:95–8. Smith 1894:7–8, commenting on Petronius' tale of Niceros: 'Many tales like this were, doubtless, current in Italy in the time of Petronius, tales told around the fire of a winter's night by slaves and rustics with, now and then, a furtive glance over the shoulder into the flickering shadows behind'; one may quibble here only with the assumption—flattering to the rationality of decent educated Romans—that the telling of such tales was confined to 'slaves and rustics'. Note now Graham Anderson's useful discussion of the audiences for fantasy more generally in the ancient world, 2019:179–87.
[2] Apuleius *Metamorphoses* 2.21–30; cf. Marmorale 1961:119–20; a more detailed discussion of the aretalogical context of Thelyphron's performance is offered at Ogden 2008:66–9.
[3] For which see Ogden 2007.

aretalogi, while Juvenal scornfully refers to Odysseus as a lying *aretalogus* as he recounts his marvellous tales of the Cyclopes and the Laestrygonians over dinner to Alcinous.[4] The marvellous stories collected by Phlegon of Tralles (author of the Publius tales discussed in Chapter 2) and the other Greek paradoxographers have also been thought to reflect the sorts of tale such *aretalogi* might have recounted at their dinners.[5]

But one might easily imagine other contexts in which such stories might be told, and Apuleius' *Metamorphoses* again offers another strong possibility here with its opening tale of the terrible *strix*-like witches Meroe and Panthia, which is exchanged between travellers, Aristomenes and Lucius, on the road.[6] Closely associated with this practice might be stories exchanged by night between travellers in inns or taverns. In this respect, it is remarkable just how frequently innkeepers appear in ancient, especially Roman, tales of witches, ghosts, werewolfism, and the macabre in general (as we have seen in Chapter 4): Meroe is herself an innkeeper, and it is in another inn that she hunts down Socrates to perform her magical butchery upon him; Augustine's Italian landladies change their guests into asses with enchanted pieces of cheese;[7] Cicero's proleptic ghost is produced when an Arcadian guest is murdered by an innkeeper for his money;[8] Galen reports—in what is best seen as an ancient urban myth—that innkeepers would murder some of their guests and feed them up to other ones as pork;[9] Aesop's supposed werewolf-thief steals a cloak from an innkeeper;[10] and it is upon Terentius' inn that Petronius' werewolf makes its attack.[11]

But other places too could attract the rehearsal of good stories, including shrines and sanctuaries. Indeed, it was in the context of sanctuaries that the term 'aretalogy' was first developed, where it was used to describe the affirmation, typically in inscription, of the deity's powers as manifest in his or her marvellous actions (as, famously, in the recording of Asclepius' marvellous cures at his healing sanctuaries, and in the so-called 'confession inscriptions' of the imperial period).[12] The point is best made by Pausanias' book: a fund of marvellous stories

[4] Suetonius *Augustus* 74; Juvenal *Satires* 15.16. For aretalogy in general see further Reitzenstein 1906, Weinreich 1909, Kiefer 1929, Sandy 1970:475–6, Scobie 1982:66–7, 1983:11–16, Totti 1985, Beck 1996, Ogden 2007:5–6.

[5] So Kiefer 1929, 24. The paradoxographers are collected by Westermann 1839 and Giannini 1965. See, in particular, the fine translation and commentary on Phlegon by Hansen, 1996.

[6] Apuleius *Metamorphoses* 1.5–19. For a shared journey as a good opportunity for a story, see Plato *Symposium* 173b: 'At any rate the road to town is a suitable one for those taking it to talk and listen'; cf. Sandy 1970:474. For the wide variety of horrors and terrors one travelling in the Roman empire might experience—in narrative at any rate—on the road, see Carabia 1995.

[7] Augustine *City of God* 18.18.

[8] Cicero *On Divination* 1.57; the same tale at Valerius Maximus 1.7 ext. 10.

[9] Galen *De alimentorum facultatibus* 3.182.1–6 Wilkins = 5.4.2, 333 *CMG*.

[10] Aesop *Fables* 419 Perry.   [11] Petronius *Satyricon* 61–2.

[12] The basic collection of aretalogical inscriptions is that of Longo 1969; for Asclepius inscriptions see also Edelstein and Edelstein 1945 and LiDonnici 1995; confession inscriptions are collected by Petzl 1994 and Strubbe 1997. The affirmation of the truth of the marvellous lies at the heart of dinner-party aretalogy too. Eucrates' guests in Lucian's *Philopseudes* repeatedly insist on the truth of their

all pinned (whether explicitly or not) to the sites, principally the religious ones, he has visited around the Greek world.[13] Long before Pausanias, the point is already well made by Herodotus' Samian material, in which he supplies us with a string of fine stories about the island, some with a distinctly folkloric feel, all of which are tied (or can be tied) to artefacts and mementos he has seen on display in the island's great temple of Hera.[14] Temple wardens (for it was surely they, the standing staff of the ancient sanctuaries, rather than the priests that came and went) must have been practised raconteurs. It was no doubt a sanctuary that was the keeper of the story of the werewolf Damarchus (Chapter 6): one might think in the first instance here of the Lykaion sanctuary itself, but the more immediate physical source of the tale in this case seems to have been, rather, Olympia. Pausanias attaches his version of the tale to the inscribed statue of Damarchus he saw there, whereas Pliny (after Varro) took the tale from a work of one 'Euagropas' on the Olympic victors, a work which was no doubt strongly grounded in that sanctuary and perhaps indeed its statues again.[15] And Pausanias as good as tells us that his tale of Euthymus and the Hero of Temesa was attached to a picture he had seen, even though the elements of the picture did not correspond with the story that he was told to accompany it (Chapter 5). He does not tell us where he saw the picture, but we have speculated that that too was at Olympia.[16] Indeed, Olympia may well have been the narrative home of many of the marvellous adventures associated with other athletes, as also discussed in Chapter 6.

Such, then, are likely to have been the home contexts of werewolf stories in the ancient world. As a traditional folkloric object, the werewolf's primary function, indeed its only duty, was to lie at the heart of a good story. The creature in itself, like the middle of the Greek verb, was more of a form than a meaning, although it may ever have evoked the polarity between the themes of wildness and civilization. But it was on the basis of stories of this kind that the more meaningful metaphorical deployments of werewolf imagery—as in the fields of aetiology, maturation, and medicine—were developed and sustained.

---

tales (and indeed this is the principal point of contention in the text). Similarly, Petronius' Niceros finishes his werewolf tale with the challenge, 'Others can make up their own mind about this, but if I'm lying, may your guardian spirits exercise their wrath upon me', while his Trimalchio finishes his corresponding tale of the *strix*-witches with the affirmation, 'I beg you to believe it. Women that know something more do exist, night-women do exist, and what is up, they can make down' (*Satyricon* 62–3).

[13] For Pausanias' relationship with his artefacts, see Arafat 1996, Habicht 1999, Hutton 2005, Pretzler 2007.

[14] E.g. the Spartan bowl and Sparta's relationship with Croesus, together with Samian piracy (Herodotus 1.70); the wooden statues of Amasis and the pharaoh's friendship with Polycrates (2.182; cf. 3.39–43); the decorations from Polycrates' *andreion* (symposium room) and the incompetence of Maeandrius (3.123); Mandrocles' picture and his boat-bridge across the Bosporus (4.87–8); Colaeus' cauldron and his voyage of discovery in the west, including his windfall trip to Tartessus (4.152). For Herodotus' interest in Samos, see Mitchell 1975.

[15] Pausanias 6.8.2; Pliny *Natural History* 8.80–2 (after 'Euagropas').   [16] Pausanias 6.6.7–11.

APPENDIX A

Homer's Circe as a Witch

In support of the discussions in Chapter 1, I take the opportunity to restate, in brief and largely tabular form, the case for reading Homer's Circe as, *inter alia*, a 'witch' and as an exploiter of 'magic'.[1]

1. The Greek words that were later to become the standard terms for 'witch', *pharmakis* (pl. *pharmakides*) and *pharmakeutria* (pl. *pharmakeutriai*), both signifying a female manipulator of *pharmaka*, 'drugs', 'poisons', or 'spells', are admittedly not applied to Circe in the *Odyssey*, but then they may simply never have entered the restricted vocabulary of oral-formulaic epic, and indeed they may not yet have come into existence at all at the time of the *Odyssey*'s composition. Circe is, however, importantly described as *polypharmakos*, 'of the many *pharmaka*',[2] and she is repeatedly shown in the manipulation of *pharmaka*.[3]

2. Circe is repeatedly described as a goddess,[4] but on one occasion, intriguingly, as a 'goddess or a woman'.[5] Possibly this is contrived merely to convey the uncertainty of Odysseus' crewman in describing her, given that he is yet to encounter her fully, but it may also be an attempt on the author's part to convey, again in the restricted language available to epic, a woman with exceptional powers, that is, a 'witch'.

3. The range of powers Circe exhibits closely maps onto those attributed to the undisputed witch Medea in the course of the sixth and fifth centuries BC (Table A.1).

4. The range of powers Circe exhibits closely maps onto those attributed to the earliest mages and sorcerers in Greek literature over the course of the first century of their attestation, beginning *c*.500 BC, when mages (*magoi*; sing. *magos*) are seemingly first mentioned by Heraclitus (Table A.2).[6] Indeed, the Greeks could not have been exposed to the Persian term *makuš*, which they borrowed to make *magos*, for very long before this.[7] It is clear that, from a Greek perspective, male 'magic' and 'sorcery' originated principally in a borrowing of the syndrome of powers already long established for female witches.

---

[1] Circe's witch status is denied by, *inter alios*, Graf 1997:30, Dickie 2001:5, 15, 34, 23–5, 128, 135, Castillo Pascual 2015:80, and Gregory (forthcoming). Hutton 2017:58, with 305–6 n.40, is also sympathetic to this line of argument.

[2] Homer *Odyssey* 10.276.   [3] Homer *Odyssey* 10.213, 236, 290, 317, 326–7, 392, 394.

[4] Homer *Odyssey* 10.136 etc.   [5] Homer *Odyssey* 10.228.

[6] Heraclitus DK 12b F14; F87 Marcovich, *c*.500 BC; if this fragment is spurious, as often thought, then the earliest extant reference to a mage will come at Aeschylus *Persians* 318 (472 BC); here a list of the commanders in Xerxes' army includes a *Magos Arabos*, which must either mean 'Arabos the mage' or 'Magos the Arab' (in the second case the proper name will nonetheless have been derived from the common noun).

[7] For the Persian *makuš*, see, e.g., the Persepolis Fortification Tablets, *PF* 758 Hallock. For the historical mages of the Persian empire see the items cited at Chapter 2 n.42.

5. From a different perspective, the Homeric Circe, in her full portrait, strikingly salutes not only a range of known folktales involving witches[8] but also at least fourteen of the hundred motifs Thompson has identified as belonging to the 'witch' in international folklore (Table A.3).[9] For all that Circe stands at the head of the Western witch tradition (and that is certainly true, whatever her status in immediate Homeric context), we must recall once again the maxim that folktales must already be considered old at the time of their earliest attestation (see Introduction).

We may be comfortable, then, in viewing the Homeric Circe as a 'witch' and considering her associations with wolf transformation, such as they are, in that context.

Table A.1 The powers of Circe in Homer and of Medea in seventh–fifth-century BC sources

THEME	HOMER'S CIRCE	MEDEA (EARLY TRADITION)
Knowledge, collection, and use of drugs, *pharmaka*	Circe is 'she of the many *pharmaka*' (*Odyssey* 10.276), and she uses them to: bewitch/transform men into wolves and lions (212–13); in a drink, to transform Odysseus' men into pigs and make them forget themselves (235–6, 394); to do the same (unsuccessfully) to Odysseus (290–1, 316–17, 326); in a salve, to transform Odysseus' men from pigs back into human form (391–2).	Aga-mede (the proto-Medea) knows *pharmaka* (Homer *Iliad* 11.738–41, *c*.700 BC). Medea rejuvenates Jason in a cauldron of drugs (*LIMC* Medea 1, *c*.630 BC); she kills Creon with *pharmaka* (Creophylus (?) at schol. Euripides *Medea* 273, *c*.550 BC). She collects noxious plants (Sophocles *Rhizotomoi* FF534–6 *TrGF*, 468–406 BC); she renders Jason invincible with drugs (Pindar *Pythians* 4.211–50, 462 BC). She offers to cure Aegeus' infertility with *pharmaka* (Euripides *Medea* 718, 431 BC) She kills Glauce and Creon by smearing incendiary *pharmaka* on the former's dress (Euripides *Medea* esp. 385, 789, 806, 1126, 1201). She uses drugs to cast sleep upon the unsleeping serpent of Colchis (*LIMC* Iason *passim*, from *c*.425 BC).

[8] For the folktale background to the Circe episode see Bolte and Polívka 1913–32: ii, 69, Radermacher 1915: 4–9, Carpenter 1946: 136–56, Germain 1954:130–50, Wildhaber 1951, Page 1973: 49–69, Heubeck and Hoekstra 1989:50–2.
[9] See Thompson 1955–8 (*MI*): iii, 285–310, nos. G200–299 for witch motifs in folklore.

Prolongation of life	Upon restoring Odysseus' men to human form, Circe makes them younger (10.395); under Circe's instructions, Odysseus acquires a double life (12.22).	Medea rejuvenates Jason in cauldron with drugs (*LIMC* Medeia 1, *c.*630 BC; Simonides F538 *PMG*/Campbell, 530–467 BC; Pherecydes FF105, 113 Fowler, *c.*456 BC).
		She rejuvenates Aeson with drugs (*Nostoi* F6 West, *c.*550 BC).
		She seeks (unsuccessfully) to extend the life of her children (Eumelus *Corinthiaca* F23 West, *c.*550 BC).
		She rejuvenates a ram in a cauldron (*LIMC* Medeia *passim*, from *c.*520 BC).
Erotic-attraction magic	Odysseus must protect himself against Circe's feminizing erotic-attraction magic (10.299–301, 34–5).	Medea is associated with spells of erotic attraction (Sophocles *Rhizotomoi* F534–6 *TrGF*, 468–406 BC).

Table A.2 The powers of the Homeric Circe in comparison with those of male mages or sorcerers of the fifth century BC[10]

THEME	HOMER'S CIRCE	MALE PRACTITIONERS (5th century BC)
Use of *pharmaka*	Circe uses *pharmaka* to transmute forms (*Odyssey* 10.212–13, 235–6, 290–1, 316–17, 326, 391–2, 394).	*Magoi* apply *pharmaka* to the river Strymon (Herodotus 7.113–14, *c.*425 BC).
Prolongation of life	Upon restoring Odysseus' men to human form, Circe makes them younger (10.395); under Circe's instructions, Odysseus acquires a double life (12.22).	*Magoi* bestow immortality (Euripides *Suppliants* 1110–11, 423 BC).

Continued

[10] This table aligns the powers Homer attributes to Circe with the magical powers attributed to male practitioners in the course of the fifth century BC; they can be variously described as 'mages' (*magoi*), 'sorcerers' (*goētes*), or 'enchanters' (*epōidoi*). It builds on incunabular versions at Ogden 2002 and 2008:36–8.

Table A.2 Continued

THEME	HOMER'S CIRCE	MALE PRACTITIONERS (5th century BC)
Erotic-attraction magic	Odysseus must protect himself against Circe's feminizing erotic-attraction magic (10.299–301, 342–5).	A man uses a doll in an erotic magical rite (Sophocles *Rhizotomoi* FF534–6 *TrGF*, 468–406 BC). Jason uses a *iynx*, a wheel of erotic attraction (Pindar *Pythians* 4.211–50, 462 BC).
Use of incantations	Circe's spell to transform Odysseus into a pig (10.320), and the necromantic prayer she instructs Odysseus to utter (526).	*Magoi* make incantations and purifications (Hippocrates *On the Sacred Disease* 1.10–12, *c.*400 BC; Euripides *IT* 1337–8, 412 BC). *Magoi* and *goētes* make deceptive incantations (Gorgias *Encomium of Helen* 10, *c.*427 BC).
Initiation	Circe sends Odysseus to visit the underworld, the characteristic conceit of mystery initiation (10.512).[11]	*Goētes* and *epōidoi* conduct initiations (Euripides *Bacchae* 233–8, 258–62, *c.*406 BC).
Invisibility	Circe travels invisibly (10.571–4).	*Magoi* make men disappear (Euripides *Orestes* 1494–8, 408 BC).
Powers of transformation	Circe perhaps transforms men into wolves and lions (212–13); she transforms Odysseus' men into pigs and makes them forget themselves (235–40, 394); she attempts the same with Odysseus (290–1, 316–17, 326); she transforms Odysseus' men from pigs back into human form (391–2).	The Dactyls as *goētes* transmute forms (*Phoronis* F2 West, *c.*500 BC; Pherecydes F47 Fowler, *c.*456 BC; Hellanicus *FGrH* 4 F89/Fowler., *c.*400 BC).
Ghost manipulation	Circe tells Odysseus how to consult ghosts (10.514–40).	Persian elders (*magoi*?) summon ghosts (Aeschylus *Persians* 598–708, 472 BC; cf. also 318); *goētes* control ghosts (Aeschylus *Choephoroe* 822, 458 BC). *Magoi* summon ghosts (Herodotus 7.43, *c.*425 BC).
Control of meteorological phenomena	Circe sends a favourable wind (11.6–8). (Cf. also the moon-drawing *pharmakis* at Aristophanes *Clouds* 749–57, 423 BC.)	*Magoi* control sun, moon, and weather (Hippocrates *On the Sacred Disease* 1.29–31, *c.*400 BC). *Magoi* and *goētes* appease winds (Herodotus 7.191, *c.*425 BC).

[11] For the link between *katabasis* and initiation, see now the Roman-era Greek rhetorical papyrus, *P.Mil.Vogl.* i 20, 18-32 = *Orphicorum Fragmenta* 713 iv Bernabé.

Table A.3 The folkloric context of Homer's Circe story

Comparanda for the general story type: ATU nos.	Comparanda for the constituent motifs: *MI* nos.:
327G a witch captures three brothers and fattens them for eating, but they are saved when the 'fool' amongst them tricks the witch's daughters	G210 witches render themselves invisible
	G211 witches in the forms of animals
	G224 witches' salve
369 a young man comes to witch's house, tricks her, and restores his father from animal form	G225 witches control animals as familiars
	G242 witches fly through the air
405 in a forest, a witch transforms a girl into a bird and keeps her in a cage; her lover finds a magic flower with which to change her, and other birds too, back	G251 witches make soul-flights
	G263 witches injure, enchant, or transform victims, in particular into animals
449 a husband is transformed into animals by his wife, but he delivers himself upon discovery of a magic wand	G264 witches entice men with offer of love and then desert or destroy them: 'La Belle Dame sans Merci'
451/a a girl rescues her brothers, whom a witch has transformed into animals	G265 witches cause animals to behave unnaturally
	G269 witches cause persons to fall from height
	G272 witches' powers compromised by steel
	G275 witches overcome by threat of sword
	G283 witches raise winds
	G299 witches calls up spirits of the dead and cause them to walk on water

Cynocephali

For all the general difficulty of drawing hard and fast lines between wolves and dogs in the ancient world and more generally, the Cynocephalus, the dog-headed man, is not something that should be allowed to intrude into debates about werewolfism. If we bear in mind the (very generous) definition of werewolfism offered in the Introduction, we can see that, by comparison with it, one critical characteristic the Cynocephalus lacks is that of transformation. Cynocephali do not change form: they are born and live and die in the same one, whether they be conceived of as one of the weird and wonderful monstrous races that inhabit the remote parts of the earth or as a species of broadly humanoid animal, apes or baboons.[1]

What was perhaps a proto-form of the Cynocephali was mentioned by the Hesiodic *Catalogue of Women.* Strabo cites Eratosthenes, who in turn cites Apollodorus' *On the Ships*: 'No one would accuse Hesiod of being ignorant, for all that he speaks of Hemicynes [Half-dogs], Macrocephali [Long-heads] and Pygmies.' All three tribes mentioned here are (from ancient Greek perspective) monstrous, and the author must surely have had them inhabiting remote parts of the earth, as was to become normal in subsequent tradition.[2]

Cynocephali proper make their first appearances in the classical tradition in the fifth century BC. We thank Strabo again for letting us know that Aeschylus (d. *c.*456 BC) referred to Cynocephali in an unidentifiable lost play; we cannot know what use he made of them.[3] Herodotus (writing before 425 BC) speaks of a mountainous part of eastern Libya dominated by large snakes and lions, amongst other wild creatures, and wild men and women: it is the home of the Cynocephali and also of the Acephali (Headless men), whose eyes are in their breasts.[4] In Aristophanes' *Knights* (424 BC) Paphlagon (that is, Cleon) taunts the Sausage-seller that, as one living on a diet suitable to dogs, he will not be able to beat him, Cleon, Cynocephalus that he is. Here the primary significance of the term is clearly to make play with the 'dog' (*kyōn*) to which Cleon (*Kleōn*), 'the Hound of Cydatheneum,' is repeatedly assimilated by Aristophanes, as most famously in the *Wasps*, a creature useful in this regard for its connotations of brazenness and shamelessness.[5]

One of the most elaborate ancient accounts of the Cynocephali was that composed by Ctesias of Cnidus in the early fourth century BC and preserved in summary by Photius.

[1] For a collation of the ancient testimonia, see Fischer and Wecker 1925. For cynocephalism in international perspective, see Kretzenbacher 1968, Karttunen 1989:180–5, White 1991 (a work of broad but on occasion shallow learning: note at 233 n.5 the misattribution of Cynocephali to the *Prometheus Bound,* together with the contention that the play itself is lost), and Steele 2012.

[2] Hesiod F153 MW = 101 Most = Strabo C43, incorporating Eratosthenes and Apollodorus *FGrH* 244 F157a+f. I do not think that anything useful for the Greek tradition can be derived from the Hittite 'dog-men' at *ANET* 360 (*pace* Burkert 1983:88 n.26).

[3] Aeschylus F431 *TrGF* = Strabo C299. Strabo makes uninformative mentions of Cynocephali also at C774-5.

[4] Herodotus 4.191.4; cf. Kretzenbacher 1968:30, White 1991:46 (where the reference is incorrectly given), 48 and Asheri et al. 2007 *ad loc.*

[5] Aristophanes *Knights* 415–16; for Paphlagon/Cleon as a dog elsewhere in the Knights see 46–8, 1017–34; cf. Taillardat 1965:403–6 §§695–7, Mainoldi 1984:156–60. For dogs as symbolic of brazenness and shamelessness more generally, see Mainoldi 1984:107–9.

He tells of the Cynocephali or Calystrii that live in the mountains on the near side of the Indus, numbering about 120,000. They have dog heads of course, but also large hairy tails sprouting from above their hips, and they are black. They live to be as old as 170 or 200. The men never bathe, washing their hands only; the women bathe once a month. They sleep on leaves or grass. Most wear animal skins, not rough but finely tanned ones; the richest alone wear linen. They live by hunting; they do not cook their meat in the normal way but expose it to the heat of the sun (biltong?). Wealth is measured in sheep. Their cave homes, high in the mountains, are impregnable. They bark like dogs, making themselves understood to each other in this way. They understand the Indian language, but can only communicate with the Indians by hand gestures. They deliver an annual tribute to the Indian king on rafts. This consists of dried fruit, purple flowers, purple dye and amber, in vast quantities. But the Indian king sends them weapons in return, every five years. Like the Indians around them, they are a just people.[6] Ctesias' influence was profound. We infer from Pliny that Megasthenes, the great authority on India who worked under Seleucus (c.300 BC), recycled Ctesias' information on the Indian Cynocephali.[7] Aelian (writing in the early third century AD) does the same.[8]

When, in his *Theaetetus* (c.369 BC), Plato mocks Protagoras' famous maxim that 'man is the measure of all things' with the observation that he might as well have declared the measure of all things to be 'a pig or a Cynocephalus or any other rather bizarre thing from amongst those that have sense', my impression is, in view of the run-on, that the term Cynocephalus designates a monstrous race still at this point, rather than an unfamiliar animal.[9] But when we come to Agatharchides of Cnidus' (second-century BC) *On the Red Sea*, we seem to have reached a turning point. This author envisages African Cynocephali as animals amongst other animals, and specifically as Hamadryas baboons: they are said to have an ugly humanoid body and a dog-head and to be untameable; more specifically, the females are said to carry their wombs outside their bodies, which, as Stanley Burstein notes, would appear to be a reference to the baboon's 'prominent ischial callosities'.[10]

Pliny himself in his sixth book (writing before AD 79) knows that the Cynocephali live south of Tergedus on the Nile, while their milk is drunk by a nomadic tribe, the Alabi, who are based adjacently to the kingdom of Meroe and are neighbours to the eight-cubit-tall Syrbotae.[11] These would appear to be animals too, as the Cynocephali mentioned in his eighth book as a class of *simia* (ape) clearly are: they are said to be 'rather fierce' (*efferatior*) in comparison to the gentler *satyri*.[12] Back in the sixth book again, Pliny immediately goes on to confuse the Cynocephali with the Cynamolgi ('Dog-milkers'). He describes the Cynamolgi—paradoxically, one might have thought—as 'dog-headed' (*caninis capitibus*) too, and reports that they are said to inhabit the same region as the Cynocephali, although he denies that they actually exist. There has evidently been some contamination of themes here: for Ctesias and Agatharchides, the Dog-milkers had been, more intelligibly, a human

---

[6] Ctesias *Indika, FGrH* 688 F45.37–43 (Auberger 1991 pp.112–13) = Photius *Bibliotheca* cod. 72 pp.47b–48a Bekker. Discussion at cf. Kretzenbacher 1968:28–9, White 1991:28–9, 48–51 (with the intriguing insight that such traditions of just dog-men may have been the origin of the designation of the 'Cynic' sect), 191–2.

[7] Ctesias *Indika, FGrH* 688 F45 p α (Auberger 1991 p.125) = Megasthenes *FGrH* 715 F29 = Pliny *Natural History* 7.23; cf. also β (Auberger 1991 p.126) = Tzetzes *Chiliades* 7.713. Discussion at White 1991:50–1, 191.

[8] Aelian *Nature of Animals* 4.46 = Ctesias *FGrH* 688 F45 p γ.

[9] Plato *Theaetetus* 161c: ὗς ἢ κυνοκέφαλος ἤ τι ἄλλο ἀτοπώτερον τῶν ἐχόντων αἴσθησιν.

[10] Agatharchides of Cnidus *On the Red Sea* Book 5, FF74a–75b Burstein (*apud* Diodorus 3.35 and Photius *Bibliotheca* cod. 250 p.455b Bekker); cf. McDermott 1938:66, Burstein 1989:121–2 (*ad loc.*).

[11] Pliny *Natural History* 6.184, 190. Discussion at White 1991:51.

[12] Pliny *Natural History* 8.216.

tribe that kept and milked dogs, just as others did with sheep and goats, and that had lived variously in India or Ethiopia.[13]

Beyond the material he takes directly from Ctesias, Aelian also tells us about the Cynoprosopi ('Dog-faces') that live between Egypt and Ethiopia. But these too are clearly a calque on the same Indian Cynocephali of Ctesias. Like their Indian fellows, they have dog-heads, they are black, they dwell in an inaccessible place, they live by hunting, and they are unable to use human speech (they squeal instead). More distinctly, their whole bodies are covered in hair and they have beards akin to the ones sported by Greek dragons (*drakontes*).[14] Separately, Aelian speaks again of some (unsituated) Cynocephali, and his material here is rather different. He speaks of their ability to detect edible food inside nuts and to strip the shell off to get at it. They will eat human cooked food, so long as it is well prepared. They will wear human clothes and take care of them. Baby Cynocephali will take milk from a human woman (a reversal here of the motif found in Pliny).[15] With these last Cynocephali too we would seem to be in ape/baboon territory, as we clearly are in the note made by Solinus (perhaps also writing in the third century AD): he speaks briefly of the Cynocephali as being counted amongst the apes. They leap around violently, have a savage bite, and are untameable.[16]

The earliest accessible recension of the *Alexander Romance*, the alpha recension of the early third century AD, included an episode of potential interest for us. Unfortunately the passage is missing from the sole Greek manuscript for this recension (A), and so we depend upon the (good) Armenian translation to know what it said. Alexander recounts his adventures beyond the Median desert in a letter to his mother Olympias:

> Then there appeared to us, about nine or ten o'clock, a man as hairy as a goat. And once again, I was startled and disturbed to see such beasts. I thought of capturing the man, for he was ferociously and brazenly barking at us. And I ordered a woman to undress and go to him on the chance that he might be vanquished by lust. But he took the woman and went far away where, in fact, he ate her. And he roared and made strange noises with his thick tongue at all our men who had run forth to reach her and to set her free. And when his other comrades heard him, countless myriads of them attacked us from the brushes. There were 40,000 of us. So I ordered that the brushes be set afire; and when they saw the fire, they turned and fled. And we pursued them and tied up 400,000 of them, but they died since they refused to eat. And they did not have human reason, but, rather, barked wildly like dogs.
>
> *Alexander Romance* (Arm.) §209 (Wolohojian trans.)

The detail that the hairy men bark like dogs seems to bring us into monstrous-race Cynocephalus territory here, but we should be clear that the men are not described by any means as 'dog-headed'. Nor does the term Cynocephalus occur in the extant Greek of the subsequent beta recension, which, as we can tell from comparing it to the Armenian,

---

[13] Pliny *Natural History* 6.195 (cf. 8.104); Ctesias *FGrH* 688 F46a–b (= Auberger 1991 pp.129–30; *apud* Aelian *Nature of Animals* 16.31 and Pollux *Onomasticon* 5.41); Agatharchides of Cnidus *On the Red Sea* FF61a-b Burstein (*apud* Diodorus 3.31 and Photius *Bibliotheca* cod. 250 pp.453b–454a Bekker). See Kretzenbacher 1968:31–2, Burstein 1989:107 n.1. For all that Pollux cites Ctesias for one point, his principal information matches Aelian's in no way (nor Pliny's, for that matter): he makes the 'Dog-' of the 'Dog-milkers' subjective rather than objective to give us a pack of (full) dogs that milk cows.

[14] Aelian *Nature of Animals* 10.25.   [15] Aelian *Nature of Animals* 10.30.

[16] Solinus 27.55.

preserves this episode quite conservatively.[17] But these creatures did eventually evolve into explicitly named Cynocephali in the Romance tradition at least from the point of the early-eighth-century A D Greek and Latin translations of the originally Syriac *Apocalypse* of pseudo-Methodius. Here the Cynocephali-as-monstrous-race have evidently come to yield to their more bestial side.[18]

Augustine (*c.* A D 400) includes the Cynocephali in a long (and predictable) list of monstrous races, such as the Acephali, the Sciapodes ('Shade-feet'), and the Pygmies, in the course of the debate as to whether they are descended from Adam and therefore part of common humanity. His conclusion is that, in general, they are. Whether this holds good for the Cyncephali more specifically, however, is less clear: 'What am I to say of the Cynocephali, whose canine heads and very barking declare them to be beasts rather than men?' Augustine's inclination appears to be to exclude them from the catalogue of problematically human races by moving them over the line into the animal kingdom (not incompatibly with the drift of the *Alexander Romance*). One senses again here Augustine's theological distaste for phenomena that cross the animal–human boundary (cf. Chapter 4).[19] Augustine is followed in this, as he often is, by the dutiful Isidore of Seville, who was influential in his own right. In his (early seventh-century A D) *Etymologies* Isidore briefly notes that the Cynocephali, whom he locates in India, are indicated by their barking to be beasts rather than men.[20]

The most glorious early Christian contribution to the tradition of the Cynocephali was the creation of St Christopher (the 'Christ-carrier'). In his mature hagiography the erstwhile Reprobus (*vel sim.*) is a Cynocephalus and a man-eating giant that can communicate only by barking. He is converted after carrying the child Christ across a river, baptized by St Babylus at Antioch and martyred in Lycia by the emperor Decius (r. A D 248–51). The earliest vestige of Christopher's Cynocephalus nature is traceable to a lost fourth-century A D Coptic *Acts of Bartholomew*: this told of one Christianos, both a Cynocephalus and an *anthrōpophagos* ('man-eater'), who was converted by the apostle.[21]

The broad outline here is a clear one: the Cynocephali began life as an ethnographic curiosity, a race of monstrous near-humans that lived on the edges of the known world (at various ends of it). In time they came to be identified, in part, with varieties of ape or baboon. From the third century A D onwards they came to be integrated in a more particular way into fantastical stories, pagan and Christian alike.

---

[17] For the Armenian text see Simonyan 1989; translation at Wolohojian 1969. For the Greek text of the beta recension see Bergson 1965 and Stoneman 2007–, the latter also with Italian translation and commentary; the Cynocephali episode falls (without the name) at 2.33.8–13. See White 1991:52–8 and Stoneman *ad loc.*, ii, 427.

[18] *Apocalypse of Pseudo-Methodius* (Gk. and Lat.) 8.10; for texts and translations of both the Greek and the Latin versions, see Garstad 2012. The original Syriac version was composed *c.* A D 692, while the Greek and Latin translations were made prior to A D 727: Garstad 2012:vii–ix.

[19] Augustine *City of God* 16.8: *Quid dicam de Cynocephalis, quorum canina capita atque ipse latratus magis bestias quam homines confitetur?* Discussion at White 1991:19, 30, 64–66, 194–5, who I think misunderstands the nuance of the passage.

[20] Isidore of Seville *Etymologies* 11.3.12–15.

[21] For the complex history of Christopher's hagiography and iconography, see Ameisenowa 1949:42–5, Kretzenbacher 1968:58–70, White 1991:34–6 and 223–6, Walter 2003:214–16, Haustein-Bartsch 2016:162–71 (with some fine reproductions of principally 19th-c. A D icons); cf. also Douglas 1992:104–9. The Coptic *Acts of Bartholomew* text is reconstructed by Zwierzina 1909; its tale is reflected in an episode of the 14th-c. A D Ethiopic *Gadla Hawâryât* or *The Contendings of the Apostles* at Budge 1898–1901: ii, 203–8. For the Anglo-Saxon reflex of the earlier St Christopher legends see Lionarons 2002.

False Werewolves: Dolon and the Luperci

I consider here—rather negatively—two further topics that scholarship has brought into the orbit of the Lykaia: those of Dolon and the Luperci.

Dolon

First we consider briefly some once influential ideas of Louis Gernet, the pioneer of the structural–anthropological approach to Greek social history and the great inspiration of the so-called 'Paris school' of Jean-Pierre Vernant, Pierre Vidal-Naquet, and Marcel Detienne.[1] The ideas in question, first published in 1936, focus on Dolon.[2]

In the *Iliad* Hector suspects that the Greeks are planning to flee and have left their ships unguarded, allowing the Trojans the opportunity to destroy them, and so he seeks a volunteer to go and spy on their camp by night.[3] The man that comes forward is the wealthy but 'bad to look at' (which in context seems to imply 'cowardly') Dolon, his name signifying 'The Tricky One' (cf. *dolos*, 'trick').[4] He agrees to the mission in exchange for Achilles' marvellous horses when the booty duly comes in. His arming scene proceeds as follows:

> At once he put his curving bow across his shoulders, and on top of this he put on the skin of a grey wolf [*rhinon polioio lykoio*], and on his head he put a cap of marten-skin, and took up his sharp spear.   Homer *Iliad* 10.331–5

As he arrives in the Greek zone he is immediately detected and ambushed by Odysseus and Diomede. He gibbers, cries, and begs for his life, offering rich ransom. Odysseus tells him not to fear for his life and interrogates him. After learning the details of his mission, he proceeds to press from him the details of the disposition of the camps of the Trojans and their allies on the plain. *Inter alia*, he learns of the newly arrived and vulnerable Thracians, under King Rhesus, and of the latter's fine horses. After they have got what they want from him, Diomede strikes his head off with a sword. They strip him of his wolfskin, his marten-skin cap, and his weapons and spread them across a tamarisk bush to help them retrace their steps. They immediately move on to find the Thracians where Dolon had told them they were, slaughter them as they sleep, and make off with Rhesus' fine horses, returning to the Greek camp via the tamarisk, where they recover the spoils. The episode has a satisfying ring composition: the attempt of a Trojan to take fine horses from the Greek side results not only in his death but in the Greeks taking fine horses from the Trojan side.

---

[1] See the introductory words of Buxton in Gordon 1981:x, xiv.
[2] Gernet 1981 (1936):125–39; see further Davidson 1979:64–6, Detienne and Svenbro 1989:158–9.
[3] Homer *Iliad* 10.299–579; cf. Hainsworth 1993 *ad loc.*
[4] 'Bad to look at': l. 316; but Hainsworth 1993 *ad loc.* prefers a more literal reading of 'ugly'. The significance of the speaking name is made explicit at [Euripides] *Rhesus* 158.

The (fourth-century BC?) pseudo-Euripidean tragedy *Rhesus* offers an account of the same episode. Here Dolon speaks of his outfit and other matters:[5]

DOLON: I'm on my way. I'll go to my house and home and clothe my body in suitable apparel, and thence I'll direct my course to the ships of the Argives.
CHORUS: What other clothing will you have in place of your current clothes?
DOLON: Clothing that is suitable to my task and my stealthy approach.
CHORUS: One must learn a clever thing from a clever man. Tell us, with what will you cover your body?
DOLON: I shall clothe my back in the skin of a wolf, and I shall place the beast's jaws around my head. I shall attach its forelegs to my arms and is back legs to my legs.[6] I shall imitate the course of the four-footed wolf, unfathomable to its enemies, as I draw near the ditch and the defences before the ships.[7] When I set foot on ground without cover, I shall go on two feet. This is how I have devised my trick [*dolos*].
CHORUS: May Hermes the son of Maia escort you there and back again safely, since he is the patron of thieves. You have your task: just succeed in it!
DOLON: I'll get back safely, and I'll kill Odysseus and bring you his head. If you have such a clear token, you'll be able to say that Dolon reached the ships of the Argives. Or otherwise I'll kill the son of Tydeus [Diomede]. Before dawn hits the land, I shall come home, with hands not unbloodied.   [Euripides] *Rhesus* 202–24

The chorus proceeds to imagine that Dolon the 'jugulator' (*sphageus*), going on all fours, will kill Agamemnon and place his head in Helen's hands.[8] But Dolon himself duly fails in his mission and is killed by Odysseus and Diomede, who also plan to behead Hector himself as he sleeps.[9] Rhesus' driver, escaping the pair's slaughter of the Thracians, reports that he had dreamed of the unfolding disaster with a vision of Rhesus' horses, his charges, being ridden by wolves that used their tails to whip them.[10] To Homer's ring composition with the prize of horses the *Rhesus* author probably adds a ring composition with decapitation, if we can infer, on the basis of Homer, that Odysseus and Diomede kill him by this method again here too (in line also with their ambitions for Hector): Dolon aspires to behead Odysseus and Diomede, but this is, rather, what they do to him.[11] But the author certainly adds a ring composition with the image of the killing wolf: Dolon the wolf plans to kill Odysseus or Diomede, but Odysseus and Diomede are seen as wolves by the driver as they are in the act of killing Dolon's Thracian allies.[12]

---

[5] For the date of the *Rhesus* see Liapes 2011:lxx–lxxv.

[6] The description of Dolon's disguise here serves as a model for the wolf disguise of Dorcon, whose name salutes Dolon's at Longus *Daphnis and Chloe* 1.20.2; cf. Liapes 2011:121 and, for the rich wolf imagery in *Daphnis and Chloe* more generally, Morgan 2004:159–60 (on 1.11).

[7] Hainsworth 1993:189 on ll.334–5 describes the *Rhesus*'s notion that Dolon should go on all fours as 'grotesque': why? At Euripides *Hecuba* 1058–9 Polymestor similarly speaks of walking on all fours.

[8] [Euripides] *Rhesus* 254–63.   [9] [Euripides] *Rhesus* 591–3 (Dolon), 605–6 (Hector).

[10] [Euripides] *Rhesus* 781–8.

[11] It has been suggested, dubiously to my mind, that the decapitation theme is entirely appropriate to Dolon as a wolf, on the basis that wolves normally kill their prey by attacking the throat: Detienne and Svenbro 1989:158–9.

[12] Eubulus (*fl. c.*375 BC) also devoted a comedy to the subject of Dolon, but the preserved fragments tell us nothing of his representation in the play (FF29–30 K–A, *apud* Athenaeus 100a, 471c); cf. Lissarrague 1980:27.

Dolon is already shown wearing a wolfskin in exactly the terms described here on vases from *c.*500 BC[13] and in particular on an appealing fragment of a vase by Euphronius of *c.*480–470 BC; long before the *Rhesus,* therefore, he is additionally shown walking on four legs.[14]

Gernet was rather more interested in the *Rhesus'* account of the episode than he was in Homer's, believing it to represent better the underlying myths and folk traditions than the epic did. He saw the *Rhesus'* Dolon material, alongside the traditions relating to Arcadia, the Luperci (for which see the next section) and the Hirpi Sorani (for which see Chapter 2), as the relics of the supposed Indo-European culture of secretive 'wolf confraternities', which we have mentioned above, and in which he believed that animal masks were worn.[15] In particular, he saw headhunting as an obligatory rite for one being initiated into such societies. I do not find the evidence to support this contention in his notes.[16] Indeed, so far as the *Iliad* is concerned, Dolon is surely wearing a wolfskin because, just like his accompanying marten-skin cap, it is déclassé, and because it marks him out as a sub-heroic, snivelling anti-warrior, capable only (potentially) of achievements through deceit as opposed to through martial valour.[17] So far as the *Rhesus* is concerned, on the other hand, Dolon is simply disguising himself as a wolf for the practical purpose of spying. There is no indication that he is some sort of transitional youth or young man; if anything, the references to his wealth suggest that he is well established in life and of a certain age.[18] There is little here to speak of werewolfism of any kind, and anything that does must, it seems, speak equally of were-martenism.[19]

Luperci

As we have seen, Augustine reports Varro as observing that 'the Luperci of the Romans arose, as it were, from the seeds of these mystery rites [*sc.* of the Lykaia]'.[20] Peter Wiseman rightly infers from this that 'Varro thought that the Luperci were originally transformed into wolves'. There is a modern misconception too that the famous Roman fertility festival of the Lupercalia was associated with some sort of werewolfism.[21] It was not, and its association with wolves of any sort is tenuous.

---

[13] *LIMC* Dolon nos. 11–12 (*c.*500–490 BC), 13 (*c.*490–480 BC). For Dolon in art see Lissarrague 1980, Mainoldi 1984:18–22, Williams 1986, and Liapes 2011:xxx–xxxi. On a Lucanian vase of *c.*390–380 BC, *LIMC* Dolon no.14, he is shown wearing a cap, which may well be the marten-skin one of the *Iliad,* but then a leopard skin instead of a wolfskin. On an Apulian vase of 340–330 BC, *LIMC* Dolon no.18, he retains the wolfskin but wears a leopard-skin bodysuit beneath.

[14] Paris, Louvre CA 1802 = Lissarrague 1980 no. 9 = *LIMC* Dolon no. 2.

[15] Gernet 1981 (1936):127; cf. also Steadman 1945 (a brief note written seemingly in ignorance of Gernet), and Chapter 6, pp.185–7.

[16] Gernet 1981 (1936):128.

[17] Hainsworth 1993:189 on ll.334–5 is dismissive of 'anthropological speculation' as to the significance of the wolfskin and the marten-skin cap alike.

[18] [Euripides] *Rhesus* 159–60, 170, 178.

[19] Kitchell 2017:193–7 most recently makes the case that the associations of the marten are significant for the characterization of Dolon, drawing attention in particular to Nicander *Theriaca* 195–9, where the marten is said to infiltrate henhouses by night and kill the hens as they sleep.

[20] Augustine *City of God* 18.17; Wiseman 1995b:85 also draws attention also to Cicero *Pro Caelio* 26, where the orator may be invoking a conceit that the Luperci were wolves in referring to them as *coitio illa silvestris,* 'that woodland pack' (cf. Chapter 3 for the association between werewolves and woods).

[21] E.g. Burkert 1983a:89; even Wiseman 1995b:87 imagines that, before the intrusion of Pan into the rite, the Luperci may have been 'wild men, like wolves'. The bibliography for the Lupercalia is vast. I have found Wiseman 1995a (cf. also 1995b:77–88) most useful; the piece incorporates a convenient

The Lupercalia rite proceeded from the sacrifice of a goat made by the Luperci priests to a god sometimes called Lupercus in a grotto called the Lupercal. The derivation of these three or four terms is obscure, though some ancients associated it with Rome's founding she-wolf, *lupa*, whose den the Lupercal grotto had supposedly been.[22] If the first element of these terms does indeed salute the 'wolf', the second element remains obscure: Servius suggested a derivation from *arceo*, 'ward off', and the *Oxford Latin Dictionary* tentatively agrees.[23] In the distinctive rite itself the Luperci ran about, naked save for animal-skin loincloths, whipping the (denuded?) women of Rome with thongs. However, these loincloths were not made of wolfskin but of goatskin, as indeed were the thongs.[24] Ovid preserves a pleasing aetiology of the rite: Juno had ordained that a failure in fertility could be ended if a sacred he-goat penetrated the matrons of Rome (*Italidas matres... sacer hirtus inito*); an Etruscan augur had found the least unacceptable way to fulfil her command, the breaking of their skins with a goatskin lash.[25] Indeed, the Luperci themselves could actually be termed *crepi*, a version of the familiar *capri*, 'goats'.[26] The animal at the heart of these celebrations was evidently the goat, not the wolf.

Ancient scholars could not agree on the identity of the god, sometime Lupercus, in whose honour the rites were performed, but he is first identified for us in Greek sources, Eratosthenes and Heraclides of Pontus, as the appropriately caprine Pan.[27] Trogus' description of the cult statue is also appropriately Pan-like: he tells us that he was dressed in a goatskin (so evidently the Luperci followed his style).[28] Ovid subsequently identifies the god as Faunus, albeit in such a way as to indicate that he is merely treating Faunus here as the *interpretatio Romana* of Pan.[29] It may seem that we are returning to the world of the

source catalogue. Further discussions at, e.g., Franklin 1921 (with care), Kerényi 1948, Michels 1953 (arguing, esp. at 49–51, for a strong connection with wolves and werewolves, and noting that the festival coincided with the lupine mating season), Duval 1977 (esp. 260–7), Holleman 1973, 1985, Harmon 1978:1441–6, Ulf 1982, Pötscher 1984, Tennant 1988, Markus 1990:131–5, Carafa 2006, McLynn 2008, Rissanen 2012:124–9, Graf 2015:163–83 and Vé 2018. For the long tradition of the foundational she-wolf herself and in particular the famous bronze *Lupa Capitolina* (an Etruscan artefact or a medieval one?), see Dulière 1979 and Mazzoni 2010 (the latter reporting the view, at p.24, that the statue boasts a facial expression 'more devastating than the Mona Lisa').

[22] For the association of the three terms, see Varro *De lingua Latina* 5.85, 6.13. For the Lupercal as the home of the she-wolf, see Ovid *Fasti* 2.381–422, Plutarch *Romulus* 21.3–8 (the rite may be performed in homage to the she-wolf, hence the sacrifice also of a dog, the enemy of the wolf, in the course of it), Dionysius of Halicarnassus *Roman Antiquities* 1.32.3–5, 1.79.7–8, Servius on Virgil *Aeneid* 8.343, *Origo gentis Romanae* 22.1; cf. Wiseman 1995a:1–2. The she-wolf of Rome eventually acquired a cult of her own—in the African and Spanish provinces, at any rate: *CIL* ii 2156 and 4603, dedicated to the *Lupa Romana* and the *Lupa Augusta*; cf. Prieur 1988:32. In due course the *lupercus* was, improbably, to become the foundation of the leprechaun: see Bisagni 2012, whose suggestion is adopted by the *Electronic Dictionary of the Irish Language* (*eDIL*) s.vv. *lupracán, luchorpán*.

[23] Servius on Virgil *Aeneid* 8.343: Pan was given the epithet Lykaios because by his protection wolves were kept away (*arcerentur*) from the flocks. *OLD* s.v. *Lupercus*. See also Franklin 1921:36.

[24] Ovid *Fasti* 2.425–52, Plutarch *Romulus* 21.3–8, Gelasius *Letter against the Lupercalia* 16. For an image of a Lupercus in a goatskin loincloth and carrying his whip, see *CIL* xiv 3624, the funerary relief of Tiberius Claudius Liberalis, reproduced at Wiseman 1995b:83 fig. 10.

[25] Ovid *Fasti* 2.425–52; cf. Wiseman 1995a:14.

[26] Festus (Paulus) 49L, cf. 42L; Wiseman 1995a:1, 14.

[27] Eratosthenes *apud* schol. Plato *Phaedrus* 244b (p.61 Ruhnk); Heraclides of Pontus F130 Wehrli, *apud* Clement of Alexandria *Stromateis* 1.108.4; cf. Wiseman 1995a:3, 10.

[28] Trogus *apud* Justin 48.1.7; cf. Wiseman 1995a:6, 12.

[29] Ovid *Fasti* 2.267–8, 303–4, 423–4 (*Quid vetat Arcadio dictos a monte Lupercos?/Faunus in Arcadia templa Lycaeus habet...*), 5.99–102; cf. Wiseman 1995a:2, 6, 12, who notes that most modern authorities have accepted Ovid on this, while himself remaining dismissive of the claim.

wolf when the Augustan authors Dionysius of Halicarnassus, Trogus, Livy, Virgil, and Ovid tell us that the god of the Lupercal was Lykaios. However, while there is evidently some knowing play with parallel lupine (pseudo-?)etymologies here, the Lykaios in question was not the Zeus of the wolves (or anything else), but (explicitly) Arcadia's other great god, Pan again, the Pan of Mount Lykaion, himself closely associated with Zeus Lykaios, and supposedly imported to Latium by the Arcadians under Evander.[30] It was doubtless on the basis of this perceived association that there arose the tradition, found not only in Varro but also in Dionysius and in Plutarch, that the Lupercalia festival was somehow derived from or equivalent to the Arcadian Lykaia.[31]

[30] Dionysius of Halicarnassus *Roman Antiquities* 1.32.3, 1.81.1, Trogus *apud* Justin 48.1.7 (also telling that the god's Latin name was Lupercus); Livy 1.5.1–2, Virgil *Georgics* 1.17 (with Servius *ad loc.*, who here claims that Pan was given the epithet Lykaios because he warded the wolves from the flocks), *Aeneid* 8.343–4 (again with Servius *ad loc.*), and Ovid *Fasti* 2.423–3, as above. Ovid also identifies Faunus with Pan at *Fasti* 2.84 and 4.650–3, as had Horace at *Odes* 1.17.1–4; cf. Wiseman 1995a:6. For Arcadian Pan and his association with the Lykaia, see Cook 1914–40:i, 87, Burkert 1983a:92, Jost 1985:456–76, esp. 474–6, 2016:41–3, Borgeaud 1988:36–7, 62–4 and Aston 2011 esp. 110–12, 210–11.
[31] Dionysius of Halicarnassus *Roman Antiquities* 1.80.1, Plutarch *Romulus* 21.3, *Caesar* 61.6, *Antony* 12.1, *Roman Questions* 68 (*Moralia* 280c).

References

Adler, A. ed. 1971. *Suidae lexicon.* 5 vols. Stuttgart.

Afzelius, A. A. 1842. *Volkssagen und Volkslieder aus Schwedens älterer und neuerer Zeit.* 2 vols. Leipzig. Trans. of vols. 1–2 of *Swenska folkets sago-häfder.* 11 vols. Stockholm, 1839–70.

Ameisenowa, Z. 1949. 'Animal-headed gods, evangelists, saints and righteous men' *Journal of the Warburg and Courtauld Institutes* 12, 21–45.

Anderson, G. 1976. *Studies in Lucian's Comic Fiction.* Leiden.

Anderson, G. 2000. *Fairytale in the Ancient World.* London.

Anderson, G. 2007. *Folktale as a Source of Graeco-Roman Fiction: The Origin of Popular Narrative.* Lewiston, NY.

Anderson, G. 2019. *Fantasy in Greek and Roman Literature.* London.

Andrén, A., K. Jennbert, and C. Raudvere eds. 2006. *Old Norse Religion in Long-Term Perspectives: Origins, Changes and Interactions.* Lund.

Arafat, K. W. 1996. *Pausanias' Greece. Ancient Artists and Roman Rulers.* Cambridge.

Arena, R. 1979. 'Considerazioni sul mito di Callisto' *Acme* 32, 5–25.

Arens, W. 1979. *The Man-Eating Myth.* Oxford.

Argenti, P. P., and H. J. Rose 1949. *The Folk-lore of Chios.* 2 vols. Oxford.

Arias, P. E. 1987. 'Euthymos di Locri' *Annali della Scuola Normale Superiore di Pisa. Classe di Lettere e Filosofia* 17, 1–8.

Armand, F. 2013. 'Les loups-garous et les eaux' *IRIS* 34, 133–45.

Asheri, D., A. B. Lloyd, and A. Corcella 2007. *Commentary on Herodotus Books I-IV.* Oxford.

Ashwin, E. A. trans., M. Summers ed. 1929. *Henry Boguet. An Examen of Witches.* London.

Ashwin, E. A. 1930. *Nicolas Remy. Demonolatry.* London.

Astbury, R. 1985. *M. Terentii Varronis saturarum Menippearum fragmenta.* Leipzig.

Aston, E. M. 2011. *Mixanthrôpoi. Animal-Human Hybrid Deities in Greek Religion.* Kernos Supplement 25. Liège.

Auberger, J. 1991 trans. *Ctésias. Histoires de l'Orient.* Paris.

Auberger, J. 1992. 'Pausanias romancier? Le témoinage du livre IV' *DHA* 18.1, 257–80.

Auberger, J. 2000. 'Pausanias et le livre 4: une leçon pour l'empire?' *Phoenix* 54, 253–81.

Azoulay, V. 2016. 'Les statues de Théogénès de Thasos: entre vénération et outrage', in C. M. d'Annoville and Y. Rivière eds. *Faire parler et faire taire les statues.* Rome. 149–96 and figs. 37–44.

Bachman, W. B., and G. Erlingsson trans. 1993. *Six Old Icelandic Sagas.* Lanham.

Baldwin, B. 1986. 'Why the werewolf urinates' *Petronian Society Newsletter* 16, 9.

Baldwin, B. 1992. 'The werewolf story as *Bulletinstil*' *Petronian Society Newsletter* 22, 6–7.

Bambeck, M. 1973. 'Das Werwolfmotiv im *Bisclavret*' *Zeitschrift für romanische Philologie* 89, 123–47.

Banks, S. E., and J. W. Binns eds. and transs. 2002. *Gervase of Tilbury. Otia Imperialia, Recreation for an Emperor.* Oxford.

Baring-Gould, S. 1865. *The Book of Werewolves.* London.

Barkan, L. 1986. *The Gods Made Flesh. Metamorphosis and the Pursuit of Paganism.* New Haven.

Bartsch, K. 1879. *Sagen, Märchen und Gebräuche aus Mecklenburg.* Vienna.

Battaglia, S. 1965. *La coscienza letteraria del medioevo.* Naples.

Baynham E. J. 2018. ' "Joining the gods": Alexander at the Euphrates: Arrian 7.27.3, *Metz Epitome* 101–102 and the *Alexander Romance*' in R. Stoneman, K. Nawotka, and A. Wojciechowska eds. *The* Alexander Romance: *History and Literature.* Ancient Narrative Supplement 25. Groningen. 189–98.

Beard, D. J. 1978. 'The berserker in Icelandic literature' in R. Thelwall ed. *Approaches to Oral Literature.* Belfast. 99–114.

Beck, R. 1996. 'Mystery religions, aretology and the ancient novel' in G. Schmeling ed. *The Novel in the Ancient World.* Leiden. 131-50.

Bedjan, P. ed. 1890–7. *Acta Martyrum et Sanctorum.* 7 vols. Leipzig.

Beekes, R. 2010. *Etymological Dictionary of Greek.* 2 vols. Leiden.

Belloni, G. G. 1986. 'Dis Pater' *LIMC* iii.1, 644.

Benediktsson, J. ed. 1950–7. *Arngrimi Jonae opera Latine conscripta.* 4 vols. Munksgaard.

Beneventano della Corte, F. 2017. 'Φάσμα. Una categoria del sovrannaturale nella cultura della Grecia antica'. Diss., Siena.

Benkov, E. J. 1988. 'The naked beast: clothing and humanity in *Bisclavret*' *Chimères* 19, 27–43.

Benveniste, E. 1938. *Les Mages dans l'ancien Iran.* Paris.

Bergson, L. 1965. *Der griechische Alexanderroman. Rezension β.* Stockholm.

Bernand, A. 1991. *Sorciers grecs.* Paris.

Bettini, M. 1989–91. 'Testo letterario e testo folclorico' in G. Cavallo, P. Fedeli, and A. Giardina eds. *Lo Spazio Letterario di Roma Antica.* 5 vols. i, Rome–Bari. 63–77.

Bickerman, E., and H. Tadmor 1978. 'Darius I, Pseudo-Smerdis and the Magi' *Athenaeum* 56, 239–61.

Bidez, J., and F. Cumont 1938. *Les Mages hellénisés.* 2 vols., Paris.

Biering, T. J. 2006. 'The concept of shamanism in Old Norse religion from a sociological point of view' in Andrén et al. 2006, 171–6.

Bill, A. H. 1931. *The Wolf in the Garden.* New York.

Biraschi, A. M. 1996. 'Καλύκα πηγή in Paus. VI 6, 11? A proposito del dipinto di Temesa' *Parola del Passato* 51, 442–56.

Bisagni, J. 2012. 'Leprechaun: a new etymology' *Cambrian Medieval Celtic Studies* 64, 47–84.

Björklund, H. 2017. 'Protecting against Child-killing Demons: Uterus Amulets in the Late Antique and Byzantine Magical World'. Diss., Helsinki.

Blackwood, A. 1908. *John Silence, Physician Extraordinary.* London.

Blaise, A. 1954. *Dictionnaire latin—français des auteurs chrétiens.* Turnhout.

Blaney, B. 1982. 'The berserk suitor: the literary application of a stereotyped theme' *Scandinavian Studies* 54, 279–94.

Blaney, B. 1993. 'Berserkr' in P. Pulsiano ed. *Medieval Scandinavia: An Encyclopedia.* New York. 37–8.

Blänsdorf, J. 1990. 'Die Werwolf-Geschichte des Niceros bei Petron als Beispiel literarischer Fiktion mündlichen Erzählens' in G. Vogt-Spira ed. *Strukturen der Mündlichkeit in der römischen Literatur.* Tübingen. 193–217.

Blom, J. D. 2014. 'When doctors cry wolf: a systematic review of the literature on clinical lycanthropy' *History of Psychiatry* 25, 87–102.

Blum, R., and E. Blum 1970. *The Dangerous Hour. The Lore and Culture of Crisis and Mystery in Rural Greece.* London.

Boardman, J. 1992. 'Lamia' *LIMC* vi.1, 189.

Boberg, I. 1966. *Motif Index of Early Icelandic Literature.* Bibliotheca Arnamagnaeana 27 Copenhagen.

Bodin, J. 1580. *De la Démonomanie des sorciers*. Paris.

Bodson, L.1980. 'Place et function du chien dans le monde antique' *Ethnozootechnie* 25, 13–21.

Boehm, F. 1932. 'Striges' *RE* 2. Reihe 4, 356–63.

Boës, J. ed. 1998. *Nicolas Rémy. La Démonolâtrie. Texte établi et annoté à partir de l'édition de 1595*. Nancy.

Boguet, H. 1590. *Discours exécrable des sorciers*. 3rd ed. Lyon.

Bohringer, F. 1979. 'Cultes d' athlètes en Grèce classique: propos politiques, discours mythiques', *REA* 81, 5–18.

Boivin, J. M. 1985. 'Le Prêtre et les loups-garous: un episode de la *Topographia Hibernica* de Giraud de Barri' in L. Harf-Lancner ed. *Métamorphose et bestiaire fantastique au moyen âge*. Paris. 51–69.

Bolte, J., and G. Polívka 1913–32. *Anmerkungen zu den Kinder- und Hausmärchen der Brüder Grimm*. 5 vols, Leipzig.

Bolton, J. D. P. 1962. *Aristeas of Proconnesus*. Oxford.

Bömer, F. 1958–63. *Die Fasten*. 2 vols. Heidelberg.

Bonnafoux, J. 1867. *Légendes et croyances superstitieuses de la Creuse*. Guéret.

Bonnechere, P. 1994. *Le Sacrifice humain en Grèce ancienne*. Kernos Suppléments 3. Liège.

Bonnechere, P. 2009. 'Le sacrifice humain grec entre norme et anormalité' in P. Brulé ed. *La norme en matière religieuse en Grèce ancienne: Actes du XIIe colloque international du CIERGA (Rennes, septembre 2007)*. Liège. 189–212.

Bonner, C. A. 1949. '*Kestos himas* and the saltire of Aphrodite' *American Journal of Philology* 70, 1–6.

Borgeaud, P. 1988. *The Cult of Pan in Ancient Greece*. Chicago. Trans. of *Recherches sur le dieu Pan*. Rome, 1979.

Borghini, A. 1991. 'Lupo mannaro: il tempo della metamorfosi (Petr. *Satyr*. lxii.3)' *Aufidus* 14, 29–32.

Böttiger, C. A. 1837. *Kleine Schriften archäologischen und antiquarischen Inhalts*. i. Dresden and Leipzig.

Boulhoul, P. 1994. 'Hagiographie antique et démonologie. Notes sur quelques *Passions* grecques (*BHG* 962x, 964, et 1165–1166)' *Analecta Bollandiana* 112, 255–304.

Bouquet, J. 1990. 'Trois histoires fantastiques' *Annales Latini montium arvernorum. Bulletin du Groupe d'Études Latines de l'Université de Clermont* 17, 17–35.

Bourgault du Coudray, D. 2006. *The Curse of the Werewolf: Fantasy, Horror and the Beast Within*. London.

Bourguet, É., ed. 1929. *Fouilles de Delphes*. iii.1. *Inscriptions de l'entrée du sanctuaire au trésor des Athéniens*. Paris.

Bouvier, D. 2015. 'Le héros comme un loup: usage platonicien d'une comparaison homérique' *Cahiers des études anciennes* 51, 125–47.

Bowie, E. L. 1994. 'The readership of the Greek novels in the ancient world' in J. Tatum ed. *The Search for the Ancient Novel*. Baltimore. 435–59.

Boyce, B. 1991. *The Language of the Freedmen in Petronius' Cena Trimalchionis*. Leiden.

Boyd, M. 2009. 'Melion and the wolves of Ireland' *Neophilologus* 93, 555–70.

Brelich, A. 1958. *Gli eroi greci*. Rome.

Brelich, A. 1967. *Presupposti del sacrificio umano*. Rome.

Brelich, A. 1969. *Paides e parthenoi*. i. Rome.

Bremmer, J. N. 1978. 'Heroes, rituals and the Trojan War' *Studi storico-religiosi* 2, 5–38.

Bremmer, J. N. 1983. *The Early Greek Concept of the Soul*. Princeton.

Bremmer, J. N. 1987. 'Romulus, Remus and the foundation of Rome' in J. N. Bremmer and N. Horsfall eds. *Roman Myth and Mythography*. London. 25–48.

Bremmer, J. N. 1997. 'Rituele ontmaagding in Simon Vestdijks "De held van Temesa"' in G. T. Jensma and Y. B. Kuiper eds. *De god van Nederland is de beste*. Kampen, 80–98.

Bremmer, J. N. 2002. *The Rise and Fall of the Afterlife*. London.

Bremmer, J. N. 2007a. ed. *The Strange World of Human Sacrifice*. Studies in the History and Anthropology of Religion 1. Leuven.

Bremmer, J. N. 2007b. 'Myth and ritual in Greek human sacrifice. Lykaon, Polyxena and the case of the Rhodian criminal' in Bremmer 2007a, 55–80. A revised and updated version in his *Collected Essays ii: The World of Greek Religion and Mythology*. 2019. Tübingen, 349–72.

Bremmer, J. N. 2008. *Greek Religion and Culture, the Bible, and the Ancient Near East*. Leiden.

Bremmer, J. N. 2016. 'Shamanism in Classical scholarship: where are we now?' in Jackson 2016, 52–78.

Bremmer, J. N. 2018. 'Method and madness in the study of Greek shamanism: the case of Peter Kingsley' *ASDIWAL. Revue genevoise d'anthropologie et d'histoire des religions* 13, 93–109.

Bremmer, J. N. 2019. *The World of Greek Religion and Mythology*. Tübingen.

Briant, P. 2002. *From Cyrus to Alexander. A History of the Persian Empire*. Winona Lake. Trans. of *Histoire de l'empire Perse. De Cyrus à Alexandre*. Paris, 1996.

Brisson, L. 1978. 'Aspects politiques de la bisexualité. L'histoire de Polycrite', in M. B. de Boer and T. A. Elridge eds., *Hommages à Maarten J. Vermaseren*. EPRO 68. Leiden. 80–122.

Bronner, S. J. 2017. *Folklore. The Basics*. London.

Bronzini, G. B. 1990. 'Themen und Motive der Volkserzählung im "Satyricon" von Petronius' in L. Röhrich hon., L. Petzoldt, and S. Top eds. *Dona folcloristica: Festgabe für Lutz Röhrich zu seiner Emeritierung*. Frankfurt am Main. 21–31.

Brown, P. 1971. 'The rise and function of the holy man in Late Antiquity' *JRS* 61, 80–101.

Bruit, L. 1986. 'Pausanias à Phigalie. Sacrifices non-sanglants et discours idéologique' *Mètis* 1, 71–96.

Brulé, P. 1987. *La Fille d'Athènes. La religion des filles à Athènes à l'époque classique. Mythes, cultes et sociétés*. Paris.

Bryce, T. R. 1983. 'The arrival of the goddess Leto in Lycia' *Historia* 32, 1–13.

Buchholz, P. 1968. *Schamanistische Züge in der altisländischen Überlieferung*. Münster.

Buck, C. D. 1955. *The Greek Dialects*. Chicago.

Budge, E. A. W., ed. and trans.1898–1901. *The Contendings of the Apostles, being the Histories of the Lives and Martyrdoms and Deaths of the Twelve Apostles and Evangelists. The Ethiopic Texts now first Edited from Manuscripts in the British Museum, with an English Translation*. 2 vols. London.

Budin, S. 2008. *The Myth of Sacred Prostitution in Antiquity*. Cambridge.

Burgess, G. S., L. C. Brook, and A. Hopkins eds. and transs. 2007. *French Arthurian literature. iv. Eleven Old French narratives*. Cambridge.

Burkert, W. 1962. '*Goes*. Zum griechischen Schamanismus' *RhM* 105, 36–55. Reprinted at Burkert 2001–11:iii, 173–90.

Burkert, W. 1972. *Lore and Science in Ancient Pythagoreanism*. Cambridge, MA.

Burkert, W. 1979. *Structure and History in Greek Mythology and Ritual*. Berkeley.

Burkert, W. 1983a. *Homo Necans*. Berkeley. Trans. of *Homo Necans*. Berlin, 1972.

Burkert, W. 1983b. 'Itinerant diviners and magicians: a neglected element in cultural contacts' in R. Hägg ed. *The Greek Renaissance of the Eighth Century BC: Tradition and Innovation*. Stockholm. 115–19.

Burkert, W. 1985. *Greek Religion*. Oxford. Trans. of *Griechische Religion der archaischen und klassischen Epoche*. Stuttgart, 1977.

Burkert, W. 1992. *The Orientalizing Revolution. Near-Eastern Influence on Greek Culture in the Early Archaic Age*. Cambridge, MA. Translation of *Die orientalisierende Epoche in der griechischen Religion und Literatur*. Heidelberg,1984.

Burkert, W. 2001–11. *Kleine Schriften*. 8 vols. Göttingen.

Burriss, E. E. 1935. 'The place of the dog in superstition as revealed in Latin literature' *Classical Philology* 30, 32–42.

Burstein, S. M., trans. 1989. *Agatharchides of Cnidus, On the Erythraean Sea*. Hakluyt Society, Second Series 172. London.

Buxton, R. G. A. 1987. 'Wolves and werewolves in Greek thought' in J. N. Bremmer ed. *Interpretations of Greek mythology*. London. 60–79. Republished with a postscript: R. G. A. Buxton *Myths and Tragedies in their Ancient Greek Contexts*. Oxford, 2013. 33–51.

Buxton, R. G. A. 2009. *Forms of Astonishment: Greek Myths of Metamorphosis*. Oxford.

Bynum, C. W. 2001. *Metamorphosis and Identity*. New York.

Byock, J. L. trans. 1990. *The Saga of the Volsungs*. London.

Byock, J. L. 1998. *The Saga of King Hrolf Kraki*. London.

Byock, J. L. 2009 trans. *Grettir's Saga*. Oxford.

Calame, C. 1997. *Choruses of Young Women in Ancient Greece*. Lanham. Trans. of *Les Choeurs de jeunes filles en Grèce archaïque*. Rome, 1977.

Calame, C. 2003. 'Le rite d'initiation tribale comme catégorie anthrolopologique (Van Gennep et Platon)' *Revue de l'histoire des religions* 220, 5–62.

Caldwell, J. R. 1940. 'The origin of the story of Bǫðvar-Bjarki' *Arkiv för nordisk filologi* 55, 223–75.

Campanile, E. 1977. *Ricerche di cultura poetica indoeuropea*. Pisa.

Campanile, E. 1979. 'Meaning and prehistory of Old Irish Cu Glas' *Journal of Indo-European Studies* 7, 237–47.

Carabia, J. 1995. 'Sorcières, loups et brigands ou les dangers des voyages' *Pallas* 43, 83–102.

Carafa, P. 2006. 'I Lupercali' in A. Carandini ed. *La leggenda di Roma. Testi, morfologia e commento*. Rome. 477–93.

Carbon, J.-M., and J. P. T. Clackson 2016. 'Arms and the boy: on the new festival calendar from Arcadia' *Kernos* 29, 19–58.

Carey, J. 2002. 'Werewolves in medieval Ireland' *Cambrian Medieval Celtic Studies* 44, 37–72.

Carnoy, E. H. 1883. *Littérature orale de la Picardie*. Paris.

Carpenter, R. 1946. *Folktales, Fiction and Saga in the Homeric Epics*. Sather Classical Lectures. Berkeley.

Casevitz, M. 2004. 'Remarques sur le sens de ἀρχαῖος et de παλαιός' *Mètis* 2, 125–36.

Casevitz, M., and J. Auberger 2005. *Pausanias. Description de la Grèce. Livre iv. La Messénie*. Budé. Paris.

Casevitz, M., J. Pouilloux, and A. Jacquemin 2002. *Pausanias. Description de la Grèce. Livre vi. L'Élide (ii)*. Budé. Paris.

Castillo Pascual, P. 2015. 'Circe *diva*: the reception of Circe in the Baroque opera' in F. Carlà and I. Berti eds. *Ancient Magic and the Supernatural in the Modern Visual and Performing Arts*. London. 79–92.

Cerchiai, L. 2000. 'Piatto pontico con demone a testa di lupo' in A. Carandini and R. Cappelli eds. *Roma. Romolo e Remo e la fondazione della città*. Milan. 226.

Chantraine P. 2009. *Dictionnaire étymologique de la langue grecque: histoire des mots*. New ed. Paris.

Charpin, F. 1978–91. *Lucilius. Satires*. 3 vols. Budé. Paris.

Cheilik, M. 1987. 'The werewolf' in M. South ed. *Mythical and Fabulous Creatures: A Sourcebook and Research Guide*. New York. 265–89.

Cherubini, L. 2009a. '*Scilicet illum tetigerat mala manus*: inganni e disinganni delle streghe in Petr. 63' *I quaderni del ramo d'oro* 2, 143–55.

Cherubini, L. 2009b. 'The virgin, the bear, the upside-down *strix*: an interpretation of Antoninus Liberalis 21' *Arethusa* 42, 77–97.

Cherubini, L. 2010a. *Strix. La strega nella cultura romana*. Turin.

Cherubini, L. 2010b. 'Hungry witches and children in Antiquity and the Middle Ages' in K. Mustakallio and C. Laes eds. *The Dark Side of Childhood in Late Antiquity and the Middle Ages*. Oxford. 67–78.

Chierici, A. 1994. 'Porsenna e Olta, riflessioni su un mito etrusco' *Mélanges de l'École française de Rome. Antiquité* 106, 353–402.

Chrimes, K. M. T. 1949. *Ancient Sparta. A Re-examination of the Evidence*. Manchester.

Christes, J. 1971. *Der frühe Lucilius. Rekonstruktionen und Interpretationen des XXVI. Buches sowie von Teilen des XXX Buches*. Heidelberg.

Citroni, M. 1984. '*Copo compilatus*: nota a Petronio 62.12' *Prometheus* 10, 33–6.

Clarke, J. R. 2007. *Looking at Laughter: Humor, Power, and Transgression in Roman Visual Culture*. Berkeley.

Clausen, W. 1994. *Virgil. Eclogues. With an Introduction and Commentary*. Oxford.

Clover, C. J. 1986. '*Vǫlsunga Saga* and the missing lai of Marie de France' in R. Simek, J. Kristjánsson, and H. Bekker-Nielsen eds. *Sagnaskemmtun: Sudies in Honour of Hermann Pálsson on his 65th birthday, 26th May 1986*. Vienna. 79–84.

Cole, S. G. 1984. 'The social function of rituals of maturation: the *koureion* and the *arkteia*' *ZPE* 55, 233–44.

Coleman, R. 1977. *Vergil. Eclogues*. Cambridge.

Coll, P. G., G. O'Sullivan, and P. J. Browne 1985. 'Lycanthropy lives on' *British Journal of Psychiatry* 147, 201–2.

Collins, D. 2008. *Magic in the Ancient Greek World*. Oxford.

Colonna, G. 1985. 'Novità sui culti di Pyrgi' *Rendiconti. Pontificia accademia Romana di archeologia* 57, 57–79.

Colonna, G. 2007. 'L'Apollo di Pyrgi, Śur/Śuri ('il Nero') e l' Apollo Sourios' *Studi Etruschi* 73, 109–13.

Cook, A. B. 1914–40. *Zeus: A Study in Ancient Religion*. 3 vols. Cambridge.

Copper, B. 1977. *The Werewolf in Legend, Fact and Art*. London.

Coppinger, R., L. Spector, and L. Miller 'What, if anything, is a wolf?' in Musiani et al. 2010a, 41–67.

Cordiano, G. 2000. 'La fine della "hierodulia" femminile a Temesa: Magno Greca nella propaganda dei Locresi Epizefirii' *Arys* 3, 115–27.

Cornell, T. J. ed. 2013. *The Fragments of the Roman Historians*. 3 vols. Oxford.

Cosi, M. ed. 2001. *L'arkteia di Brauron e i culti femminili*. Bologna.

Cosquin, E. 1887. *Contes populaires de Lorraine comparés avec les contes des autres provinces de France et des pays étrangers, et précédés d'un essai sur l'origine et la propagation des contes populaires européens*. 2 vols. Paris.

Crampon M. 1936. *Le Culte de l'arbre et de la forêt en Picardie*. Mémoires de la Société des antiquaires de Picardie 46. Paris.

Crane, G. 1988. *Calypso. Background and Connections in the Odyssey*. Beiträge zur klassischen Philologie. Frankfurt am Main.

Crane, S. 2013. *Animal Encounters. Contacts and Concepts in Medieval Britain*. Philadelphia.

Crawford, M. H. ed. 1996. *Roman Statutes*. 3 vols. London.

Crum, R. 1933. 'The werewolf again' *Classical Weekly* 26, 97–8.

Curletto, S. 1987. 'Il contesto mitico-religioso antenato/anima/uccello/strega nel mondo greco-latino' *Maia* 39, 143–56.

Currie, B. 2002. 'Euthymos of Locri: a case study in heroization in the Classical Period' *JHS* 122, 24–44. Reprinted as 'Euthymos di Locri: uno studio sull' eroizzazione nel periodo classico' *Polis* 1 (2003) 85–102.

Dalley, S., trans. 1989. *Myths from Mesopotamia*. Oxford.

Dambielle, H. 1907. *La Sorcellerie en Gascogne*. Auch.

D'Assier, A. 1883. *Essai sur l'humanité posthume et le spiritisme par un positiviste*. Paris. Trans. (H. S. Olcott) as *Posthumous Humanity: A Study of Phantoms*. London, 1887.

D'Autilia, M. I. 2003. 'Il licantropo: Un topos del "racconto reaviglioso" tra Petronio e oralità folklorica' *Annuario delle attività della Delegazione della Valle del Sarno dell' A.I.C.C.* 2, 93–111.

D'Autun, J. 1678. *L'Incredulité sçavante et la credulité ignorante*. Lyon.

Davidson, H. R. E. 1986. 'Shape-changing in the Old Norse sagas' in Otten 1986, 142–60. Originally published in J. R. Porter and W. M. S. Russell eds. *Animals in Folklore*. London, 1978. 126–42 and 258–9.

Davidson, H. R. E. and A. Chaudri eds. 2003. *A Companion to the Fairy Tale*. Cambridge.

Davidson, H. R. E., ed., and P. Fisher trans. 1980. *Saxo Grammaticus. History of the Danes, Books 1–9*. 2 vols. Cambridge. [Latterly reprinted in a single volume, albeit preserving the separate paginations.]

Davidson, M. E. 1979. 'Dolon and Rhesus in the *Iliad*' *QUCC* 1, 61–6.

Davies, M., and Kathirithamby, J. 1986. *Greek Insects*. London.

De Blécourt, W. 2007a. ' "I would have eaten you too": werewolf legends in the Flemish, Dutch and German area' *Folklore* 118, 23–43.

De Blécourt, W. 2007b. 'A journey to Hell: reconsidering the Livonian "werewolf" ' *Magic, Ritual and Witchcraft* 2, 49–67.

De Blécourt, W. 2009. 'The werewolf, the witch, and the warlock: aspects of gender in the Early Modern period' in A. Rowlands ed. *Witchcraft and Masculinities in Early Modern Europe*. London. 191–213.

De Blécourt, W. 2013a. 'Monstrous theories: werewolves and the abuse of history' *Preternature* 2, 188–212.

De Blécourt, W. 2013b. 'Wolfsmenschen' in Ranke and Bausinger 1975–2015, xiv, 975–86.

De Blécourt, W., ed. 2015a. *Werewolf Histories*. Basingstoke.

De Blécourt, W. 2015b. 'The differentiated werewolf: an introduction to cluster methodology' in de Blécourt 2015a, 1–24.

De Block, R. 1877. 'Le loup dans les mythologies de la Grèce et de l'Italie anciennes' *Revue de l'instruction publique en Belgique*, 20, 145–58 and 217–234.

De Borries, J. 1911. *Phrynichi sophistae* Praeparatio sophistica. Leipzig.

De Lancre, P. 1612. *Tableau de l'inconstance des mauvais anges et demons*. Paris. Trans. (G. Scholz-Williams) as *On the Inconstancy of Witches*. Tempe, 2006.

Delcourt, M. 1938. *Stérilités mystérieuses et naissances maléfiques dans l'antiquité classique*. Liège.

Dench, E. 1995. *From Barbarians to New Men: Greek, Roman, and Modern Perceptions of Peoples from the Central Apennines*. Oxford.

Deonna, W. 1925. 'Orphée et l'oracle de la tête coupée' *REG* 38, 44–69.

De Roguin, C.-F. 1999. 'Apollon Lykeios dans la tragédie: dieu, protecteur, dieu tueur, "dieu de l'initiation" ' *Kernos* 12, 99–123.

Deroy, L. 1985. 'Le nom de Circé et les "portulans" de la Grèce archaïque' *Les Études classiques* 53, 185–91.

De Sanctis, G. 1909–10. 'L'eroe di Temesa' *Atti dell'Accademia delle scienze di Torino* 45, 164–72. Reprinted in his *Scritti minori*. 6 vols. Rome, 1966–72. i, 21–9.

De Smedt, C. ed. 1889–93. *Catalogus codicum hagiographicorum latinorum antiquiorum saeculo XVI qui asservantur in Bibliotheca nationali Parisiensi*. 3 vols. Brussels.

Detienne, M. 2003. 'At Lycaon's table', in M. Detienne ed. *The Writing of Orpheus*. Baltimore. 115–22. Trans. of 'La Table de Lycaon' *Modern Language Notes* 106 (1991) 742–50.

Detienne, M., and J. Svenbro 1989. 'The feast of wolves, or the impossible city' in M. Detienne and J.P. Vernant eds. *The Cuisine of Sacrifice among the Greeks*. Chicago. 148–63. Trans. of *La Cuisine du sacrifice en pays grec*. Paris, 1979.

De Vaan, M. A. C. 2008. *Etymological Dictionary of Latin and the other Italic Languages*. Leiden.

Devlin, J. 1987. *The Superstitious Mind: French Peasants and the Supernatural in the Nineteenth Century*. New Haven

Dickie, M. W. 1990. 'Talos bewitched: magic, atomic theory and paradoxography in Apollonius' *Argonautica* 4.1638–88' *Papers of the Leeds International Latin Seminar* 6, 267–96.

Dickie, M. W. 1991. 'Heliodorus and Plutarch on the evil eye' *CP* 86, 17–29.

Dickie, M. W. 1995. 'The Fathers of the Church and the evil eye' in H. Maguire ed. *Byzantine Magic*. Washington, DC, 9–34.

Dickie, M. W. 2001. *Magic and Magicians in the Greco-Roman World*. London.

Diels, H., and W. Kranz eds. 1951. *Die Fragmente der Vorsokratiker* i. 6th ed. Berlin.

Di Fazio M. 2013. 'Gli Hirpi del Soratte' in G. Cifani ed. *Tra Roma e l' Etruria. Cultura, identità e territorio dei Falisci*. Rome. 231–64.

Diggle, J. 1984. *Euripidis fabulae*. i. Oxford.

Dillinger, J. 2015. ' "Species", "phantasia", "raison": werewolves and shape-shifters in demonological literature' in de Blécourt 2015, 142–58.

Dodd, D. B., and C. A. Faraone eds. 2003. *Initiation in Ancient Greek Rituals and Narratives*. London.

Dodds, E. R. 1951. *The Greeks and the Irrational*. Berkeley.

Donecker, S. 2012. 'The werewolves of Livonia: lycanthropy and shape-changing in scholarly texts, 1550–1720' *Preternature* 1, 289–322.

Doody, A. 2016. 'The authority of Greek poetry in Pliny's *Natural History* 18.63–65' in F. Cairns and R. Gibson eds. *Papers of the Langford Latin Seminar* vol. 16. Prenton. 247–68.

Doroszewska, J. 2017. 'The liminal space: suburbs as a demonic domain in Classical literature' *Preternature* 6, 1–30. Reprinted, with revisions, at D. Felton ed. *Landscapes of Dread in Classical Antiquity. Negative Emotion in Natural and Constructed Spaces*. London, 2018. 185–208.

Douglas, A. 1992. *The Beast Within: A History of the Werewolf*. Avon. Republished as *The Beast Within: Man, Myths and Werewolves* (London, 1993).

Douglas, N. 1915. *Old Calabria*. London.

Dowden, K. 1989. *Death and the Maiden: Girls' Initiation Rites in Greek Mythology*. London.

Drew, K. F. 1991. *The Laws of the Salian Franks*. Philadelphia.

Drexler, W. 1894–7. 'Lykaon (3)' *ML* ii.2, 2169–73.

Ducat, J. 1997. 'La cryptie en question' in Y. Garlan hon., P. Brulé and J. Oulhen eds., *Esclavage, guerre, économie en Grèce ancienne. Hommages a Yvon Garlan*. Rennes. 43–74.

Dulière C. 1979. *Lupa Romana. Recherches d' iconographie et essai d' interpretation*. i. *Texte*. Brussels.

Dunbabin, T. J. 1948. *The Western Greeks: The History of Sicily and South Italy from the Foundation of the Greek Colonies to 480 B.C*. Oxford.

Dundes, A. ed. 1965. 'What is folklore?' in A. Dundes ed. *The Study of Folklore*. Englewood Cliffs, NJ. 1–3.

Dundes, A. 1980. *Interpreting Folklore*. Bloomington, IA.

Duni, M. 2015. ' "What about some good wether?" Witches and werewolves in sixteenth-century Italy' in de Blécourt 2015a, 121–41.

Dunn, C. W. 1960. *The Foundling and the Werewolf: A Literary-Historical Study of Guillaume de Palerne*. Toronto.

Duval, Y.-M. 1977. 'Des Lupercales de Constantinople aux Lupercales de Rome' *Revue des Études Latines* 55, 222–70.

Eckels, R. P. 1937. 'Greek Wolf-Lore'. Diss., Pennsylvania.

Edelstein, E. J., and L. Edelstein 1945. *Asclepius. Collection and Interpretation of the Testimonies*. 2 vols. Baltimore.

Eidinow, E. 2018. ' "The horror of the terrifying and the hilarity of the grotesque": daimonic spaces—and emotions—in ancient Greek literature' *Arethusa* 51, 209–35.

Eidinow, E. 2019. 'Consuming narratives: the politics of cannibalism on Mt. Lykaion' *Classica et Mediaevalia* 67, 63–89.

Eighteen-Bisang, R., and E. Miller 2013. *Bram Stoker's Notes for Dracula: A Facsimile Edition*. Jefferson, NC.

Eisler, R. 1951. *Man into Wolf*. London.

Elderkin, G. W. 1940. 'Bronze statuettes of Zeus Keraunios' *AJA* 44, 225–33.

Eliade, M. 1964. *Shamanism. Archaic Techniques of Ecstasy*. London. Trans. of *Le Chamanisme et les techniques archaïques de l'extase*. Paris, 1951.

Elliot, J. E. 1995. 'The Etruscan wolfman in myth and ritual' *Etruscan Studies* 2, 17–34.

Endore, S. G. 1933. *The Werewolf of Paris*. New York.

Epstein, J. 1995. *Altered Conditions: Disease, Medicine and Story-telling*. London.

Evelyn-White, H. G. 1914. *Hesiod*. LCL. Cambridge, MA.

Fahy, T. A. 1989. 'Lycanthropy: a review' *Journal of the Royal Society of Medicine* 82, 37–9.

Falivene, M. R. 2011. '4. The *Diegeseis* Papyrus: archaeological context, format and contents' in B. Acosta-Hughes, L. Lehnus, and S. Stephens eds. *Brill's Companion to Callimachus*. Leiden.

Faraone, C. A. 1999. *Ancient Greek Love Magic*. Cambridge, MA.

Faraone, C. A. 2003. 'Playing the bear and the fawn for Artemis: female initiation or substitute sacrifice?' in Dodd and Faraone 2003, 43–68.

Farber, W. 1983. 'Lamaštu' *Reallexikon der Assyriologie* 6, 439–46.

Farnell, L. R. 1896–1909. *The Greek Cults*. 5 vols. Oxford.

Faure, M. 1978. 'Le *Bisclavret* de Marie de France, une histoire suspecte de loup-garou' *Revues des Langues Romances* 83, 345–56.

Fedeli, P. 1995. 'Il mistero della metamorfosi: Un licantropo nel *Satyricon*' in R. Rafaelli ed. *Il mistero nel racconto classico. Convegno del XIII Mystfest*. Urbino. 45–51.

Felton, D. 1999. *Haunted Greece and Rome*. Austin.

Felton, D. 2013. 'Apuleius' Cupid considered as a lamia (*Metamorphoses* 5.17–18)' *Illinois Classical Studies* 38, 229–44

Felton, D. 2018. ed. *Landscapes of Dread*. London.

Ferlampin-Acher, C. ed. and trans. 2012. *Guillaume de Palerne*. Paris.

Field, E. 1896. *The Second Book of Tales*. New York.

Fincel, J. 1556. *Wunderzeichen: Warhafftige Beschreibung und gründlich verzeichnus schröcklicher Wunderzeichen und Geschichten, die von dem Jar an M.D.XVIII bis auff jetziges Jar M.D.LVI geschehen und ergangen sind nach der Jarzal.* Jena.

Fincel, J. 1559. *Der ander Teil Wunderzeichen: gründlich verzeuchnis schröcklicher Wunderzeichen und Geschichten, so innerhalb viertzig Jaren sich begeben haben.* Leizpig.

Finch, R. G. ed. and trans. 1965. *Vǫlsunga saga.* London.

Finlay, A., and A. Faulkes transs. 2011. *Snorri Sturluson. Heimskringla.* i. *The Beginnings to Óláfr Tryggvason.* London.

Fischer, C. T., and O. Wecker 1925. 'Kynokephaloi' *RE* xii, 24–6.

Foerster, R. 1893. *Scriptores physiognomonici Graeci et Latini.* ii. Leipzig.

Fontenrose, J. 1959. *Python.* Berkeley.

Fontenrose, J. 1968. 'The hero as athlete', *CSCA* 1, 73–104.

Forbes-Irving, P. M. C. 1990. *Metamorphosis in Greek Myth.* Oxford.

Fortenbaugh, W. W., et al. 1992. *Theophrastus of Eresus. Sources for his Life, Writings, Thought and Influence.* 2 vols. Leiden.

Fortune, D. 1930. *Psychic Self-Defense.* London.

Fowler, R. F. 2000–13. *Early Greek Mythography.* 2 vols. Oxford.

Franchi de' Cavalieri, P. 1908. *Hagiographica.* Studi e Testi 19. Rome.

Frangoulidis, S. 2008. *Witches, Isis and Narrative.* Berlin.

Franklin, A. M. 1921. 'The Lupercalia'. Diss., Columbia.

Frassinetti, P. 1955. *Fabularum Atellanarum fragmenta.* Turin.

Frazer, Sir James G. 1898. *Pausanias' Description of Greece.* 6 vols. Cambridge.

Frazer, Sir James G. 1929. *The* Fasti *of Ovid.* 5 vols. London.

Frenaye, F. 1947 trans. Carlo Levi, *Christ Stopped at Eboli.* London.

Friedlaender, L. ed. and trans. 1906. *Petroni* Cena Trimalchionis. Leipzig.

Frost, B. J. 1973. *The Book of the Werewolf.* London.

Frost, B. J. 2003. *The Essential Guide to Werewolf Literature.* Madison, WI.

Gaide, F. 1995. 'Les histories du loup-garou et des *striges* dans la *Cena Trimalchionis* ou la narration du "vécu": deux joyaux du Latin vulgaire' in L. Callebat ed. *Latin vulgaire—Latin tardif.* iv. Hildesheim. 715–23.

Gantz, T. 1993. *Early Greek Myth.* Baltimore.

Garstad, B., ed. and trans. 2012. *Pseudo-Methodius. Apocalypse* and *An Alexandrian World Chronicle.* Cambridge, MA.

Gaster, M. 1900. 'Two thousand years of a charm against the child-stealing witch' *Folklore* 11, 129–62.

Gauger, J.-D. 1980. 'Phlegon von Tralleis, *mirab.* iii: zu einem Dokument geistigen Widerstandes gegen Rom' *Chiron* 10, 225–61.

Geerard, M. 1974–9. *Clavis patrum Graecorum.* 3 vols. Turhhout.

Gentili, B., and F. Perusino eds. 2002. *Le orse di Brauron: Un rituale di iniziazione femminile nel Santuario di Artemide.* Pisa.

George, A. 1999. *The Epic of Gilgamesh.* London.

George, A. 2003. *The Babylonian Gilgamesh Epic. Introduction, Critical Edition and Cuneiform Texts.* 2 vols. Oxford.

Georgoudi, S. 1999. 'À propos du sacrifice humain en Grèce ancienne: remarques critiques' *Archiv für Religionsgeschichte* 1, 61–82.

Germain, G. 1954. *Genèse de l'Odyssée.* Paris.

Gernet, L. 1981. 'Dolon the wolf' in L. Gernet, *The Anthropology of Ancient Greece.* Baltimore and London. 125–39. Trans. of *Anthropologie de la Grèce ancienne.* Paris, 1968. Originally published as 'Dolon le loup', *Annuaires de l'Institut de philologie orientales et slaves IV (Mélanges Franz Cumont)* 1936, 189–208.

Gershenson, D. E. 1991. *Apollo the Wolf-god*. McLean, VA.

Gerstein, M. R. 1974. 'Germanic *warg*: the outlaw as werewolf' in G. J. Larson ed. *Myth in Indo-European Antiquity*. Berkeley. 131–56.

Gianelli, G. 1924. *Culti e miti della Magna Grecia*. Florence.

Giannini, A. 1965. *Paradoxographorum graecorum reliquiae*. Milan.

Gilhus, I. S. 2006. *Animals, Gods and Humans: Changing Attitudes to Animals in Greek, Roman and Early Christian Ideas*. London.

Ginzburg, C. 1990. *Ecstasies: Deciphering the Witches' Sabbath*. London. Trans. (R. Rosenthal) of *Storia notturna. Una decifrazione del sabba*. Turin, 1989.

Ginzburg, C., and B. Lincoln 2020. *Old Thiess, a Livonian Werewolf: A Classic Case in Comparative Perspective*. Chicago.

Glare, P. G. W. ed. 1982. *Oxford Latin Dictionary*. Oxford.

Glauser, J. 1993. 'Ála flekks saga' in P. Pulsiano ed. *Medieval Scandinavia. An Encyclopedia*. New York. 6–7.

Gordon, R. L. ed. 1981. *Myth, Religion and Society. Structuralist Essays by M. Detienne, L. Gernet, J,-P. Vernant and P. Vidal-Naquet*. Cambridge.

Gordon, R. L. 1987. 'Lucan's Erictho' in M. Whitby, P. Hardie, and M. Whitby eds. *Homo Viator: Classical Essays for John Bramble*. Bristol. 231–41.

Gordon, R. L. 1999. 'Imagining Greek and Roman Magic' in V. Flint, R. L. Gordon, G. Luck, and D. Ogden *Witchcraft and Magic in Europe*. ii. *Ancient Greece and Rome*. London. 159–75.

Gordon, R. L. 2015. 'Good to think: wolves and wolf-men in the Graeco-Roman world' in de Blécourt 2015, 25–60.

Gourmelen, L. 2003. 'Le crime de Lykaon: enjeux et significations d'un récit de la mort (Pausanias viii, 2)' in G. Jacquin and A.M. Callet-Bianco eds. *Le Récit de la mort: Écriture et histoire*. Paris. 15–33.

Gourmelen, L. 2004. *Kékrops, le roi-serpent. Imaginaire athénien, représentations de l'humain et de l'animalité en Grèce ancienne*. Paris.

Grabow, E. 1998. *Schlangenbilder in der griechischen schwartzfiguren Vasenkunst*. Münster.

Graesse, J. G. T. ed. 1850. *Jacobus de Voragine. Legenda aurea*. Leipzig.

Graf, F. 1985. *Nordionische Kulte. Religionsgeschichtliche und epigraphische Untersuchungen zu den Kulten von Chios, Erythrai, Klazomenai und Phokaia*. Rome.

Graf, F. 1997. *Magic in the Ancient World*. Cambridge, MA. Translation of *La Magie dans l'antiquité gréco-romaine*. Paris, 1994. Note also the German edition, *Gottesnähe und Schadenzauber: die Magie in der griechisch-römischen Antike*. Munich, 1996—a revised version of the French original.

Graf, F. 2000. 'The Locrian Maidens' in R. G. A. Buxton ed. *Oxford Readings in Greek Religion*. Oxford. 250–70. Trans. of 'Die lokrischen Mädchen' *Studi storico-religiosi* 2 (1978) 61–79.

Graf, F. 2015. *Roman Festivals in the Greek East: from the Early Empire to the Middle Byzantine Era*. Cambridge.

Greenfield, R. P. H. 1988. *Traditions of Belief in Late Byzantine Demonology*. Amsterdam.

Gregory, A. (forthcoming). 'Was Homer's Circe a witch?' in J. E. Decker and D. A. Layne eds. *Otherwise than the Binary: Towards Feminist Reading of Ancient Greek Philosophy, Magic and Mystery Traditions*. Leiden. [*vel sim.*]

Grimm, Brüder. 1986. *Kinder- und Hausmärchen, gesammelt durch die Brüder Grimm*. 3 vols. Göttingen. [The standard edition of the original 1812–15 work.]

Guazzo, F. M. 1608. *Compendium maleficarum*. Milan. Trans. (M. Summers), London, 1929.

Guðmundsdóttir, A. 2007. 'The werewolf in Medieval Icelandic literature' *Journal of English and Germanic Philology* 106, 277–303.

Guðnason, B. ed. 1982. *Danakonunga sögur*. Reykjavik

Guillaume d'Auvergne (Guillelmus Alverni) 1674. *Opera omnia*. 2 vols. Paris.

Guimier Sorbets, A. M., M. Jost and Y. Morizot 2008. 'Rites, cultes et religions. Le site de Lycosoura' *Ktema* 33, 87–209.

Gunnell, T. 1994. *The Origins of Drama in Scandinavia*. Cambridge.

Gwynn, A. ed. 1955. *The Writings of Bishop Patrick, 1074–1084*. Scriptores Latini Hiberniae 1. Dublin.

Habicht, C. 1999. *Pausanias' Guide to Ancient Greece*. Berkeley.

Hainsworth, J. B. 1993. *The Iliad: A Commentary*. iii. Books 9–12. Cambridge.

Halleux, R., and J. Schamp. 1985. *Les Lapidaires grecs*. Budé. Paris.

Halliday, W. 1928. *Plutarch. The Greek Questions*. Oxford.

Hallock, R. T. 1969. *Persepolis Fortification Tablets*. University of Chicago Oriental Institute Publications xcii. Chicago.

Halm-Tisserant, M. 1993. *Cannibalisme et immortalité: L'enfant dans le chaudron en Grèce ancienne*. Paris.

Hamilton, H. C. ed. 1948. *Chronicon domini Walteri de Hemingburgh*. 2 vols. London.

Handley-Schachler, M. 1992. 'Achaemenid Religion, 521–465 BC' Diss., Oxford University.

Hansen, P. A. ed. 2005. *Hesychii Alexandrini lexicon*. iii. Berlin.

Hansen, W. F. 1988. 'Folklore' in M. Grant and R. Kitzinger eds. *Civilization of the Ancient Mediterranean: Greece and Rome*. 3 vols. New York. ii, 1121–30.

Hansen, W. F. 1996. *Phlegon of Tralles' Book of Marvels*. Exeter.

Hansen, W. F. 2002. *Ariadne's Thread: A Guide to International Tales Found in Classical Literature*. Ithaca.

Hard, R. trans. 2015. *Eratosthenes and Hyginus. Constellation Myths*. Oxford.

Harden, A. 2017. ' "Wild men" and animal skins in archaic Greek imagery' in T. Fögen and E. Thomas eds. *Interactions between Animals and Humans in Graeco-Roman Antiquity*. Berlin. 369–88.

Harf-Lancner, L. 1985. 'La métamorphose illusoire: des théories chrétiennes de la métamorphose aux images médiévales du loup-garou' *Annales ESC* 40, 208–26.

Harmon, D. P. 1978. 'The public festivals of Rome' *ANRW* ii.16.2, 1440–68.

Harrington, F. H., and C. S. Asa 2003. 'Wolf communication' in Mech and Boitani 2003a, 66–103.

Harris, H. A. 1964. *Greek Athletes and Athletics*. London.

Hartley, B. 2014. 'Novel Research: Fiction and Authority in Ptolemy Chennus'. Diss., Exeter.

Haupt, M. 1869. 'Excerpta ex Timothei Gazaei libris de animalibus' *Hermes* 3, 10–30, 174.

Haustein-Bartsch, E., ed. 2016. *Von Drachenkämpfern und anderen Helden. Kriegerheilige auf Ikonen*. Recklinghausen.

Haxthausen, A. 1856. *Transkaukasia: Andeutungen über das Familien- und Gemeindeleben und die socialen Verhältnisse einiger Völker zwischen dem Schwarzen und Kaspischen Meere. Reiseerinnerungen und gesammelte Notizen*. 2 vols. Leipzig.

Heath, M. 1998. 'Hermogenes' Biographers' *Eranos* 96, 44–54.

Heckel, W. 1988. *The Last Days and Testament of Alexander the Great: A Prosopographic Study*. Historia Einzelschriften. Stuttgart.

Hedreen, G. 2016. *The Image of the Artist in Archaic and Classical Greece: Art, Poetry, and Subjectivity*. New York.

Heinrichs, J. 2015. 'Military integration in late archaic Arkadia: new evidence from a bronze *pinax* (ca. 500 BC) of the Lykaion' in W. Heckel, S. Müller, and G. Wrightson eds. *The Many Faces of War in the Ancient World*. Cambridge. 1–89.

Henrichs, A. 1981. 'Human sacrifice in Greek religion: three case studies' in J. Rudhardt and O. Reverdin eds. *Le Sacrifice dans l'antiquité*. Entretiens fondation Hardt 27. Geneva. 195–235.

Hertz, W. 1862. *Der Werwolf*. Stuttgart.

Heubeck, A., and A. Hoekstra. 1989. *A Commentary on Homer's Odyssey*. ii. Oxford.

Heusler, A. and W. Ranisch 1903. *Eddica minora. Dichtungen eddischer Art aus den fornaldarsögur und anderen Prosawerken zusammengestellt und eingeleitet*. Dortmund.

Heyworth, S. J. 2007. *Cynthia: A Companion to the Text of Propertius*. Oxford.

Hild, J. A. 1877–1919. 'Genius' in C. Daremberg and E. Saglio eds. *Dictionnaire des antiquités grecques et romaines*. 5 vols. Paris. ii.2, 1488–94.

Hilgenfeld, H. trans. 1908. 'Syrische Lebensbeschreibung des heiligen Symeons' in H. Lietzmann, *Das Leben des heiligen Symeon Stylites*. Texte und Untersuchungen zur Geschichte der altchristlichen Literatur xxxii.4. Leipzig. 80–187.

Hodgson, E. 2016. 'Rewriting the werewolf: transformations of Bisclavret in *Guillaume de Palerne*' *French Studies Bulletin* 37, 9–13.

Höfler, O. 1934. *Kultische Geheimbünde der Germanen*. Frankfurt. Partial English translation at Ginzburg and Lincoln 2020:33–45.

Höfler, O. 1976. 'Berserker' in H. Beck et al. eds. *Reallexikon der Germanischen Altertumskunde* 2nd ed. ii, 298–304.

Hollander, L. M. trans. 1936. *Old Norse Poems. The Most Important Non-skaldic Verse not included in the Poetic Edda*. New York.

Hollander, L. M. 1964. trans. Snorri Sturluson. *Heimskringla: The History of the Kings of Norway*. Austin.

Holleman A. W. J. 1973. 'Ovid and the Lupercalia' *Historia* 22, 260–8.

Holleman A. W. J. 1985. 'Lupus, Lupercalia, lupa' *Latomus* 44, 609–14.

Holtsmark, A. 1968. 'On the werewolf motif in *Egil's saga Skallagrímssonar*' *Scientia Islandica* 1, 7–9.

Hopkins, A. 2005. Melion *and* Biclarel. *Two Old French Werewolf Lays*. Liverpool Online Series. Critical Editions of French Texts. Liverpool.

Hordern, J. H. 2004. *Sophron's Mimes. Text, Translation and Commentary*. Oxford.

Hornblower, S. 2015. *Lykophron: Alexandra*. Oxford.

Hough, C. 1994–5. 'OE *wearg* in Warnborough and Reighburn' *Journal of the English Place-Name Society* 27, 14–20.

Hughes, D. D. 1991. *Human Sacrifice in Ancient Greece*. London.

Hull, D. B. 1964. *Hounds and Hunting in Ancient Greece*. Chicago.

Hunink, V. 1997. *Apuleius of Madauros. Pro se de magia*. 2 vols. Amsterdam.

Hutchinson, G. O., ed. 2006. *Propertius. Elegies, Book IV*. Cambridge.

Hutton, R. 2001. *Shamans. Siberian Spirituality and the Western Imagination*. London.

Hutton, R. 2017. *The Witch. A History of Fear, from Ancient Times to the Present*. New Haven.

Hutton, W. 2005. *Describing Greece. Landscape and Literature in the* Periegesis *of Pausanias*. Cambridge.

Hyde, W. 1903. *De Olympionicarum statuis a Pausania commemoratis*. Halle.

Ideler, J. L. ed. 1842. *Physici et medici Graeci minores*. 2 vols. Berlin.

Immerwahr, W. 1891. *Die Kulte und Mythen Arkadiens*. 1. *Die arkadischen Kulte*. Leipzig. [The only volume published.]

Ingemark, C. A., and D. Ingemark, 2013. 'More than scapegoating: the therapeutic potential of stories of child-killing demons in ancient Greece and Rome' in C.A. Ingemark ed. *Therapeutic uses of Storytelling: An Interdisciplinary Approach to Narration as Therapy*. Lund. 75–84.

Isler, H. P. 1981. 'Acheloos', *LIMC* i.1, 12–36.

Ivančik, A. I. 1993. 'Les guerriers-chiens: Loups-garous et invasions scythes en Asie Mineure' *Revue de l'histoire des religions* 210, 305–30.

Jackson, P. ed. 2016. *Horizons of Shamanism: A Triangular Approach*. Stockholm Studies in Comparative Religion 35. Stockholm.

Jacoby, F. et al. 1923– eds. *Die Fragmente der griechischen Historiker*. Multiple volumes and parts. Berlin and Leiden.

Jacoby, M. 1974. *Wargus, vargr, 'Verbrecher', 'Wolf.' Eine sprach- und rechtsgeschichtliche Untersuchung*. Uppsala.

Jameson, M. H. 1980. 'Apollo Lykeios at Athens' *Archaiognosia* 1, 213–36. Reprinted in his *Cults and rites in Ancient Greece: Essays on Religion and Society*. Cambridge, 2014. 41–61.

Jannot, J.-R. 2005. *Religion in Ancient Etruria*. Madison, WI. Trans. of *Devins, dieux et démons: regards sur la religion de l'Etrurie antique*. Paris, 1998.

Jeanmaire, H. 1913. 'La cryptie lacédémonienne' *REG* 26, 121–50.

Jeanmaire, H. 1939. *Couroi et courètes: Essai sur l'éducation spartiate et sur les rites d'adolesccence dans l'antiquité hellénique*. Lille.

Johnston, M. 1931. 'Vergil, *Eclogues* 53–4' *Classical Weekly* 24, 103.

Johnston, M. 1932. 'The werewolf in Calabria' *Classical Weekly* 25, 183.

Johnston, S. I. 1991. 'Crossroads' *ZPE* 88, 213–20.

Johnston, S. I. 1995. 'Defining the dreadful: remarks on the Greek child-killing demon' in M. Meyer and P. Mirecki eds. *Ancient Magic and Ritual Power*. Leiden. 361–87.

Johnston, S. I. 1999a. *Restless Dead. Encounters between the Living and the Dead in Ancient Greece*. Berkeley.

Johnston, S. I. 1999b. 'Songs for the ghosts: magical solutions to deadly problems' in D. R. Jordan, H. Montgomery, and E. Thomassen eds. *The World of Ancient Magic*. Papers from the Norwegian Institute at Athens 4. Bergen. 83–102.

Jones, G. 1972. *Kings, Beasts, and Heroes*. London.

Jónsson, F. ed. 1920. *Konungs skuggsjá: Speculum regale*. Copenhagen.

Jost, M. 1985. *Sanctuaires et cultes d'Arcadie*. Paris.

Jost, M. 1989. 'Image de l'Arcadie au iiie s. av. J.-C.: Lycophron, *Alexandra* v.479–83' in P. Lévèque hon., M.-M. Mactoux and E. Geny eds. *Mélanges Pierre Lévêque*. ii. *Anthropologie et société*. Paris. 285–93.

Jost, M. 2002. 'À propos des sacrifices humains dans le sanctuaire de Zeus du mont Lycée' in R. Hägg ed. *Peloponnesian Sanctuaries and Cults: Proceedings of the Ninth International Symposium at the Swedish Institute at Athens, 11–13 June 1994*. Stockholm. 183–6.

Jost, M. 2005. 'Deux mythes de métamorphose en animal et leurs interpretations: Lykaon et Kallisto' *Kernos* 18, 347–70.

Jost, M. 2016. 'Les sources littéraires relatives au mont Lycée, d'Hésiode à Tzetzès' *Classica et Mediaevalia* 65, 23–54.

Jost, M. et al. 2008. 'Rites, cultes et religion. Le site de Lycosoura' *Ktema* 33, 93–209.

Kahil, L. 1977. 'L'Artémis de Brauron: rites et mystères' *Antike Kunst* 20, 86–120.

Kahil, L. 1983. 'Mythological repertoire of Brauron' in W. Moon ed. *Ancient Greek Art and Iconography*. Madison.

Kahil, L. 1984. 'Artemis' *LIMC* ii.1, 618–753.

Kahil, L., et al. eds. 1981–99. *Lexicon Iconographicum Mythologiae Classicae*. 9 vols. Zurich and Munich.

Kaiser, E. 1964. 'Odyssee-Szenen als Topoi. ii. Der Zauber Kirkes und Kalypsos' *Museum Helveticum* 21, 197–224.

Karttunen, K. 1989. *India in Early Greek Literature*. Helsinki.

Kassel, R., and C. Austin. 1983–. *Poetae Comici Graeci*. 8+ vols. Berlin.

Keck, P. E. et al. 1988. 'Lycanthropy: alive and well in the twentieth century' *Psychological Medicine* 18, 113–20.

Keen, A. G. 1998. *Dynastic Lycia: A Political History of the Lycians and their Relations with Foreign Powers c. 545–362 B.C.* Leiden.

Kerényi, K. 1948. 'Wolf und Ziege am Fest der Lupercalia' in J. Marouzeau hon., *Mélanges de philologie, de littérature et d'histoire anciennes: offerts à J. Marouzeau par ses collègues et élèves étrangers*. Paris. 309–17. Republished in his *Niobe: Neue Studien über antike Religion und Humanität* (Zurich 1949), 136–47.

Kiefer, A. 1929. *Aretalogische Studien*. Leipzig.

Kindstrand, J. F. 1981. *Anacharsis: The Legend and the* Apophthegmata. Uppsala.

Kitchell, K. F. 2017. '"Animal literacy" and the Greeks: Philoctetes the hedgehog and Dolon the weasel' in T. Fögen and E. Thomas eds. *Interactions between Animals and Humans in Graeco-Roman Antiquity*. Berlin. 183–204.

Kittredge, G. L. ed. 1903. *Arthur and Gorlagon*. Boston. Reprinted from *Studies and Notes in Philology and Literature* 8 (1903) 149–275.

Kleberg, T. 1957 *Hôtels, restaurants et cabarets dans l'antiquité romaine*. Uppsala.

Knight, R. 2001. 'Werewolves, monsters and miracles: representing colonial fantasies in Gerald of Wales' *Topographia Hibernica*' *Studies in Iconography* 22, 55–83.

Koehler, K., H. Ebel, and D. Varzopoulos 1990. 'Lycanthropy and demonomania: some psychopathological issues' *Psychological Medicine* 20, 629–33.

Korenjak, M. 1996. *Die Ericthoszene in Lukans Pharsalia: Einleitung, Text, Übersetzung, Kommentar*. Frankfurt.

Kotter, B., and R. Volk eds. 1969–2013. *Die Schriften des Johannes von Damaskos*. 7 vols. Patristische Texte und Studien 7, 12, 17, 22, 29, 61, 68. Berlin and New York.

Kovacs, D. 1995. *Euripides*. ii. *Children of Heracles, Hippolytus, Andromache, Hecuba*. LCL. Cambridge, MA.

Kramer, H., and J. Sprenger 1487. *Malleus maleficarum*. Speyer.

Kratz, D. M. 1976. 'Fictus lupus: the werewolf in Christian thought' *Classical Folia: Studies in the Christian Perpetuation of the Classics* 30, 57–80.

Krauskopf, I. 1987. *Todesdämonen und Totengötter im vorhellenistischen Etrurien. Kontinuität und Wandel*. Studi Etruschi 16. Florence.

Krauskopf, I. 1988. 'Aita/Calu' *LIMC* iv.1, 394–9.

Kremer, P. 2006. *Der Werwolf von Bedburg. Versuch einer Rekonstruktion des Hexereiprozesses aus dem Jahr 1589*. Bonn.

Krenkel, W. 1970. *Lucilius. Satiren*. 2 vols. Leiden.

Kretzenbacher, L. 1968. *Kynokephale Dämonen südosteuropäischer Volksdichtung*. Munich.

Kristensen, E. T. 1893. *Danske Sagn*. 7 vols. Aarhus.

Kroll, W. 1937. 'Etwas von Werwolf' *WS* 55, 168–72.

Kumaniecki, K. 1929. *De Satyro peripatetico*. Krakow.

Kunstler, B. 1991. 'The werewolf figure and its adoption into the Greek political vocabulary' *CW* 84, 189–205.

Laborde, J.-B. 1935-6. 'Les "brouches" (sorcières) en Béarn, Gascogne et Pays Basque (Histoire et Folklore)' *Revue historique et archéologique du Béarn et du Pays Basque* 163 (1935) 5–23; 164 (1935) 105–30; 165 (1935) 230–49; 166 (1935) 285–309; 167 (1936)18–34; 168 (1936) 71–86. Reprinted as *Les brouches en Béarn, Gascogne et Pays basque: histoire et folk-lore*. Bouhet, 2005.

Lagerholm, Å. ed. 1927. *Drei lygisǫgur: Egils saga einhenda ok Ásmundar berserkjabana, Ála flekks saga, Flóres saga konungs ok sona hans.* Altnordische Saga-Bibliothek, 17. Halle.

Lai, W. 1992. 'From folklore to literate theater: Unpacking "Madame White Snake"' *Asian Folklore Studies* 51, 51–66.

Laing, S. trans. 1844. *Heimskringla or The Chronicle of the Kings of Norway by Snorri Sturlson.* London.

Langerwerf, L. 2009. 'Drimakos and Aristomenes. Two stories of slave rebels in the Second Sophistic' in S. Hodkinson ed. *Sparta: Comparative Approaches.* Swansea. 331–59.

Lansens, T. P. A. 1855. 'Vlämische Segen und Gebraüchen' *Zeitschrift für deutsche Mythologie und Sittenkunde* 3, 161–72.

Lanzillotta, L. R. 2007. 'The early Christians and human sacrifice' in Bremmer 2007a, 81–102.

Larson, L. M. trans. 1917. *The King's Mirror (Speculum regale—Konungs skuggsjá).* New York.

La Sorsa, S. 1915. 'Superstizioni, pregiudizi e credenze popolari Pugliesi' *Lares* 4, 49–67. [*Non vidi.*]

La Torre, G. F. 1997. [untitled round-table contribution] in *Mito e storia in Magna Grecia. Atti del XXXVI convegno di studi sulla Magna Grecia.* Taranto. 366–72, with pl. ix.1.

Latouche, J. [pseudonym of O. F. Crawfurd] 1875. *Travels in Portugal.* London.

Latte, K. 1967. *Römische Religionsgeschichte.* 2nd ed. Munich.

Laugrand, F., and J. Oosten 2010. *The Sea Woman. Sedna in Inuit Shamanism and Art in the Eastern Artic.* Chicago.

Launey, M. 1941. 'L'athlète Théogenes et le *hieros gamos* d'Héracles Thasien' *RA* 119 (1941 ii), 22–49.

Lawson, J. C. 1910. *Modern Greek Folklore and Ancient Greek Religion.* Cambridge.

Lawson, J. C. 1926a. 'περὶ ἀλιβάντων (part i)' *CR* 40, 52–8.

Lawson, J. C. 1926b. 'περὶ ἀλιβάντων (part ii)' *CR* 40, 116–21.

Lebrun, R. 2001. 'Syro-Anatolica scripta minora I' *Le Muséon* 114, 245–53.

Lecouteux, C. 2003. *Witches, Werewolves and Fairies. Shapeshifters and Astral Doublers in the Middle Ages.* Rochester. Trans. of *Fées, sorcières et loups-garous au Moyen Age: histoire du double.* Paris, 1992.

Lefèvre, E. 2003. 'Petrons Spuknovellen 61.8–64.1' in J. Herman and H. Rosén eds. *Petroniana. Gedenkschrift für Hubert Petersmann.* Heidelberg. 147–57.

Leinweber, D. W. 1994. 'Witchcraft and lamiae in *The Golden Ass*' *Folklore* 105, 77–82.

Lent, F., trans. 1915. 'The Life of Simeon Stylites.' *Journal of the American Oriental Society* 35, 111–98.

Leshock, D. B. 1999. 'The knight of the werewolf: Bisclavret and the shape-shifting metaphor' *Romance Quarterly* 46, 155–65.

Letta, C. 1972. *I Marsi e il Fucino nell'antichità.* Milan.

Leutsch, E. L. von., and F. G. Schneidewin 1839–51. *Corpus paroemiographorum Graecorum.* 2 vols. Göttingen.

Lévêque, P. 1961. 'Sur quelques cultes d'Arcadie: princesse-ourse, hommes-loups et dieux-chevaux' *Information historique* 23, 93–108.

Levi, C. 1945. *Cristo si è fermato a Eboli.* Rome.

Lévi, É. 1854–6. *Dogme et rituel de la haute magie.* 2 vols. Paris. Trans. (A. E. Waite) as *Transcendental Magic, its Doctrine and Ritual.* London, 1896.

Liapes, V. 2011. *A Commentary on the* Rhesus *attributed to Euripides.* Oxford.

Liberman, A. 2003. 'Berserkir: a double legend' in R. Simek and J. Meurer eds. *Scandinavia and Christian Europe in the Middle Ages: Papers of the 12th International Saga Conference.* Bonn. 337–40.

Liberman, A. 2005. 'Berserks in History and Legend' *Russian History/Histoire russe* 32, 401–11.

Liberman, A. 2016. *In Prayer and Laughter. Essays on Medieval Scandinavian and Germanic Mythology, Literature and Culture*. Moscow.

Liddell, H. G., R. Scott, and H. S. Jones eds. 1968. *A Greek-English Lexicon*. 9th ed. with supplement. Oxford.

LiDonnici, L. R. 1995. *The Epidaurian Miracle Inscriptions. Text, Translation and Commentary*. Atlanta.

Liebrecht, F. ed. 1856. *Des Gervasius von Tilbury* Otia imperialia. Hanover.

Lilja, S. 1976. *Dogs in Ancient Greek Poetry*. Helsinki.

Lincoln, B. 1975. 'Homeric λύσσα, "wolfish rage"' *Indogermanische Forschungen* 80, 98–105.

Lincoln, B. 2018. *Apples and Oranges. Explorations in, on and with Comparison*. Chicago.

Lindow, J. 1977. Review of Jacoby 1974, *Speculum* 52, 382–5.

Lionarons, J. T. 1998. *The Medieval Dragon: The Nature of the Beast in Germanic Literature*. Enfield Lock.

Lionarons, J. T. 2002. 'From monster to martyr: the Old English legend of Saint Christopher' in T. S. Jones and D. A. Srunger eds. *Marvels, Monsters, and Miracles: Studies in the Medieval and Early Modern Imaginations*. Kalamazoo. 167–82.

Lissarrague, F. 1980. 'Iconographie de Dolon le loup' *Revue archéologique* [no serial no.] 3–30.

Litavrin, G. G. 2003. *Кекавмен, Советы и Рассказы*. 2nd ed. Moscow.

Littlewood, R. J. 2006. *A Commentary on Ovid* Fasti, *Book* vi. Oxford.

Lloyd-Jones, H. 1983. 'Artemis and Iphigenia' *JHS* 103, 87–102.

Longo, V. 1969. *Aretalogie nel mondo greco*. i. *Epigraphi e papyri*. Genoa.

Lopez, B. H. 1978. *Of Wolves and Men*. London.

Luchini, V., A. Galov, and E. Randi 2004. 'Evidence of genetic distinction and long-term population decline in wolves (*Canis lupus*) in the Italian Apennines' *Molecular Ecology* 13, 523–35.

Luck, G. 1999. 'Witches and sorcerers in Classical literature' in V. Flint, R. L. Gordon, G. Luck, and D. Ogden. *Witchcraft and Magic in Europe*. ii. London. 91–158.

Ma, J. 2008. 'The return of the Black Hunter' *Cambridge Classical Journal* 54, 188–208.

Maass, E. 1907. 'Der Kampf um Temesa' *Jahrbuch des Deutschen Archäologischen Instituts* 22, 18–53.

Macchioro, R. 2019. *Le redazioni latine della* 'Passio Tryphonis martyris'. *Traduzioni e riscritture di una leggenda bizantina*. Quaderni di 'hagiographica' 16. Florence.

McCone, K. R. 1987. 'Hund, Wolf und Krieger bei den Indogermanen' in W. Meid ed. *Studien zum indogermanischen Wortschatz*. Innsbruck. 111–54.

McCracken P. 2012. 'Skin and sovereignty in Guillaume de Palerne' *Cahiers de recherches médiévales et humanistes* 24, 361–75.

McDermott, W. C. 1938. *The Ape in Antiquity*. Baltimore.

McDonough, C. 1997. 'Carna, Proca and the *strix* on the Kalends of June' *TAPA* 127, 315–44.

McDougall, M. V. 1984. 'Wolves and Folklore. A Study of Petronius' *Satyricon* 62. MA diss., University of Wellington.

McGlynn, M. P. 2009. 'Bears, boars and other socially constructed bodies in *Hrólfs saga kraka*' *Magic, Ritual and Witchcraft* 4, 152–75

Mackay, C. S., ed. and trans. 2006. *Henricus Institoris and Jacobus Sprenger. Malleus maleficarum*. 2 vols. Cambridge.

McKeown, J. C. 1989. *Ovid: Amores. Text, Prolegomena and Commentary*. Leeds.

McLynn N. 2008. 'Crying Wolf: The Pope and the Lupercalia' *JRS* 98, 161–75.

McPhee, I. 1990. 'Kallisto' *LIMC* v.1, 940–4.

Madar, M. 1990. 'Estonia 1: werewolves and poisoners' in B. Ankarloo and G. Henningsen eds. *Early Modern European Witchcraft: Centres and Peripheries*. Oxford. 257–72.

Maddoli, G., ed. 1982. *Temesa e il suo territorio. Atti del convegno di Perugia e Trevi*. Taranto.

Magnus, O. 1555. *Historia de gentibus septentrionalibus*. Rome.

Mainoldi, C. 1984. *L'image du loup et du chien dans la Grèce ancienne d'Homère à Platon*. Paris.

Maisonneuve, M. N. 1985. 'Le Loup dans le monde gréco-romain'. Thèse de l'université, Paris IV. [*Non vidi*.]

Maiuri, A. 1945. La cena di Trimalchione *di Petronio Arbitro*. Naples.

Maltby, R. 2002. *Tibullus*: Elegies. *Text, Introduction and Commentary*. Cambridge.

Marbach, E. 1929. 'Soranus' *RE* ii.3, 1130–3.

Marcinkowski, A. 2001. 'Le loup et les grecs' *Ancient Society* 31, 1–26.

Marinatos, N. 2000. *The Goddess and the Warrior: The Naked Goddess and the Mistress of Animals in Early Greek Religion*. London.

Markus, R. A. 1990. *The End of Ancient Christianity*. Cambridge.

Marmorale, E. V. 1961. *Petronii Arbitri* Cena Trimalchionis. 2nd ed. Florence.

Marx, F. 1904–5. *C. Lucilii carminum reliquiae*. 2 vols. Leipzig.

Maturin, C. R. 1824. *The Albigenses. A Romance*. 4 vols. London.

Mazzoni, C. 2010. *She-Wolf: The Story of a Roman Icon*. Cambridge.

Mech, L. D., and L. Boitani eds. 2003a. *Wolves. Behavior, Ecology and Conservation*. Chicago.

Mech, L. D., and L. Boitani. 2003b. 'Wolf social ecology' in Mech and Boitani 2003a, 1–34.

Melchert, H. C., ed. 2003. *The Luwians*. Leiden.

Mele, A. 1983. 'L'eroe di Temesa tra Ausoni e Greci' in *Forme de contatto e processi di trasformazione nelle societa antiche*. Atti del convegno di Cortona (24–30 maggio 1981). Pisa and Rome. 848–88.

Ménard, P. 1984. 'Les Histoires de loup-garou au Moyen Age' in M. de Riquer, hon. *Symposium in honorem Prof. M. de Riquer*. Barcelona. 209–38.

Mentz, F. 1933. 'Die klassischen Hundenamen' *Philologus* 88, 104–29, 181–202, 415–42.

Mentzer, S. M., D. G. Romano, and M. E. Voyatzis. 2017. 'Micromorphological contributions to the study of ritual behavior at the ash altar to Zeus on Mt. Lykaion, Greece' *Archaeological and Anthropological Sciences* 9, 1017–43.

Merkelbach, R. 1970. Review of Piccaluga 1968, *Gnomon* 42, 182–5.

Merlen, R. H. A. 1971. *De canibus: Dog and Hound in Antiquity*. London.

Messerschmidt F. 1930, 'Probleme der etruskischen Grabmalerei des Hellenismus', *JdI* 45, 62–90.

Metsvahi, M. 2001. 'Werwolfprozesse in Estland und Livland im 17. Jahrhundert. Zusammenstösse zwischen der Realität von Richtern und von Bauern' in J. Beyer and R. Hiiemäe eds. *Folklore als Tatsachenbericht*. Tartu. 175–84.

Metsvahi, M. 2015. 'Estonian werewolf history' in de Blécourt 2015, 206–27.

Metzger, N. 2011. *Wolfsmenschen und nächtliche Heimsuchungen. Zur kulturhistorischen Verortung vormoderner Konzepte von Lykanthropie und Ephialtes*. Remscheid.

Metzger, N. 2012. 'Zwischen Mensch und Wolf. Zur Lykanthropie in der spätantiken Medizin' *Les Études classiques* 80, 135–56.

Metzler, D. 1982 'Zum Schamanismus in Griechenland' in D. Metzler, C. Müller-Wirth, and B. Otto eds., J. Thimme hon., *Antidoron Jürgen Thimme*. Karlsruhe. 75–82.

Meuli, K. 1935. 'Scythica' *Hermes* 70: 121–76.

Meyer, E. 1927. 'Lykaion' *RE* xiii.2, 2235–44.

Meyer, K. 1894. 'The Irish *mirabilia* in the Norse "Speculum regale"' *Folk-lore* 5, 299–316.

Micha, A. ed. 1990. *Guillaume de Palerne: Roman du xiiie siècle*. Geneva.

Michelant, H. ed. 1876. *Guillaume de Palerne*. Paris.

Michels, A. K. 1953. 'iii. The topography and interpretation of the Lupercalia' *TAPA* 84, 35–59.

Migne, J. P., ed. 1857–1904. *Patrologiae cursus completus. Series Graeca*. Paris.

Migne, J. P., ed. 1884–1904. *Patrologiae cursus completus. Series Latina*. Paris.

Milin, G. 1991. 'La "Vita Ronani" et les contes de loup-garou aux xiie et xiiie siècles' *Le Moyen-age* 97, 259–73.

Milin, G. 1993. *Les Chiens de Dieu: La representation du loup-garou en Occident, xie–xxe siècles*. Brest.

Miller, C. H. 2007. 'Part I. "Fragments of Danish History" (*Skjöldunga saga*)' *American Notes and Queries* 20.3, 3–33.

Miller, S. M. 1942. 'Werewolves and "ghost words" in Petronius: *matavita tau*' *Classical Philology* 37, 319–21.

Milne, F.A. trans. 1904. 'Arthur and Gorlagon' *Folk-lore* 15, 40–60. Reprinted in Otten 1986, 234–55.

Mitchell, B. M. 1975. 'Herodotus and Samos' *JHS* 95, 75–91.

Moreau, A. 1989. 'Lupus duplex. Première partie: l'énigme de Lykomède' *Connaissance Hellénique. Revue de culture grecque pour non-spécialistes* 41, 26–35.

Moreau, A. 1990a. 'Lupus duplex. Deuxième partie: les hommes-loups dans la mythologie grecque' *Connaissance Hellénique. Revue de culture grecque pour non-spécialistes* 42, 32–45.

Moreau, A. 1990b. 'Lupus duplex. Troisième partie: du mythe au conte' *Connaissance Héllénique. Revue de culture grecque pour non-spécialistes* 43, 49–58.

Moreau, A. 1997. 'Le loup-garou (i)' *Connaissance Hellénique. Revue de culture grecque pour non-spécialistes* 73, 69–79.

Moreau, A. 1998. 'Le loup-garou (ii)' *Connaissance Hellénique. Revue de culture grecque pour non-spécialistes* 74, 6–17.

Moreau, A. 2004. ed. *Mythes grecs*.ii. *L'initiation*. Montpellier.

Moretti, L. 1957. *Olympionikai: I vincitori negli antichi agoni Olimpici*. Rome.

Morgan, J. R. 2004. *Longus. Daphnis and Chloe*. Oxford.

Moselhy, H. F., and J. F. Macmillan 2014. 'Lycanthropy, mythology and medicine' *Irish Journal of Psychological Medicine* 11, 168–70.

Most, G. W., ed. and trans. 2006–7. *Hesiod*. LCL. 2 vols. Cambridge, MA.

Murgatroyd, P. 1980. *Tibullus I. A Commentary on the First Book of the Elegies of Albius Tibullus*. Pietermaritzburg.

Murphy, T. 2004. *Pliny the Elder's Natural History. The Empire in the Encyclopaedia*. Oxford.

Musiani, M., L. Boitani, and P. C. Paquet eds. 2010a. *The World of Wolves. New Perspectives on Ecology, Behaviour and Management*. Calgary.

Musiani, M., L. Boitani, and P. C. Paquet eds. 2010b. 'Introduction' in Musiani et al. 2010a, 1–11.

Musti, D., and M. Torelli eds. 1991. *Pausania. Guida della Grecia. Libro IV. La Messenia*. Milan.

Myers, S. K. 1996. 'The poet and the procuress: the *lena* in Latin love elegy' *JRS* 86, 1–21.

Nagy, J. 1990. 'Hierarchy, heroes and heads: Indo-European structures in Greek myth' in L. Edmunds ed. *Approaches to Greek Myth*. Baltimore. 200–38.

Napier, A. ed. 1883. *Wulfstan. Sammlung der ihm zugeschriebenen Homilien nebst Untersuchungen über ihre Echtheit*. Berlin.

Nardi, E. 1960. *Case 'infestate da spiriti' e diritto Romano e moderno*. Milan.

Negri, M., 1982. 'Lupi Sabinorum lingua vocantur hirpi' *Acme* 35, 199–203.

Nilsson, M. P. 1967. *Geschichte der griechischen Religion*. i. 3rd ed. Munich.

Ní Mheallaigh, K. 2014. *Reading Fiction with Lucian*. Cambridge.

Nock, A. D. 1950. 'Tertullian and the Ahori' *VC* 4, 129–41.

Oates, C. 1989. 'Metamorphosis and lycanthropy in Franche-Comté, 1521–1643' in M. Feher ed. *Fragments for a History of the Human Body*. 3 vols. New York. i, 305–63.

O'Donnell, E. 1912. *Werwolves* [*sic*]. London.

Ogden, D. 1997. *The Crooked Kings of Ancient Greece*. London.

Ogden, D. 2001. *Greek and Roman Necromancy*. Princeton.

Ogden, D. 2002. Review of M. W. Dickie *Magic and Magicians in the Greco-Roman World* (London, 2001) and A. Moreau and J.-C. Turpin eds. *La magie*. 4 vols. (Montpellier, 2001), *CR* 52, 129–33.

Ogden, D. 2004. *Aristomenes of Messene. Legends of Sparta's Nemesis*. Swansea. 113–22.

Ogden, D. 2007. *In Search of the Sorcerer's Apprentice. The Traditional Tales of Lucian's Lover of Lies*. Swansea.

Ogden, D. 2008. *Night's Black Agents*. London.

Ogden, D. 2009. *Magic, Witchcraft and Ghosts in the Greek and Roman Worlds: A Sourcebook*. 2nd ed. New York.

Ogden, D. 2011. *Alexander the Great: Myth, Genesis and Sexuality*. Exeter.

Ogden, D. 2013a. *Drakōn: Dragon Myth and Serpent Cult in the Greek and Roman Worlds*. Oxford.

Ogden, D. 2013b. *Dragons, Serpents and Slayers in the Classical and Early Christian Worlds: A Sourcebook*. New York.

Ogden, D. 2017. *The Legend of Seleucus*. Cambridge.

Ogden, D. 2018. 'John Damascene on dragons and witches (*De draconibus et strygibus*, PG 94, 1599–1604): a translation with select commentary' *Pegasus. Journal of the Exeter Classics Department* 60, 16–25.

Ogden, D. 2019a. 'Niceros, Hermotimus and Bisclavret: werewolves, souls and innkeepers' in J. R. Morgan hon., I. Repath and F.-G. Herrmann eds. *Some Organic Readings in Narrative, Ancient and Modern, Gathered and Originally Presented as a Book for John*. Ancient Narrative Supplementum 27. Groningen. 255–79.

Ogden, D. 2019b. 'Lies too good to lay to rest: The survival of pagan ghost stories in early Christian literature' in D. Romero-González, I. Muñoz-Gallarte, and G. Laguna-Mariscal eds., *Visitors from beyond the Grave: Ghosts in World Literature*. Humanitas Supplementum. Coimbra. 55–70.

Oliphant, S. G. 1913. 'The story of the *strix*: ancient' *TAPA* 44, 133–49.

Oliphant, S. G. 1914. 'The story of the *strix*: Isidorus and the glossographers' *TAPA* 44, 49–63.

Oring, D., ed. 1986. *Folk Groups and Folklore Genres. An Introduction*. Logan, UT.

Orth, F. 1910. *Der Hund im Altertum*. Schleusingen.

Otten, C. F., ed. 1986. *A Lycanthropy Reader*. Syracuse, NY.

Otto, W. F. 1910. 'Genius' *RE* vii, 1155–70.

Otto, W. F. 1913. 'Hirpi Sorani' *RE* viii, 1933–5.

Packard, J. M. 2003. 'Wolf behavior: reproduction, social and intelligent' in Mech and Boitani 2003a, 35–65.

Page, D. L. ed. 1962. *Poetae melici Graeci*. Oxford.

Page, D. L. 1973. *Folktales in Homer's Odyssey*. Cambridge, MA.

Pais, E. 1908. 'The legend of Euthymos of Locri' in E. Pais *Ancient Italy. Historical and Geographical Investigations*. Chicago. 39–51 [= 'La leggenda di Eutimo di Locri e del heroon di Temesa' in his *Ricerche di storia e di geografia dell 'Italia antica*. Turin, 1908. 43–56; also = his *Italia antica. Ricerche di storia e geografia storica* ii. Bologna, 1922. 79–91]

Pais, E. 1909. 'La lotta di Eutimo di Locri a Temesa' *Klio* 9, 385–94.

Pálsson, H. ed., and A. Faulkes trans. 2012. *Snorri Sturluson, The Uppsala Edda*. London.

Panaino, A. 2011. 'Erodoto, i magi e la storia religiosa iranica' in R. Rollinger et al. eds. *Herodot und das Persische Weltreich*. Wiesbaden. 343–70.

Panayotakis, C. 1995. *Theatrum Arbitri: Theatrical Elements in the* Satyrica *of Petronius*. Leiden.

Papachatzis, N. D. 1963–9. *Παυσανίου Ἑλλάδος Περιήγησις*. 4 vols. Athens.

Papathomopoulos, M. 1968. Antoninus Liberalis. *Les Métamorphoses*. Budé. Paris.

Pape, W., and G. E. Benseler 1911. *Wörterbuch der griechischen Eigennamen*. 3rd ed. Brunswick, 1911.

Parker, R. C. T. 1996. *Athenian Religion. A History*. Oxford.

Parker, R. C. T. 2008. *Polytheism and Society at Athens*. Oxford.

Pàroli, T. 1986. 'Lupi e lupi mannari, tra mondo classico e germanico, a partire da Petronio 61–62' in *Semiotica della novella latina. Atti del seminario interdisciplinare 'La novella latina,' Perugia, 11–13 aprile 1985*. Materiali e contribute per la storia della narrativa Greco-Latina 4. Rome. 281–317.

Parry, H. 1992. *Thelxis. Magic and Imagination in Greek Myth and Poetry*. Lanham.

Pasarić, M. 2015. 'Dead bodies and transformations: werewolves in some South Slavic folk traditions' in de Blécourt 2015, 238–56.

Patera, M. 2005. 'Comment effrayer les enfants: le cas de Mormô/Mormolukê et du mormolukeion' *Kernos* 18, 371–90.

Patera, M. 2015. *Figures grecques de l'épouvante de l'antiquité au présent: peurs enfantines et adultes*. Mnemosyne Suppl. 376. Leiden.

Paule, M. T. 2017. *Canidia, Rome's First Witch*. London.

Pauly, A., G. Wissowa, W. Kroll et al. eds. 1894–1978. *Realencyclopädie der klassischen Altertumswissenschaft*. Multiple volumes and parts. Munich.

Pearson, L. 1962. 'The pseudo-history of Messenia and its authors' *Historia* 11, 397–426.

Pélékidis C. 1962. *Histoire de l'éphébie attique. Des origines à 31 avant J-C*. Paris.

Perlman, P. 1983. 'Plato's *Laws* 833C–834D and the bears of Brauron', *GRBS* 24, 115–30.

Perlman, P. 1989. 'Acting the she-bear for Artemis' *Arethusa* 22, 111–34.

Peronaci, A. 1974. [untitled round-table contribution] in *Metaponto. Atti del xiii convegno di studi sulla Magna Grecia*. Naples. 269–74.

Perrochat, P. 1952. *Pétrone. Le festin de Trimalcion: commentaire exégétique et critique*. 2nd ed. Paris.

Perry, B. E. 1952. *Aesopica*. Urbana, IL.

Perry, B. E. 1967. *The Ancient Romances*. Berkeley.

Petrakos, V. 1999. 'Ἀνασκαφὴ 'Ραμνοῦντος' *Πρακτικά* 154, 1–31.

Pettazzoni, R. 1940. 'Carna' *Studi Etruschi* 14, 163–72.

Petzl, G. 1994. *Die Beichtinschriften Westkleinasiens*. Epigraphica Anatolica 22. Bonn.

Peucer, C. 1560. *Commentarius de praecipuis generibus divinationum*. 2nd ed. Wittenberg.

Pfeiffer, R. 1965. *Callimachus*. 2nd ed. 2 vols. Oxford.

Phillips, A., and M. M. Willcock eds. and transs. 1999. *Xenophon and Arrian: On Hunting*. Warminster.

Phillips, J. 1953. 'Odysseus in Italy' *JHS* 73, 53–88.

Piccaluga, G. 1968. *Lykaon. Un tema mitico.* Rome.

Piccaluga, G. 1976. 'I Marsi e gli Hirpi' in P. Xella ed., R. Garosi hon., *Magia. Studi di storia delle religioni in memoria di Raffaella Garosi.* Rome. 207–31.

Pinna, T. 1978. 'Magia e religione nella *Cena Trimalchionis*' in G. Solinas ed. *Studi di filosofia e di storia della cultura.* Pubblicazioni dell'Istituto della facoltà di lettere dell' università di Cagliari. Sassari. 449–500. [*Non vidi.*]

Pinotti, P. 2003. 'In compagnia dei lupi. Storie antiche e interpretazioni moderne del rapporto tra umani, lupi e lupi mannari' in F. Gasti and E. Romano eds. *Buoni per pensare: gli animali nel pensiero e nella letteratura dell'antichità.* Atti della ii giornata ghisleriana di filologia classica, Pavia, 18–19 aprile 2002. Como. 83–125.

Pirenne-Delforge, V. 2008. *Retour à la source. Pausanias et la religion grecque.* Kernos Suppléments 20. Liège.

Pischel, R. 1888. 'Zu Petronius, *Satirae* 62' in M. J. Hertz hon. *Philologische Abhandlungen: Martin J. Hertz zum siebzigsten Geburstag von ehemaligen Schülern dargebracht.* Berlin. 69–80.

Pitrè, G. 1889. *Usi e costumi credenze e pregiudizi del popolo Siciliano.* iii. Palermo.

Pluskowski, A. G. 2005. 'The tyranny of the gingerbread house: contextualising the fear of wolves in Medieval northern Europe through material culture, ecology and folklore' *Current Swedish Archaeology* 13, 141–60.

Pluskowski, A. G. 2006. *Wolves and the Wilderness in the Middle Ages.* Woodbridge.

Pluskowski, A. G. 2015. 'Before the werewolf trials: contextualising shape-changers and animal identities in Medieval north-western Europe' in de Blécourt 2015a, 82–118.

Poliakoff, M. B. 1987. *Combat Sports in the Ancient World.* New Haven.

Pötscher, W. ed. 1964. *Theophrastus. De pietate.* Leiden.

Pötscher, W. 1984. 'Die Lupercalia—eine Strukturanalyse' *Grazer Beiträge* 11, 221–49.

Pouilloux, J. 1954. *Recherches sur l'histoire et les cultes de Thasos.* 2 vols. Paris.

Pretzler, M. 2007. *Pausanias. Travel Writing in Ancient Greece.* London.

Prieur, J. 1988. *Les Animaux sacrés dans l'antiquité: art et religion du monde méditerranéen.* Rennes.

Propp, V. I. 1958. *Morphology of the Folktale.* Bloomington, IA.

Propp, V. I. 1984. *Theory and History of Folklore.* Manchester.

Przyluski, P. 1940. 'Les confréries de loups-garous dans les sociétés indo-européennes' *Revue de l'histoire des religions* 121, 128–45.

Puiggali, J. 1986. 'Une histoire de fantôme (Xénophon d'Ephèse V 7)' *RhM* 129, 321–8.

Radermacher, L. 1915. *Die Erzählungen der Odyssee.* SAWW clxxviii. Vienna.

Radt, S.L. 2002–11. *Strabons Geographika, mit Übersetzung und Kommentar.* 10 vols. Göttingen.

Ramos, E. 2014. 'The Dreams of a Bear. Animal Traditions in the Old Norse-Icelandic Context'. MA diss., University of Iceland.

Ranke, K. 1934. *Die zwei Brüder: eine Studie zur vergleichenden Märchenforschung.* FFC 114. Helsinki.

Ranke, K., and H. Bausinger eds. 1977–2015. *Enzyklopädie des Märchens.* 15 vols. Berlin.

Rasmussen, K. 1926. *Rasmussens Thulefahrt.* Frankfurt.

Reeder, E. D. ed. 1995. *Pandora. Women in Classical Greece.* Princeton.

Reiner, E. 1938. *Die rituelle Totenklage der Griechen.* Tübinger Beiträge zur Altertumswissenschaft 30. Tübingen.

Reinhard, J. R., and V. E. Hull 1936. 'Bran and Sceolang' *Speculum* 11, 42–58.

Rémy, N. 1592. *Dæmonolatreiæ libri tres.* Lyons.

Rémy, N. 1595. *La Démonolâtrie.* Nancy. French translation of Rémy 1592.

Resnick, I. M., and K. F. Kitchell Jr. 2007. '"The sweepings of Lamia": transformations of the myths of Lilith and Lamia' in A. Cuffel and B. Britt eds. *Religion, Gender, and Culture in the Pre-modern World*. Basingstoke. 77–104.

Rhodes, P. J. 1981. *A Commentary on the Aristotelian* Athenaion Politeia. Oxford.

Ribbeck, O. 1873. *Comicorum Romanorum praeter Plautum et Terentium fragmenta*. Leipzig.

Richter, W. 1978. 'Wolf' *RE* Suppl. xv, 960–87.

Ridley, R. A. 1976. 'Wolf and werewolf in Baltic and Slavic tradition' *Journal of Indo-European Studies* 4, 321–32.

Rini, A. 1929. 'Popular superstitions in Petronius and Italian superstitions of to-day' *Classical Weekly* 22, 83–6.

Rissanen, M. 2012. 'The Hirpi Sorani and the wolf cults of Central Italy' *Arctos* 46, 115–35.

Rives, J. B. 1995. 'Human sacrifice among pagans and Christians' *JRS* 85, 65–85.

Roberts, K. 1999. 'Eine Werwolf-Formel. Eine kleine Kulturgeschichte des Werwolfs' in U. Müller and W. Wunderlich eds. *Dämonen, Monster, Fabelwesen*. St. Gallen. 565–81.

Rogge, C. 1927. 'Mitteilungen zu Petron' *Philologische Wochenschrift* 47, 1021–3.

Rohde, E. 1925. *Pysche*. London. Trans. of *Pysche*. 8th ed. Freiburg, 1920.

Romano, D. G. 2005. 'A new topographical and architectural survey of the sanctuary of Zeus at Mt. Lykaion' in E. Østby ed. *Ancient Arcadia. Papers from the Third International Seminar on Ancient Arcadia*. Athens. 381–96.

Romano, D. G. 2008. 'Cult digs. The sanctuary of Zeus on Mt Lykaion' *Current World Archaeology* 30, 42–8.

Romano, D. G. 2019. 'Mt. Lykaion as the Arcadian Birthplace of Zeus' in T. S. Scheer ed. *Natur—Mythos—Religion im antiken Griechenland/Nature—Myth—Religion in Ancient Greece*. Stuttgart. 219–37.

Romano, D. G., and M. E. Voyatzis 2010. 'Excavating at the birthplace of Zeus: the Mt. Lykaion excavation and survey project' *Expedition* 52.1, 9–21.

Roscher, W. H. ed. 1884-1937. *Ausfürliches Lexikon der griechischen und römischen Mythologie*. 7 vols. Leipzig.

Roscher, W. H. 1896. *Das von der 'Kynanthropie' handelnde Fragment des Marcellus von Side*. Leipzig.

Rose, H. K. 1923. 'On the original significance of the *genius*' *CQ* 17, 57–60.

Rose, K. F. C. 1971. *The Date and Author of the* Satyricon. Leiden.

Rouveret, A. 1990. 'Tradizioni pittorische magnogreche' in G. Pugliese Carratelli ed. *Magna Grecia*. iv. Milan. 317–50.

Roy, J. 2011. 'On seeming backward: how the Arkadians did it' in S. D. Lambert ed., N. R. E. Fisher hon., *Sociable Man: Essays on Ancient Greek Social Behaviour in Honour of Nick Fisher*. Swansea. 67–85.

Rupp, W. L. 2007. 'Shape of the Beast: The Theriomorphic and Therianthropic Deities and Demons of Ancient Italy'. PhD thesis, Florida State University.

Russell, W. M. S., and C. Russell 1978. 'The social biology of werewolves' in J. R. Porter and W. M. S. Russell eds. *Animals in Folklore*. Cambridge. 143–82, 260–9.

Rutherford, I. 2001. *Pindar's Paeans: A Reading of the Fragments with a Survey of the Genre*. Oxford.

Ryan, W. G., trans. 1993. *Jacobus de Voragine. The Golden Legend. Readings on the Saints*. 2 vols. Princeton.

Rychner, J. ed. 1966. *Les lais de Marie de France*. Paris.

Salanitro, M. 1998. 'Il racconto del lupo mannaro in Petronio: tra folclore e letteratura' *Atene e Roma* 43, 156–67.

Salapata, G. 2006. 'The tippling serpent in the art of Laconia and beyond' *Hesperia* 75, 541–60.

Sale, W. 1962. 'The story of Callisto in Hesiod' *RhM* 105, 122–41.

Sale, W. 1975. 'The temple legends of the *arkteia*' *RhM* 118, 265–84.

Sandy, G. N. 1970. 'Petronius and the tradition of interpolated narrative' *TAPA* 101, 463–76.

Schäublin, C. 1995. 'Lupercalien und Lichtmess' *Hermes* 123, 117–25.

Scheer, T. S. ed. 2009. *Tempelprostitution im Altertum*. Berlin.

Schefold, K., and F. Jung 1989. *Die Sagen von den Argonauten, von Theben und Troia in der klassischen und hellenistischen Kunst*. Munich.

Schjødt, J. P. 2003. 'Myths as sources for rituals—theoretical and practical implications' in M. C. Ross ed. *Old Norse Myths, Literature and Society*. Odense. 261–78.

Schjødt, J. P. 2006. 'The notion of berserkir and the relation between Óðinn and animal warriors' in J. McKinnell, D. Ashurst, and D. Kick eds. *The Fantastic in Old Norse/Icelandic Literature: Sagas and the British Isles*. 2 vols. Durham. ii, 886–92.

Schmeling, G. L. 2011. *A Commentary on the* Satyrica *of Petronius*. Oxford.

Schmeling, G. L., and J. H. Stuckey 1977. *A Bibliography of Petronius*. Leiden.

Schmidt, M. 1972. 'Ein neues Zeugnis zum Mythos vom Orpheushaupt' *Antike Kunst* 15, 128–37.

Scholz, H. H. 1937. *Der Hund in der griechisch-römischen Magie und Religion*. Berlin.

Schorn, S. 2018. *Studien zur hellenistischen Biographie und Historiographie*. Berlin.

Schuster, M., 1930. 'Der Werwolf und die Hexen' *WS* 48, 149–78.

Schwenn, F. 1924. 'Lamia' *RE* xii.1, 544–6.

Scobie, A. S. 1978. 'Strigiform witches in Roman and other cultures' *Fabula* 19, 74–101.

Scobie, A. S. 1982. 'Trimalchio en "Folklore"' *Hermeneus* 54, 62–71.

Scobie, A. S. 1983. *Apuleius and Folklore: Toward a History of ML3045, AaTh567, 449A*. London.

Sconduto, L. A. 2004. *Guillaume de Palerne. An English Translation of the 12th Century French Verse Romance*. Jefferson, NC.

Sconduto, L. A. 2008. *Metamorphoses of the Werewolf. A Literary Study from Antiquity through the Renaissance*. Jefferson, NC.

Scudder, B. trans. 2004. *Egil's Saga*. London.

Sébillot P. 1897, 'Traditions et coutumes du Périgord' *Revue des traditions populaires* 12, 657–67.

Sébillot P. 1904–7. *Le Folk-lore de France*. 4 vols. Paris.

Shero, L. R. 1938. 'Aristomenes the Messenian' *TAPA* 69, 500–31.

Simon, E. 1973. 'Die Tomba dei Tori und der etruskische Apollonkult' *Jahrbuch des Deutschen archäologischen Instituts* 88, 27–42.

Simonsen, M. 2015. 'The werewolf in nineteenth-century Denmark' in de Blécourt 2015, 228–37.

Simonyan, H. 1989. *Patmowt'iwn Ałek'sandri Makedonac'woy, haykakan xmbagrowt'yownner*. Yerevan.

Small, S. 2013. 'The Medieval werewolf model of reading skin' in K. L. Walter ed. *Reading Skin in Medieval Literature and Culture*. New York. 81–98.

Smith, K. F. 1894. 'An historical study of the werwolf [*sic*] in literature' *Publications of the Modern Language Association of America* 9.1, 1–42.

Smith, K. F. 1913. *The Elegies of Albius Tibullus*. New York.

Smith, M. S. 1975. *Petronius. Cena Trimalchionis*. Oxford.

Snell, B., Kannicht, R., and Radt, S., 1971–2004. *Tragicorum Graecorum fragmenta*. 5 vols. Göttingen.

Sourvinou-Inwood, C. 1987. 'Myth as history: the previous owners of the Delphic oracle' in J. N. Bremmer ed. *Interpretations of Greek Mythology*. London, 215–41.

Sourvinou-Inwood, C. 1988a. '"Myth" and history: on Herodotus iii.48 and 50–3' *Opuscula Atheniensia* 17, 167–82.

Sourvinou-Inwood, C. 1988b. *Studies in Girls' Transitions. Aspects of the Arkteia and Age Representation in Attic Iconography*. Athens.

Sourvinou-Inwood, C. 1990. 'Ancient rites and modern constructs: on the Brauronian bears again' *BICS* 37, 1–14.

Spaeth, B. S. 2010. '"The terror that comes in the night": the night hag and supernatural assault in Latin literature' in E. Scholi and C. Walde eds. *Sub imagine somni: Nighttime Phenomena in Greco-Roman Culture*. Florence. 231–58.

Spaeth, J. W. 1933. 'Petronius and H.M. Tomlinson: the werewolf again' *Classical Weekly* 26, 98–9.

Spaeth, J. W. 1935. 'In the werewolf tradition' *Classical Weekly* 28, 125–6.

Spier, J. 1993. 'Medieval Byzantine amulets and their tradition' *Journal of the Warburg and Coutauld Institutes* 56, 25–62.

Spotte, S. 2012. *Societies of Wolves and Free-ranging Dogs*. Cambridge.

Stahl, M. 1983. 'Tyrannis und das Problem der Macht' *Hermes* 111, 202–20.

Steadman, S. H. 1945. 'A note on the Rhesus' *Classical Review* 59, 6–8.

Steele, K. 2012. 'Centaurs, satyrs, and Cynocephali: Medieval scholarly teratology and the question of the human' in A. S. Mittman and P. J. Dendle eds. *The Ashgate Research Companion to Monsters and the Monstrous*. Farnham.257–74.

Steindorf, L. 1985. 'Wolfisches Heulen. Ein Motiv im mittelalterlichen slavischen Quellen' *Byzantino-Slavica* 46, 40–9.

Stenbock, E. S., Count, 1893. 'The other side: a Breton legend' *The Spirit Guide* 4.2, 52–68.

Stoker, B. 1897. *Dracula*. London.

Stoker, B. 1914. *Dracula's Guest and Other Weird Stories*. London.

Stoneman, R. 2007–. *Il Romanzo di Alessandro*. 3 vols. Milan.

Stramaglia, A. 1989. 'La scena di necromanzia nella novella di Telifrone (Apuleio, *Metamorfosi* ii.27–30) e la figura del sacerdote-mago egiziano nella narrativa Greco-latina'. Graduation thesis. Bari.

Stramaglia, A. 1999. *Res inauditae, incredulae. Storie di fantasmi nel mondo greco-latino*. Bari.

Stratton, K. B. 2007. *Naming the Witch. Magic, Ideology and Stereotype in the Ancient World*. New York.

Strubbe, J. 1997. *ΑΡΑΙ ΕΠΙΤΥΜΒΙΟΙ. Imprecations against Desecrators of the Grave in the Greek Epitaphs of Asia Minor*. A Catalogue. Bonn.

Suard, F. 1980. '*Bisclavret* et les contes du loup-garou: essai d'interprétation' in J. de Caluwé ed., C. Foulon hon., *Mélanges de langue et littérature françaises du moyen âge et de la Renaissance offerts à Charles Foulon*. 2 vols. Rennes. ii, 267–76.

Summers, M. trans. 1928. H. Kramer and J. Sprenger. *Malleus maleficarum*. London.

Summers, M. 1933. *The Werewolf*. London. Republished as *The Werewolf in Lore and Legend*. Mineola, NY, 2003.

Sundquist, O., and A. Hultgård 2004. 'The lycophoric names of the 6th- to 7th-century Blekinge rune stones and the problem of their ideological background' in A. van Nahl, L. Elmevik and S. Brink eds. *Namenwelten: Orts- und Personennamen in historischer Sicht*. Berlin. 583–602.

Susanetti, D. 1999. 'Amori tra fantasmi, mummie e lenoni: Sicilia e Magna Grecia nel romanzo di Senofonte Efesio' in G. Avezzù and E. Pianezzola eds. *Sicilia e Magna Grecia. Spazio reale e spazio immaginario nella letteratura greca e latina*. Padua. 127–69.

Szilágyi, J. G. 1994. 'Olta' *LIMC* vii.1, 35–7.

Taillardat, J. 1965. *Les images d'Aristophane. Études de langue et de style*. Paris.

Talbert, R. J. A. ed. 2000. *Barrington Atlas of the Greek and Roman World*. Princeton.

Tennant P. M. W. 1988. 'The Lupercalia and the Romulus and Remus legend' *Acta Classica* 31, 81–93.

Thomas, P. H. 1960. *Incerti auctoris epitoma* Rerum gestarum Alexandri Magni *cum* Libro de morte testamentoque Alexandri. Leipzig.

Thompson, R. 1828. 'The wehr wolf: a legend of Limousin' in his *Tales of an Antiquary*. 3 vols. London. i, 232–60.

Thompson, S. 1955–8. *Motif-Index of Folk-Literature*. 2nd ed. 6 vols. Bloomington, IN.

Thompson, S. 1977. *The Folktale*. Berkeley.

Thorpe, B. ed. 1840. *Ancient Laws and Institutes of England*. London.

Ting, N. 1966. 'The holy man and the snake woman: a study of a lamia story in Asian and European literature' *Fabula* 8, 145–91.

Tituli Asiae Minoris. Vienna, 1901–.

Todd, J. H. 1848. *Leabhar Breathnach annso sis: The Irish Version of the* Historia Britonum *of Nennius*, ed. with trans. Irish Archaeological Society. Dublin.

Tolley, C. 2007. 'Hrólfs saga kraka *and Sámi bear rites*' *Saga-Book* 31, 5–21.

Tomberg, K. 1968. 'Die *Kaine Historia* des Ptolemaios Chennos'. Diss., Bonn.

Tomlin, R. S. O. 1988. 'The curse tablets' in B. Cunliffe, ed. *The Temple of Sulis Minerva at Bath*. ii. *The Finds from the Sacred Spring*. Oxford University Committee for Archaeology monograph no. 16. Oxford. 59–277; also published separately (but preserving original pagination) as *Tabellae Sulis: Roman Inscribed Tablets of Tin and Lead from the Sacred Spring at Bath* (monograph no. 16, fascicule 1).

Totti, M. 1985. *Ausgewählte Texte der Isis- und Sarapis-Religion*. Studia Epigraphica 12. Hildesheim.

Touchefeu-Meynier, O. 1968. *Thèmes odysséens dans l'art antique*. Paris.

Trampedach, K. 2017. 'Die Priester der Despoten. Herodots persische Magoi' in H. Klinkott and N. Kramer eds. *Zwischen Assur und Athen. Altorientalisches in den Historien Herodots*. Stuttgart. 197–218.

Treadgold, W. T. 1988. *The Byzantine Revival, 780–842*. Stanford.

Tremoli, P. 1975. '*Matavita tau* (Petron. *Sat.* 62.9): greco o latino?' in L. A. Stella hon. *Studi triestini di antichità in onore di Luigia Aurelia Stella*. Trieste. 439–54.

Tuczay, C. A. 2015. 'Into the wild—Old Norse stories of animal men' in de Blécourt 2015a, 61–81.

Tupet, A.-M. 1976. *La Magie dans la poésie latine*. i. *Des origins à la fin du règne d'Auguste*. Paris.

Tupet, A.-M. 1986. 'Rites magiques dans l'antiquité romaine' *ANRW* ii.16.3, 2591–675.

Turner, V. 1967. *The Forest of Symbols*. Ithaca.

Tzschucke, K. H. 1806–7. *Pomponii Melae* De situ orbis *libri tres*. 7 vols. Leipzig.

Ulf, C. 1982. *Das römische Lupercalienfest: ein Modellfall für Methodenprobleme in der Altertumswissenschaft*. Impulse der Forschung 38. Darmstadt.

Ullmann, M. 1976. 'Der Werwolf: ein griechisches Sagenmotif in arabischer Verkleidung' *Wiener Zeitschrift für die Kunde des Morgenlandes* 68, 171–84.

Ustinova, Y. 2002a. 'Lycanthropy in the Sarmatian warrior societies: the Kobyakovo torque' *Ancient West and East* 1, 102–23.

Ustinova, Y. 2002b. ' "Either a *daimon*, or a hero, or perhaps a god": mythical residents of subterranean chambers' *Kernos* 15, 267–88.

Ustinova, Y. 2004a. 'Jason the shaman' in J. Gebauer, E. Grabow, F. Jünger, and D. Metzler eds., K. Stähler hon., *Bildergeschichte. Festschrift für K. Stähler*. Möhnsee. 507–14.

Ustinova, Y. 2004b. 'Truth lies at the bottom of a cave: Apollo Pholeuterios, the pholarchs of the Eleats, and subterranean oracles' *Parola del Passato* 59, 25–44.

Ustinova, Y. 2009. *Caves and the Early Greek Mind*. Oxford.

Uther, H.-J. 2004. *The Types of International Folktales. A Classification and Bibliography.* 3 vols. FFC 284–6. Helsinki.

Valentini Pagnini, R. 1981. '*Lupus in fabula.* Trasformazioni narrative di un mito' *Bollettino di Studi Latini* 11, 3–22.

Van Gennep, A. 1909. *Les Rites de passage*. Paris.

Van Mal-Maeder, D. 2001. *Apuleius Madaurensis. Metamorphoses, Livre II. Texte, introduction et commentaire.* Groningen.

Van Thiel, H. 1971-2. *Der Eselroman.* Zetemata: Monographien zur klassischen Altertumswissenschaft 54. 2 vols. Munich.

Vé, K. K. 2018. 'La cité et la sauvagerie: les rites des Lupercales' *Dialogues d'histoire ancienne* 44, 139–90.

Veenstra, J. R. 2002. 'The ever-changing nature of the beast: cultural change, lycanthropy and the question of substantial transformation (from Petronius to Del Rio)' in J. N. Bremmer and J. R. Veenstra eds. *The Metamorphosis of Magic from Late Antiquity to the Early Modern Period.* Leuven.133–66.

Verkerk, D. 2001. 'Black servant, black demon: color ideology in the Ashburnham Pentateuch' *Journal of Medieval and Early Modern Studies* 31, 57–78.

Vermeule, E. 1979. *Aspects of Death in Early Greek Art and Poetry.* Berkeley.

Vernant, J.-P. 1981. 'The myth of Prometheus in Hesiod' in Gordon 1981, 43–56. Trans. of 'Le mythe prométhéen chez Hésiode' in J.-P. Vernant *Mythe et société en Grèce ancienne.* Paris, 1974. 177–94.

Vernant, J.-P. 1989. 'At man's table: Hesiod's foundation myth of sacrifice' in M. Detienne and J.-P. Vernant eds. *The Cuisine of Sacrifice among the Greeks.* Chicago. 21–86. Trans. of 'À la table des hommes' in *La Cuisine du sacrifice en pays grec.* Paris, 1979. 37–132.

Vestdijk, S. 1962. *De held van Temesa: een roman uit Groot-Griekenland (528–448 v. Chr.).* The Hague.

Vian, F. 1952. *La Guerre des Géants. Le mythe avant l'époque hellénistique.* Paris.

Vidal-Naquet, P. 1981a. 'The Black Hunter and the origin of the Athenian *ephebeia*' in Gordon 1981, 147–62. Trans. of 'Le Chasseur noir et l'origine de l'ephébie athénienne' *Annales ESC* 23 (1968) 47–64.

Vidal-Naquet, P. 1981b. 'Recipes for Greek adolescence' in Gordon 1981, 163–85. Trans. (with alterations) of 'Le cru, l'enfant grec et le cuit' in J. le Goff and P. Nora eds. *Faire de l'histoire* (Paris, 1973) 137–68.

Villeneuve, R. 1960. *Loups-garous et vampires*. Paris.

Viltanioti, I. F. 2012. 'La Démone Yellô dans la Grèce ancienne, byzantine et moderne' in J. Ries and H. Limet eds. *Anges et démons.* Louvain-la-Neuve. 173–89.

Visintin, M. 1992. *La vergine e l' eroe. Temesa e la leggenda di Euthymos di Locri.* Bari.

Voltmer, R. 2015. 'The judge's lore? The politico-religious concept of metamorphosis in the peripheries of western Europe' in de Blécourt 2015a, 159–84.

Von Bruiningk, H. 1924. 'Der Werwolf in Livland und das letzte im Wendeschen Landgericht und Döptschen Hofgericht i. J. 1692 deshalb stattgehabte Strafverfahren' *Mitteilungen aus der livländischen Geschichte* 22, 163–220.

Von Schlegel, C. H. J. 1830. *Reisen in mehrere russische Gouvernements in den Jahren 178*, 1801, 1807 und 1815.* v. Meiningen.

Von See, K. 1961. 'Berserker' *Zeitschrift für deutsche Wortforschung* 17, 129–35.

Walsh, P. G. 1970. *The Roman Novel: The* Satyricon *of Petronius and the* Metamorphoses *of* Apuleius. Cambridge.

Walter, C. 2003. *The Warrior Saints of Byzantine Art and Tradition*. Aldershot.

Ward, D. 1975. 'Bärensohn' in Ranke and Bausinger 1975–2015, i, 1232–5.

Warmington, E. H. 1935–40. *Remains of Old Latin*. 4 vols. LCL. Cambridge, MA.

Waszink, J. H. 1947. *Quinti Septimi Florentis Tertulliani De Anima*. Edited with an Introduction and Commentary. Amsterdam.

Wathelet, P. 1986. 'Homère, Lykaon et le rituel du mont Lycée' in J. Ries and H. Limet eds. *Les Rites d'initiation*. Louvain-la-Neuve. 285–97.

Watson, L. C. 2003. *A Commentary on Horace's Epodes*. Oxford.

Watson, L. C. 2004. 'Making water not love: Apuleius *Metamorphoses* 1.13–14' *CQ* 54, 651–5.

Wawn, A., trans. 2000. 'The Saga of the People of Vatnsdal' in Ö. Thorsson ed. *The Sagas of the Icelanders*. New York. 185–269.

Wayne, R. K. 2010. 'Recent advances in the population genetics of wolf-like canids' in Musiani et al. 2010a, 15–38.

Weber-Lehmann C. 1995, 'Polyphem in der Unterwelt? Zur Tomba dell'Orco II in Tarquinia', *RhM* 102, 71–100.

Weiler, G. 2007. 'Human sacrifice in Greek culture' in K. Finsterbusch et al. eds. *Human Sacrifice in Jewish and Christian Tradition*. Leiden. 35–64.

Weinreich, O. 1909. *Antike Heiligungswunder: Untersuchungen zum Wunderglauben der Griechen under Römer*. RGVV 8.1. Giessen.

West, D. R. 1991. 'Gello and Lamia: two Hellenic daimons of Semitic origin' *Ugarit-Forschungen* 23, 361–8.

West, D. R. 1995. *Some Cults of the Greek Goddesses and Female Daemons of Oriental Origin*. Alter Orient und Altes Testament 233. Neukirchen-Vlyun.

West, M. L. 1997. *The East Face of Helicon. West Asiatic Elements in Early Greek Poetry and Myth*. Oxford.

West, S. 2004. 'Herodotus on Aristeas' in C. Tuplin ed. *Pontus and the Outside World*. Leiden. 43–67.

Westermann, A. 1839. *Scriptores rerum mirabilium Graeci*. Brunswick.

White. D. G. 1991. *Myths of the Dog Man*. Chicago.

Wiggermann, F. A. M. 2000. 'X. Lamaštu, daughter of Anu, a profile' in M. Stol and F. A. M. Wiggermann, *Birth in Babylonia and the Bible: Its Mediterranean Setting*. Groningen. 217–53.

Wildhaber, R. 1951. 'Kirke und die Schweine' in K. Meuli hon. *Festschrift K. Meuli*. Basel. 233–6.

Williams, D. 1986. 'Dolon' *LIMC* iii.1, 660–4.

Winkler, J. J. 1980. 'Lollianos and the desperadoes' *JHS* 100, 155–81.

Winkler, R. 1909. 'Über Hexenwahn und Hexenprozesse in Estland während der Schwedenherrschaft' *Baltische Monatsschrift* 67, 321–55.

Wiseman, T. P. 1995a. 'The god of the Lupercal' *JRS* 85, 1–22.

Wiseman, T. P. 1995b. *Remus: A Roman Myth*. Cambridge.

Wissowa, G. 1884–90 'Hirpi Sorani' *ML* i, 2694.

Wolohojian, A. M. trans. 1969. *The Romance of Alexander the Great by Pseudo-Callisthenes. Translated from the Armenian Version*. New York.

Woodward, I. 1979. *The Werewolf Delusion*. London.

Wright, M. R. 1981. *Empedocles: The Extant Fragments*. New Haven.

Yarnall, J. 1994. *Transformations of Circe. History of an Enchantress*. Urbana.

Zaganiaris, N. J. 1980. 'Le chien dans la mythologie et la literature gréco-latines' *Platon* 32, 52–87.

Zancani Montuoro, P. 1968–9. 'Ricerche intorno a Temesa. 1. Hera e il demone' in U. Zanotti-Bianco ed. *Atti e memorie della società Magna Grecia* 9–10. Rome. 7–19.

Zhmud, L. 1997. *Wissenschaft, Philosophie und Religion im frühen Pythagoreismus.* Berlin.

Zolotnikova, O. 2005. 'The cult of Zeus Lykaios' in E. Østby, ed. 2005. *Ancient Arcadia. Papers from the Third International Seminar on Ancient Arcadia.* Athens. 105–19.

Zwierzina, K. 1909. 'Die Legenden der Märtyrer vom unzerstörbaren Leben' *Innsbrucker Festgruss von der philosophischen Fakultät.* Innsbruck. 130–58.

General Index

Abaris 65, 126–7
Acanthis 38, 40, 59, 192, 208
Acephali 216, 219
Aelian 16–17, 23–4, 49, 70, 141–4, 148–52,
    201, 217–18
[Aeschines] 144–5, 152
Aeson 41, 93, 213
Aesop 16, 31, 54, 59, 75, 83–4, 100, 128, 131,
    133, 135, 157, 207, 209
Aëtius of Amida 71–2, 74
Aetolia, Aetolians 68–9, 87, 168
Agatharchides of Cnidus 217–18
Agnar 116
Aita 61–2, 64, 80, 162–5; see also Hades
Alcmene 5, 49, 54, 172, 199
Alcyoneus 147–51, 156, 164
Alexander the Great 50–2, 87; Alexander
    Romance 27, 141, 218–19
Ali, Spotted 58–9, 91, 104
Aliano 105
Alibas 147, 159, 162, 206
Alphonse 57, 91, 104, 106, 190
Alybas 142, 147, 159, 206
Amenemhet III 26
Amphitryon 5, 154, 199
Anchises 22
Andania 86
Andromeda 146–9
Androphagoi 25, 101
anguipedes 37, 160
Anthia 153–4
Anthids 17, 83, 100–1, 103, 105, 128, 166–7,
    174–87, 190–7, 203, 205
Anthus 179, 181–2, 194
Antoninus Liberalis 23, 32, 49, 147–8, 150–2,
    156, 158, 164
Aphrodite 21–2, 24
Apollo 22–4; Delphic 16, 24, 145, 147, 160,
    185–6, 190, 198, 201; Hyperborean 126–7;
    Lykēgenēs 23; Lykeios, Lykios 24, 69, 184; of
    Soracte 62–4, 104
Apollodorus (mythographer) 1, 16, 50, 52, 86,
    146, 150, 153–4, 167, 170–1, 174, 176,
    187–9, 203
Apollonius (paradoxographer) 126–7
Apollonius of Tyana 32, 73–8, 93, 99, 127, 160,
    200, 207

Apuleius 2, 3, 5, 27, 37–8, 43–52, 59, 70, 76,
    82–3, 97, 106, 123, 132–3, 135, 208–9
Arcadia, Arcadians 7, 9, 14, 17, 20–1, 26, 59, 70,
    83, 86, 100–1, 103, 105–6, 123, 125, 128, 131,
    133, 166–205, 209, 222–4;
    see also Lykaia, Lykaion
Arcas 167–9, 170, 188, 204
Archonides 70
aretalogy 208–9
Arignotus 76
Arimaspians 126
Aristeas of Proconnesus 65, 109–10, 125–8
Aristomenes (Apuleius) 44–6, 48, 83, 209
Aristomenes (comic poet) 65
Aristomenes of Messene 85–8, 107, 206
Ariston 154, 199
Aristotle, [Aristotle] 17, 23, 39, 70, 74–5, 88,
    100, 127–8, 151, 184, 200
Arkteia 188–90
Armenia 134
Arruns 63, 104
Artemidorus 15–16, 134
Artemis 21–3, 183, 188–90
Arthex 98–9
Arthur 56; Arthur and Gorlagon 10, 57–8,
    105, 130–1
Astrabacus 154, 161, 199
Athamas 16, 178, 193
athletes 198–203, see Cleomedes, Damarchus,
    Euthymus, Milo, Taurosthenes, Theogenes
Augustine 20, 24, 85, 99–101, 103–7, 110, 121,
    123–5, 134–5, 180–2, 191, 194–6, 209,
    219, 222
Autolykos 94, 187
Auvergne 94–5
Axius 151, 185

baboons 216–19
baboutziarios 101
Babylus, St 219
Bardanes Turcus 4–5
Baring-Gould, Sabine 13, 79, 89
bawd-witches 17, 28, 35–41, 59, 67, 82, 101;
    see also Acanthis, Dipsas, Tibullus
bears, bearskins 15, 53, 91, 113–17, 183,
    185, 188–90
beggars 38, 45, 74–8, 81, 93–4, 99, 207

Beowulf 115, 137
Bera 115
berserkers 79, 113–16, 122, 190
Bisclavret (*Bisclavret*) 8, 10–11, 14, 55, 84, 96,
    104, 113, 129–36, 190–1, 207
Bjarkamál 116
Bjarkarímur 116–17
Bjorn 115–16
blackness 25–6, 33, 70, 72, 76, 78, 92, 105, 138,
    147, 161–2
Blackwood, Algernon 122
Bodvar Bjarki 114–16
Boguet, Henri 95, 118–19
Bois d'Orville 106
Bonnel, Jules 106
Book of Settlements 117
Brande 57, 91
Brauron, Brauronia 189–90
bread 3, 74, 93, 99, 102, 107, 207
Briareus 87
bubo (eagle owl) 42–4
bulls 114, 117, 199–201
bullets, silver 96
Burchard of Worms 7, 24
Byzantium *see* Constantinople

Caeadas 87
Callimachus 137, 139–40, 145, 152–5, 198–9,
    201, 206
Callirhoe 145
Callisto 167–9, 188–90, 204
Calu *see* Aita
Canidia 35, 42
cannibalism 16, 20, 37, 98, 100–1, 135, 167, 197;
    see also sacrifice, human
Canute 7
Carna 29, 33
Carthage 179
Cassandra 154
Caucon 86–7
Cecrops 172
Cerberus 39–40, 60
Cercidas 70
Charlemagne 34
Chaucevaire 84, 129, 192
cheese 99, 123–4, 134, 209
Christianos 219
Christopher, St 219
Chrysapha relief 161
Cimon 144–5, 152
Circe 5, 13, 18–24, 28, 59, 99, 123, 125, 131, 180,
    191, 208, 211–15
Clearchus of Soli 127–8, 144
Cleomedes of Astypalaea 198, 220–2
Cleomenes I 70

Cleostratus 147, 150, 156
Clovis 34
Colchis 27, 42, 167, 212; *see also* Medea
confession inscriptions 209
confraternities of werewolves 187, 222
Conopium 16
Constantinople 4
Constantius 112
Corinth 160, 186–7
Corneto 61, 162
Coroebus 160, 198
Coutras 70, 91, 105
Cranae 29, 33
Crawfurd, Oswald 96, 102, 105
Creon 212
Cresimus 27
Crisa 150–1
crop-charming 27
Ctesias of Cnidus 216–18
curses 5, 13, 36, 54–9, 77, 85, 89–91, 98–9,
    103–4, 115, 120, 179, 183, 185, 201
Cynamolgi 217
cynanthropy 71, 74; *see also* dogs
Cynocephali 75, 216–19
Cynoprosopi 218
Cyprus 96
Cyranides 4, 32, 101, 192

Dactyls, Idaean 64, 66, 214
Damarchus 1, 14, 167, 178–83, 191–8, 202–5,
    207, 210
D'Assier, Adolphe 122
Datius 112
D'Autun, Jacques 119
De Ingantaib Érenn 111
death 14, 60–4, 76, 134, 152–3, 162, 164; 'social
    death' 182–3, 201–2; *see also* Aita, Hades
decapitation 58, 70, 220–1; *see also* heads, talking
defecation 2
Deianeira 163
Delphi 16–17, 24, 140, 145, 147, 150, 161, 164,
    185–6, 189, 199–200, 204
Demaenetus *see* Damarchus
Demaratus 154, 199
Demeter Melaina 177
demons (*daimones*), devils 13–14, 20, 26, 32, 35,
    62, 68, 73–8, 93, 99, 101–3, 111–12, 118–19,
    124–5, 127, 134, 137–8, 142, 145–8, 152, 154,
    159, 161–2, 164, 206–8; the Devil, Satan 7, 34,
    78, 91–2, 102–3, 106–7, 118–19; *see also* Hero
    of Temesa
Diomede 123, 125, 220–1
Dipsas 40–1, 192
Dis Pater 63–4
Dog-heads *see* Cynocephali

dogs 15–16, 19, 20, 22, 36–8, 42, 47, 54, 60–1, 64, 70–81, 83, 87, 93, 95, 98–9, 107, 114, 120, 122, 129, 131, 161, 177, 187, 207–8, 223; *see also* Cynocephali
Dolon 185–6, 220–2
doors, doorways 30–1, 33–4, 45–6, 48, 105, 125, 153
Douglas, Norman 72–3

ectoplasm 122
Edict of Rothari 34
Egil's Saga 113, 117
Egypt, Egyptians 16, 26–7, 49, 59, 74–5, 129, 218
Elgfrodi (Elk-Frodi) 115–16
Eliduc (*Eliduc*) 50, 52, 97
empousa 77
Endore, Guy 12, 54, 78, 83, 96
ephebes, *ephebeia* 147, 150, 157, 166, 183–90, 193, 195
Ephesus 73–8, 81, 99, 127, 207–8
Ephialtes (incubus) 101
Ephialtes (of Athens) 88
epilepsy 153
Eratosthenes, [Eratosthenes] 100, 168, 174, 188–9, 204, 216, 223
Erictho 35, 37, 41–2
Etruria, Etruscans 64, 80, 162–5, 223
Euagropas 100, 179–183, 204, 210
Euanthes 101, 179, 182, 194, 204
Eurybatus 148–51, 157, 164
Eurycleia 93–4
Eurylochus 18–21
Euthycles of Locri 201
Euthymus 14, 78, 137–65, 198, 201–2, 205–6

Faliscan 62–3
Fenrir 122
Festus 28–9
fetch see *fylgja*
Field, Eugene 96
Fincel, Hiob 4, 88
Flemish Folk Tale Bank 12
folklore, folktales 1, 8–14, 18, 28, 46, 49, 59, 70–1, 78, 84, 91–2, 97, 99, 100, 102–3, 112, 114, 117, 161, 166, 196, 200, 203, 205, 210, 212, 215; *see also* Grimm
Fortune, Dion 122
foxes 6–7, 87–8, 129
fylgja, fylgjur 117

Gagliano 105
Galen 133–4, 209
Gallizenae 47
Gallû 32

Garutti brothers 118
Gello, *gelloudes* 31–2, 35
Gelon of Syracuse 16
Gerald of Wales 10, 55, 89–90, 104, 106, 111, 183, 191
Germanus of Auxerre 112
Gervase of Tillbury 7, 10, 35, 84, 94–5, 98, 129, 192
Gervasius and Protasius 112
ghosts 3, 13, 26–7, 36, 39–41, 60–81, 87, 89, 108, 111–12, 124, 133, 135, 137, 152–4, 161–2, 164, 206–9, 214; *see also* demons, souls
Gilgamesh 22, 72
Glaucus 50–2
goats, goatskins 46, 48, 75, 98–9, 107, 168–9, 190, 197, 218, 223
goēs, goētes 25, 49, 64–7, 80, 213–14; *see also* sorcerers
Gordiana 78
Gorlagon see *Arthur and Gorlagon*
graves *see* tombs
Gregory the Great 112
Grenier, Jean 70, 91–2, 105, 192
Grettir's Saga 113–14
Grimm, Brothers, 'The Story of a Boy who Went forth to Learn Fear' (no. 4) 112; 'The Wolf and the Seven Young Kids' (no. 5) 46–8; 'The Wonderful Musician' (no. 8) 200; 'The Three Snake Leaves' (no. 16) 49–50, 97; 'Little Red Riding Hood' (no. 26) 46; 'The Six Swans' (no. 49) 90; 'The Werewolf' (no. 214) 84–5
Guazzo, Francesco Maria 119
Guillaume d'Auvergne 10, 85, 94–5, 105, 111, 118
Guillaume de Palerne 10, 55, 57, 91, 104, 106, 190–1
Gunnar 117

Hades 61, 65, 80, 146, 162; *see also* Aita
hair, hairiness 41, 53, 76, 135, 171, 218; *see also* hearts, wolfskins
hamartia 54
hamramr 117
Hariwulfr (Hariulfus) 114
heads, talking 68–70
hearts, hairy 85–9, 107, 206
Hecate 37–8, 49, 61
Hecuba 162
Heimskringla see Snorri Sturluson
Helen 27, 221
Hemicynes 216
Hera 23–4, 53, 188, 210
Heracles 5, 49, 74, 87, 144, 146, 148–50, 152, 154, 164, 172, 199–201
Hermotimus of Clazomenae 127–31

Hero of Temesa 14, 26, 60, 73, 77–8, 80, 89, 137–65, 197–8, 202, 206, 208, 210
Herodotus 13, 24–7, 59, 64–7, 80, 85, 101, 126, 144, 154, 178, 185–6, 191, 198–9, 208, 210, 213–14, 216
Hesiod, [Hesiod] 54, 61, 67, 100, 154, 167–8, 175–6, 188–9, 204, 206, 216
Hesione 146–50
Hildegard of Bingen 113
Hirpi Sorani 62–4, 80, 104, 222
Hjalti 115–16
Hleidargard 115–17
Homer 3, 13, 15, 18–24, 27–8, 37, 59, 61–2, 94, 99, 113, 123, 131, 161, 177, 187, 191, 208, 211–15, 220–2; see also Circe, Odysseus
Howard the Halt's Saga 117
Hrolf's Saga 113–16
Hrotswitha 6
husband-blinding spells 39
Hvit 115
Hyginus 50, 52, 167–8, 171, 188
Hyperboreans 23, 126–7

ingestion 13, 98–103, 115, 196
initiation 86, 114, 166, 184–90, 214, 222; see also maturation
inns, innkeepers 2–3, 45, 49, 83–4, 95, 123, 128, 131–6, 207, 209; see also landladies, Meroe, Terentius
Inuit 120–1
Iphigenia 146, 189
Ireland 56, 89, 94, 110–11, 117, 131, 223; see also Ossory
Ishtar 22–3, 72
Ishullanu 22
Isidore of Seville 21, 33, 181–2, 194, 219

Joana 74, 96, 102, 105
John Damascene 31–3, 46, 125
John of Salisbury 11
Jürgensburg 120

Kaikinos 141, 144, 148–9, 152, 156, 199
Kalabros 138, 148, 156–7, 164, 206
Kalmar 91
Keban 131
Kekaumenos 32
Konungs skuggsjá 55–6, 104
Kramer and Sprenger 105, 118
krypteia 166, 183–7, 190, 193, 195

La Creuse 98
Lamashtu 32–3
Lamia, lamias 32, 35, 44, 53–4, 77, 160–1, 198; Lamia-Sybaris 147–52, 156–60, 164

landladies 99, 106, 133, 209; see also inns, innkeepers, Meroe
Landnámabók 115, 117
Lansens, T. P. A. 134
Laodamia 153
Laomedon 146–8
Latouche, John see Crawfurd
Lawson, J. C. 96
Lebanon, Mt 53–4
Lemburg 120
leprechauns 223
Leto 22–4
Levi, Carlo 105
Lévi, Éliphas 121
lions 18–20, 22, 74–5, 212, 214
Listerlandet 114
liver, wolf's 101, 192
Locri, Eastern 154, 197
Locri, Ozolian 155
Locri, Western (Epizephyrii) 137, 140–2, 144, 148–9, 151; see also Euthymus
lotion, magic 57, 70, 72, 91
Lucania 158
Lucian 27, 37–8, 44, 76, 78, 112, 132, 159, 199, 208–10
Lucius (Apuleius) 43, 82, 132, 209
Lucius of Patras 44
lupa 43, 223; lupa Romana 223; lupulae 43
lupomanaro (lupo mannaro) 7, 74
lupus 63, 158, 162
Lybas 139, 142, 147, 158, 206
Lycophron (Alexandra) 149, 170–1, 204
Lyka 138, 149, 156–8, 161, 206
Lykaia 5, 9–10, 60, 83, 101, 128, 166–7, 172, 175–6, 178–80, 184–5, 188–9, 193–8, 203, 205, 207, 220, 222, 224
Lykaina 61
Lykaion, Mt 14, 26, 166, 168–9, 172–4, 176–7, 180, 188, 195–7, 204–5, 210, 224
Lykaios see Pan, Zeus
lykanthrōpia, lykanthrōpos 4–5, 101
Lykaon 1, 4, 7, 9, 14, 23, 54, 86, 100, 103, 131, 160, 166–77, 180, 186, 188–91, 194–6, 202–6
Lykaonians 4
Lykas 158
Lyko 61
Lykomedes 187
Lykomids 86
lykophōs (twilight) 2, 177, 192
Lykophron (son of Periander) 186–7
Lykoreia 177
lykos (word) 4, 75, 113, 158, 176–7, 180
Lykos (Athenian) 86–7
Lykos (Messenian) 202
Lykosoura 103, 172–3, 175–7

Machates 153
Macrocephali 216
maga 20–1, 180
Magnus, Olaus 95, 99
magos 31, 67, 211, 213–14
Maidens, Locrian *see* Locri (Eastern)
Malleus maleficarum see Kramer and Sprenger
Mallory 191
Marcellus of Side (Sidetes) 4, 6, 13, 71–2, 74, 80, 191, 208
Marie de France; *see* Bisclavret, Eliduc
Marrok 191
maturation 9, 166, 178, 184–90, 192–195, 205, 210; *see also* initiation
Maturin, C. R. 73, 89
Maximus of Tyre 125–6
Mecone 175–6
Medea 27, 36–7, 40–2, 67, 93, 192, 208, 211–13
Megara 133
Melanchlainoi 25–6
Melion 10, 55–6, 84, 104, 106, 130–1
Melissa of Corinth, wife of Periander 154, 186
Melissa of Tarentum 2–3, 132
Melitene 35
Menestratus 148–50
Meroe and Panthia 2, 44–9, 59, 83, 133, 209
Metapontum 74, 126–7, 159
Milo of Croton 17, 198, 200–2, 204
Milograd culture 24
Minos 50, 52
Mistress of Animals 21–4, 121
Moeris 13, 26–7, 59, 67, 80, 92, 103, 191, 208
Molossians 171–2; Molossian dog 74–5, 87
moon 2, 39–41, 68, 84, 94, 102, 107, 191–2, 206, 214
Mormolyke 61
Mustafa Pasha 4

Natalis 59, 89, 183
Nennius of Bangor 111
Nessus 164
Neuri 13, 24–7, 59, 64–7, 80, 101, 185, 191, 208
Nicander 22, 150–2, 222
Niceros 1–3, 30, 42–3, 61, 68, 93, 98–9, 103, 132–3, 135, 191, 206, 208, 210
Nicolaus of Damascus 170–1, 174, 203–4
Njal's Saga 117
Nyctimus 169–71, 177

Odin 114, 117
O'Donnell, Elliot 80
Odysseus 18–21, 62, 94, 123, 137, 139–40, 142, 164, 180, 187, 209, 211–14, 220–1
Oebotas of Dyme 201

Olympia 137, 139–40, 142, 172, 179–80, 194, 199–201, 204, 210; *see also* athletes
Orcus 2, 61, 68
oreinoi 185
Orestes 76
Orpheus 70, 76
Orvieto 61, 162–3
Oscan 158
Ossory 55, 89–90, 104, 106, 111, 183, 191, 196
Ovid 23, 27, 29–33, 35, 40–2, 44, 89, 93, 103, 164, 171–2, 174, 176, 188, 192, 208, 223–4

Palermo 92; see also *Guillaume de Palerne*
Pamphile 38, 43–4
Pan 222–4; Lykaios 180, 223–4
Pandora 176
Panthia *see* Meroe
Paphlagon 216
Patrick, Bishop of Dublin 10, 94, 110, 127
Patrick, St 55, 104
Pausanias 26, 73, 77, 80, 85–7, 89, 100–1, 137–65, 173, 175–7, 179–83, 188–9. 191, 193–5, 198–202, 204, 206–10
Periander 154, 186
Périgord 92, 106
Persephone 61, 162–3
Perseus 146, 148–9, 152
Petronius Arbiter 1–3, 7–11, 13–14, 30–1, 33, 41–3, 49, 61, 68, 80, 83, 93, 98–9, 103, 128–36, 191–2, 206–10
Petronius (werewolf) 11
Peucer, Kaspar 106, 119
phantasticum 124
pharmaka (drugs, spells) 27, 65, 211–13
pharmakeia, pharmakos (scapegoating) 78, 152, 201
pharmakis (witch) 31, 49, 211, 214
phasma 74–7
Phigalia 177
Philinnion 76, 153
Philip V 179
Philostratus 13, 70, 73–8, 80, 93, 99, 127, 207–8
Phlegon of Tralles 17, 68–71, 76, 153, 209
pigs 19–21, 99, 106, 133, 212, 214
Plato, [Plato] 65–7, 74, 100, 159, 178–9, 181–2, 184, 193, 203–4, 217
Plautus 5–6, 33, 76, 112, 152, 199
Pliny the Elder 5, 10–11, 17, 33, 44, 54, 83, 85–6, 100–1, 103, 105, 107, 126, 128, 131, 140, 152, 163, 179–83, 191, 194–6, 198, 202, 207, 210, 217–18
Pliny the Younger 2, 112, 153
Plutarch, [Plutarch] 85, 141–3, 159, 177, 184–6, 223–4

Polites 57, 73, 78, 140, 143, 155, 164, 206;
    see also Hero of Temesa
Polybius 179, 181–2, 193
Polycritus 69
Polydamna 26–7
Polyidus 50–2
Polykaon 86
Polyxena 162
Ponte de Lima 102
potion, magic 19, 42, 57, 93, 99, 192
Praestantius 124
Prometheus 175–6
Prose Edda see Snorri Sturluson
Proselenos 31
prostitution 43; sacred, 144
Protesilaus 77, 153
Proteus 66, 77
proverbs 6, 27, 41, 133, 140–3
Psamathe 198
Psellus, Michael 72
psychagōgeō, psychagōgoi 65–6
Ptolemy Chennus 87–8
Ptolemy I Soter 50–2, 87
Pythagoras, Pythagoreans 73–4, 109, 123,
    125–7, 177, 181, 200
Python 145, 160, 185–6

Raimbaud de Poinet 94, 98
Rémy, Nicolas 11
Reprobus 219
Rhanaeus 119
Rhesus 220–2
Rhianus of Bene 85–6, 206
rings 95; magic 56–7, 68, 104, 130
Ronan, St 131
root-cutters (rhizotomoi) 27, 36, 212–14

sacrifice, human 14, 21, 25–6, 30, 41, 54, 100–1,
    145–7, 154, 160, 162, 166–7, 169–70, 172,
    176, 178–83, 188, 190, 193–8, 202, 205–7;
    see also cannibalism
Salaparuta 92
Salic Law 34
Samos 210
sapling, magic 57–8, 105
Satan see Devil
Saxo Grammaticus 8, 116
Scamander 144–5, 152
scapegoat see pharmakeia
schol. Germanicus Aratea 169, 188
schools 16, 199–201
Sciapodes 219
screech-owl see strix-witch
Scythia, Scythians 25, 101, 110, 126
Sedna 121

Sena 47
serpents see snakes
Servius 6, 63–4, 170, 173, 188, 223
Sextus Pompey 35
shamanism, shamans 13–14, 65, 77–8, 81,
    108–31, 136, 201
Siggeir 58, 90, 113, 201
Sigmund 50–2, 58, 90–1, 96–8, 104, 113,
    187, 201
Signy 58
Sigurd 115
Simeon Stylites 53
Simon Magus 41
Sinfjötli 50–2, 90–1, 96–8, 104, 113, 187
Skjöldunga saga 116
Skuld 115–16
Slavic 78
snakes 6, 22, 27, 32–3, 41–2, 49–52, 61, 68, 97,
    117, 133, 147, 157, 160–5, 185, 198, 212, 216;
    'Three Snake Leaves' see Grimm; see also
    anguipedes, Lamia, Python
Snorri Sturluson, Prose Edda 8, 116;
    Heimskringla 114, 117
Socrates (Apuleius) 45–8, 83, 133, 209
Socrates (philosopher) 6, 66
sophists 66
Soracte 62–4, 104
sorcerers 18, 25–7, 49, 56, 58–9, 60, 65–6,
    91–2, 104, 118–29, 207–8, 211, 213–14;
    Egyptian 27; see also goēs, magos
souls 37, 65–8, 76–7, 80, 108, 161, 172, 177;
    soul-projection 12–14, 31–3, 81, 85, 89,
    109–36, 201, 215; see also ghosts
Sparta, Spartans 70, 85–7, 166, 183–4, 187, 199,
    206, 210
sponge, magic 45–6, 48–9
stag 15, 20, 56, 130
Statius 160, 168
statues 16, 24, 74, 137, 140, 150, 177, 180,
    199–201, 204, 210, 223
Stenbock, Count 107
sterility 199, 201
Stoker, Bram, Dracula 12, 79; 'Dracula's
    Guest' 79, 96; 'The Judge's House' 112
stoning 78, 201
Storolf 117
Strabo 65, 140–3, 148–9, 151, 155, 198–200, 216
strix-witches 13, 28–54, 59, 125–6, 209, 210
Suda 65, 142–3, 159, 171, 189
Summers, Montague 4, 13
Sybaris (Lamia) see lamias
Sybaris (youth) 138, 147–9, 152, 156–7, 164, 206

Tarouca 102–3
Taurosthenes of Aegina 198, 201, 204

Temesa *see* Hero of Temesa
teras 201
Terentius 2, 132, 209
Tertullian 112
Thelyphrons 47–52, 59, 97, 208
Theogenes of Thasos 142, 198–202
Theophane 167
Theophrastus 179, 181–2, 193
Thespiae 147–8, 150, 156, 160
Thessalians, Thessaly 5, 43–7, 59
Thiess, Old 99, 102, 120
Thièvres 106
Thomson, Richard 95
Thon 26
Thorbjorn Hornklofi 113
thunderbolts 140, 162, 168–72, 175–6
Tibullus 13, 17, 36–40, 44, 59, 67, 72, 82, 101
Timothy of Gaza 16, 131, 174
Tityos Painter 62, 163
tombs 2, 26, 37, 39–40, 49–52, 65, 67, 68, 71–2,
    80, 93, 112, 153, 159, 162–3, 198, 202
Torslunda 114
Trapezus 168–71, 174
Trimalchio 1–3, 30–1, 42–3, 83, 133,
    208, 210
Troy 144, 146–8, 153–5, 160
Trypho, St 78
Tungus 109–10

Ulf 117
úlfahamir 90
úlfheðnar 113–14
urination 83, 128, 150, 206

Varro 20, 24, 100–1, 123, 133, 180–3, 191–2,
    194–5, 204, 210, 222
Vatnsdæla saga 114
Verrius 28
versipellis 3, 5–7, 9, 41, 47–8, 54, 59, 83, 89,
    93, 99, 179
Virgil 13, 22, 26–7, 59, 63, 67, 80, 92, 103–4, 170,
    173, 208, 224

Völsunga saga 10, 50, 52, 58, 90, 96–7, 104,
    115, 200
vrikolakas 78

water 20, 83, 103, 105–7, 128, 179–84, 194–6,
    205; *see also* Axius, Kaikinos, Kalabros,
    Lamia-Sybaris, Lyka, Scamander
weasels 5, 47–52, 97
Webster, John 88
werewolf *passim*; derivation of English word 7–8
'were-women' 53
werewulf 7–8
wife, unfaithful 2, 39, 49, 51–2, 56–8, 96, 104,
    127–33, 136, 191, 207, 215
William of Malmesbury 106
witches 18–59, 60, 67, 72, 76, 81–3, 91, 95, 101,
    103, 106, 109, 115, 117–19, 125–6, 133, 153,
    192, 207–15; *see also* Brande, Circe,
    Hvit, Skuld
wolf, wolves *passim*; as animal of choice for
    transformation 14–17; lone 17, 100, 103;
    red 17, 68–71, 91, 105; white 71
wolfskin 14, 26, 58, 61–2, 64, 70, 73, 77, 80,
    89–92, 96–7, 105, 113–15, 118, 134–5, 137–65,
    186, 198, 202, 206, 220, 222–3; drum 92;
    wolf-head cap 61
woods 3, 13, 15, 26, 58, 63, 67, 86, 89, 94, 97,
    102–5, 117, 129, 134, 190, 200, 222
wound, identifying 13, 92–8, 102, 107, 119–20,
    131, 207
Wulfila 9
Wulfstan 7

Xenophon of Ephesus 153

Ypres 134

Zatchlas 27, 49, 51
Zeus 5, 54, 140, 150, 154, 199–200;
    Hoplosmios 70; Lykaios 54, 100, 123,
    167–82, 188–9, 193–4, 198, 203, 206, 224;
    Sosipolis 198